THE SCHOOLS HISTORY PROJECT

S·H·P

OFFICIAL TEXT

MODERN AMERICA

THE USA, 1865 TO THE PRESENT

Joanne de Pennington
Series Editor: Ian Dawson

Hodder Murray

A MEMBER OF THE HODDER HEADLINE GROUP

In the same series

Britain 1783–1851	Charlotte Evers and Dave Welbourne	ISBN 0 7195 7482 X
Communist Russia Under Lenin and Stalin	Chris Corin and Terry Fiehn	ISBN 0 7195 7488 9
The Early Tudors: England 1485–1558	David Rogerson, Samantha Ellsmore and David Hudson	ISBN 0 7195 7484 6
Fascist Italy	John Hite and Chris Hinton	ISBN 0 7195 7341 6
The Reign of Elizabeth: England 1558–1603	Barbara Mervyn	ISBN 0 7195 7486 2
Weimar and Nazi Germany	John Hite and Chris Hinton	ISBN 0 7195 7343 2

The Schools History Project

The project was set up in 1972, with the aim of improving the study of history for students aged 13–16. This involved a reconsideration of the ways in which history contributes to the educational needs of young people. The Project devised new objectives, new criteria for planning and developing courses, and the materials to support them. New examinations, requiring new methods of assessment, also had to be developed. These have continued to be popular. The advent of GCSE in 1987 led to the expansion of Project approaches into other syllabuses.

The Schools History Project has been based at Trinity and All Saints College, Leeds, since 1978, from where it supports teachers through a biennial Bulletin, regular INSET, an annual Conference and a website (www.tasc.ac.uk/shp).

Since the National Curriculum was drawn up in 1991, the Project has continued to expand its publications, bringing its ideas to courses for Key Stage 3 as well as a range of GCSE and A level specifications.

America/the USA are used interchangeably throughout this book. American spelling has been used in quotes from other sources, where appropriate.

Although every effort has been made to ensure that website addresses are correct at time of going to press, Hodder Murray cannot be held responsible for the content of any website mentioned in this book. It is sometimes possible to find a relocated web page by typing in the address of the home page for a website in the URL window of your browser.

Papers used in this book are natural, renewable and recyclable products. They are made from wood grown in sustainable forests. The logging and manufacturing processes conform to the environmental regulations of the country of origin.

Orders: please contact Bookpoint Ltd, 130 Milton Park, Abingdon, Oxon OX14 4SB. Telephone: (44) 01235 827720. Fax: (44) 01235 400454. Lines are open from 9.00 to 6.00, Monday to Saturday, with a 24-hour message answering service. Visit our website at www.hodderheadline.co.uk.

© Joanne de Pennington, 2005
First published in 2005 by Hodder Murray, an imprint of Hodder Education,
a member of the Hodder Headline Group
338 Euston Road, London NW1 3BH

Impression number 10 9 8 7 6 5 4 3 2 1
Year 2010 2009 2008 2007 2006 2005

Layouts by Janet McCallum
Artwork by Oxford Designers and Illustrators Ltd
Typeset in 10/12 Walbaum by Fakenham Photosetting, Norfolk
Printed and bound in Great Britain by J.W. Arrowsmith Ltd, Bristol

A catalogue record for this title is available from the British Library

ISBN-10: 0 7195 7744 6
ISBN-13: 9780719577444

Contents

Acknowledgements

Dedication
To Alan, Nick and Jane, Gillian, Charles and Ian for their constant support and good ideas

Photo credits

Cover *background* Popperfoto.com, *inset* photo courtesy FDR Library; **p.2** Library of Congress (LC-B811-557); **p.7** *t* © Bettmann/Corbis, *b* © Corbis; **p.8** © Bettmann/Corbis; **p.10** Brown Brothers; **p.12** *t & c* © Corbis, *b* Library of Congress (LC-USZ62-121735); **p.13** © Elliott Erwitt/ Magnum Photos; **p.15** © Bettmann/Corbis; **p.17** *t* © Bettmann/Corbis, *b* © Corbis; **p.18** *t* Department of Special Collections, University of Chicago Library, *bl* © Corbis, *br* Library of Congress (LC-MS-44669-31); **p.23** *t* Library of Congress (LC-USZ62-55222), *b* Collection of the New-York Historical Society (# 41800); **p.25** © Bettmann/Corbis; **p.26** *t* Western History Collections, University of Oklahoma, *b* © Bettmann/Corbis; **p.28** *both* © Corbis; **p.29** *t* Amon Carter Museum, Fort Worth, Texas, Acquisition in Memory of Rene d'Harnoncourt, Trustee, Amon Carter Museum, 1961–1968, *b* © Corbis; **p.31** *t* Peter Newark's American Pictures, *b* Christie's Images/Bridgeman Art Library; **p.32** *t* Peter Newark's American Pictures, *b* The South Dakota Art Museum Collection; **p.34** *t* United Artists/ The Kobal Collection, *b* Arizona Office of Tourism; **p.37** Brown Brothers; **p.38** Pocumtuck Valley Memorial Association, Memorial Hall Museum, Deerfield, Massachusetts; **p.40** *t* © Corbis, *b* © Hulton-Deutsch Collection/ Corbis; **p.41** *t* © Corbis, *b* © Bettmann/Corbis; **p.42** © Corbis; **p.43** Keystone Mast Collection, UCR/California Museum of Photography/University of California at Riverside; **p.44** Library of Congress (LC-USZ62-75203); **p.46** *t* Library of Congress (LC-USZ62-26205), *b* photo courtesy New York State Library; **p.47** © Underwood & Underwood/ Corbis; **p.49** *tl* National Archives (196-GS-369), *tr* © Minnesota Historical Society/Corbis, *b* © Bettmann/Corbis; **p.55** US Naval Historical Foundation; **p.57** © Bettmann/ Corbis; **p.58** © Bettmann/Corbis; **p.59** Courtesy Frederic Remington Art Museum, Ogdensburg, New York; **p.60** *t* Brown Brothers, *b* The Art Archive/ Culver Pictures; **p.61** *t* © Corbis, *b* Library of Congress (LC-USZ62-28092); **p.63** *t* Culver Pictures, *b* National Archives (NWCTC-59-INV15E205-86220212/69); **p.66** The Art Archive/Imperial War Museum; **p.67** Copyrighted 2005, Chicago Tribune Company. All rights reserved.; **p.70** Culver Pictures; **p.71** all © Bettmann/Corbis; **p.73** © Corbis; **p.75** *tl & b* © Bettmann/ Corbis, *tr* Library of Congress (LC-USZ62-22160); **p.78** Brown Brothers; **p.82** Library of Congress (LC-USZ62-11430); **p.85** Culver Pictures; **p.86** *l* photo courtesy FDR Library, *r* © Bettmann/Corbis; **p.87** © Corbis; **p.90** *t* © Bettmann/Corbis, *b* © Underwood & Underwood/Corbis; **p.92** © Bettmann/Corbis; **p.94** Library of Congress (LC-USZ62-8705); **p.95** © Bettmann/Corbis; **p.96** © Corbis; **p.97** © Bettmann/Corbis; **p.100** © Bettmann/Corbis; **p.102** photo courtesy FDR Library; **p.106** © Corbis; **p.108** *t* © Corbis, *b* Smithsonian American Art Museum/ Art Resource/Scala, Florence; **p.109** Library of Congress (LC-USZ62-90003); **p.111** © Corbis; **p.113** © Bettmann/Corbis; **p.118** photo courtesy FDR Library; **p.119** © Underwood & Underwood/Corbis; **p.120** *t* Library of Congress (LC-USZ62-96791), *bl* Brown Brothers, *br* photo courtesy FDR Library; **p.121** © Bettmann/Corbis; **p.122** © Corbis; **p.124** photo courtesy FDR Library; **p.125** © Bettmann/Corbis; **p.129** Culver Pictures; **p.132** RKO/The Kobal Collection; **p.134** Library of Congress (LC-USZ62-17308); **p.136** *t* © Corbis, *b* Getty Images; **p.137** © Corbis; **p.138** *t* With permission from the Evening Standard (photo: Centre for the Study of Cartoons and Caricature, University of Kent), *b* photo courtesy FDR Library; **p.140** Printed by permission of the Norman Rockwell Family Agency Copyright © 1943 the Norman Rockwell Family Entities (photo: The Curtis Publishing Company); **p.141** photo courtesy FDR Library; **p.142** © Bettmann/Corbis; **p.148** National Archives (NWDNS-208-COM-132); **p.149** © Corbis; **p.153** *tl & tr* photo courtesy Harry S. Truman Library, *bl* © Corbis, *br* Library of Congress (LC-USZ62-95951); **p.155** *tl* Library of Congress (LC-USW3-034282-C), *tr* © Corbis; **p.156** *l* National Archives (NWDNS-44-PA-389), *r* National Archives (NWDNS-44-PA-229); **p.157** © K.J. Historical/Corbis; **p.160** *t* © Bettmann/Corbis, *b* photo courtesy Harry S. Truman Library; **p.166** *t* photo courtesy FDR Library, *b* Getty Images; **p.167** *t* © Corbis, *b* © Bettmann/Corbis; **p.168** *l* Digital image © 1996 Corbis; Original image courtesy of NASA/Corbis, *r* Time Life Pictures/Getty Images; **p.169** *t* © Nick Gunderson/Corbis, *b* AP/Wide World Photos; **p.170** © Yevgeny Khaldei/Corbis; **p.171** © Bettmann/Corbis; **p.175** Winston Churchill Memorial & Library at Westminster College, Fulton, Missouri; **p.177** © Bettmann/Corbis; **p.179** *l* Courtesy of the George C. Marshall Research Library, Lexington, Virginia, *r* © Bettmann/ Corbis; **p.180** AP/Wide World Photos; **p.186** © Bettmann/Corbis; **p.187** Time Life Pictures/Getty Images; **p.188** © Willy McNamee/Corbis; **p.190** *t* AP/Wide World Photos, *b* from *Herblock's Special for Today* (Simon & Schuster, 1958) reproduced courtesy of The Herb Block Foundation; **p.191** © Collection Corbis KIPA; **p.192** The Art Archive/Culver Pictures; **p.193** © Bettmann/Corbis; **p.194** *t* © Bettmann/Corbis, *b* © Corbis; **p.196** AP/Wide World Photos; **p.197** © Bettmann/Corbis; **p.203** National Archives (NWDNS-111-SC-651408); **p.204** *t* Library of Congress (LC-USZ62-130601), *b* AP/Wide World Photos; **p.206** *l* © Jules Feiffer, *r* © Lynn Goldsmith/ Corbis; **p.212** © Elliott Erwitt/Magnum Photos; **p.214** © Bettmann/Corbis; **p.215** Courtesy the Hagley Museum and Library (Photo: Alex Henderson); **p.217** *tl* 20th Century Fox/The Kobal Collection, *tr* Peter Newark's American Pictures, *cr* Time Life Pictures/Getty Images, *br* © Corbis; **p.219** AP/Wide World Photos; **p.221** *t & b* © Bettmann/Corbis; **p.223** AP/Wide World Photos; **p.224** Rube Goldberg is the ® & © of Rube Goldberg Inc.; **p.225** *t* Federal Civil Defense Agency, *b* National Archives (397-MA-160); **p.227** AP/Wide World Photos; **p.233** The Art Archive/Culver Pictures; **p.237** © Bettmann/ Corbis; **p.238** AP/Wide World Photos; **p.239** *t* © Bettmann/Corbis, *b* AP/ Wide World Photos; **p.241** Black Star/Katz; **p.243** © Bettmann/Corbis; **p.248** Lyndon Baines Johnson Library (photo by Yoichi R. Okamoto); **p.251** from *Herblock: A Cartoonist's Life* (Times Books, 1998) reproduced courtesy of The Herb Block Foundation (photo: Centre for the Study of Cartoons and Caricature, University of Kent); **p.253** *t* AP/Wide World Photos, *b* © Bettmann/Corbis; **p.258** courtesy the George Bush Presidential Library & Museum; **p.261** AP/Wide World Photos; **p.263** AP/Wide World Photos; **p.264** *t* from *Herblock: A Cartoonist's Life* (Times Books, 1998) reproduced courtesy of The Herb Block Foundation, *b* © Jules Feiffer; **p.266** © Corbis; **p.271** SARGENT © 1986 Austin American -Statesman. Reprinted with permission of UNIVERSAL PRESS SYNDICATE. All rights reserved.; **p.272** © Corbis; **p.276** © Bettmann/Corbis; **p.277** © Eugene Richards/Magnum Photos; **p.278** © Ira Wyman/Corbis Sygma; **p.281** *t* courtesy Ronald Reagan Library, *b* AP/Wide World Photos; **p.282** AP/Wide World Photos; **p.283** Cameraphoto Arte Venezia/Bridgeman Art Library; **p.285** *tl & br* © Bettmann/Corbis, *tr* Time Life Pictures/Getty Images, *bl* AP/Wide World Photos; **p.286** © Reuters/Corbis; **p.287** all © Reuters/Corbis.

t = top, *b* = bottom, *l* = left, *r* = right, *c* = centre

Every effort has been made to contact copyright holders, but if any have been inadvertently overlooked the publishers will be pleased to make the necessary arrangements at the earliest opportunity.

Using this book

This is an in-depth study of the USA, 1865 to the present. It contains everything you need for examination success and more. It provides all the content you would expect, as well as many features to help both independent and class-based learners. So, before you wade in, make sure you understand the purpose of each of the features.

Focus routes

On every topic throughout the book, this feature guides you to produce the written material essential for understanding what you read and, later, for revising the topic (e.g. pages 5, 21, 85). These focus routes are particularly useful for you if you are an independent learner working through this material on your own, but they can also be used for class-based learning.

Activities and Discussion

The activities offer a range of exercises to enhance your understanding of what you read to prepare you for examinations. They vary in style and purpose. There are:

- a variety of essays (e.g. pages 50, 135)
- source investigations (e.g. pages 144, 238)
- examination of historical interpretations, which is now central to A level history (e.g. pages 130, 249)
- decision-making exercises which help you to see events from the viewpoint of people at the time (e.g. pages 8, 57, 256)
- exercises to develop Key Skills such as communication and research skills (e.g. pages 28, 113).

These activities help you to analyse and understand what you are reading. They address the content through the key questions that the examiner will be expecting you to have investigated.

Overviews, summaries and key points

In such a large book on such a massive topic, you need to keep referring to the big picture. Each chapter begins with an overview and each chapter ends with a key-points summary of the most important content of the chapter.

Learning trouble spots

Experience shows that time and again some topics cause confusion for students. This feature identifies such topics and helps students to avoid common misunderstandings (e.g. page 74). In particular, this feature addresses some of the general problems encountered when studying history, such as assessing sources (e.g. pages 112, 203); understanding interpretations (e.g. pages 152, 192); and explaining contemporary ideas (e.g. page 174).

Charts

The charts are our attempts to summarise important information in note or diagrammatic form (e.g. pages 42, 87). There are also several grid charts that present a lot of information in a structured way (e.g. page 123). However, everyone learns differently and the best charts are the ones you draw yourself! Drawing your own charts in your own way to summarise important content can really help understanding (e.g. pages 56, 101), as can completing assessment grids (e.g. page 244).

Glossary

We have tried to write in an accessible way but occasionally we have used advanced vocabulary. These words are often explained in brackets in the text but sometimes you may need to use a dictionary. We have also used many general historical terms as well as some that are specific to the study of the USA, 1865 to the present. You won't find all of these in a dictionary, but they are defined in the glossary on page 292. The first time a glossary word appears in the text it is in SMALL CAPITALS like this.

Talking points

These are asides from the normal pattern of written exercises. They are discussion questions that invite you to be more reflective and to consider the relevance of this history to your own life. They might ask you to voice your personal judgement (e.g. pages 94, 148); to make links between the past and present (e.g. pages 16, 34); or to highlight aspects of the process of studying history (e.g. pages 15, 51, 207).

Modern American history is an increasingly popular A level history topic. The content is deeply relevant, but the actual process of studying history is equally relevant to the modern world. Throughout this book you will be problem solving, working with others, and trying to improve your own performance as you engage with deep and complex historical issues. Our hope is that by using this book you will become actively involved in your study of history and that you will see history as a challenging set of skills and ideas to be mastered rather than as an inert body of factual material to be learned.

The nation expands, 1865–1919

The Declaration of Independence, July 1776

'We hold these truths to be self-evident: That all men are created equal; that they are endowed by their Creator with certain inalienable rights; that among these are life, liberty, and the pursuit of happiness ...'

The authors of the Declaration went on to devise a Constitution, which created the structure and powers of government – the Executive (the President), the Legislative (Congress with a House of Representatives and a Senate) and the Judiciary (with the Supreme Court at its head). The Constitution could, provided certain conditions were met, have Amendments added to it. Since 1791 only 27 Amendments have been passed.

SOURCE 1 Battleground photo of some of the CONFEDERATE dead laid out after the Battle of Antietam, where 6000 soldiers were killed in one day, in September 1862

This new United States of America had rebelled successfully against British rule. It was determined to be a different kind of nation to those of Europe. For its first century, until 1865, it concentrated on domestic policies – establishing its boundaries, exploiting its resources, creating an economy through trade and manufacture. Then came the Civil War of 1861–65. Eleven southern states, the Confederacy, broke away from the northern or Unionist states to form their own republic. The Civil War started as the North attempted to prevent this secession – to keep the United States united. But in addition the Civil War became a war about slavery. The Confederacy wanted to keep slavery. The ownership of enslaved black people was the basis of their economy and society. However, after decisive defeats at Antietam and Gettysburg the Confederacy surrendered. More than 620,000 Americans had died. Slavery in the USA was at an end and was abolished by the Thirteenth Amendment. Now the FEDERAL government had the unprecedented task of trying to re-establish a united nation.

Section 1 therefore investigates how, between 1865 and 1919, the USA faced up to twin challenges:

a) could the USA now really become the land of the free

b) would the USA build up its power and play a part in wider world events?

By the end of Section 1 you will have developed clear answers to the following questions:

■ A   Were all Americans free and equal by 1919?

Did black Americans become free citizens after the Civil War? (Chapter 1)

Did agricultural and industrial workers benefit as the US economy developed? (Chapter 3)

What was the fate of Native Americans as settlers moved West?
(Chapter 2)

Did the USA liberate Cuba and the Philippines?
(Chapter 4)

■ B   To what extent was the USA's power established, 1865–1919?

Did the end of slavery make the USA more powerful? (Chapter 1)

How did industrialisation make the USA so wealthy?
(Chapter 3)

What influence did the myths of the West have on Americans? (Chapter 2)

Why did the USA become involved with other nations after 1890?
(Chapter 4)

1

Were black Americans really made free and equal by the abolition of slavery, 1865–1915?

CHAPTER OVERVIEW 'I felt like a bird out of a cage. Amen. Amen. Amen. I could hardly ask to feel any better than I did that day.'
This is Houston H. Holloway, a slave, speaking in 1865 on the day that freedom for slaves was declared. Only twenty years old, he had already been sold three times during his short life.

SOURCE 1.1 'Emancipated Negroes Celebrating the Emancipation Proclamation of President Lincoln', from *Le Monde Illustré*, 21 March 1863

DISCUSS

Think about the chapter title. What ideas do you have about the likely answer to the question? Have you any ideas about what topics you would need to include in an essay answering the question?

What was Emancipation?

The dictionary definition of emancipation is 'to set free, especially from legal, social, or political restrictions'. The Emancipation Proclamation was signed by President Lincoln on 1 January 1863. It was issued as a war measure and ensured that slavery would end when the South was finally defeated. As news of the Proclamation spread across the country it was greeted with rejoicing. Black churches, whose slave congregations had seen themselves like the Biblical Israelites waiting for God to help them return to their Promised Land, resounded with the singing of 'Sound the loud trumpet o'er Egypt's dark sea. Jehovah has triumphed, his people are free'. Two years later the North won the Civil War and the Thirteenth Amendment, ending slavery, was passed.

However, the federal government in WASHINGTON DC in 1865 had to face the realities of the South's long-held attitudes and behaviour towards black Americans. The newly united nation was divided about the idea that a black freedman could also be a citizen. Would legal changes be sufficient to make slaves into citizens? Would legal changes be enough to make real and practical the ideals and practice of an equal life for former slaves? This chapter will help you answer these questions by looking at:

A What was slavery? (pp. 6–7)

B What problems resulted from the abolition of slavery? (p. 8)

C How did a slave become a citizen? (p. 9)

D Was legal action enough to make slaves into citizens? (pp.10–12)

E How did discrimination develop between black and white citizens, 1877–1915? (pp. 13–18)

F Review: Were black Americans really made free and equal by the abolition of slavery, 1865–1915? (pp. 18–19)

FOCUS ROUTE

As you work through this chapter complete your own copy of the table below to help you answer the question in the chapter title. An example has been done for you.

Events or Evidence	Slaves become citizens and had freedom and equality	Slaves become citizens but were *not* free and equal
Emancipation Proclamation, 1863		Slaves were freed from slavery, but had no constitutional right to citizenship

A   What was slavery?

■ 1A Slaves were property

A slave was not a citizen, but the property, for life, of his or her owner.

A slave was refused the basic rights of the law and society.

A slave was unable to leave his or her master to find alternative work.

Slave families could be split up and sold to different owners.

A slave was not paid cash or educated, but rather given food, clothing and accommodation as his or her owner deemed fit.

Slaves were punished, often by whipping, for disobedience, laziness or trying to escape.

Female slaves were often sexually exploited by their white owners. Any children from these 'relationships' were known as mulattos.

Slavery was peculiar to the South. The Northern states had made slavery illegal.

FOCUS ROUTE

Use the following questions as a basis for making notes on pages 6–7.

1 Why was the abolition of slavery likely to create problems for white Southerners?
2 Why would it be difficult for freed slaves to adjust to a free life?

Traditionally, Southern society was based on the ownership of slaves; its PECULIAR INSTITUTION. The economy of the South relied on cotton and tobacco, both labour-intensive in their cultivation. As long as cotton and tobacco could be sold at a profit there was little incentive to diversify into industrial production, or to find alternatives to slave labour. As capital was tied up in slave ownership, slaves became a measure of wealth, and a sign of status. The large plantation owners, with 500 or more slaves, were the social and political elite of the South (although most slaves were owned by small farm holders).

The South did not need or welcome immigrants, as the North did, as long as they had unwaged slaves to exploit. Around 4 million slaves lived in the South (out of a total American population in 1860 of 31 million) and were controlled not only by force, by their lack of civil rights, their lack of education, and their lack of access to wealth, but also by attitudes. The paternalistic and superior attitudes of white Southerners meant that slaves were portrayed as childlike, dependent, and inferior. Their colour and African heritage, arriving in the USA by force not choice, meant they were regarded as inferior to any white person, however poor or ill-educated they were.

What were the reactions to emancipation?

SOURCE 1.2 A fugitive slave, whose daughter had been taken from him and sold years before

Now, no more of dat ... Dey can't sell my wife and child any more. Bless de Lord.

7

WERE BLACK AMERICANS REALLY MADE FREE AND EQUAL BY THE ABOLITION OF SLAVERY, 1865–1915?

SOURCE 1.3 *The First Vote*, by Alfred R. Waud, *Harper's Weekly*, 16 November 1867. This painting shows the key black voters who, for the first time, could exert black political power: the artisan with his tools, the successful town dweller and the soldier

SOURCE 1.4 Two members of the Ku Klux Klan in their disguises, *Harper's Weekly*, 19 December 1868

THE KU KLUX KLAN

The Klan used their frightening disguise, intimidation, beatings and lynching to oppose equality for black people. They became known and feared after 1865 in the South, but their organisation was eventually weakened by federal government prosecutions. It was revived in 1915 and grew considerably in the 1920s.

ACTIVITY

Use Sources 1.2–1.4 to answer the following questions.

1 What hopes might slaves have of their new freedom?
2 What problems might they have in turning these hopes into a reality?

DISCUSS

1 If you were a newly freed slave what would you want for yourself?
2 If you were a newly freed slave what would you expect the government to do for you?
3 If you were a newly freed slave how would you a) hope and b) fear that people might behave towards you?

8

WERE BLACK AMERICANS REALLY MADE FREE AND EQUAL BY THE ABOLITION OF SLAVERY, 1865–1915?

FOCUS ROUTE

As you work through Section B:

a) Make a list of the problems that resulted from the abolition of slavery.

b) Make notes on why it would be difficult to solve these problems.

SOURCE 1.5 An influential Radical Republican senator, Thaddeus Stevens, in a speech given on 18 December 1865

We have turned, or are about to turn loose four million slaves without a hut to shelter them or a cent in their pockets. The infernal laws of slavery have prevented them from acquiring an education, understanding the common laws of contract, or of managing the ordinary business of life. This Congress is bound to provide for them until they can take care of themselves. If we do not furnish them with homesteads, and hedge them around with protective laws; if we leave them to the legislation of their late masters, we had better have left them in bondage.

TALKING POINT

What does Lincoln's biography (below) tell you about the standards expected of an American president?

 # What problems resulted from the abolition of slavery?

In his second Inaugural Address in March 1865, President Lincoln recognised that the Civil War had led to much pain for everyone:

'…With malice toward none; with charity for all; with firmness in the right, as God gives us to see the right, let us strive on to finish the work we are in, to bind up the nation's wounds …'

The UNION victory confirmed the abolition of slavery, but binding the wounds created by abolition would not be achieved painlessly, given that slavery had been the social and economic basis of the Southern states for more than one hundred years.

SOURCE 1.6 A former slave, Frederick Douglass, writing in the magazine, *The Atlantic Monthly*, December 1865

Slavery … has steadily exerted an influence upon all around it favourable to its own continuance … Custom, manners, morals, religion, are all on its side everywhere in the South; and when you add the ignorance and servility of the ex-slave to the intelligence and accustomed authority of the master, you have the conditions, not out of which slavery will grow again, but under which it is impossible for the federal government to wholly destroy it, unless the federal government be armed with despotic powers … The true way, and the easiest, is to make our government entirely consistent with itself, and give to every loyal citizen the elective franchise – a right and power which will be ever present, and will form a wall of fire for his protection.

DISCUSS

'If you were the President in 1865 …'
Discuss with a partner or a small group what a president would have to do to create real freedom and equality for the emancipated slaves.

1 What problems would a president face?
2 What would different sections of society need?
3 What would be the priorities?
4 What would be the most difficult things to change?

Abraham Lincoln (1809–65)
This photo shows the Lincoln Memorial in the centre of Washington DC. The statue of Lincoln within looks towards the memorial to George Washington and to the Capitol, where Congress meets. This photograph was taken on the day of the March to Washington, in 1963, organised by Martin Luther King to demand a Civil Rights Act. It was the day of his famous 'I have a Dream' speech (see Chapter 12).

Lincoln demonstrated the American ideal that anything was possible. Born into poverty in a Kentucky log cabin in 1809, largely self-taught and experienced at hard physical work, he managed to be elected to the legislature of Illinois and to become a lawyer by the age of 27. He became a Congressman ten years later. Although he detested slavery he did not, at that stage, want to abolish it across the nation. By 1856, he had joined the Republican Party and so impressed them that he won the party nomination and the presidential election in 1860. He was admired for his common sense, caution and sincerity, and took the nation into a civil war only when there was no alternative. By 1861, he believed that it was impossible to have a nation that was half free and half slave. At the end of the Civil War his ideas were victorious, but before he had the opportunity to reunite the nation he was assassinated by a Confederate soldier, John Wilkes Booth, only five days after the surrender of the South. His ideas, his actions and his words at Gettysburg and in his Inaugural Addresses have meant that he is regarded as one of America's greatest presidents.

FOCUS ROUTE

1 List the purposes of Reconstruction.
2 In what ways did the federal government try to help freed slaves?
3 Which of their actions was most important?

C How did a slave become a citizen?

The end of the Civil War gave the federal government the opportunity to do more than merely end slavery. It could make freed slaves into equal citizens. The Radical Republicans, who were in the majority in Congress, were determined to make emancipation a reality by amending the Constitution and translating freedom into citizenship; even if it meant opposing the new president, Andrew Johnson. Reconstruction was the name given to the federal government's attempt to aid the freed slaves, who were uneducated, unskilled, and without the ownership of property, land, or savings. Reconstruction began in 1865 and lasted for twelve years.

■ 1B Making slaves into citizens – using the law and the Constitution

Year	Presidents	Acts and Amendments	Agencies
1863		Emancipation Proclamation	
1865	Vice-President Andrew Johnson became president after the assassination of Lincoln.	Thirteenth Amendment – abolished slavery everywhere in the USA, and gave Congress power to ensure this through legislation.	Bureau of Refugees, Freedmen and Abandoned Lands (the Freedmen's Bureau) – this was a federal agency which lasted for four years, supplied food, medical services and schools to freedmen, and also negotiated work contracts between them and their former masters. It was an example of social welfare by the state.
1866		Civil Rights Act – as a response to the BLACK CODES of some Southern states (laws designed to limit the rights and freedom of former slaves) this Act granted citizenship to anyone born in the USA (except Native Americans). Fourteenth Amendment – a four-part amendment which: a) confirmed the rights to citizenship; b) forbade STATES from abridging the 'privileges and immunities' of citizens; c) forbade states from depriving any person of life, liberty or property without 'due process of law'; d) forbade states from denying citizens the 'equal protection of the laws'.	
1868	U. S. Grant (Republican) becomes president.		
1870		Fifteenth Amendment – forbade states from denying anyone the right to vote 'on account of race, color, or previous condition of servitude', but left states free to restrict SUFFRAGE on other grounds such as illiteracy or poverty.	
1870–71		Enforcement Acts and Ku Klux Klan Act – these were passed in response to increased violence in the South against freedmen. It became a federal criminal offence for an individual to restrict the civil and political rights of others. In order to control the Ku Klux Klan martial law could be enforced and *habeas corpus* (the right to trial) suspended.	
1872	Presidential election – U.S. Grant re-elected		
1875		Civil Rights Act – a law to guarantee black Americans equal accommodation in public places, but lacked powers of enforcement.	
1876	The disputed results of the presidential election led to political negotiation. In return for Democratic support for the Republican candidate, Rutherford B. Hayes, the Democrats, who now controlled the South, were able to obtain the end of military control there. It was the effective end of the Reconstruction period and of federal protection for freed slaves.		

FOCUS ROUTE

1 Why did so many freedmen continue to do the same work after abolition?

2 Was legal action enough to make slaves into citizens? Make a list of the evidence from Section D which suggests:
   a) that it was
   b) that it was not.

TALKING POINTS

1 Why was the violence of the Ku Klux Klan so powerful in slowing progress to real equality?

2 What does violence do to people; both to those who suffer from it, and those who initiate it (think of fear, aggression, intimidation, disrespect for others' differences)?

D Was legal action enough to make slaves into citizens?

The abolition of slavery had been long desired by slaves, but when abolition came suddenly, it left both North and South, and the government, unprepared for the reality of how to release people from servitude into self-sufficiency. The devastation and distress caused by the Civil War also meant that at first life was slow to change in the South.

For the new ex-slave citizens there was deep pleasure at being able to live with their families, to enjoy their communities, to make choices about employment and residence, and to be formally educated for the first time. However, servitude had left most freedmen with few, if any, savings and therefore they were unable to purchase land or acquire many possessions. They could travel to work in the industries of the North, but most had little choice but to remain as paid labourers or to become sharecroppers working on the land as before.

Over time some freedmen did succeed in saving enough money to buy their own land, even becoming businessmen or using their education to become politicians and professionals. However, for many freedmen and their families, the effect of generations of intimidation was insidious and encouraged passive behaviour. Southern white society, which had owned black workers as property and controlled them by force, could not easily forget habits of superiority. The rise of the Ku Klux Klan (see page 7) was a continuation of such attitudes towards non-white people. It made the creation of equal citizens, regardless of their colour, more difficult to achieve.

Being a sharecropper (see Source 1.7) meant that a family rented land, and received a house, tools and sometimes seed. In return they gave the landlord (usually a white farmer) one half, or as much as two-thirds, of the crop. Most sharecroppers, needing clothes and other supplies, had to borrow against their first crop, relied on credit, and so fell into debt easily. This system kept the black cotton producers in an inferior position. Its attraction was the short-term benefit to both groups, but the reliance on cotton led to problems when prices were low (for example, the fall in cotton prices in the 1870s). The shortage of money for investment also restricted diversification into grain and livestock production.

SOURCE 1.7 A black sharecropper family outside their house, with a formally dressed white landlord in the background

STRENGTHS

- Freedom guaranteed by presidential proclamation, by law and by Constitutional Amendments
- The overwhelming desire of slaves to be free and to enjoy their freedom
- Ex-slaves acquired legal rights as equal citizens
- The Bureau of Refugees, Freedmen and Abandoned Lands provided support by setting up schools, supplying work, clothes and food
- Military rule in the rebel Southern states and the desire of Radical Republicans in Congress to ensure the rights of freedmen
- Solidarity of the Afro-American culture, through the blending of different African ethnic groups and languages, continued after emancipation
- Abolition was thought to be morally right by most of the USA

WEAKNESSES

- Slaves had been refused education by most of their owners before emancipation, and were consequently disadvantaged
- There was no redistribution of confiscated Southern lands so most freedmen had no economic AUTONOMY, and many could only work as paid labourers or sharecroppers
- Entrenched attitudes about white supremacy and stereotypical images of lazy, 'childlike' blacks prevented the value of black Americans being realised
- The traumatic experience of Civil War and the speed of abolition hampered the development of equality
- The implementation of new laws was difficult for the small, federal government bureaucracy

OPPORTUNITIES

- The enthusiasm and political power of Radical Republicans who supported abolition
- Political power through suffrage resulted in large numbers of black voters in some Southern states being willing to elect black Congressmen and Senators
- Marriages between freed people allowed the creation of socially acceptable family groups, with, for the first time, their own surnames and identity
- The continuing strength of the Christian Church as a focus for black communities
- The right to travel, to find and choose work
- The right to the benefits of work, including being paid and using that money freely

THREATS

- The traditional attitude of many Southern whites that black people were inferior and always would be
- Violence and intimidation through groups like the Ku Klux Klan
- Social structure in the South still valued land ownership above the artisan, the entrepreneur and the industrialist
- Due to economic recession after 1873 many people in the North were more focused on their immediate problems than the racial integration problems of the South
- Competition for unskilled work between freedmen and white labourers

ACTIVITY

Study Chart 1C and answer the following questions.

1 a) Work in pairs. Identify what you think were the two most significant elements in each section of Chart 1C.
   b) Join another pair and compare your conclusions. Justify your choices, but try to reach agreement.
2 Which was the greater:
   a) the strengths or the weaknesses of abolition?
   b) the opportunities created by abolition or the threats facing freedmen?
3 Look at Sources 1.8 to 1.11. Which parts of Chart 1C do they support?
4 Why was the abolition of slavery such a problematic issue:
   a) for individuals
   b) for American society?

SOURCE 1.8   Letter written in 1865 by Jourdan Anderson to his former master in Tennessee who wanted Jourdan to return to work for him. However, Jourdan was now being paid $25 a month, his children were being educated, and he and his wife Mandy were comfortable with their new life, so Jourdan set out conditions for his return (in F. M. Binder and D. M. Reimers, *The Way We Live*, Vol. II, 4th edn, 2000, pp.17–18)

... we have concluded to test your sincerity by asking you to send us our wages for the time we served you ... I served you faithfully for thirty-two years, and Mandy twenty years ... our earnings would amount to $11,680. Add to this the interest for the time our wages have been kept back, and deduct what you paid for our clothing, and three doctor's visits for me, and pulling a tooth for Mandy, and the balance will show what we are in justice entitled to ... We trust the good Maker has opened your eyes to the wrongs which you and your fathers have done to me and my fathers, in making us toil for you for generations without recompense. Here, I draw my wages every Saturday night; but in Tennessee there never was any pay-day for the Negroes any more than for horses and cows ... please state if there would be safety for my Milly and Jane ... both good-looking girls. You know how it was with poor Matilda and Catherine. I would rather stay here and starve – and die, if it came to that – than have my girls brought to shame by the violence and wickedness of their young masters ...

SOURCE 1.9 *The Freedmen's Bureau*, from *Harper's Weekly*, 25 July 1868. This was the desired image of the Freedmen's Bureau as the active supporter of racial peace

SOURCE 1.10 *The Freedman's Bureau!* a Democratic campaign poster from 1866. Not everyone valued the efforts of the Bureau to integrate freed slaves into society. Note the stereotypical image of the central character, against the equally stereotypical white farmer, and the supposed largesse of the Bureau

SOURCE 1.11 'This is a White Man's Government', from *Harper's Weekly*, 5 September 1868. Here the newly freed slave is overwhelmed by the combined, but very different demands of (from left to right) an Irish immigrant (competition for unskilled work), a Confederate veteran (anxious to protect his Southern traditions) and a WALL STREET financier (eager to make profits from manufacture and the railroad)

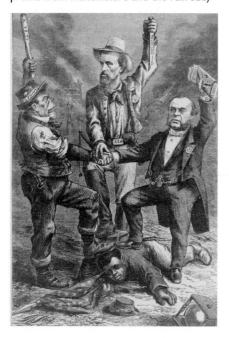

The end of Reconstruction

The military success of the North in the Civil War meant that the Southern states had to accept re-union into the United States. The defeated states were divided into five military areas, although it was always recognised that military control was a temporary situation. This control was gradually removed as the Southern states ratified the Amendments to the Constitution over slavery and citizenship. As the memory of the Civil War faded, government and individuals' energies turned towards industrial and business expansion rather than continuing to consolidate the rights of black citizens. The influence of the Radical Republicans, who supported citizens' rights for everyone, was also waning in Congress. The Democrats, with their traditional attitudes about white supremacy, gradually gained control of Southern state legislatures. At the same time election disputes, in 1876, led to compromises to allow the Republican Rutherford B. Hayes to become president. These compromises meant the withdrawal of all military control in the Southern states. It signalled the end of the Reconstruction period, and hence of direct federal intervention in the government of the former Confederate states.

FOCUS ROUTE

Make notes to answer the following questions:

1 Why was discrimination possible after 1877?
2 What was the process by which black and white people were segregated?
3 How did black Americans respond?

E | How did discrimination develop between black and white citizens, 1877–1915?

SOURCE 1.12 Separate and unequal – drinking fountains were an example of deliberate public discrimination against black citizens

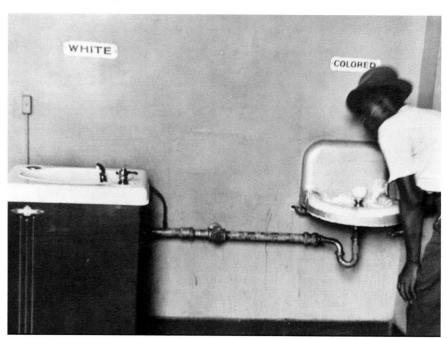

After 1877, the federal government left states to uphold the Amendments that had given the rights of citizenship to freed slaves. But the next 40 years were particularly difficult for black Americans. States and communities enforced disenfranchisement (the loss of the right to vote) and social separation. At the same time, opportunities for education and wealth acquisition were restricted. Violence, and the failure to use the law to stop discrimination, were used to maintain white supremacy. There were black activists and educators who challenged this supremacy, trying to find the most effective way to improve the lives of black citizens. Some hoped for at least a gradual, grudging acceptance of black rights, whilst others thought that attitudes had to be changed by direct public action.

Discrimination by the states

The Fifteenth Amendment (1870) stated that no one should be denied the right to vote by reason of their race, colour or previous condition of servitude. In South Carolina, in the 1880 presidential election, 70 per cent of eligible blacks voted. In the 1896 presidential election this number dropped to eleven per cent; a pattern repeated across the Southern states. What caused this? Apathy and indifference on the part of black voters now that the novelty of abolition had worn off? Or was it the result of political decisions to interpret the Amendment so as to diminish its intent?

Reconstruction had failed to counter decades of belief in white superiority. Many Southern whites could not accept that freed slaves should have the honourable rights of citizenship, or that they should have the ability to choose political leaders. So states found ways to interpret the law to reflect this, particularly through the requirement to register as a voter prior to elections.

TALKING POINT

The words of the Declaration of Independence of 1776
Remember the words of the Declaration of Independence of which Americans are so proud:

'We hold these truths to be self-evident, that all men are created equal, that they are endowed by their Creator with certain unalienable Rights, that among these are Life, Liberty, and the Pursuit of Happiness.'

How could Americans reconcile these words with the ill-treatment of freed slaves who became citizens? You might be able to understand the difficulties immediately after the Civil War, but why did inequality persist?

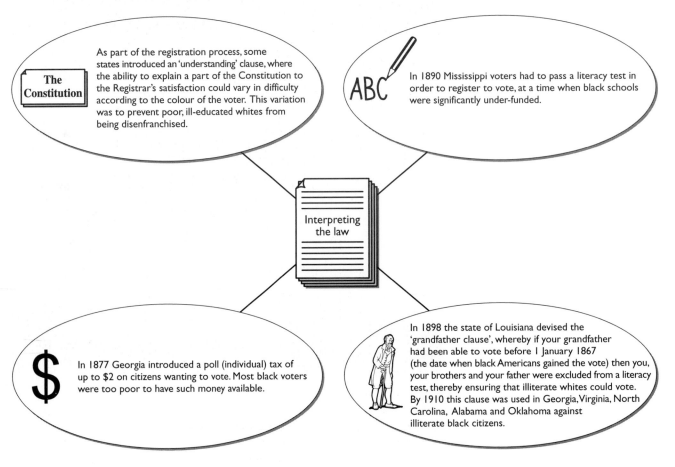

The Constitution

As part of the registration process, some states introduced an 'understanding' clause, where the ability to explain a part of the Constitution to the Registrar's satisfaction could vary in difficulty according to the colour of the voter. This variation was to prevent poor, ill-educated whites from being disenfranchised.

ABC

In 1890 Mississippi voters had to pass a literacy test in order to register to vote, at a time when black schools were significantly under-funded.

Interpreting the law

$

In 1877 Georgia introduced a poll (individual) tax of up to $2 on citizens wanting to vote. Most black voters were too poor to have such money available.

In 1898 the state of Louisiana devised the 'grandfather clause', whereby if your grandfather had been able to vote before 1 January 1867 (the date when black Americans gained the vote) then you, your brothers and your father were excluded from a literacy test, thereby ensuring that illiterate whites could vote. By 1910 this clause was used in Georgia, Virginia, North Carolina, Alabama and Oklahoma against illiterate black citizens.

What were the results?

1 Few Southern blacks were able to vote or become political leaders and represent their communities at state or national level.
2 There was little political opportunity, or public support, for legislation to be passed to benefit black people.
3 This political ineffectiveness reinforced images of black inferiority and white superiority.
4 Many Southern blacks accepted the situation as being too difficult to change (and anyway it was better than slavery).
5 Neither the federal government nor the Supreme Court enforced the spirit of the Amendment, since there was no political pressure to do so.

■ 1E Economic discrimination

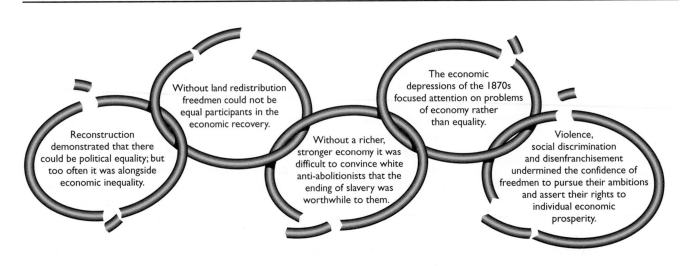

Reconstruction demonstrated that there could be political equality; but too often it was alongside economic inequality.

Without land redistribution freedmen could not be equal participants in the economic recovery.

Without a richer, stronger economy it was difficult to convince white anti-abolitionists that the ending of slavery was worthwhile to them.

The economic depressions of the 1870s focused attention on problems of economy rather than equality.

Violence, social discrimination and disenfranchisement undermined the confidence of freedmen to pursue their ambitions and assert their rights to individual economic prosperity.

SOURCE 1.13 In the years following Reconstruction the lynching of black Americans became increasingly common

Lynching (see Source 1.13) was murder, usually by hanging, by groups claiming the right to exercise justice on behalf of society. Afro-Americans were usually the victims. It is estimated that between 1889 and 1918, 2558 black men were lynched – nearly a hundred a year – although virtually none of the murderers were tried and convicted. Although such murders lessened after the First World War, they only really ended with the passing of the Civil Rights Act in 1964 (see Chapter 12, page 244). In the 1930s one of the most famous songs of the black blues singer Billie Holliday was 'Strange Fruit', which began:

'Southern trees bear strange fruit,
Blood on the leaves and blood at the root,
Black bodies swinging in the southern breeze,
Strange fruit hanging from the poplar trees.'

It is said that Billie Holliday was so affected by this song that she could only sing it at the end of her act and was always physically sick afterwards. Audiences sat in shocked silence as it ended. Congress never passed an actual anti-lynching law because presidents feared alienating political support in the Southern states.

Discrimination by society

By 1900 about 90 per cent of black or Afro-Americans lived in the South. Most relied on farming, usually as labourers or sharecroppers, or on domestic service for their employment. White attitudes towards black people were reinforced by the doctrines of Social Darwinism that became popular at the end of the nineteenth century.

Social Darwinism

Following on from Charles Darwin's theories about evolution in *The Origin of Species*, published in 1859, the philosopher Herbert Spencer applied the theory to society. He argued that human progress needed the 'survival of the fittest'. He said that government action to support the poor and weak interfered with such survival and went against the laws of nature. White supremacists used these arguments to justify their perception of a shiftless, black 'Sambo' cartoon-type image. His dark colour and different racial origins justified his being treated as an inferior in society. These beliefs were popular in an age when colonial

TALKING POINTS

1 Is the way black Southerners were being treated familiar to you in the way other minority groups have been, or are being, treated? (Think about women, disabled people, refugees, religious minorities, etc.)

2 How can such behaviour be best challenged? (This was the problem faced by black activists in the twentieth century.)

ACTIVITY

Put yourself in the shoes of a black American in the 1870s. Note down which aspects of society you would want to fight against. How might you go about your campaign?

---

imperialism promoted white rule by European countries in Africa, and later by the USA in the Pacific and Caribbean.

As black citizens were losing their basic political rights so it became easier to segregate white and black individuals. A railroad company in Florida, in 1887, was the first to introduce segregated carriages.

The *Plessy v. Ferguson* case

In 1892, Homer A. Plessy, light-skinned but deemed to be black because he had one-eighth black ancestry (i.e. as only seven-eighths white he was known as an octoroon), deliberately challenged the Louisiana state law requiring railroad companies to provide separate facilities on their trains for black and white passengers. Refusing to leave a 'white carriage' he was arrested. The local Judge Ferguson ruled against Plessy's plea that his rights (under the Fourteenth Amendment) were being violated. The case was taken to the Supreme Court and the Justices agreed with Judge Ferguson and ruled against Plessy. They argued that the enforced separation of the races was not a mark of inferiority and that the Amendment referred only to state and federal governments not to individuals and organisations (such as railroad companies). The Court deemed that 'separate but equal' facilities were sufficient to be within the law. However, the one dissenting judge, John Harlan (a Southerner and former slave-owner) believed that there was prejudice, and the intent was to keep black passengers away from white ones. He predicted that the decision would 'stimulate aggression, more or less brutal, upon the admitted rights of the colored citizens'.

Here was more Reconstruction legislation being ignored – specifically the Civil Rights Act (1875), which guaranteed black people equal accommodation in public places, and the Fourteenth Amendment (1866), which granted citizenship to freed slaves. Not only were they ignored, but also the Supreme Court supported these attitudes in the *Plessy v. Ferguson* case. The ruling was a disaster for black civil rights since states could now interpret 'equal' in whatever way they wanted. In 1899 the ruling was extended to schooling so that black children became trapped in a segregated system of education. In practice this meant under-funded schools and a reinforcement of inequality in expectations and attitudes. It was not until 1954 that desegregation was slowly begun; not until 1957 that there was another Civil Rights Act; and not until 1964 that there was a fully-enforced, effective Civil Rights Act.

Challenging discrimination

Such discrimination by state laws became known as 'Jim Crow' laws (supposedly named after a popular black minstrel music hall act). This discrimination:

- created a bi-racial Southern society
- meant that racial SEGREGATION was approved by the highest court in the land
- reinforced and entrenched images of the inferior status and work of Afro-Americans
- encouraged the gradual flow of black workers to the industrial North where segregation was less systemised
- meant that new ways had to be found to challenge laws and attitudes.

ACTIVITY

Make notes on the following:

a) How did each of the people described on pages 17–18 challenge discrimination?
b) What kinds of needs were they meeting?
c) How effective were their challenges?

You will need to think about: the social and political environments in which they lived; the fears and hopes of their communities; the role and importance of education; how change is able to occur in society.

Booker T. (Taliaferro) Washington (1856–1915)
Born a slave in Virginia, with a black mother and a white father (whom he never knew), Washington became the most well-known leader of Afro-Americans before the First World War. After emancipation he quickly realised the importance of education and struggled through great poverty to attend college. His commitment and enthusiasm led to him setting up the respected Tuskegee Institute in Alabama, in 1881. It became a model for education linked to vocational training for black students. Later, he helped set up the National Urban League to help black workers adjust to industrial, urban life. He believed that hard work and financial success would weaken discrimination – that there was no racial prejudice in the American dollar. In *Up from Slavery* and his speeches, he urged acceptance that change was a slow process; as in this speech in 1895, which critics called the Atlanta Compromise:
'Our greatest danger is that in the great leap from slavery to freedom we may overlook the fact that the masses of us are to live by the productions of our hands … No race can prosper till it learns that there is as much dignity in tilling a field as in writing a poem. It is at the bottom of life we must begin, and not at the top. Nor should we permit our grievances to overshadow our opportunities.'

■ 1F How should a black leader behave at the end of the nineteenth century?

WAS IT SUFFICIENT THAT WASHINGTON:

- was a respected leader (the only black leader to dine with President Roosevelt and take tea with Queen Victoria)
- gained the financial support of white industrialists such as Andrew Carnegie
- made the Tuskegee an effective institution for improving the knowledge and skills of hundreds of black students and the communities to which they returned
- subtly raised black pride in work well done
- was pragmatic at a time of violent reaction and white intransigence?

OR SHOULD HE HAVE:

- fought for political change to end discrimination
- used his oratory and organisational skills to encourage the majority black population in the South to react in a more aggressive way
- challenged the segregation laws
- raised the expectations of black people?

THE CONSENSUS VIEW IS THAT:
- in the circumstances of the time, his behaviour and beliefs were the most appropriate and possibly the only possible stance to take
- self-help may not have been the most dramatic or the quickest route to equality, but at least it did give individuals pride and some economic power.

DISCUSS

What is your view of Washington's actions? Were they well-judged or too great a compromise? At the end of the book you may want to review these, and decide if Washington's tactics were effective, or damaging, in the long-term fight for civil rights.

W. E. B. Du Bois (1868–1963)
As a free black man born in the North, Du Bois had a very different life from Washington. After gaining degrees at Fisk (an all black college), at Berlin and from the prestigious Harvard University, he became a lecturer in sociology. Although initially sympathetic to incremental change, by 1900 he was arguing for more active resistance to discrimination. He urged the use of legal and political processes through unceasing agitation. He helped to organise the Niagara Conference of 1905, which pledged the militant pursuit of civil rights, and helped to found the National Association for the Advancement of Colored People (NAACP) in 1909, the most important American civil rights organisation of the twentieth century. Du Bois continued to write powerfully against discrimination, particularly through his editorship of the journal *The Crisis*. His frustration at the slow pace of change eventually resulted in him moving to Ghana where he died in 1963.

Ida B. Wells (1862–1931)

A journalist and militant campaigner, she too was a founder member of the NAACP. Her writings were particularly directed against lynching after having seen two friends murdered. However, her fierce condemnations led to the destruction of her paper's printing presses by a mob and this forced her out of Memphis.

Recognising the power of women's protests, she encouraged more aggressive demands by women's and church groups. She travelled to Britain and wrote articles there that were critical of the Southern states. As she hoped, this raised awareness of discriminatory practices in America. Knowing that lynching often took place after accusations of a black man raping a white woman, she challenged the conventional picture of Southern white male chivalry: 'True chivalry respects all womankind, and no one who reads the record as it is written in the faces of the million mulattos in the South, will for a minute conceive that the Southern white man had a very chivalrous regard for the honor due to women of his own race or respect for the womanhood which circumstance placed in his power'.

Nannie Helen Burroughs (1883–1961)

She advocated the 'three Bs' – the Bible, the Bath and the Broom as much as the 'three Rs' (Reading, Writing and Arithmetic). One of many women who worked in black communities, especially through the Church, to improve ordinary lives, Burroughs set up a girls' school in Washington in 1909. She believed that vocational skills and hard work were necessary to fight discrimination because they would enable women to earn a living and self-respect.

Madam C. J. Walker (1867–1919)

Born as Sarah Breedlove and the first free member of her sharecropper family, she started working as a cook and laundress, both typical occupations for black women. However, she was also enterprising and inventive. Devising a hair cream suitable for black women's hair she made it at home, sold it door-to-door, and, because of its success, went on to devise a complete hair-care system. She hired Afro-American girls as agents and sold her products in churches and women's clubs as white stores refused to stock them. Reputed to be the first female black millionaire, she donated money to the Tuskegee Institute, to anti-lynching campaigns and the NAACP. In 1998, the US Postal Service issued a stamp in her honour. She was an early example of black pride, and of black communities meeting their own particular needs.

DISCUSS

Is it reasonable to criticise the politicians of the time for their failure to overcome the problems that resulted from the abolition of slavery? How long does it really take for attitudes to change?

F Review: Were black Americans really made free and equal by the abolition of slavery, 1865–1915?

This chapter has looked at how far slaves, freed as a result of the Civil War, were able to become free and equal citizens. Historians disagree about how successful Reconstruction was; but all would agree that it set in place both the legal framework to allow former slaves to become citizens and the rebuilding of a different society in the South. However, twelve years was too short a time to change conservative traditional attitudes about the roles of black and white Southerners. The range of problems to be tackled after the Civil War demanded too much of the bureaucratic system at the time, so that injustices, violence and corruption persisted. Some historians have argued that the reaction to abolition actually made racism more embedded in American society. The failure to wholly integrate freedmen and value their contributions to society, made the fight for black civil rights both long and painful.

ACTIVITY

Were black Americans really set free by the abolition of slavery?

Copy and complete the table below, about the effectiveness of different factors between 1877 and 1915, which might have created full freedom and equality for former slaves.

	Reuniting the Northern and Southern states	Enabling slaves to become effective citizens	Superficial or long-term change
Constitutional or legal changes			
Influence of religion			
Agricultural economy of the South			
Industrial economy of the North			
Racist attitudes			
Enforcement of the law			
Violence			
Reconstruction policies			

ACTIVITY

Select three key events in the history of black Americans between 1865 and 1915. What does your choice tell you about the extent to which black Americans had really gained freedom and equality?

KEY POINTS FROM CHAPTER 1

Were black Americans really made free and equal by the abolition of slavery, 1865–1915?

1 The Civil War started as an argument about maintaining the unity of the states system and ended as a fight for the abolition of slavery.

2 The period known as Reconstruction (1865–77) was aimed at unifying the North and South, and at coping with the realities of life for newly freed black Americans.

3 The early years of Reconstruction demonstrated that it was possible to successfully challenge racist ideas, but deep-seated prejudice combined with economic and social patterns continued to diminish for decades the rights and opportunities of black Americans, especially in the South.

4 The Northern states continued the wartime pattern of industrialisation suggesting that the power of economic and political demands was clearly stronger than that of civil rights in directing change in the USA from the 1870s.

5 Constitutional and legal changes provided a framework for enabling freed slaves to be citizens.

6 Racist attitudes about white superiority motivated deliberate disenfranchisement and social discrimination.

7 Afro-Americans found it difficult to challenge such reactions, deprived as many of them were of equality in education, employment opportunities, wealth and political power.

8 Black communities were able to demonstrate that self-help was a possible way of fighting for a better life.

2

How significant was the settlement of the West, 1865–1900?

CHAPTER OVERVIEW

■ 2A 'Westward I go free' – the USA gets bigger

The US Census Bureau defines the USA West region as the states of Alaska, Arizona, California, Colorado, Hawaii, Idaho, Montana, Nevada, New Mexico, Oregon, Utah, Washington and Wyoming.

The West can also be categorised as follows:
The South West states: Arizona, California, Colorado, New Mexico, Nevada and Utah.
The Pacific North West states: Idaho, Montana, Oregon, Washington.
The West coast states: California, Oregon and Washington.

The area can also be divided into two regions: Pacific States and Mountain States (which also relate to the time zones of the same name).

The West is more vaguely defined as:
- anywhere west of the Mississippi
- everywhere west of the Great Plains (i.e. the Rockies and westwards)
- everywhere west of the 100 degrees line of longitude
- anywhere west of the Appalachians (i.e. most of the land mass!)
- some Americans say it just depends on where you are standing when you answer the question!

The Civil War ended in 1865. It had re-created the political unity of the existing states, but the political nation we call the United States of America was still incomplete. The population lived from the Atlantic to the Missouri River, and from the Pacific to the Sierra Nevada mountains. In between was what was known as the West, about half the area of the USA, but with only one per cent of the population (see Chart 2A). However, between 1865 and 1900 the West was dramatically changed through settlement and the exploitation of its resources.

> 'The future lies that way to me, and the earth seems more unexhausted and richer on that side ... Eastward I go only by force; but westward I go free ... I must walk towards Oregon, and not toward Europe.'

Henry Thoreau, one of America's most famous nineteenth-century philosophers, wrote this just weeks before he died. He had never travelled beyond the Missouri, but sensed the idea of exciting freedom offered by the empty area on the map known as the West. It was an emotional force, as much as an economic one that persuaded American citizens to move into the lands west of the Mississippi River. This chapter will investigate how significant this settlement was both for the peoples of the West and the rest of America, and why the West gained such a mythical status in the later history of the USA.

A Manifest destiny – why go West? (pp. 21–24)

B How did the West become the nation's bread basket? (pp. 25–26)

C How was Native American culture destroyed? (pp. 27–29)

D How were myths about the West created and maintained? (pp. 30–34)

E Review: How significant was the settlement of the West, 1865–1900? (pp. 35–36)

ACTIVITY

1 This chapter evaluates the significance of the settlement of the West. Make a list of the criteria you would use to evaluate the significance of an event in history.

2 What are your current ideas about how significant the settlement of the West was? Brainstorm as many ideas as you can, working in pairs or small groups.

FOCUS ROUTE

As you work through Section A make notes on the following questions.

1 What were:
   a) the practical reasons
   b) the emotional reasons
   for people moving to the West?

2 What changes were likely to result from this movement of population?

DISCUSS

Which groups of Americans do you think believed in this manifest destiny and which were excluded?

A Manifest destiny – why go West?

Many Americans believed in 'manifest destiny'; a God-given right to settle the continent. The first use of the term can be found in the magazine *Democratic Review*, in July 1845:

> 'the fulfilment of our manifest destiny [is] to overspread the continent allocated by Providence for the free development of our yearly multiplying millions'.

This idea of 'destiny' encouraged the notion of expansion and linked the developing American nationalism with geography. America did not have Europe's ancient ruins and medieval cathedrals as symbols of civilisation, but it did have immense, dramatic, unspoilt landscapes in the West. To most Americans these landscapes symbolised America's freedom as a republic. This republic was free, untainted by aristocracy and the corruption of the past (unlike the 'Old World' of Europe), and was full of natural energy and boundless vistas.

SOURCE 2.1 One of America's favourite songs, 'America the Beautiful', written in 1893, reflected the ideas of a wonderful land

America the Beautiful
O beautiful for spacious skies
For amber waves of grain
For purple mountain majesties
Above the fruited plain

America! America!
God shed his grace on Thee
And crown thy good with brotherhood
From sea to shining sea.

■ **2B Population density, 1870 and 1890**

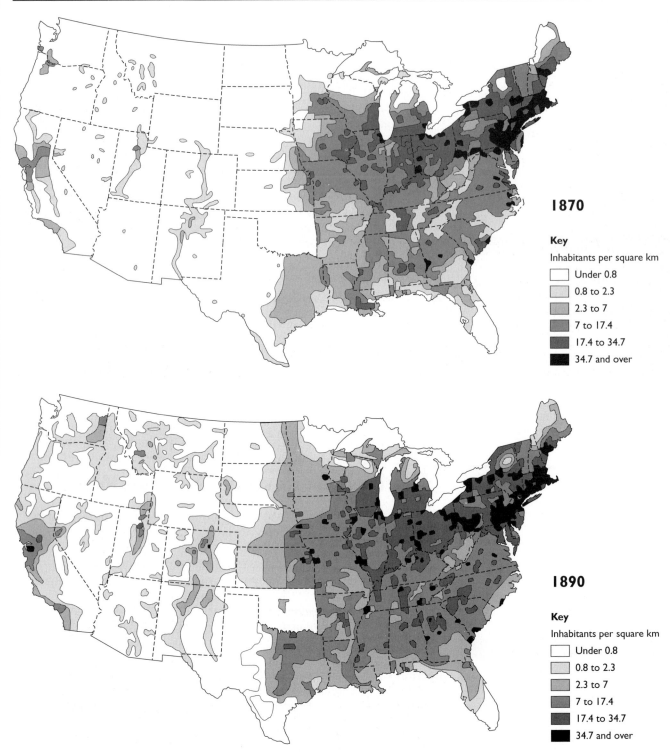

1870

Key

Inhabitants per square km

- Under 0.8
- 0.8 to 2.3
- 2.3 to 7
- 7 to 17.4
- 17.4 to 34.7
- 34.7 and over

1890

Key

Inhabitants per square km

- Under 0.8
- 0.8 to 2.3
- 2.3 to 7
- 7 to 17.4
- 17.4 to 34.7
- 34.7 and over

ACTIVITY

1 What is meant by the phrase 'manifest destiny'?

2 Using Sources 2.2–2.4 decide who would be attracted to the possibilities of travelling West. Here are some possibilities to consider:

Young men eager to make their fortune / entrepreneurs / Eastern industrialists with finance for investment / families wanting more land / those feeling overwhelmed by the growth of cities and industry in the east / immigrants from farming areas in Germany and Scandinavia / single women / farming families / those disliking physical work / unskilled immigrants

SOURCE 2.2 Cattle on the open range in the 1880s

SOURCE 2.3 A poster entitled *California the Cornucopia of the World*, 1870s

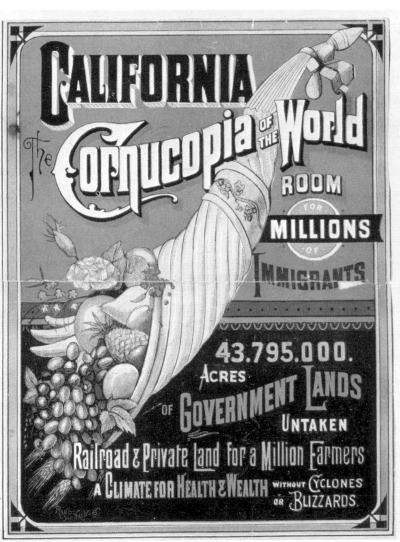

SOURCE 2.4 Theodore Roosevelt (later President in 1901) describing Dakota, in a letter to his sister in New York, 1884 (quoted in E. Morris, *The Rise of Theodore Roosevelt*, 1979, pp. 274–75)

It certainly has a desolate, grim beauty of its own, that has a curious fascination for me. The grassy, scantily wooded bottoms through which the winding river flows are bounded by bare, jagged buttes; their fantastic shapes and sharp, sheer edges throw the most curious shadows, under the cloudless, glaring sky ... my days I would spend alone, riding through the lonely rolling prairies and broken lands.

DISCUSS

Sources only become evidence when they are used to answer questions or investigate topics. What different questions or topics could you use Sources 2.2–2.4 to investigate?

■ 2C The federal government encourages settlement of the West

1 By purchase, treaty, annexation and war during the nineteenth century, the federal government had promoted and increased the land area and population of the West.

2 It passed laws that helped settlers gain land. The Homestead Act of 1862 said that farmers could have free land by staking a claim and living on it for five years, or by buying it for $1.25 an acre after six months. Single women could apply under the same conditions as men.

3 It offered practical help by protecting overland migrants from Native American and outlaw raids, and helped to supply migrant parties.

4 Using the US army it imposed legal, social and political patterns of acceptable behaviour on the Western lands.

5 It financed, and encouraged others to build roads, railroads and stagecoach routes. The first trans-continental railroad was created on 10 May 1869. Coming from the east the Union Pacific Railroad Company built 1086 miles, from Omaha, and met the Central Pacific Railroad Company line built along 689 miles, from Sacramento in the West.

6 It initiated scientific explorations and published their reports. Such reports had detailed maps, scenic landscape and scientific illustrations.

In 1862, the US government passed the Pacific Railway Act, which allowed railway companies to take sufficient materials for its building and for 'stations, buildings, workshops, and depots, machine shops, switches, side tracks, turn tables, and water stations', from the land alongside the railway line. It said that 'The US shall extinguish as rapidly as may be the Indian titles to all lands falling under the operation of the Act'. The government provided cash bonds to facilitate the constructions, to be repaid in 30 years' time. Between 1850 and 1871 an estimated 155 million acres were granted by Congress for railroad construction.

■ 2D Routes of six major transcontinental railroads

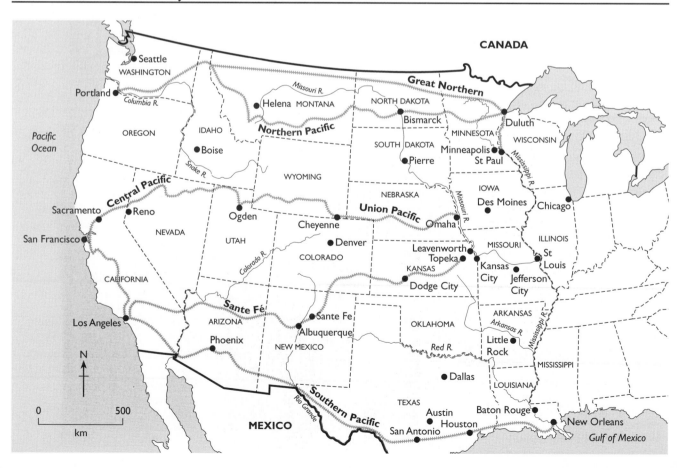

FOCUS ROUTE

1 List the factors that enabled agricultural production to increase so rapidly.
2 Why was this development significant, then and since?

B How did the West become the nation's bread basket?

Remember the 'amber waves of grain' in the song 'America the Beautiful' (page 21)? This was a real image seen by anyone who travelled to the West as agricultural production increased enormously within twenty years. The West not only supplied the grain needs of the USA – its own 'bread basket' – but by 1890 the USA was exporting so much grain that it was seen as the bread basket of industrial Europe.

SOURCE 2.5 Grain production, 1866–1898 (in millions of bushels)

	1866	1880	1898
Wheat	152	500	675
Corn	730	1500	2330

The varied climate and terrain in the West meant that a range of crops could be grown and that there was sufficient space to raise beef cattle on open ranges. By 1900, farm commodities formed three-quarters of all American exports. It was estimated that a quarter of all agricultural products were exported, which included 34 per cent of wheat, ten per cent of corn and 68 per cent of cotton. However, there were other key reasons why farming was so successful:

- farms and ranches produced huge surpluses (grain, cattle) to sell
- a transport network developed to move the surplus around the country
- markets for these surpluses were growing, especially with the rapid industrialisation taking place in the East. There was a growing population in the East, partly because of immigration, that needed the West's produce.

Mechanical inventions increased productivity, and so did new land being cultivated for the first time. Between 1870 and 1900, 225 million acres of improved land were added to American farms. After 1873, fearful of becoming bankrupt, the National Pacific Railroad Company sold 483,000 acres of its land at $5 an acre. Most of it was bought by only 23 people, who went on to create bonanza farms in the Red River Valley of the Dakotas. These farms of 10,000 acres needed 250 farmhands each; a stark contrast to the small farms of Homestead Act settlers. A similar development took place in California. These large-scale farms applied industrial production techniques: the use of machinery for mass production; professional management; specialisation; and cheap labour. Although many had failed by the end of the century they produced immense quantities of grain at the height of their success.

SOURCE 2.6 Combine reaper-thresher harvesting prairie wheat c. 1880. Note the number of horses

ACTIVITY

1 Look at Sources 2.6–2.8. What can you learn from them about why agricultural production and farming communities increased so rapidly?

SOURCE 2.7 A late nineteenth-century Oklahoma homestead family still living in a sod house (one with a roof made of grass sods), but also using the products of industrialisation – a reaper, a windmill for pumping water from underground, a sewing machine, and possibly catalogue-bought clothes

SEARS, ROEBUCK AND COMPANY

The Sears, Roebuck and Company catalogue was started in the 1890s. The mail order company offered a catalogue of nearly 800 pages, in three languages, and sold a staggering range of goods. These included groceries, household utensils, farm implements, pianos, clothes, footwear and books; all sold at lower prices than rural stores. It created a national market and enabled isolated rural families to enjoy manufactured, labour-saving products. Its popularity was aided by free rural mail delivery from 1897.

SOURCE 2.8 A Sears, Roebuck and Company catalogue cover, 1897

FOCUS ROUTE

1 Identify the main methods used by the government to take control of Native Americans.

2 Why did the government wish to control the Native Americans? (Your answer should include reference to manifest destiny.)

3 Explain why this period was so significant for Native Americans.

SOURCE 2.10 Chief Washakie, of the Shoshone Indian tribe, c. 1870–75

The white man kills our game, captures our furs and sometimes feeds his herds upon our meadows … Every foot of what you proudly call America, not very long ago belonged to the red man. The Great Spirit gave it to us … But the white man had, in ways we know not of, learned some things we had not learned; among them, how to make superior tools and terrible weapons … and there seemed no end to the hordes of men that followed … from other lands across the sea.

C How was Native American culture destroyed?

SOURCE 2.9   Chief Washakie of the Shoshone Indians commented

The white man who possesses this whole vast country from sea to sea, who roams over it at pleasure and lives where he likes, cannot know the cramp we feel in this little spot.

The Native Americans, who had lived in the West for hundreds of years, saw their traditions and culture damaged and even destroyed by the white settlement of the West. Native American tribes were vulnerable because their nomadic lifestyle (which relied heavily on horses and the buffalo or bison) was completely at odds with the attitudes of homesteaders and ranchers who settled on 'their' land. The Native Americans lost the battle for grasslands, water and bison. Between 1864 and the final stand by the Lakota Ghost Dance movement of 1890 the tribes were defeated by the army who had superior numbers and technology. Tribes were left struggling for food, and with little choice but to acquiesce in a variety of assimilation practices to make them more 'acceptable' members of American society (even though they were not granted citizenship rights until 1924).

■ 2E The federal government establishes control over Native Americans' lives

1865–67	Sioux war against white miners and the US army
1867–68	Policy of 'small reservations' adopted for Native Americans
1873	Discovery of silver in Comstock Lode in Nevada leads to influx of miners. Invention of barbed wire allows land to be fenced off
1874	Discovery of gold in Dakota leads to Black Hills gold rush
1875	Sioux ordered to leave Powder River hunting land, and war results
1876	General Custer defeated at the Battle of Little Bighorn by the Sioux
1879	Ute tribe surrenders and forced to accept territorial loss in Colorado. Carlisle School for Indians established in Pennsylvania
1883	Fewer than 200 buffalo left in the West
1884	US Supreme Court defines Indians as wards under government protection
1887	Dawes Severalty Act ends communal ownership of Indian lands and gives Native Americans individual plots of land
1890	Sioux massacred at battle of Wounded Knee in South Dakota. Last battle of Plains Indians

■ 2F The reservations policy

The policy gave our tribes no say over our own affairs, leaving us in need of government food handouts because the land was unproductive.

It ignored our native history, combining groups that were hostile towards one another on the same reservations. It weakened our traditional lifestyles.

Pressure from white farmers, miners and speculators seeking land increased, and this made it difficult for the government to keep our reservations intact.

They argued that this was done for our future welfare, but the establishment of the Friends of the Indian movement showed that the main concern was to bring us into mainstream society, whatever the cost to our own culture and landholdings.

SOURCE 2.11 'Before and after' photos of Apache Indian children at the Carlisle Indian School in 1886

Children, like the ones shown in Source 2.11, were being 'Americanised' in US Training and Industrial Schools and boarding schools because:

• professional educators saw schooling as a social engineering tool to create an integrated and patriotic nation (like the Tuskegee Institute for black students in Alabama, see page 17).
• of the influence of Euro–American and Christian views challenging the traditional family structures and values of Native Americans
• it was an attempt to weaken tribal distinctiveness and dissent.

The Dawes Severalty Act of 1887 encouraged tribes away from communal land ownership into more acceptable private land ownership, with each family granted 160 acres. Surplus land was sold at five cents an acre.

SOURCE 2.12 H. Evans, *The American Century*, p. 7

… The Dawes Act suffered from a defect basic to the democracy that spawned it. Nobody took much notice of what the Indians really wanted. The obverse of the glorious expansion west was that for the Indian, the American dream was a nightmare: oppression instead of democracy, poverty instead of prosperity, despair instead of hope, contraction instead of expansion, confinement instead of freedom.

ACTIVITY

Using Sources 2.10–2.13 and Charts 2E and 2F:

1 Identify the different methods that the government used to establish its superiority over the Native Americans.
2 Which actions do you think did most to destroy Native American culture and resistance?

TALKING POINTS

It is interesting to compare American behaviour towards native peoples with that of Canadian behaviour. There, the process of assimilation was deliberately slower, native peoples had citizenship rights, were protected by the Royal Mounted Police from white aggression and inter-marriage was encouraged and tolerated. It has been argued though, that in the long-term such assimilation was just as likely to weaken traditional life.

1 How far should traditional ways of life and values be protected by the majority group in society?
2 Does it matter if minority groups are diminished or disappear?

SOURCE 2.13 *Crow Creek Agency, Dakota Territory* by William Fuller, 1884, showing the 'ideal' changes for Indian life; from nomadic hunting and tepee homes to a Euro-American model of neatly-fenced frame houses, tidy fields and suited braves riding saddled horses

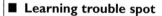

ACTIVITY

Personal research
Find out more about the dramatic clashes between the tribes and the army at Little Big Horn, Wounded Knee, Sand Creek and about Chief Joseph's rebellion. Dee Brown's book, *Bury my Heart at Wounded Knee*, has done much to generate another view of the treatment of Native Americans.

SOURCE 2.14 Chief Joseph of the Nez Perce tribe said 'I never said the land was mine to do with as I chose. The one who has the right to dispose of it is the one who has created it. I claim a right to live on my land, and accord you the privilege to live on yours.'

ACTIVITY

Improvise a conversation *c.* 1890 between a white settler and a Native American who has been sent to a reservation. Try to explain to each other your attitudes and also your feelings about what has happened to the West.

■ **Learning trouble spot**

Were there any protests?
These changes did not happen without comment. Helen Hunt Jackson's *A Century of Dishonor*, 1881, shocked its readers with the story of the brutality and deceit shown to the tribes. However, the end of the nineteenth century was not a time when dissent was appreciated or valued. The imposition of territorial order on the movement of others deemed as inferiors allowed white Americans to believe in the superiority of their manifest destiny and rights to mobility. Native Americans were the most obvious victims of these attitudes, but Chinese immigrants also suffered. Hired mainly to work on railroad construction they were paid at much lower rates than other workers, creating resentments that they competed unfairly for jobs. There were riots against Chinese immigrants in Los Angeles in 1871 and Denver in 1880. In 1882 President Hayes signed the Chinese Exclusion Act restricting immigration from China and limiting the opportunity to become a naturalised citizen.

How were myths about the West created and maintained?

The West had more than political and financial importance. It contributed to a unique and lasting image of America, which mingled fact and imagination. Settling the West meant losing the wilderness and that 'uncivilised' part of the American continent. To some Americans this meant losing the essence of America – freedom.

What is a frontier?

A frontier can be:

- a border between countries or a dividing line within a country
- the edge of civilisation
- a region with more than two, and less than six, people per square mile (US Census Bureau definition).

In 1890, the US Census Bureau declared 'Up to and including 1880 the country had a frontier of settlement, but at present the unsettled area has been so broken into by isolated bodies of settlement there can hardly be said to be a frontier line. In the discussion of its extent, its westward movement, etc. it cannot, therefore, any longer have a place in the census reports.'

So, officially, there was no longer a frontier. For the first time in American history there was no large tract of unsettled land. Then in 1893, the young historian Frederick Jackson Turner, presented a conference paper entitled 'The Significance of the Frontier in American History'. Turner had grown up in Wisconsin, where the pioneering life was still remembered, but in contrast, had been educated in the East at the Johns Hopkins University in Baltimore, where the influences of European manners and expectations were still strong. Turner's key points aroused much debate. He claimed:

- at the deepest root of America's past had been 'the existence of an area of free land'
- that accessible land, as in the West, acted as a safety valve against social discord and violence
- the harshness of the frontier created self-reliant individuals, who were invaluable to a nation like the USA
- that America's development had been different from that of Europe as it had no hierarchy or aristocracy relying on privileges of birth to create social class
- that the USA had a unique form of democracy. It was the abundance of Nature and its resources (so visible in the West) that made Americans free.

His ideas encouraged people, and notably the presidents of the time, to think that if frontiers and all they represented had made the USA unique, then perhaps the USA should have new frontiers, frontiers that were outside the geographic boundary of the nation. Turner's ideas also helped to create an idea or myth of the frontier lands – that 'the West' was different. It was essential to the image of a strong America.

FOCUS ROUTE

1 Explain in your own words Turner's arguments about why the frontier was so important in American history.
2 Why did the myth of the West appeal to **a)** politicians and **b)** ordinary Americans at the end of the nineteenth century?

Whose West was being portrayed?

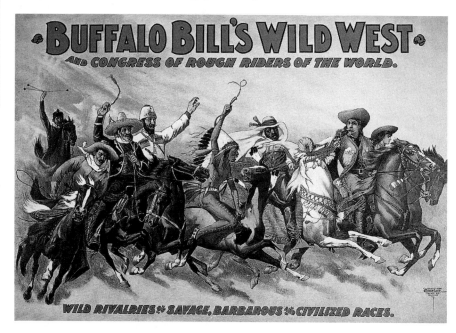

SOURCE 2.16 Owen Wister's novel, *The Virginian, Horseman of the Plain*, was written in 1902 and dedicated to Wister's friend President Theodore Roosevelt. It became the archetypal cowboy story (best read aloud for full dramatic effect!)

The Virginian's pistol came out, and his hand lay on the table, holding it unaimed. And with a voice as gentle as ever, the voice that sounded almost like a caress, but drawling a very little more than usual, so that there was almost a space between each word, he issued his orders to the man Trampas: 'When you call me that, smile!'
And he looked at Trampas across the table. Yes, the voice was gentle. But in my ears it seemed as if somewhere the bell of death was ringing; and silence, like a stroke, fell on the large room.

SOURCE 2.15 A poster advertising 'Buffalo Bill's Wild West Show'. William Frederick Cody led an adventurous life as a gold miner, Pony Express rider, Civil War veteran, army scout during the Indian wars and hero of dime novels (see Sources 2.16 and 2.18). In 1873, he began producing shows featuring cowboys and Indians (now known as Native Americans) enacting real events and the imaginary ones of the novels. They were immensely successful for 30 years, travelling across the USA and Europe. However, in spite of having Chief Sitting Bull as a star in 1885, they were also a source of the negative stereotyping of the Native American life continued in later films and television

SOURCE 2.17 A painting by Frank Tenney Johnson entitled *Singing 'Em to Sleep*, 1926. A classic image of the lone cowboy on the range

SOURCE 2.18 Front cover of the dime novel *Diamond Dick: Wild Bill's Last Trail*. Dime novels were cheap adventure stories

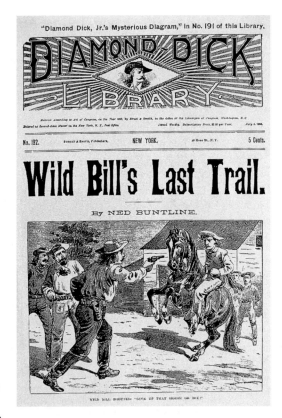

SOURCE 2.19 An extract from *The Women's West*, by S. Armitage and E. Jameson, 1987, p. 9

Hisland. In a magnificent western landscape, under perpetually cloudless skies, a cast of heroic characters engage in dramatic combat, sometimes with nature, sometimes with each other. Occupationally, these heroes are diverse: they are mountain men, cowboys, Indians, soldiers, farmers, miners and desperadoes, but they share one distinguishing characteristic – they are all men. It seems that all rational demography has ended at the Mississippi River; all the land west is occupied only by men.

It is easy to see how these images became popular, especially in the industrial East far away from the real West. Heroism, mixed with violence and romantic costumes, provided a visual myth to match the ideas about the moral value of the freedom of the frontier. Stories of lawless mining towns and gunfights between ranchers and farmers over rights to water and land were both real and dramatised. The lone cowboy like the Virginian became the typical image of this imagined and mythical West. He was independent, self-reliant, tough and unafraid of the harshness of the land and the violence of others. But – where were the women?

SOURCE 2.20 Harvey T. Dunn's painting, *The Prairie is my Garden*, 1950

... the refined lady, the helpmate and the bad woman. The lady, who may be a schoolteacher, a missionary, or merely a woman of some civilised taste, is defined as too genteel for the rough-and-ready West. She is either uncomfortable, unhappy, or is driven literally crazy by the frontier ... the strong and uncomplaining helpmate adapts to the West, but in the process becomes a work-worn superwoman, losing all her individuality. The bad woman has both glamour and power, but she loses them along with her life as she comes rapidly to her appropriate end – a bad one.

Source 2.20 shows an image not often seen in Western pictures, both truthful and mythical. It gives some indication of the isolation of prairie life, although the sunshine and flowers diminish the prairie's harshness. Gardens represented peace and the cultivation of the wilderness. Women were the gardeners of the West, not only in a practical sense, but in that they also brought the civilising influences needed to raise and educate a family; the essence of a good society. This woman looks determined, if a little stern; a female heroine of the West, able to cope with its harshness, but also able to provide gentleness, care and order amidst its wildness.

ACTIVITY

1 What images of women fitted the myth of the West?
2 Why were women excluded from most representations of the West?

ACTIVITY

You can perhaps see why the West has been called Hisland (Source 2.19). You can get another perspective by reading novels about women in the West, for example, Willa Cather's *O Pioneers*, Agnes Smedley's *Daughter of Earth*, or Laura Ingalls Wilder's *Little House on the Prairie* (and others in that series).

The appeal of the myth of the West

As the reality of industrialisation and business, the demands for women's suffrage and labour unions, and unhealthy sprawling cities spread across the country, so there was a reaction to the mechanistic, rational, controlled life that these things represented. The wide-open spaces of the West, where men could be men and women knew their place, was a much more exciting, satisfying image of America. It was a land of restless settlers, ambitious ranchers, migrants seeking work and gold-hungry miners. Myths survive on nostalgia; a desire for an imagined past that is better than the present. People believed that the West was pure, in contrast to the industrial East, which seemed to be sterile, corrupt and over civilised. Violence was acceptable in the imagined West, when it was between gunfighters or the army and Native Americans, but not in the real East if it came from labour unions trying to improve working conditions. The mythical West seemed to provide the moral and social lessons needed for a better society. Even at his worst the imagined Western hero was, for many Americans, preferable to a disciplined factory worker (especially if he was a foreign factory worker).

These ideas were exploited by writers, photographers, magazine illustrators and painters. The vocabulary of conflict evident in much Western life and literature became part of everyday speech – 'show down', 'last stand', 'round-up'. The early film industry had cowboy confrontations as a mainstay of their production. The film *Stagecoach* made in 1939, with John Wayne as its star, was one of the most famous (see Source 2.22). The story was typical of the time. The stagecoach with its odd mix of passengers (drunken doctor, thieving banker, criminal but brave cowboy, good time girl) was pursued by 'Red Indians', crossing the arid but magnificent landscape of Monument Valley in Utah. It was to be rescued by the timely arrival of the US cavalry. The stark contrast between good and evil, between law and disorder, took place amidst America's natural grandeur and uniqueness; the land of manifest destiny.

SOURCE 2.22 A still from the 1939 film, *Stagecoach*

SOURCE 2.23 This photograph appears on the Arizona Office of Tourism website as a promotional image to encourage visitors to the state

Study Source 2.23.

1 With a partner list the features that are being used in this image to paint a particular picture of the West. Are these features fact or fiction?

2 Does the myth of the West have any meaning or importance today? Think of examples of Western-style clothes (denim jeans), listening to music (country and western), watching Western films. What is attractive to people about them? Do you think they are still presenting an image, rather than the reality, of the Western states of the USA?

■ **Learning trouble spot**

What is the difference between history and myths?

Both history and myths tell stories about the past. Both try to impose some order on the past. But historians use facts in context. They try to decipher, not ignore, the relationship between facts. So a historian telling the story of the settlement of the West would recognise that there were many people involved, including ones usually ignored by the myth-makers, such as law-abiding cowboys, black settlers and single women. Historians do not change facts. They recognise that 'the past is a foreign country. They do things differently there'. Whatever happened in the past is in a different context from today's world.

Mythmakers use actual events and people, but feel free to change the details, or the sequence of events or to add or ignore characters, so that the emphasis they want to make is clearer. They do not put their stories into the context of the past with its behaviour, expectations, attitudes or knowledge. So myths, even if appealing or reassuring stories, are essentially false interpretations of the past, designed to satisfy the needs of the time in which they were created. They are often used in wartime or when a nation or community need reassurance. The West's heroic, independent men, with the iconic image of the cowboy, fitted the image of America at a time, from the beginning of the twentieth century onwards, when it was beginning to assert, by force, its place in the world.

ACTIVITY

Do you remember being asked at the beginning of this chapter to think about how we determine whether an event is significant (page 21)? This Activity will help you summarise your ideas about how significant the settlement of the West was. In the table below are six criteria for significance. Your task is to complete the other two columns.

1 Copy and complete the table below. In the middle column write the aspects of settlement that meet each criterion. You can use one aspect more than once. Some of the chief results of settlement are in Chart 2G but you may think of others.

2 Now look back through this chapter to find evidence to support your choices.

Criteria for significance	Aspect of the settlement of the West	Evidence
1 **Importance** – was it important to people living at the time?		
2 **Profundity** – how deeply were people's lives affected?		
3 **Quantity** – how many lives were affected?		
4 **Durability** – for how long were people's lives affected?		
5 **Relevance** – does understanding this event help us to understand the world today?		
6 **Consequences** – what significant changes did this event lead to?		

DISCUSS

1 Do you agree with the criteria used in the Activity or would you suggest others?

2 Do you think that any of them are more important than others?

■ 2G Effects of the settlement of the West

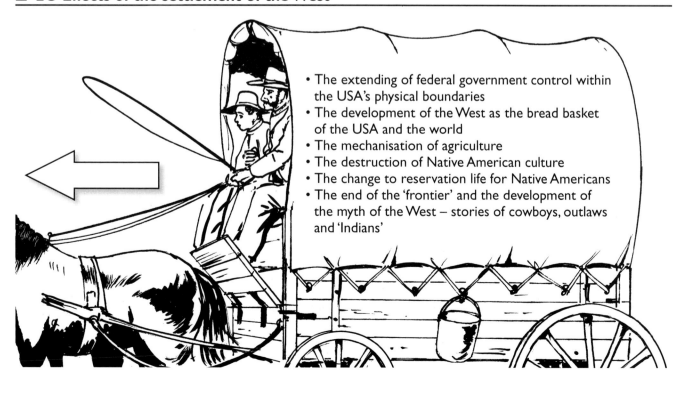

- The extending of federal government control within the USA's physical boundaries
- The development of the West as the bread basket of the USA and the world
- The mechanisation of agriculture
- The destruction of Native American culture
- The change to reservation life for Native Americans
- The end of the 'frontier' and the development of the myth of the West – stories of cowboys, outlaws and 'Indians'

ACTIVITY

How significant was the settlement of the West, 1865–1900?
First work in pairs or small groups.

1 Brainstorm an answer to this question and summarise it in five or six lines. That's the basis of your introduction.
2 Decide what each of your main paragraphs will be about – will they be about **topics**, such as the destruction of Native American culture, or will you use **criteria for significance** as your paragraphs?
3 Brainstorm an introductory sentence for each paragraph – make sure that each sentence directly answers the question.
4 Now jot down what else you want to put in each paragraph.
5 Now take a paragraph each and write them in full. Then work together to review each one.

KEY POINTS FROM CHAPTER 2

How significant was the settlement of the West, 1865–1900?

1 The settlement of the West completed the political unity of continental USA.

2 The expansion westwards was driven by a range of factors that were opportunistic, practical and emotional, including immigration and industrialisation pressures in the East, and opportunities for wealth creation in the West.

3 Wealth generated in the East was invested in the building of transcontinental railroads and the opening of new markets in the West.

4 The demands of farming and ranching led to innovation and inventions. Agricultural production increased rapidly, making the USA a much richer nation. The West supplied not only American but also European needs, making the West the bread basket of the industrial world.

5 Native Americans saw their way of life damaged, then eroded and almost totally destroyed in the settlement of the West.

6 The federal government encouraged expansion, but at the expense of restrictions on the lives and rights of Native Americans.

7 The reality and images of the West were used to create a mythical West for twentieth-century Americans.

8 The end of the 'Frontier' in the West encouraged ideas about finding new American frontiers beyond the continent.

3

Was industrialisation a blessing or a blight for the USA, 1880–1917?

CHAPTER OVERVIEW

SOURCE 3.1   An immigrant woman working as a poorly-paid seamstress in a cramped workshop typical of cities like New York or Chicago

ACTIVITY

Think about what you would expect the blessings and curses of industrialisation to be. Make a list, using your knowledge of the impact of industrialisation in Britain or other countries, including modern-day examples. Sources 3.1 and 3.2 might give you some ideas.

WAS INDUSTRIALISATION A BLESSING OR A BLIGHT FOR THE USA, 1880–1917?

38

SOURCE 3.2 An early general store selling mass-produced consumer goods

Interior E.E. Brown's Store — Bernardston Mass.

The Civil War created the demand for guns, ammunition, rail lines, uniforms, bedding and tents, quickly and in great amounts. When the War ended in 1865 industrial production kept on growing – no longer for the benefit of soldiers, but for America's increasing, and increasingly urban-based, population. Such growth brought immense wealth to some. It brought desperate poverty to others. This chapter will explore how the growth of industry made the USA a rich and powerful nation by the time of the First World War and will also assess whether industrialisation was a curse or a blessing for the American people. Did the benefits of industrialisation outweigh the costs of the resulting social problems?

A What were the key features of America's industrial revolution? (pp. 39–42)

B What problems were caused by industrialisation? (pp. 43–46)

C Were the problems of industrialisation resolved? (pp. 47–48)

D Review: Was industrialisation a blessing or a blight for the USA, 1880–1917? (pp. 49–50)

FOCUS ROUTE

As you work through this chapter keep a record of evidence of the effects of industrialisation in your own copy of the following table.

What were the blessings – the positive results of industrialisation?	What were the curses – the negative results of industrialisation?

39

WAS INDUSTRIALISATION A BLESSING OR A BLIGHT FOR THE USA, 1880–1917?

FOCUS ROUTE

Make notes about the key features of industrialisation in the USA, under the following headings:
- the types of products manufactured
- the systems by which goods were made
- the factors that led to rapid industrial growth.

A What were the key features of America's industrial revolution?

The importance of steel

Steel was an essential product for industrial development. It was used for rail lines, bridges, rail engines and carriages, vehicles, ships, oil refineries, building structures and much more. It was the typical industrial product.

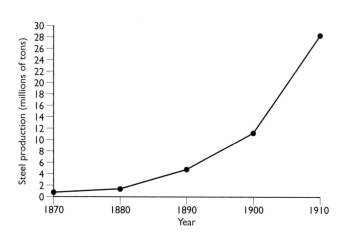

SOURCE 3.3 Steel production, 1870–1910

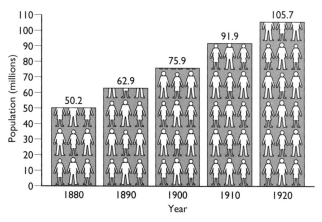

SOURCE 3.4 Population growth, 1880–1920

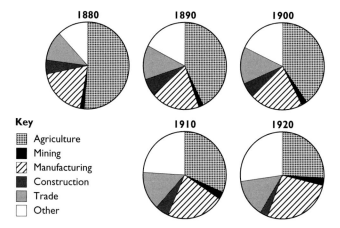

SOURCE 3.5 Immigration, 1881–1920

1870	
City	Population
New York	942,292
Philadelphia	674,022
Brooklyn, New York	419,921
St Louis	310,864
Chicago	298,977
Baltimore	267,354
Boston	250,526
Cincinnati	216,239
New Orleans	191,418
San Francisco	149,473

1910	
City	Population
New York	4,766,883
Chicago	2,185,283
Philadelphia	1,549,008
St Louis	687,029
Boston	670,585
Cleveland	560,663
Baltimore	558,485
Pittsburgh	533,905
Detroit	465,766
Buffalo	423,715

SOURCE 3.6 Urban growth of the ten largest cities by population, in 1870 and 1910

Key
- Agriculture
- Mining
- Manufacturing
- Construction
- Trade
- Other

SOURCE 3.7 Division of labour, 1880–1920

SOURCE 3.8 Gross National Product, 1880–1920

40

WAS INDUSTRIALISATION A BLESSING OR A BLIGHT FOR THE USA, 1880–1917?

ACTIVITY

Look at the statistical Sources 3.3–3.8 on page 39 and answer the following questions:

1 What changes occurred in:
   a) steel production
   b) population growth
   c) the growth of cities?
2 How were these changes interrelated?
3 Look at the pie chart for the division of labour (Source 3.7). What changes were happening
   a) to the total workforce
   b) to each of the sectors?
4 Note the changes in the GNP (Gross National Product – a country's annual total value of goods produced and services provided) shown in Source 3.8.
5 What was the cumulative effect of all these changes?

Andrew Carnegie (1835–1919) – a case study in industrial wealth

Two of Carnegie's principles: 'The man who dies rich dies disgraced' and 'Give with warm hands'.

Steel made Andrew Carnegie one of the richest men in the world; so rich that he gave away $350 million. Arriving in America in 1848 as a poor Scottish immigrant, Carnegie started work in a railroad company and by the Civil War was selling iron. The fortune that he made from this was invested in an ironworks. He began to use the new, British-invented Bessemer converters to make better and cheaper steel from iron. Steel rails were in great demand as the railroads spread across the USA. Just as importantly, Carnegie brought all the processes of steel manufacturing together – smelting, refining, rolling – in his Homestead Steelworks in Pennsylvania. This was to become the model for efficient and profitable production. As the demand for rails decreased he switched production to provide for new markets in cities and industries: bridges, the first skyscrapers (also made possible by the invention of the Otis elevator), machinery, wire, pipes, and armour plating for the US navy. In 1900, he sold his steel empire to the banker J. P. Morgan for $480 million.

Carnegie had now accumulated great wealth. In 1889, he published a collection of his writings, *The Gospel of Wealth*, in which he outlined his philanthropic philosophy. As a typical self-made man he was especially interested in helping those willing to help themselves. So his list of charitable priorities was headed by universities, free libraries, hospitals, parks, concert halls, swimming baths, churches (an order of priority objected to by some clergy!), and he gave to other countries including Britain. He set up the Carnegie Endowment for International Peace for research and the advancement of knowledge.

However, he was criticised; on the one hand for being a socialist and giving away so much to the benefit of society, and on the other hand, for obtaining his wealth by paying low wages and demanding long hours from his workers and by crushing competition, thereby damaging many individual businesses and their employees.

TALKING POINTS

1 Does the source of philanthropic generosity matter?
2 Is any gift better than no gift at all to those in need?
3 Do Carnegie's ideas and practical actions outweigh ethical considerations about how he treated his workers?

John D. Rockefeller (1839–1937)

Rockefeller bought his first oil refinery in 1862 and eight years later set up the Standard Oil Company of Ohio. He ruthlessly eliminated competitors, used fixed prices, paid fierce attention to manufacturing processes and negotiated with immense skill. By the 1880s he controlled 85 per cent of all American oil production and by 1899 had a fortune of $200 million. He expanded into iron, copper, coal, shipping and banking. By 1913 he had become the world's first billionaire. Like Carnegie he became a philanthropist, giving away an

estimated $530 million; notably to medicine, black educational institutions and support for the Baptist Church. His PHILANTHROPY is still continued by his family today.

How did corporations make profits?

The 1870s and 1880s became known as the 'Gilded (golden) Age' because of the seeming worship of money and ostentation, aided by corrupt politics and business dealings. Huge monopoly corporations like Standard Oil were created.

Corporations

A corporation raised money by selling STOCK to investors, but kept the daily administration with managers rather than stockholders. Corporations were able to prosper because the Supreme Court ruled that they had protection under the law, and because the government was willing to tax imports. This meant less competition and higher profits for American manufacturers, but also that consumers had to keep paying high prices. An amazing range of products was controlled by monopolies or corporations: sewage pipes, lamps, pottery, glass, shot, rivets, sugar, candy, starch, preserved fruits, glucose, vapour stoves, chairs, lime, rubber, screws, chains, harvesting machinery, pins, salt, type (a block used for printing), brass tubing, hardware, silk and many more. Such combinations of companies also controlled the railroads and freight companies essential for the distribution of goods.

In order to keep making profits, and pay back investors, corporations needed:

- Congress to keep TARIFFS high, making foreign imports more expensive than domestic products
- to keep squeezing out foreign competition
- to maintain the same price (for example, $28 per ton for steel) to be charged by all producers
- to pay low wages whilst demanding long working days from their workers.

Carnegie and other industrialists became known as 'Robber Barons' for their willingness to take from the poor (their workers) to enrich themselves and their investors. The lack of rules and regulations by the state produced a 'vacuum', encouraging freedom of action for risk takers and the ambitious. It became standard practice to combine companies into corporations, then control them by creating holding companies, set up in states where regulation was weak. There were some attempts made before 1900 to control industry. The Sherman Anti-Trust Act of 1890 was intended to prevent any organisation that was 'in restraint of trade', but few companies were prosecuted, and it was used as a union-controlling measure. By 1890, the richest group in America were the bankers and stockbrokers rather than the individual company bosses.

The importance of invention

Carnegie had shown that entrepreneurial skills were necessary for wealth creation, Rockefeller the need for efficient management, and Morgan for financial expertise to run companies successfully. However, just as important were the inventors, the technology designers and the organisers of production.

J. P. Morgan (1837–1913)
Skilful financiers were essential for creating corporate wealth and J. P. Morgan was the best known. He inherited around $12 million, but increased his fortune through his skill as a banker, being the major force behind complicated deals and the creation of large companies. The US Steel Corporation, created by the sale of Carnegie's company, was the first billion-dollar corporation in history. Morgan's declared interest was with the companies not with the public good. Rather than helping those in need he used his money to donate paintings, which he loved to acquire, to the Metropolitan Museum of Art and other galleries.

Henry Ford (1863–1947)
Henry Ford was the inventor of mass transport with his Model T Ford car, the 'quintessential machine of the twentieth century'. His influence on industrial production was immense. Ford's ambition was to build a car so cheap (less than $500) that it could be sold in thousands. He realised that though the profit from one car may be small, massive sales of one design (and one colour – black) would result in great profits. So, as a systems engineer, Ford designed his manufacturing system. Rail lines, conveyor belts and assembly lines moved components when and where they were needed, saving human time and energy. The system meant that unskilled workers could be employed. Using time and motion studies he demanded standardisation of components, of the manufacturing process and of the most effective working space. The result was that instead of producing one car every twelve hours, by 1924 cars were coming off the assembly line every 24 seconds. By 1918, half of all the cars in the world were Model Ts and by 1924 the cost was down to $300. When production ceased in 1928, 15.5 million had been sold in the USA.

42

WAS INDUSTRIALISATION A BLESSING OR A BLIGHT FOR THE USA, 1880–1917?

Thomas Edison (1847–1931)
Edison, like Carnegie, was a believer in self-improvement. Interested in science and technology from childhood, he became a telegrapher at the beginning of the communications revolution. He began devising ways to improve the telegraph system and invented the phonograph to reproduce sound and make records. He invented the first moving pictures (the beginning of the cinema), the first safe incandescent light bulb for domestic use, developed all the components of the electrical system – bulbs, sockets, switches, voltage regulators, wires, junction boxes, power meters, and created the giant General Electric Company. He improved batteries for the new automobiles, provided scientific advice during the First World War, including work on how to detect submarines (invaluable for the Second World War) and found an alternative to natural rubber for Firestone's car tyres. He was regarded as the symbol of America's ingenuity and the country's greatest inventor. On the day of his funeral all the electric lights in the USA were dimmed for one minute.

ACTIVITY

1 What benefits did the expansion of industry bring? (Consider wealth, opportunities, new products, new ways of living.)
2 Who do you think benefited most?

TALKING POINTS

1 What criteria would you use to decide on the historical significance of an individual?
2 Can you think of anyone other than Edison who has contributed so much to daily life today?

■ 3A American industrialisation

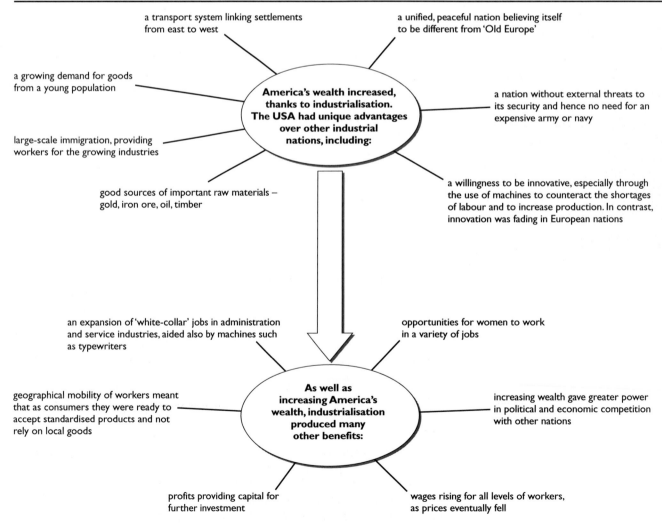

a transport system linking settlements from east to west

a unified, peaceful nation believing itself to be different from 'Old Europe'

a growing demand for goods from a young population

America's wealth increased, thanks to industrialisation. The USA had unique advantages over other industrial nations, including:

a nation without external threats to its security and hence no need for an expensive army or navy

large-scale immigration, providing workers for the growing industries

good sources of important raw materials – gold, iron ore, oil, timber

a willingness to be innovative, especially through the use of machines to counteract the shortages of labour and to increase production. In contrast, innovation was fading in European nations

an expansion of 'white-collar' jobs in administration and service industries, aided also by machines such as typewriters

opportunities for women to work in a variety of jobs

geographical mobility of workers meant that as consumers they were ready to accept standardised products and not rely on local goods

As well as increasing America's wealth, industrialisation produced many other benefits:

increasing wealth gave greater power in political and economic competition with other nations

profits providing capital for further investment

wages rising for all levels of workers, as prices eventually fell

B # What problems were caused by industrialisation?

43

WAS INDUSTRIALISATION A BLESSING OR A BLIGHT FOR THE USA, 1880–1917?

FOCUS ROUTE

1   List the problems that resulted as America changed from a rural and agricultural nation to an industrial, urban-based one.
2   At the end of Section B:
    a) review your list of problems, and add details and evidence to justify your choices.
    b) Try to list the problems in order of importance as you think they would have affected
        i)   individuals
        ii) society
        iii) the government.

ACTIVITY

Write a campaigning article for a newspaper in 1900, identifying the problems resulting from industrialisation and demanding action by the government to solve these problems.

Immigration

Most immigrants were from Europe and disembarked in New York after their cheap steamship passage. Between 1880 and 1910, 8.4 million immigrants arrived from southern and eastern Europe. By 1900, New York had more Italians than Naples, and twice as many Irish as Dublin, and by 1914 the Jewish population was 1.4 million out of a city population of 4.7 million. Chinese and Japanese immigrants usually arrived in San Francisco. In California by 1880 one-tenth of the population were Chinese.

Immigration was a major reason why the USA was able to progress so quickly with industrialisation. Immigrants came as workers. Just as importantly they became consumers. America was unique amongst industrial nations – neither Britain nor Germany had the advantage of migrant workers, in such numbers, at a time when industry needed them. Immigrants came for many reasons – religious persecution (Russian and German Jews), poverty (eastern and southern Europeans), famine (Irish), revolution (Mexicans), and often, like North European farmers, to join friends and family who had already become settlers. Many were attracted by the idea of a land of freedom and opportunity.

Whilst immigrants might be welcomed by employers as cheap and willing labour, they were an easy target for Americans who were fearful and resentful of the rapid changes brought by industrialisation. They knew that immigrants were used as strike-breakers, that they appeared to contribute to the overcrowding in cities, were vulnerable to manipulation by unscrupulous politicians and increased racial and ethnic conflict. It was easy for critics to see their distinctive cultural and religious interests as un-American. In a land of increasing wealth and a growing middle class, their poverty and lack of skills (although, ironically, that was just what mass production manufacture required) set them apart, and diminished their social worth. Social stratification developed within cities. The new streetcars (trams) enabled the middle classes to move away from the overcrowded, unsanitary centres, leaving them for poor workers and so further isolating them in ethnic ghettos.

The reality of life in America was often a shock to new arrivals. As one Italian immigrant said, having been led to believe that the streets were paved with gold, 'First the streets weren't paved with gold, second they weren't paved at all, and third I was expected to pave them'. Settling in this new country was hard. Moving from a peasant outdoor life, unregulated by clocks, to a disciplined, machine-controlled life was difficult. Low wages meant that wives and children also had to work. Working conditions were often harsh.

SOURCE 3.9 Immigrants arriving at Ellis Island in New York, c. 1905

SOURCE 3.10 Count Vay de Vaya und Luskod was a Hungarian nobleman who travelled in America between 1903 and 1906. He visited his countrymen working in Pittsburgh steelworks, and noted conditions and attitudes (in O. Handlin, *This Was America*, 1949, pp.407–41)

Fourteen thousand chimneys are silhouetted across the sky ... On every hand are burning fires and spurting flames. Nothing is visible save the forging of iron and the smelting of metal ... thousands of immigrants wander here from year to year. Here they fondly seek the realization of their cherished hopes ... This is scarcely work for mankind. Americans will hardly take anything of the sort;

only immigrants rendered desperate by circumstances ... In making a tour of these prisons, wherever the heat is most insupportable, the flames most scorching, the smoke and soot most choking, there we are certain to find compatriots bent and wasted with toil. Their thin, wrinkled, wan faces seem to show that in America the newcomers are of no use except to help to fill the moneybags of the insatiable millionaires ... everything has a value, except human life ... Why? Because human life is a commodity the supply of which exceeds demand.

Trade Unions

In the 1880s the National Labor Union banned membership to 'parasites, professional gamblers, stockbrokers, prostitutes, lawyers, bankers, and liquor dealers'. An interesting list, clearly regarded as being different characters from the working man. There were three main attempts to organise workers: the Knights of Labor union led by Terence Powderley from 1878, the American Federation of Labor (AFL), led by Samuel Gompers from 1886, and the Industrial Workers of the World (IWW) or 'Wobblies' led by William 'Big Bill' Haywood organised in 1905. Socialism was popular in Europe amongst workers at the time and Eugene V. Debs founded the Socialist Party of America in 1901. It had some popularity, but failed to consolidate its influence into actual political power in America.

A sense of threat was typical of the 1880s and early 1890s, when workers saw little alternative but to use violence to win or defend rights. In one year, 1886, there were 1400 strikes involving 500,000 workers. Why were strikes necessary and so often violent? Partly because rational argument was never enough to change conditions. The government was prepared to interpret the law to support employers, and to use force to do so. Federal troops were used against strikers, who had no such force at their disposal. At Carnegie's Homestead Steelworks, the manager, Henry Clay Frick, cut wages in 1892 and refused to accept union negotiation. In an attempt to break the union's power Pinkerton (private) detectives were used to smuggle in strike-breakers, who were then attacked by the strikers. The company called in the militia, armed with rifles and the new Gatling machine gun. The strike collapsed, with union leaders excluded from future employment. It was the end of unionisation in the Carnegie works until the middle of the twentieth century.

The Pullman strike was the first national strike in the USA and it paralysed the rail system. The Pullman company cut wages, but refused to lower rents for the houses where employees were required to live. The dispute, led by the American Railway Union (ARU), escalated. President Cleveland claimed that mail deliveries were threatened and ordered in federal troops. Rioting was followed by the troops firing into the crowd and killing four people. Union leaders were arrested. The strike gradually ended, but the company rents were not lowered. The federal government had shown itself willing to shoot its own citizens. The Omnibus Indictment Act, used against the ARU, permitted the legal banning of strikes and remained in force until the passing of the Wagner Act in 1935.

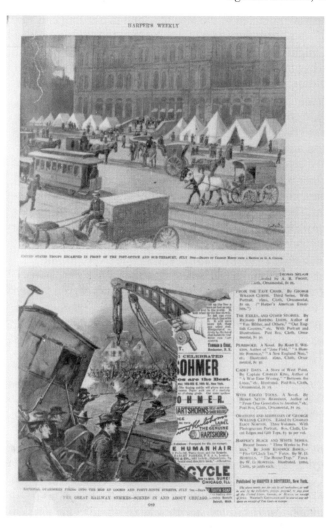

SOURCE 3.11 A torn newspaper report on the Pullman strike, 1894, which spread from Chicago

We mean to make things over, we are tired of toil for nought,
With but bare enough to live upon, and ne'er an hour for thought;
We want to feel the sunshine, and we want to smell the flowers,
We are sure that God has willed it, and we mean to have eight hours,
We're summoning our forces from the shipyard, shop and mill.
Eight hours for work, eight hours for rest, eight hours for what we will.

SOURCE 3.13 Writing in the *New Orleans Daily Democrat*, the journalist A. C. Buell could already see the problems in August 1877, quoted in J. Lorence, *Enduring Voices*, Vol. II, 4th edn, 2000, p.59

The most striking fact developed by this movement is the terrible antipathy which has grown up among the poor and laboring classes against those who possess great wealth ... John Jones and William Smith, laborers, regard William H. Vanderbilt, Jay Gould and Tom Scott, capitalists, as their natural enemies, whose welfare means their loss and whose downfall would redound to their gain.

Haymarket Bomb, 1886

This was a culmination of workers' frustrations combined with the arguments of anarchists against any form of organised government. During a mass demonstration in Chicago a bomb was thrown into a group of police. The subsequent trial of eight anarchists, four of whom were hanged (although their responsibility for the bombing is still disputed), exposed the deep divisions in this new industrialised, urban society.

Investigative journalism

Journalists in mass market journals began to expose some of the unpleasantness of industrialisation. 'Muck-rakers' was President Roosevelt's description of these journalists, but they could be effective as well as dramatic.

SOURCE 3.14 In 1906 Upton Sinclair published *The Jungle*, about the meat packing industry in Chicago. The intention was to raise public condemnation of the way workers (mainly immigrants) were required to work in dangerous and degrading conditions (quoted in J. Lorence, *Enduring Voices*, Vol. II, 4th edn, 2000, p.143)

Worst of any, however, were the fertilizer men, and those who served in the cooking room. These people could not be shown to the visitor – for the odor of the fertilizer men would scare away any ordinary visitor at a hundred yards, and as for the other men, who worked in the tank rooms full of steam, and in some of which there were open vats near the level of the floor, their peculiar trouble was they fell into the vats: and when they were fished out, there was never enough of them left to be worth exhibiting – sometimes they would be overlooked for days, till all but the bones of them had gone out to the world as Durham's Pure Leaf Lard! ...

But his sickening description of food processing provoked the most protest. Sausage production, for example

meat that had tumbled on the floor, in the dirt and sawdust, where the workers had trampled and spit uncounted billions of consumption germs ... rats were a nuisance, and the packers would put poisoned bread out for them, they would die, and then rats, bread and meat would go into the hoppers together ... There was no place for the men to wash their hands before they ate their dinner, and so they [washed] them in the water that was to be ladled into the sausage ...

Ida Tarbell wrote for the popular McClure's magazine and between 1902 and 1904 used her carefully researched investigations of Rockefeller's Standard Oil Company to expose the widespread business corruption that had enabled the millionaire to amass his wealth. She described Rockefeller as 'money-mad' and said 'Our national life is on every side distinctly poorer, uglier, meaner, for the kind of influence he exercises'. Her articles were praised for their high standard of investigation and their analysis, in language understandable to all, of the complexities of the Rockefeller business empire.

ACTIVITY

Create a discussion between either a striking worker and a manufacturer or between a striker and a worker who does not want to strike.

1 What would each want?
2 What would each fear?
3 Why would their views differ?

DISCUSS

1 Compare Ida Tarbell's words on Rockefeller's success, with the description given on page 40.
2 What does the comparison tell you about the importance of gathering a number of sources in order to successfully interpret and assess the past?

46

WAS INDUSTRIALISATION A BLESSING OR A BLIGHT FOR THE USA, 1880–1917?

SOURCE 3.15 The Standard Oil Company as an octopus. The greedy octopus uses its tentacles to ensnare (from top left to right:) Congress, the state legislatures, taxpayers, and is reaching out to the ultimate seat of power, the White House

SOURCE 3.16 Front page of the *New York Tribune*, 26 March 1911. The failings of health and safety legislation and inspection were horribly highlighted by the deaths of 146 textile workers in New York in 1911. The locking of fire doors and the inadequacy of the fire department's equipment forced many to jump to their deaths or to die in the fire

Farming

Farmers in the West objected to the power of bankers and corporations. Farmers traditionally saw themselves as independent and self-sufficient, but many relied on loans to get them through the farming year. However, falling agricultural prices, together with higher prices charged for grain storage and transportation, meant less income for repaying loans. Many farmers blamed the railroads and bankers for these problems. They joined together into Farmers' Alliances, creating unity for themselves through co-operation and mutual self-respect, presenting themselves as the only truly functional and productive Americans. The Alliances became the People's Party or Populists. They joined with the Democrats in the 1896 presidential election, but were defeated. One of their leaders, Ignatious Donnelly, said in 1892:

'We meet in the midst of a nation brought to the verge of moral, political and material ruin. Corruption dominates the ballot box, the legislature, the Congress and touches even the ermine of the bench. The people are demoralized … The newspapers are subsidized or muzzled; public opinion silenced; business prostrate, our homes covered with mortgages, labor impoverished, and the land concentrated in the hands of the capitalists … We breed two classes – paupers and millionaires.' (in H. Zinn, *A People's History of the United States*, 1995, pp.282–83)

47

WAS INDUSTRIALISATION A BLESSING OR A BLIGHT FOR THE USA, 1880–1917?

FOCUS ROUTE

As you work through Section C make notes on the following questions:

1 What were the aims of the Progressives?
2 What changes took place that benefited Americans as workers and as consumers?

C Were the problems of industrialisation resolved?

By the 1890s it was clear that industrialisation had created many problems as well as bringing wealth to some. The depression of 1893–97, with an estimated twenty per cent of the workforce unemployed, 16,000 businesses closed and over 600 banks failing, accelerated the demands for a positive government response. However, there was confusion about the role of government. It was clearly responsible for supporting business and industry for the good of the nation, but could the government, at the same time, protect those used and abused by the realities of rapid industrial growth?

Jane Addams (1860–1935)

The 1893 depression exposed the limitations of relying on charity resources to help the poor. There were groups and individuals trying to improve unhealthy city conditions by working directly with the poor. Jane Addams established one of the first settlement houses at Hull House in Chicago in 1889. In her book *Twenty Years at Hull House*, she wrote of her experiment to solve the problems amongst immigrant workers. She and her co-founder, Ellen Gates Starr, both young, well-educated and middle class, established Hull House as a community resource, to try to meet the needs of the poor. This included: setting up a kindergarten; putting on evening classes for working children; opening kitchens to sell cheap, healthy food; providing boarding apartments for factory girls and health visitors for babies; and giving short breaks to elderly women forced to live in the Poorhouse. They wished to demonstrate kindness and practical help, to bring people together to give pleasure to the young and comfort to the aged. Jane Addams was also an active campaigner for the Consumer's League, Women's Trade Union and the NAACP. She was a lifelong crusader for world peace and in 1931 was awarded the ultimate honour of the Nobel Peace Prize.

ACTIVITY

Copy Chart 3B and draw lines linking the topics that are interrelated. You will have created a spider diagram showing the complex results of industrialisation.

ACTIVITY

Make a list identifying the priorities for a government that wished to reduce the problems resulting from industrialisation. Use Chart 3B as a guide to the problems and challenges.

■ 3B The challenges of industrialisation

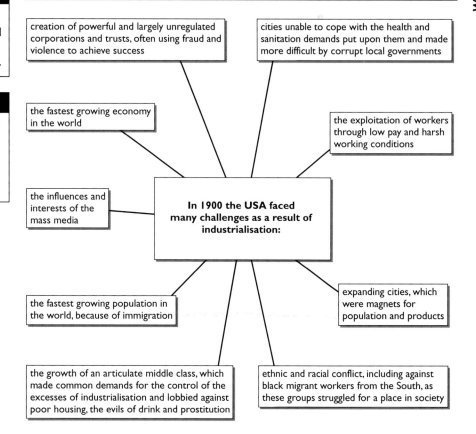

creation of powerful and largely unregulated corporations and trusts, often using fraud and violence to achieve success

cities unable to cope with the health and sanitation demands put upon them and made more difficult by corrupt local governments

the fastest growing economy in the world

the exploitation of workers through low pay and harsh working conditions

the influences and interests of the mass media

In 1900 the USA faced many challenges as a result of industrialisation:

the fastest growing population in the world, because of immigration

expanding cities, which were magnets for population and products

the growth of an articulate middle class, which made common demands for the control of the excesses of industrialisation and lobbied against poor housing, the evils of drink and prostitution

ethnic and racial conflict, including against black migrant workers from the South, as these groups struggled for a place in society

48

WAS INDUSTRIALISATION A BLESSING OR A BLIGHT FOR THE USA, 1880–1917?

■ 3C Social, legal and constitutional changes 1900–17

1903	National Women's Trade Union League founded
1905	*Lochner v. New York* overturns law restricting the length of the working day
	Industrial Workers of the World (IWW or Wobblies) founded as a labour union
1906	Pure Food and Drug Act
	Meat Inspection Act
1908	*Muller v. Oregon* upholds regulation of working hours for women
1909	NAACP formed
1912	Progressive Party formed
1913	Sixteenth Amendment passed legalising federal income tax
	Federal Reserve Act establishes central banking system
1914	Federal Trade Commission set up to investigate unfair trade practices
	Mother's Day becomes a national holiday
1916	Margaret Sanger forms New York Birth Control League
	Law setting eight-hour working day for railroad workers
1917	Literacy test required for all immigrants

PRESIDENTS

Theodore 'Teddy' Roosevelt (1900–08)

William Taft (1908–12)

Woodrow Wilson (1912–20)

Who were the Progressives?

The social welfare changes that were pursued after 1900 were largely the result of the ideas and activities of the Progressives. The Progressives were not a political party (until the 1912 presidential election), nor an organised group. They were a collection of groups who influenced change in the first part of the twentieth century. They were reacting to the social effects of industrialisation on ordinary people and to the way the nation was governed. President Theodore Roosevelt, prompted by a miners' strike and his active involvement in arbitration for a settlement, declared that citizens should have a 'Square Deal', especially by the regulation of businesses. He went on to use this phrase in the 1904 presidential campaign, as a shorthand for Progressive policies, with his argument that the federal government should have an activist role (this had not happened since 1865).

Some Progressives were writers and thinkers, like the philosopher William James and the educator John Dewey. James favoured pragmatism; active involvement in problems, rather than theoretical ideas, should guide reform. Dewey believed in learning by doing, not by rote. As in Britain, with Charles Booth and Seebohm Rowntree, they emphasised scientific investigation, collecting information and facts as the basis for action. The result was the setting up of commissions of inquiry, for example into child labour. Groups worked in different areas: to improve the lives of immigrants and the poor (like Jane Addams); for women's suffrage; for the rights of farmers against bankers (like the Populists); and against the evils of drink and prostitution (the Purity Crusade). Their common aim was that of improving society with justice for all.

Women's suffrage demands became part of the Progressive movement. Women's commitment to national life could demonstrate their right to have the vote. By their practical actions they could show equality as citizens and their worthiness as equal representatives with men in choosing governments. Susan B. Anthony and Carrie Chapman Catt were successive leaders of the movement for women's suffrage. Their campaign involved them in demands for a range of social changes. In 1920, their efforts resulted in the passing of the Nineteenth Amendment, giving women the right to vote.

■ 3D The Progressives did make some differences to society ...

✓ by establishing the principle of public intervention to change society

✓ by raising awareness of poverty, injustice, workers' health and safety and urban problems

✓ by making politicians and businessmen aware of the need to consider public opinion

✓ by demonstrating practical and effective ways to help the poor

✓ by encouraging government to take responsibility to protect consumers

✓ by encouraging decisions to be made for ethical reasons, not just the profit of the few

✓ by working at local, state and national level

■ 3E ... but they did not solve all the problems of industrial society

✗ they did not end the influence of business and commerce on government

✗ the courts still had much control over social welfare issues

✗ there was little change in the status of black workers in the North as well as the South

✗ agencies helping those in need were often under-resourced

ACTIVITY

Look back to your priorities in the Activity on page 47. To what extent did government actions meet the priorities you identified?

The abolition of slavery had shown that governments could take the lead in reforming society. The reforms of the early twentieth century showed that freedom, in terms of health and justice, was also a part of being a citizen and could be enforced by an activist state. The first three presidents of the twentieth century, Theodore Roosevelt, William Taft and Woodrow Wilson, initiated and approved a series of legal, constitutional and social changes which reflected the demands of the Progressives. They were to be continued in the New Deal policies of Franklin D. Roosevelt in the 1930s.

DISCUSS

Discuss what Sources 3.17–3.19 tell you about the impact of industrialisation in the USA.

D Review: Was industrialisation a blessing or a blight for the USA, 1880–1917?

SOURCE 3.17 Scene in Hester Street, New York City, 1903

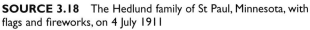

SOURCE 3.18 The Hedlund family of St Paul, Minnesota, with flags and fireworks, on 4 July 1911

SOURCE 3.19 An advertisement for the Kodak folding pocket camera costing $10

Holidays are Kodak Days

The long evenings of Christmas-tide are made doubly delightful by taking flash-light pictures of one's friends.

Picture taking by daylight or flash-light is easy with a Kodak.

Kodaks $5.00 to $35.00.

Catalogues free of dealers or by mail.

EASTMAN KODAK CO.

Rochester, N. Y.

Industrialisation had consequences for workers, employers and financiers that were not predictable in 1880:

- the growth of cities and the problems that resulted
- the influx of immigrants and their impact in creating a pluralistic American society
- a consumer society with new expectations of an acceptable standard of living
- production beyond domestic needs, pushing America to a new involvement with the world
- a change in the role and authority of the president
- a new agenda for government, to take responsibility for the social welfare of its citizens.

50

WAS INDUSTRIALISATION A BLESSING OR A BLIGHT FOR THE USA, 1880–1917?

ACTIVITY

Working with a partner, imagine yourself as an immigrant steel worker or a Ford assembly line worker. Look back over the last 30 years of your working life. Draw up a table to compare and contrast your life in 1877 and 1917, under the following headings:

  Type of work done / Method of production / The benefits of industrialisation to you and your family / What you think you have lost because of industrial working patterns / Your hopes for the future for your children.

This type of activity will also make you realise what you *don't* know about life between 1877 and 1917. Try to make some time to find out more about those aspects that particularly interest you. The bibliography on page 293 will help you.

ACTIVITY

Essay

Using the information in this chapter, and your own reading, write an essay that answers the question:

  Was industrialisation a blessing or a blight for the USA, 1880–1917?

You will need to write paragraphs on:

- what is meant by industrialisation
- the problems it created
- resolving the problems
- how it changed different aspects of the USA, for example, national wealth, goods produced, methods of production, standard of living, the role of government
- your assessment of the impact of industrialisation on the USA by 1917.

KEY POINTS FROM CHAPTER 3   **Was industrialisation a blessing or a blight for the USA, 1880–1917?**

1 Industrialisation made the USA economically powerful in the world by 1917.

2 Industrial growth in the 1880s was made possible by a combination of extensive raw materials, the influx of immigrant workers, ambitious and successful entrepreneurs, and the limited role of government.

3 Industrialisation meant great wealth for a few and poverty for many.

4 Labour unions fought to improve conditions and levels of pay, but were undermined by a surplus of workers, the use of government troops by some employers and the difficulty of uniting workers across such a diverse and immense country.

5 Industrialisation led to the rapid growth of cities, which were often overcrowded and unhealthy.

6 By the 1890s unchecked industrial expansion was creating social welfare problems.

7 The Progressive movement, through organisations and individuals, and with ideas and practical schemes, changed the attitude of government towards social welfare.

8 By 1900, social welfare problems needed government regulation and legislation.

9 The powers of the presidency and especially those of Theodore Roosevelt, William Taft and Woodrow Wilson were enhanced by welfare and business reforms.

10 President Theodore Roosevelt's 'Square Deal', promised in the 1904 election, was a forerunner of President F. D. Roosevelt's 'New Deal' in the 1930s and President Harry Truman's 'Fair Deal' in 1949, protecting the citizen against over-mighty business and promoting social welfare legislation.

4

From jellyfish to eagle? Why did the USA change its foreign policy, 1890–1919?

CHAPTER OVERVIEW

'The big fat Republic that is afraid of nothing because nothing up to the present day has happened to make her afraid, is as unprotected as a jellyfish.' (Rudyard Kipling, the English writer of stories about imperial India, speaking in 1891, about the USA.)

An unprotected jellyfish! This is hardly the impression given by twenty-first-century America, the only nation that has deliberately dropped nuclear bombs on an enemy and that, in 2002, spent more on its defence than all of the EU countries combined. How did a nation that, in 1890, had a navy that was smaller than that of Sweden, Turkey or the Netherlands and was quite unprepared to defend itself, become the strongest military power in the world? The answer is foreign policy; the making of deliberate choices to protect a nation's world power and maintain its self-interest. Once America was involved in world affairs then the impact of events, often beyond America's control, demanded further decisions and actions which, in turn, led to America's current military strength.

However, in 1890 there was no inevitability that America would become the military power that it is today. Although a perceptive observer might have wondered about the effects of America's rapid industrialisation, to become a global power America needed not just an enormous increase in military and naval strength, but also a change in people's ideas about America and its role within the rest of the world. This chapter will consider how and why events and policies began to change American foreign policy. Just how far had the USA gone in its transformation from jellyfish to eagle by 1919?

A Why was the USA a 'jellyfish' in 1890? (pp. 52–55)

B Was the Spanish–American War of 1898 a turning point in American foreign policy? (pp. 56–59)

C How did America extend its power in the world, 1898–1917? (pp. 60–61)

D Why did America go to war in 1917? (pp. 62–65)

E Why didn't the USA sign the Treaty of Versailles? (pp. 66–67)

F Review: From jellyfish to eagle? Why did the USA change its foreign policy, 1890–1919? (pp. 67–68)

TALKING POINTS

1 This chapter's question asks 'why?' – it is asking you to explain causes. Think back to other causal questions you have tackled. What are the different aspects of causation that you need to think about?
2 Can you work out in advance what the shape of the answer will be, even if you don't know any of the content yet?

FOCUS ROUTE

At key points in this chapter you will be reminded to complete your own copy of this table, which focuses on the key question in the chapter title.

	1898 – the Spanish–American War	1917 – entering the First World War
1 How did US foreign policy change?		
2 Why did US foreign policy change?		

Why was the USA a 'jellyfish' in 1890?

FOCUS ROUTE

Make notes to answer the following questions:

1 Why did the USA have a foreign policy of non-involvement during most of the nineteenth century?
2 What did the Monroe Doctrine say and why was it important?
3 Why did Hawaii become an American state?

Non-intervention

The USA's foreign policy had been formed by its early statesmen. In 1780, John Adams, foreign envoy to Europe and vice-president to Washington said, with reference to Europe, 'Our business with them, and theirs with us, is commerce, not politics, much less war'. George Washington, the first president, told Congress to beware of 'foreign alliances' with foreign governments.

So non-involvement and non-intervention, in other governments' internal affairs and their wars (but not in their trade), was America's policy. Such inward-looking attitudes were appropriate for a rural, agricultural nation. When industrialisation began, America had sufficient raw materials available – ores, coal, timber, water power – not to need imports. The Pacific and the Atlantic Oceans were also immense natural barriers and, if war occurred in Europe, the strength of the British navy (usually an ally of America because of their shared history), provided a barrier for the USA against dangers. Hence there was no need to create a strong US navy. There was no need for a strong army either, as no state on America's borders (Canada, Mexico, Central and South America) was a major threat. America had secure boundaries as a result of two agreements. The 1818 British–American Convention fixed the Canadian border and the 1819 Transcontinental Treaty with Spain confirmed Florida as American territory. A border with the Spanish lands in the south-west and west to the Pacific was also agreed.

In 1823, the Monroe Doctrine was announced by President Monroe and John Quincy Adams, his secretary of state (the equivalent of the British foreign minister). It established the scope of American interests in the early nineteenth century. The Doctrine stated that:

1 US policy was to avoid becoming involved in European wars unless American interests were involved
2 the 'American continents' were not to be colonised by any European powers
3 any such attempts at colonisation would be regarded as 'unfriendly' acts.

This Doctrine seemed to indicate a disinterest in foreign affairs. Certainly the USA did not fight in overseas wars until 1898. However, the USA was asserting itself as the pre-eminent power in Central and South America. There were numerous diplomatic incidents and interventions, usually relating to fishing rights, border disputes and internal disorder that threatened American interests, including ones in Venezuela, British Guiana and Chile.

Industrialisation and the need to trade added another focus of interest, but also created a dilemma for politicians. Could the USA support demands from traders and the navy for strategic Pacific bases, yet also avoid becoming an imperialist power? Could the government maintain America's constitutional ideals of life, liberty and the pursuit of happiness for all? The conflict of commercial interests and political attitudes could be seen in Hawaii in the 1890s.

1 Who would want to cross the Pacific and why?
2 Why should its vastness be both a problem and an advantage to the USA before 1919? Consider: raw materials, markets, protecting trade, creating a navy, responding to competition, having a political role in the area.

■ **4A The Pacific**

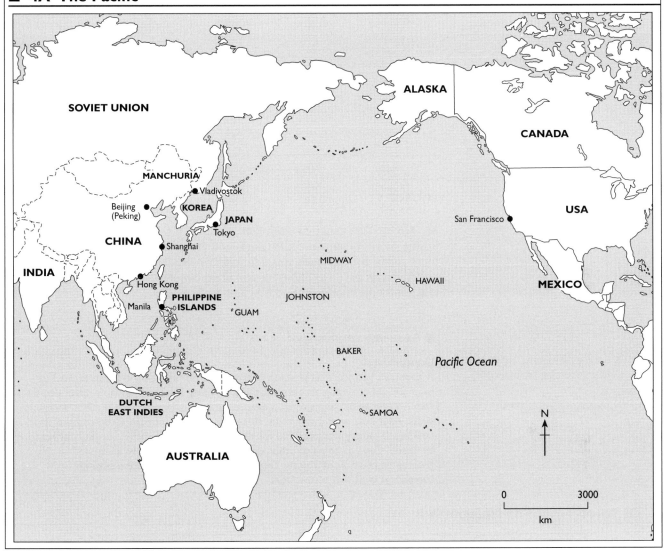

IMPERIALISM

Imperialism can be defined as the imposition of control over other peoples, through annexation, military conquest or economic domination. It was used to ensure political control over markets and sources of raw materials by major European nations, especially Britain, Germany, Spain, France and the Netherlands. These were nations who traditionally had strong navies and relied on manufacturing and trade for their wealth.

Hawaii

If you use Chart 4A and trace the routes from the USA to Japan, to Australia and to the Philippines you can see why the Hawaiian Islands became known as the 'crossroads of the Pacific'. The Americans established missionaries and settlers there. As sugar production (the islands' main crop) increased, the treaties of 1857 and 1887 allowed cheap, duty-free sugar into the USA. In return, Hawaii was required to accept both American economic domination and political protection. The USA also gained the use of one of Hawaii's best harbours, Pearl Harbor (the scene of Japan's attack on the US fleet in 1941). When Hawaiian sugar lost its duty-free status in 1890, prices rose, production fell and unemployment increased. The new queen of the islands, Liliuokalani, led a rebellion. American residents called for help from the USA. The marines arrived and within three days the rebels surrendered. The US government planned to annex Hawaii because of its important location, but was opposed by those who feared that America would become an imperial power, no better than the Europeans. However, the war with Spain in Cuba strengthened the arguments for annexation. Hawaii was annexed in July 1898 and became the fiftieth state of the USA in 1959.

ACTIVITY

Identify how each of the following developments might have affected foreign policy decision-makers:
a) industrialisation
b) the end of the 'frontier'
c) Social Darwinism, manifest destiny and ideas about racial superiority.

What changes were affecting foreign policy makers' ideas?

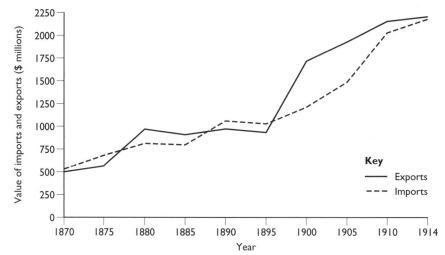

SOURCE 4.1 Imports and exports, 1870–1914

By 1878 the USA exported more than it imported (see Source 4.1), requiring it to seek more consumers for its goods and more raw materials for producing those goods. In 1893 there was a four-year economic depression, which together with the ideas about the end of the 'frontier' made Americans anxious to pursue expansion both for trade and national pride.

TALKING POINT

Why were many Americans opposed to their country becoming an imperialist power?

■ **Learning trouble spot**

Geopolitics
A country's geographical position in the world can affect political decisions. For example, either having access to the sea, or being landlocked, would affect decisions about the need for, and size of, a navy. In turn, that decision would affect decisions about what resources (navy, army, citizen force) were needed to defend the state, how much money was required for those resources, and how that money was to be raised. Can you think of other decisions that would follow, all related to the geographic position of a state? Think about Britain's geopolitical position and compare it with that of the USA.

■ **4B Involvement or Isolationism**

Some of these ideas overlapped during the first part of the twentieth century, but they centred on the competing ideas of worldwide involvement or isolationism as a regional power. Like all changes there were unpredictable elements which combined together to produce new demands and situations. They in turn swayed emotions and decisions. These arguments about America's role were to continue throughout the century, until the overwhelming Allied victory of the Second World War after which isolationism was no longer an option.

UNPREDICTABLE INFLUENCES

• The influence of individuals with new ideas, especially Mahan's ideas about sea power.

• The aggressive expansionist ideas of Theodore 'Teddy' Roosevelt, Henry Cabot Lodge and other politicians, which during the 1890s gradually gained support from presidents Harrison, Cleveland and McKinley, and from Congress.

• The actions of states with foreign territorial interests:
– Spain, which had territories in the Caribbean and the Pacific
– European states involved in the 'scramble for Africa' after the mid-1880s
– Japanese and Chinese competition for power in Korea.

OPTIONS

• Ignore the rest of the world and remain a regional power, or seek global order and stability through influence and military power.

• Become a colonising power (like Britain and Germany were and Japan and Russia wanted to be) and thus be in political and economic competition with other great nations in the world.

• Pursue 'open-door' policies, which meant being in economic competition with other nations, rather than taking control of other peoples. Open-door policies were designed to allow all nations to trade in a particular area.

Alfred Thayer Mahan (1840–1914)
Alfred Thayer Mahan was a captain in the American navy who, by writing *The Influence of Seapower upon History 1600–1812* in 1890, became the navy's leading strategist. He believed the USA needed to treat the sea as a highway:

• for transport of goods via a merchant navy
• to create a powerful navy to protect American commerce abroad
• to establish overseas bases for supplying coal, water and other necessities for crews.

He wanted a canal across Central America to join the Caribbean and the Pacific to improve both trade and access to the Pacific. These ideas gave a focus to American policy abroad. Congress agreed and provided funds in 1890 for three new battleships; the beginning of the navy's expansion. By 1914, the USA had the world's third largest battleship fleet after Britain and Germany.

55

FROM JELLYFISH TO EAGLE? WHY DID THE USA CHANGE ITS FOREIGN POLICY, 1890–1919?

ACTIVITY

Complete your own version of the table below to identify the influences and ideas that explain why foreign policy changed during the 1890s.

Influence	Idea
Mahan	
Roosevelt	
Cabot Lodge	
McKinley	

SOURCE 4.2   Theodore Roosevelt, as assistant secretary to the navy, speaking to the Naval War College, Newport, Rhode Island in June, 1897 (in E. Morris, *The Rise of Theodore Roosevelt*, 1979, p.594)

All the great masterful races have been fighting races; and the minute that a race loses the hard fighting virtues, then … it has lost its proud right to stand as the equal of the best … Cowardice in a race, as in an individual is the unpardonable sin … Better a thousand times to err on the side of the over-readiness to fight, than to err on the side of tame submission to injury, or cold-blooded indifference to the misery of the oppressed … No triumph of peace is so great as the supreme triumphs of war … It may be that at some time in the dim future of the race the need for war will vanish; but that time is yet ages distant. As yet, no nation can hold its place in the world, or can do any work really worth doing, unless it stands ready to guard its rights with an armed hand.

SOURCE 4.3   Henry Cabot Lodge, a Republican Senator from Massachusetts speaking in the 1890s about the Anglo-Saxon 'race', quoted in H. Zinn, *A People's History of the United States*, 1995, p.291

The great nations are rapidly absorbing for their future expansion and their present defense, all the waste places of the world. It is a movement which makes for civilization and the advancement of the race. As one of the great nations of the world the US must not fall out of the line of the march.

SOURCE 4.4   President McKinley had experienced the horrors of the Civil War, unlike Roosevelt and Cabot Lodge who had only read about the drama, quoted in H. Zinn, *A People's History of the United States*, 1995, p.297

The President [McKinley] did not want war; he had been sincere and tireless in his efforts to maintain the peace. By mid-March, however, he was beginning to discover that, although he did not want war, he did want what only a war could produce; the disappearance of the terrible uncertainty in American political and economic life, and a solid base from which to resume the building of the new American commercial empire.

56

FROM JELLYFISH TO EAGLE? WHY DID THE USA CHANGE ITS FOREIGN POLICY, 1890–1919?

Was the Spanish–American War of 1898 a turning point in American foreign policy?

FOCUS ROUTE

1 Briefly summarise American foreign policy before the 1890s.
2 Explain in what ways:
 a) the invasion of Cuba
 b) the fight for the Philippines
 were turning points in America's foreign policy.
3 Why was there opposition to these changes in policy?
4 Complete your Focus Route table from page 51.

ACTIVITY

Wars rarely happen for just one reason. Think of a jigsaw and how all the pieces fit together to make a complete picture.

1 As you work through Section B identify the 'pieces' that led to the Spanish–American War in 1898.
2 Create a jigsaw-type diagram with each 'piece' containing information that explains how it helped lead to war.
3 Compare your diagram with that of a partner, and discuss the differences. Do you both agree on the most important 'pieces'? Have either of you thought of less obvious reasons for the War?

'The Play for Peace'

Act 1 – The fight for Cuba

Why was America concerned about Cuba? Cuba was on America's doorstep and according to the Monroe Doctrine was in the USA's sphere of interest. However, it was controlled by a foreign power, Spain. Spain had once controlled the greatest empire in the Americas, as far as the Philippines in the Pacific. Now little of it was left. To the Spanish any further losses would weaken its political stability, and it became a matter of honour to defend its possessions. Yet Cuban revolutionaries were demanding independence. Spain did offer the rebels some concessions, but not enough. The USA was unsure of how to react to either Spain or the rebels until two incidents, and the way they were interpreted, resulted in war against Spain.

SOURCE 4.5 Map of the Caribbean

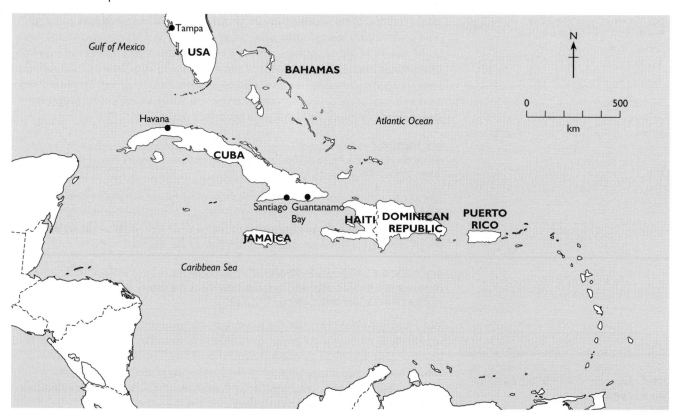

Incident 1

The Spanish ambassador in Washington wrote a private letter criticising President McKinley. Its contents were made public, which embarrassed the Spanish government and angered the American public.

Incident 2

SOURCE 4.6 The explosion of the *Maine*, 15 February 1898

Whilst on a 'friendly' visit to Havana harbour, the American battleship *Maine* exploded, with the loss of 266 crew. Immediately the American press accused the Spanish of sabotage. A Spanish investigation concluded that the explosion was due to a fault on the ship, whilst a US Naval Court of Inquiry said it was caused by a mine. There was a growing sense that if Spain remained in power in Cuba, they posed a military, and possibly an economic, threat to the USA. The incident ignited war passions and urged on by the press, by Vice-President Roosevelt and by Congress, the president ordered a blockade of Cuba. War was declared on 25 April. Subsequent and less biased investigations concluded the *Maine* exploded because of a coal bunker fire close to where shells were stored; a known design problem on this type of ship.

Act 2 – Defeating Spain

In April 1898, US forces launched a double attack on Spanish territories. The navy attacked Spain in the Philippines and defeated its fleet outside Manila. In Cuba American troops landed near Santiago and Spanish troops were blockaded in Havana. After seventeen days of fighting the Spanish forces surrendered. Neither side fought particularly well. Spanish commanders were fearful of defeat, knowing its wider impact on Spanish imperial power, yet they used weak military and naval strategies. The American navy were impressive, but the army commanders had never organised such a war. There were shortages of weapons and transport, a lack of basic training for hastily enlisted volunteers, and ill-prepared supply lines and medical care.

As was to happen in the First World War, the contribution of black troops was largely ignored in stories of the Spanish–American War. This was a time when assumptions about the superiority of the white race over other 'inferior' or non-white races was increasing.

Did America benefit from the Spanish–American War?

The terms of the **Treaty of Paris** in 1898 clearly showed the USA as the victors. It stated that:

1 Cuban independence was recognised, but the USA influenced its constitution and was allowed possession of Guantanamo Bay.

ACTIVITY

Why did America go to war? Listed below are the immediate reasons for America's war with Spain.

1 Rank them in order of importance for:
   a) a politician
   b) an industrialist
   c) an anti-imperialist.
   i) To ensure that the Cubans gained independence from Spain.
   ii) To punish Spain for the sinking of the *Maine*.
   iii) To assert American authority in the Caribbean.
   iv) To assert American authority and influence in the Pacific.
   v) To become a territorial power, like European states.
   vi) To permit the practice of the American values of freedom and the pursuit of happiness.
2 Is the order the same for each, and if not, why not?

58

FROM JELLYFISH TO EAGLE? WHY DID THE USA CHANGE ITS FOREIGN POLICY, 1890–1919?

SOURCE 4.8 Emilio Aguinaldo

ACTIVITY

The USA had gained control over the Philippines, but had never fought a war like this, against a foreign state and outside its land mass. What was it going to do with these new possessions? Was it becoming an imperial power? Using Sources 4.9 and 4.10 identify the objections to America becoming an imperialistic power.

SOURCE 4.10 H. Zinn, *A People's History of the United States*, 1995, p.308, quoting the popular American writer Mark Twain on the war in the Philippines

We have pacified some thousands of the islanders and buried them; destroyed their fields; burned their villages, and turned their widows and orphans out-of-doors; furnished heartbreak by exile to some dozens of disagreeable patriots; subjugated the remaining ten millions by Benevolent Assimilation, which is the pious new name for the musket; we have acquired property in the three hundred concubines and other slaves of our business partner, the Sultan of Sulu, and hoisted our protecting flag over the swag. And so, by these Providences of God – and the phrase is the government's, not mine – we are a World Power.

2 Spain lost the last pieces of her American empire by ceding Puerto Rica in the Caribbean and the Pacific island of Guam (part of the Mariana group) to the USA.
3 The USA was able to purchase the Philippine Islands for $20 million.

The USA had demonstrated its areas of interests, as set out in the Monroe Doctrine, and also had the Pacific bases so much desired by Mahan. However, views on the war differed. According to John Hay, secretary of state, it had been 'A splendid little war', whereas the author Sherwood Anderson said it had been 'like robbing an old Gypsy woman in a vacant lot at night after a fair'.

SOURCE 4.7 H. Zinn, *A People's History of the United States*, 1995, p.302

Even before the Spanish flag was down in Cuba, US business interests set out to make their influence felt. Merchants, real estate agents, stock speculators, reckless adventurers, and promoters of all kinds of get-rich schemes flocked to Cuba by the thousands.

Act 3 – Controlling the Philippines

The defeat of the Spanish in the Philippines in 1898 had been made possible by the assistance of the Filipino independence leader, Emilio Aguinaldo. However, when the USA refused independence to the islands, a vicious three-year war began with Aguinaldo leading guerrilla opposition to the American army. A 1902 US Senate Committee exposed the brutality of both sides, with an estimated 4300 Americans killed and 50,000–200,000 Filipino deaths. In 1901, Aguinaldo was captured and a civil government, under William Taft, was established. The islands were promised independence, but did not achieve it until July 1946. The treatment of the Filipinos by American soldiers led to a reaction against imperialism within the USA.

SOURCE 4.9 A comment by the English observer, James Bryce, in 1897 during the debate about the annexing of Hawaii (in P. Foner and R. Winchester (eds.), *The Anti-Imperialist Reader: a Documentary History of Anti-Imperialism in the United States,* Vol. I, 1984, pp.98–9)

What have the United States to gain by territorial extension? ... one of the noblest parts of her mission in the world has been to show the older peoples and states an example of abstention from the quarrels and wars and conquests that make so large and so lamentable a part of the annals of Europe. Her remote position and her immense power have, as I have said, delivered her from that burden of military and naval armaments, which presses with crushing weight upon the peoples of Europe. It would be, for her, a descent from what may be called the pedestal of wise and pacific detachment on which she now stands, were she to yield to that earth hunger which has been raging among the European states, and to imitate the aggressive methods, which some of them have pursued. The policy of creating great armaments and of annexing territories beyond the sea would be, if a stranger may venture to say so, an un-American policy, and a complete departure from the maxims – approved by long experience – of the illustrious founders of the republic.

The Anti-Imperialist League was formed in 1898 as a result of the Spanish–American War. William James ('Goddamn the US for its vile conduct in the Philippine Isles') was supported by prominent Americans such as the industrialist Andrew Carnegie, the social activist Jane Addams, the author Mark Twain, the labour leader Samuel Gompers, as well as a wide mix of society businessmen, politicians and intellectuals. They were brought together by their reaction to American behaviour in the Philippines and they claimed that the annexation of the Philippines was against American values and its principles of independence and self-determination. They objected because:

• if tyranny was established abroad then it could become easy to allow tyranny at home
• of the cost of colonies (navy, army, governing, country's debts)
• there was no need to 'own' people in order to trade with them

- cheap labour might be in competition with American industry
- being an imperial power contradicted the American values as expressed in the Declaration of Independence: 'that all men are created equal' and that governments derive their powers from the consent of the governed.

Ironically this was the time of permitted aggressive racism in the USA (see Chapter 1).

THE SPANISH–AMERICAN WAR AND THE RISE OF THEODORE ROOSEVELT

In 1898, the army had only 26,000 men and was in desperate need of more soldiers. Theodore Roosevelt raised his own regiment, the 1000-strong First US Volunteer Cavalry. The men were handpicked by Roosevelt and included cowboys, frontiersmen, lumberjacks, two English aristocrats and adventurers of all kinds. They were involved in the charge for San Juan Hill, the drama of which captured the imagination of the press. Roosevelt's energy, ambition and patriotism made him a national hero. The War won the Republican Party much public support and Roosevelt particularly benefited. He became vice-president in 1900 and when President McKinley was assassinated in September 1901, Roosevelt became, at 41, the youngest American president.

SOURCE 4.11 Remington's impression of Roosevelt (on horseback) and the Rough Riders on Kettle Hill

ACTIVITY

1 What, for the USA, were the:
   a) short-term
   b) long-term
   effects of the Spanish–American War? Here are some suggestions, but you should also add ones of your own.
   Possible benefits: more land for settlement; control of other countries and peoples; safe sea routes; safe bases for traders and the navy; influence in the Pacific; influence in the Atlantic; defeat of Spain; to give freedom to the Cubans and to the Filipinos; a practice for the navy and army in a 'real' fighting situation; personal glory and ambition; exciting copy for the newspapers; proof that white Anglo-Saxon races were superior.

2 Which of these effects was the most important?

3 Review your list of effects. Was the Spanish–American War a turning point for US foreign policy?

ACTIVITY

From jellyfish to eagle?
   a) How far had the USA moved from jellyfish to eagle?
   b) Where would you place America on this continuum in 1898?
   c) Explain your decision.

| **America the jellyfish** – avoiding all external contact except trade. | America reluctantly involved in foreign conflicts within its sphere of influence, in defence of trade. | America reluctantly involved worldwide to solve international problems. | **America the eagle** – enthusiastically committing forces to external conflicts to gain resources and influence. |

60

FROM JELLYFISH TO EAGLE? WHY DID THE USA CHANGE ITS FOREIGN POLICY, 1890–1919?

FOCUS ROUTE

Why was America involved in:

a) Latin America
b) Asia?

Theodore Roosevelt (1858–1919)
Theodore Roosevelt revelled in his position as president. It seemed the natural culmination to a career in which he had tried to raise standards in public life in the federal civil service and the New York Police Department. He had extended his political skills as governor of the state of New York. He thrived on change and drama. Here's an example in a story he enjoyed retelling. In March 1886 aged 28, he and two fellow cowboys chased three boat thieves for a hundred miles downstream in desolate Dakota in freezing winter weather. When Roosevelt caught up with them he insisted on making a formal arrest and taking them to the nearest jail eight days' travel away. Desperately short of food, fearful of currents, ice floes and thawing mud, he still found time to read the poetry of Matthew Arnold and Tolstoy's *Anna Karenina*. He insisted on re-enacting the capture for a local photographer (complete with a rifle and wearing a buckskin costume), and much impressed the local doctor, Dr Stickney, who reacted like many others on meeting Roosevelt, 'He was all teeth and eyes … He was scratched, bruised, and hungry, but gritty and determined as a bulldog … He impressed me and puzzled me … I told my wife that I had met the most peculiar and at the same time the most wonderful man I ever came to know'.

C How did America extend its power in the world, 1898–1917?

The Founding Fathers of the USA had not expected the nation to be involved in foreign affairs and made little provision in the Constitution for foreign policy decisions and control, except that the Senate had to review and approve treaties. Presidents and those who influenced them became the major directors of policy. None more so than Theodore Roosevelt, who relished the opportunities for foreign policy control that the 1898 Spanish–American War had given him. He boasted, 'The biggest matters, such as the Portsmouth Peace [ending the Russo–Japanese War of 1905], the acquisition of Panama, and sending the fleet around the world I managed without consultations with anyone; for when a matter is of capital importance, it is well to have it handled by one man only.'

After 1898, the USA maintained its interests in Latin America, ready to intervene in order to maintain regional stability and establish the USA's HEGEMONY (leadership by one state over a number of other states). President Roosevelt outlined this in his annual message to Congress in 1904 (Source 4.12).

SOURCE 4.12 Roosevelt's annual message to Congress, 1904

… it is not true that the US feels any land hunger or entertains any project as regards the other nations of the Western Hemisphere save as for their welfare … [but] the adherence of the US to the Monroe Doctrine may force the United States, however reluctantly, in flagrant cases of such wrongdoing or impotence, to exercise as an international police power … We would interfere with them only in the last resort, and then only if it became evident that their inability or unwillingness to do justice at home and abroad had violated the rights of the US or had invited foreign aggressions to the detriment of the entire body of American nations.

Between 1901 and 1920 the three presidents – Roosevelt, Taft and Wilson – pursued similar policies towards American interests in Latin America and the Far East. They rejected making territorial claims on Latin America, but clearly stated that for a combination of reasons – economic, political, paternalistic, elitist and probably racist – there should be stability and order on America's doorstep. So the USA sorted out the debts of the Dominican Republic, took over land in Panama to build the canal link to the Pacific, opposed Mexican revolutionaries and generally tried to support American trade, business and engineering interests, whilst keeping out competing countries, which included Britain and Germany.

The markets of the Far East, especially in China, were tempting and the USA continued to support open-door policies with trading open to all. Taft used 'dollar diplomacy' (private funds used for diplomatic and financial investment in China) to counteract the increasing power of Japan in the region. There were tensions with Japan after the fall of the Manchu dynasty in China in 1911. The USA was anxious to preserve Chinese independence, although not to the extent of military intervention.

SOURCE 4.13 President William Taft in his home state of Ohio in 1911. He had been the first governor of the Philippines

SOURCE 4.14 Woodrow Wilson was the Democratic president, 1912–20; a former academic with a strong Presbyterian faith

---

ACTIVITY

In 1900 Roosevelt wrote, 'I have always been fond of the African proverb "Speak softly and carry a big stick".'

Explain the cartoon, *The World's Constable* (Source 4.15):
a) Which countries and which characters can you see in the cartoon?
b) Which of these are symbols, and what do they stand for?
c) What is the message of the cartoon?

SOURCE 4.15 *The World's Constable*, 1905

THE WORLD' CONSTABLE

62

FROM JELLYFISH TO EAGLE? WHY DID THE USA CHANGE ITS FOREIGN POLICY, 1890–1919?

FOCUS ROUTE

1 As you study Section D create a timeline to show the events and ideas that led to America's involvement in the First World War and its support for the Allies.
2 Complete your Focus Route table from page 51.

D Why did America go to war in 1917?

Why was the USA neutral until 1917?

The USA believed the war that broke out in 1914 was a European dispute over the balance of power in that continent. Wilson insisted that the USA was neutral, but he became a central figure in attempts to negotiate a peace. Wilson's ideals were of democracy, open-door trading and diplomacy. He believed that only the USA, because of its 'exceptionalism' as a free republic, could lead such a world. In January 1917 Wilson had argued for 'peace without victory'; unrealistic given the nature of the War and the strength of Europe's rivalries over territory and commerce. As one of his advisors had reported after a visit to Europe in 1914, 'The situation is extraordinary. It is jingoism [extreme nationalism] run stark mad ... There is too much hatred, too many jealousies'.

The USA also stayed out of the conflict because of the increase in peace movements within America:

- the Women's Peace Party with Jane Addams, Carrie Chapman Catt and other suffragists
- the American Union Against Militarism set up by Progressive pacifists
- peace initiatives funded by Carnegie and Ford
- the Socialist Party's criticisms, led by Eugene V. Debs
- black Americans who saw it as a white imperialist war.

Their arguments focused on the corruption of war, the loss of young lives, the interruption to domestic reforms and the inadequacy of war as a solution to wrongs. In the 1916 presidential election Wilson used the slogan, 'He kept us out of the war'. However, this meant that he was later criticised for not alerting the American public to the likelihood of war. It was claimed that he failed to prepare the nation militarily, resulting in it taking almost a year to get troops into France.

SOURCE 4.16 In January 1917 Wilson spoke to Congress

Only a peace between equals can last, only a peace the very principle of which is equality and a common participation in a common benefit ... Victory would mean peace forced upon the loser, a victor's terms imposed upon the vanquished. It would be accepted in humiliation, under duress, at an intolerable sacrifice, and would leave a sting, a resentment, a bitter memory upon which terms of peace would rest, not permanently, but only as upon a quicksand. Only a peace between equals can last.

Why did the policy of neutrality end?

Wilson failed to realise the practical difficulties of claiming to be a neutral nation. In practice, neutrality was impossible as long as America was still trading with the combatants. Trade with Britain and France rose from $753 million to $2.75 billion between 1914 and 1916. Trade with Germany dropped from $345 million to only $29 million. American banks provided loans of $2.3 billion to the Allies, but only $27 million to Germany. Was this neutral behaviour? Germany didn't think so, although it was the British navy's blockade of German ports that forced most American trade to be with the Allies. The initial German response was for U-boats (submarines) to attack American ships without warning, but this was curtailed after American protests at the sinking of the *Lusitania* in May 1915.

The German suspension of U-boat attacks lasted for the best part of two years. However, the USA declared war on Germany on 6 April 1917. The two main incidents that led to the USA entering the war came as the culmination of a growing sense that German militarism had to be defeated in order to allow the American ideas of a democratic world to be realised.

ACTIVITY

Study Source 4.16.

1 What were Wilson's reasons for advocating 'peace without victory'?
2 Why was this policy unsuccessful?

DISCUSS

1 Theodore Roosevelt said that Wilson's peace plans were 'a product of men who want everyone to float to heaven on a sloppy sea of universal mush'. Do you agree with Roosevelt?
2 In the light of later history, was Wilson right in advocating 'peace without victory'?

LUSITANIA

The German embassy in the USA published an advertisement in newspapers warning travellers on British ships crossing the Atlantic of the risks of such travel. On the same day the liner, *Lusitania* sailed from New York to Liverpool. Off the Irish coast she was hit by a U-boat torpedo and sank in only eighteen minutes with the loss of 1200 of her 1257 passengers – 128 of whom were Americans. America was shocked that civilians were now enemy targets. Wilson demanded that Germany protect passenger ships, and later threatened to end diplomatic relations if similar incidents were repeated. Germany accepted limitations on U-boat use, but both sides realised that any repetition could result in war between the two countries.

SOURCE 4.17 The *Lusitania* leaving New York, May 1915

Incident one: Germany resumed unrestricted submarine warfare

By January 1917, the Russian army was showing weaknesses and the Allied troops were flagging. Despite the risk of America entering the conflict, the Germans decided to seize their chance of victory. They restarted unrestricted submarine warfare in the hope that this would reduce Allied resources and lead to a rapid German victory. From 1 February all shipping around Britain and France would be attacked on sight.

Incident two: the Zimmermann Telegram

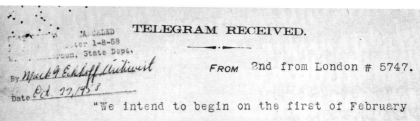

TELEGRAM RECEIVED.

FROM 2nd from London # 5747.

"We intend to begin on the first of February unrestricted submarine warfare. We shall endeavor in spite of this to keep the United States of America neutral. In the event of this not succeeding, we make Mexico a proposal of alliance on the following basis: make war together, make peace together, generous financial support and an understanding on our part that Mexico is to reconquer the lost territory in Texas, New Mexico, and Arizona. The settlement in detail is left to you. You will inform the President of the above most secretly as soon as the outbreak of war with the United States of America is certain and add the suggestion that he should, on his own initiative, invite Japan to immediate adherence and at the same time mediate between Japan and ourselves. Please call the President's attention to the fact that the ruthless employment of our submarines now offers the prospect of compelling England in a few months to make peace." Signed, ZIMMERMANN.

ACTIVITY

1 What are the key points in the telegram (Source 4.18)?
2 How long did Zimmermann expect the War to last?
3 Why might this telegram lead to America entering the War?
4 What do you think Zimmermann might have ignored or underestimated about America entering the War?

SOURCE 4.18 A photocopy of the original decoded Zimmermann Telegram, 25 February 1917, sent by the German Foreign Secretary, Zimmermann, to the German minister in Mexico (the 'President' is the President of Mexico)

64

FROM JELLYFISH TO EAGLE? WHY DID THE USA CHANGE ITS FOREIGN POLICY, 1890–1919?

TALKING POINTS

1 How do you think a neutral state should behave? With whom should they trade? How should they treat violations of their neutrality? What if their innocent citizens are killed in the conflict?

2 These are not easy questions to answer in theory, and much harder to deal with in practice. In the First World War Switzerland and Sweden were neutral. How did they behave?

DISCUSS

Do you think that the USA entering the First World War in 1917 was a bigger turning point in American foreign policy than the Spanish–American War of 1898?

The declaration of war

In early March, President Wilson, on his own authority, ordered that all merchant ships should be armed, and that the navy should fire on U-boats. Germany responded by sinking five American ships in one week. There was no alternative but for the president to ask Congress for a declaration of war on Germany.

SOURCE 4.19 Wilson asks Congress to declare war, 1917, in J. Lorence, *Enduring Voices*, 4th edn., 2000, p.184

With a profound sense of the solemn and even tragical character of the steps I am taking and of the grave responsibilities which it involves, but in unhesitating obedience to what I deem my constitutional duty, I advise that Congress declare the recent course of the Imperial Government to be in fact nothing less than war against the government and people of the United States; that it formally accept the status of belligerent which has thus been thrust upon it; and that it take immediate steps not only to put the country in a more thorough state of defense but also to exert all its power and employ all its resources to bring the Government of the German Empire to terms ...

When he was applauded by Congress he commented, 'My message today was a message of death for our young men. How strange it seems to applaud it.' And he was right. By the end of the War in November 1918 there had been 48,909 American deaths in battle, as many again from disease, and 230,000 wounded.

The American contribution to the fighting

■ 4C The Western Front, France, 1918

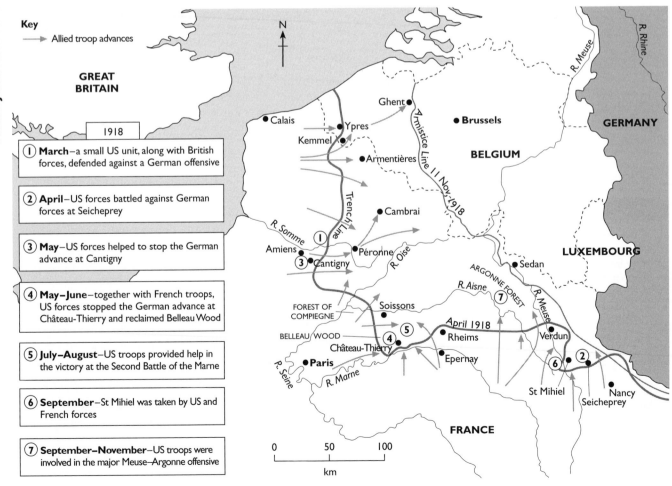

Key
→ Allied troop advances

1918

① **March**–a small US unit, along with British forces, defended against a German offensive

② **April**–US forces battled against German forces at Seicheprey

③ **May**–US forces helped to stop the German advance at Cantigny

④ **May–June**–together with French troops, US forces stopped the German advance at Château-Thierry and reclaimed Belleau Wood

⑤ **July–August**–US troops provided help in the victory at the Second Battle of the Marne

⑥ **September**–St Mihiel was taken by US and French forces

⑦ **September–November**–US troops were involved in the major Meuse–Argonne offensive

TALKING POINTS

1   The USA lost 48,909 soldiers in the First World War. On 1 July 1916 Britain lost 20,000 in one day on the Somme. Can you judge the American contribution on the number of dead alone?

2   What else needs to be considered to make a balanced assessment of their contribution to the Allied victory?

The American Expeditionary Force (AEF) was put under the control of General Pershing. He had been concerned that the lack of military preparation before 1917 had prolonged the war into 1918. Even after American soldiers landed in France they relied on British and French weapons (though made in America) and had their own weapons only in time to fire a salute at the armistice celebrations. However, the navy provided vital destroyer-ship escort across the Atlantic for food and industrial goods. Although relatively untrained, the American soldiers brought a much needed infusion of energy and morale into the Allied campaign. They halted the German advance on Paris in July 1918 and played a decisive role in eastern France in September. Germany realised that it would not be able to counter the reality of American intervention and called for an armistice. It was signed at 11.00 a.m. on 11 November 1918 – the eleventh hour of the eleventh day of the eleventh month.

At home, the government had mobilised the population to produce weapons, ammunition and uniforms. Food conservation was introduced with propaganda slogans like 'If U fast U beat U boats – if U feast U boats beat U'. The contribution made by women was given recognition in the passing of the Nineteenth Amendment in 1920, giving federal voting rights to all women. Government powers increased with controls on unions, arms production, housing and fuel, all designed to support the war effort.

ACTIVITY

From jellyfish to eagle?
  a) How far had the USA moved from jellyfish to eagle?
  b) Where would you place America on this continuum in 1917?
  c) Explain your decision.

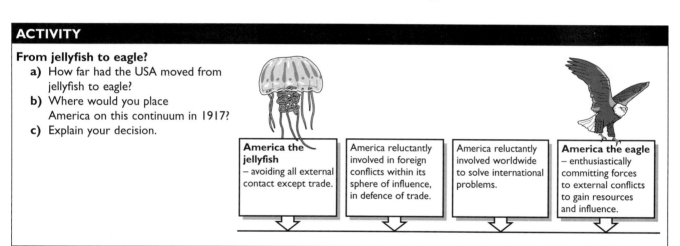

America the jellyfish – avoiding all external contact except trade.

America reluctantly involved in foreign conflicts within its sphere of influence, in defence of trade.

America reluctantly involved worldwide to solve international problems.

America the eagle – enthusiastically committing forces to external conflicts to gain resources and influence.

66

FROM JELLYFISH TO EAGLE? WHY DID THE USA CHANGE ITS FOREIGN POLICY, 1890–1919?

E Why didn't the USA sign the Treaty of Versailles?

SOURCE 4.20 *The Signing of the Peace in the Hall of Mirrors,* Versailles, 28 May 1919, by Sir William Orpen

SOURCE 4.21 An extract from Wilson's speech in St Louis, Missouri, 5 September 1919, in J. Lorence, *Enduring Voices*, 4th edn, 2000, p.187

This nation went into this war to see it through to the end, and the end has not come yet. This is the beginning, not of the war, but of the processes which are going to render a war like this impossible. It is a great treaty, it is a treaty of justice, of rigorous and severe justice, but do not forget that there are many other parties to this treaty than Germany and her opponents ...
America is made up of the peoples of the world. All the best bloods flow in her veins, all the old affections, all the old and sacred traditions of peoples of every sort throughout the world circulate in her veins, and she has said to mankind at her birth: 'We have come to redeem the world by giving it liberty and justice.' Now we are called upon before the tribunal of mankind to redeem that immortal pledge.

President Wilson spent the first half of 1919 in Versailles, France, negotiating at the peace conference. He had already called for a 'peace without victory' and had set out his FOURTEEN POINTS as a basis for a treaty. The key point was to create a league of nations as the basis for a new international, moral order and to prevent future wars. Such a league would encourage the American values of democracy and free trade, would curb UNILATERALISM, i.e. make states consult about foreign affairs, and be able to mediate in disputes. It would make the First World War the 'war to end all wars'. The Treaty of Versailles did create the League of Nations, but Wilson did not achieve 'peace without victory' as many of the key terms punished Germany by, for example, imposing huge reparations and depriving Germany of its colonies.

Once the negotiations were over, Wilson faced another argument as there was considerable opposition in Congress to ratifying and signing the Treaty. Wilson toured America to rally popular support. Source 4.21 is typical of the speeches he made at the time.

SOURCE 4.22 Congressman Victor Berger writing in his local paper, 1919, in J. Lorence, *Enduring Voices*, 4th edn, 2000, p.175

This was the worst imperialistic war ever known in the history of the world ... As for America in particular – what have we gained in this war and by this war? What has America gained except billions of debts and a hundred thousand of cripples? And we have lost most of our political democracy. Can anyone think of a single thing, worthwhile, that we have gained through this war?

ACTIVITY

1 What were Wilson's main arguments in Source 4.21 for signing the Treaty?
2 Using Sources 4.22–4.24 and the text above, identify the reasons why America did not sign the Treaty.
3 Review your answer to the Activity 'From jellyfish to eagle' on pages 59 and 65. Had the USA retreated towards its traditional foreign policy by 1919?

67

FROM JELLYFISH TO EAGLE? WHY DID THE USA CHANGE ITS FOREIGN POLICY, 1890–1919?

SOURCE 4.24 *Interrupting the Ceremony,* by McCutcheon, c. 1920. The harmony of a union between Uncle Sam and his European bride, encouraged by the League of Nations, is violently disrupted by an angry Senate, arguing that such unions were against the US Constitution and a threat to the American nation

SOURCE 4.23 The journal *The New Republic* criticises the Treaty of Versailles, Vol. XIX, 17 May 1919

The world which will result from this document can by no stretch of language be made to agree with the picture which the President had in mind when he went to Paris, or when he spoke in the days of his glory of what was to be accomplished … The treaty is the work of the European governments, mitigated at a few points no doubt by Mr Wilson. But the settlement which we are now asked to guarantee … is one made by European governments in the spirit of the traditional diplomacy of Europe. In the meshes of that diplomacy it would be reckless folly for a nation placed as ours is to entangle itself … the immediate task for Americans is to decide coolly just how they will limit their obligations under the Covenant. That they must be limited seems to us an inescapable conclusion.

Woodrow Wilson suffered a massive stroke in October 1919. For the next six months he never met his Cabinet and all communication with him was through his wife and doctor.

However, through them he continued to insist that Democrats must not compromise about the terms of the ratification. After two attempts at ratification in November 1919 and March 1920, both of which failed because of Republican opposition and the Democrat's failure to compromise, it was accepted that no further attempt was viable. Instead, Congress passed a resolution in July 1921 formally ending the War, but without signing any peace treaty. Wilson's attempt to match American values and 'exceptionalism' to the complex realities of the post-war world had failed. The USA never signed the Treaty of Versailles nor joined the League of Nations. The Democrats refused to select Wilson as their presidential candidate in 1920 and the Republican Warren Harding won a landslide victory on a platform of a return to 'normalcy'.

■ **Learning trouble spot**

Understanding individuals
Woodrow Wilson died in 1924. His character can be seen as a confused mixture of idealism, arrogance and disillusionment. He was an idealist but also a traditional Southerner and unsympathetic to racial equality in his own administration. This is not a mixture that we would expect today, but Wilson's apparently contradictory attitudes have to be seen in the context of his time.

One of the problems about studying the past is understanding how people were affected by their upbringing, education and the events and ideas of the time. You can gain some insight into others' lives by reading 'around' a subject, looking at contemporary photos or paintings, reading novels and biographies. However, you will always have to be aware that you are studying the past with your modern 'head' and that that will inevitably influence both how you think today, and how you view the past.

TALKING POINTS

1 When you are answering a causal question it is vital to remember that events could have happened differently. It is helpful to ask yourself 'what if…?' What if there had been: no war against Spain in Cuba; no Theodore Roosevelt; no German U-boat attacks on American shipping? Would American foreign policy have developed in the same way?

2 How far can one individual change a nation's foreign policy? Did Presidents Theodore Roosevelt, William Taft and Woodrow Wilson have unique influences upon America's foreign policy?

F | # Review: From jellyfish to eagle? Why did the USA change its foreign policy 1890–1919?

America's involvement in the world had expanded enormously between 1890 and 1919. At the end of the nineteenth century the USA was concerned about its own domestic 'manifest destiny'. As the West was settled it was inevitable that adventurers and traders would look beyond the nation's geographical boundaries. Such expansion needed direction from government to be successful. What could not be anticipated was the way in which foreign policy changes for the benefit of American trade and security would entangle the USA in situations beyond its control. The dilemma for policy makers, after the flurry of military and naval success in 1898 in Cuba, was how this success could, and should, be used. The stark choice of isolationism or entanglement, as outlined by the republic's early statesmen, had become much more complicated by 1919.

68

FROM JELLYFISH TO EAGLE? WHY DID THE USA CHANGE ITS FOREIGN POLICY, 1890–1919?

Write an essay answering the following question:
  Why did America change its foreign policy, 1890–1919?
Use the following to help you:

• your completed Focus Route table from page 51
• your completed charts from the Activity 'From jellyfish to eagle?' (pages 59, 65 and 66)
• Chart 4D below.

■ 4D Why did America's foreign policy change?

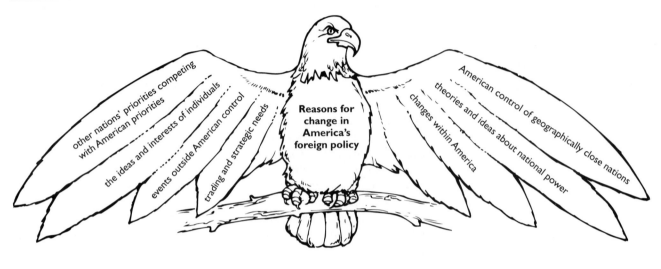

other nations' priorities competing with American priorities

the ideas and interests of individuals

events outside American control

trading and strategic needs

Reasons for change in America's foreign policy

American control of geographically close nations

theories and ideas about national power

changes within America

KEY POINTS FROM CHAPTER 4

From jellyfish to eagle? Why did the USA change its foreign policy, 1890–1919?

1 The settlement of the West encouraged America to look beyond its immediate borders for markets and settlements.

2 The search and need for new markets meant greater involvement with the rest of the world. New policies required military and naval support.

3 US policies were influenced by ideas of Social Darwinism and racial superiority.

4 It became possible for determined presidents like Roosevelt and Wilson to initiate changes in foreign policy.

5 America's attitude to imperialism was much debated during the 1890s and 1900s. America rejected establishing territorial control, but did impose its political and military will in Latin America, the Caribbean and the Philippines.

6 The Spanish–American War of 1898 and fighting in the First World War were turning points in American foreign policy as both entangled the USA further into international politics.

7 The First World War exposed the problems of neutrality for a globally active industrial nation.

8 The First World War demonstrated the immense possibilities of American industrial production, commitment and the potential power of the state.

9 Congress' rejection of the Treaty of Versailles led to the isolationist policies of the 1920s and 1930s and had long-term significance for world peace.

10 By 1920, the USA had built up its navy and army, although this made it a threat to other nations.

Section 1 Review: The nation expands, 1865–1919

■ A   Were all Americans free and equal by 1919?

Did black Americans become free citizens after the Civil War? (Chapter 1)

Did agricultural and industrial workers benefit as the US economy developed? (Chapter 3)

What was the fate of Native Americans as settlers moved West? (Chapter 2)

Did the USA liberate Cuba and the Philippines? (Chapter 4)

■ B   To what extent was the USA's power established, 1865–1919?

Did the end of slavery make the USA more powerful? (Chapter 1)

How did industrialisation make the USA so wealthy? (Chapter 3)

What influence did the myths of the West have on Americans? (Chapter 2)

Why did the USA become involved with other nations after 1890? (Chapter 4)

ACTIVITY

1 These charts introduced Section 1 (page 3). Using the information from the last four chapters, write a summary answer, perhaps of two or three sentences or a paragraph, for each of the questions.

2 Discuss the following statements with your group. Write your own brief response to each one, and then review your opinion at the end of Sections 2 and 3.

Statement One
By 1919 the USA had become 'the land of the free'.

Statement Two
The future supremacy of the USA in the world had been established by 1919.

3 Choose **three** images that you would put on the cover of a book on the history of the USA, 1865–1919 and explain your choices.

Prosperity, collapse, destruction and victory, 1920–45

By 1919 the key developments in American history had been:

- the growth of technology and the wealth created by industrialisation
- the emergence of the **USA** as a reluctant international power
- the slow progress to civil rights for minorities
- the increase in presidential authority and changing use of executive power.

What might happen next?

SOURCE I   Revere Beach, Boston

Will more and more Americans live richer, fuller lives?

SOURCE 2   Charles Evan Hughes and Ariste Briand at the Washington Conference

Will the USA advance or retreat in international affairs?

SOURCE 3   The lynching of black Americans

Will the USA speed up its progress towards equality for all its people?

SOURCE 4   President Franklin D. Roosevelt broadcasting to the nation

What role will emerge for the president of such a powerful country?

5

Internationalism or isolationism – did the USA pursue an inconsistent foreign policy, 1920–39?

CHAPTER OVERVIEW

TALKING POINTS

1 What is a consistent foreign policy? Do you agree with the following definition?

- One that is based on principle.
- One that has consistent aims.
- One that has consistent attitudes to events.
- One that is known to the rest of the world.
- One that is flexible, but clear in its purpose.

2 What would be the hallmarks of an inconsistent policy?

The majority of Americans had never wanted to be involved in the First World War. Once it had ended they were happy to return to immediate concerns. There were certainly plenty of real or imagined dangers – the pandemic of flu in 1918–19; the apparent menace of communism after the Russian Revolution of 1917; the supposed threat of black workers migrating north and taking jobs from white men. Many Americans wanted a return to the certainties of 1914 and especially to a foreign policy that entailed avoiding involvement in foreign wars. For the twenty years to 1939 the USA therefore tried to remain internationally uninvolved, but failed because trade continued to be a focus of both business and political ambition. These twenty years would prove that in the unstable post-war world of Europe and Asia it was impossible to separate making money from being a political player.

This chapter will look at foreign policy between the end of one war and the start of another and ask whether it was really as inconsistent as it seemed. The policies were driven by the urge to retain and extend economic global power, but also by a desire for peace, until the disastrous Wall Street Crash of October 1929. This made economic recovery and stability the deciding factors in foreign policy. The 1930s saw military aggression and political dictatorship used in Europe and Asia as the tools for this recovery. Could the USA resist involvement?

A Why was 'never again' the feeling in 1920? (p. 73)

B How did the policy of 'independent internationalism' support American global interests, 1920–32? (pp. 74–78)

C Getting involved – being a 'good neighbour' in Latin America (p. 79)

D Did the USA retreat into isolationism in the 1930s? (pp. 80–83)

E Review: Internationalism or isolationism – did the USA pursue an inconsistent foreign policy, 1920–39? (pp. 83–84)

ACTIVITY

In your work in Chapter 4 you looked at how foreign policy decisions differ from domestic ones. Before you start this chapter revise some of that knowledge:

1 Why was it difficult for the USA to deal with other countries?
2 The main 'players' involved in making American decisions were the president, the secretary of state, Congress, the military and public opinion. How might their priorities differ?
3 There were constraints on the making of foreign policy. Consider how:
   a) financial stability and the costs of war, and
   b) logistical preparation (of men, ammunition, food supplies, medical care)
   might have practical implications for policy decisions.

FOCUS ROUTE

INTERNATIONALISM   ISOLATIONISM

As you work through this chapter use a simple chart like this to record evidence for America adopting either internationalist or isolationist policies.

FOCUS ROUTE

1 How did each of the five topics in Chart 5A influence foreign policy in the immediate post-war period? (Think in terms of isolationism or internationalism.)
2 Write a paragraph explaining why the term 'a mixed legacy' might be a good description of the impact of the First World War.

■ **5A The legacy of the Great War**

1 INDUSTRIAL GROWTH

War had taught government how to mobilise workers and increase production with union support, use the new labour sources of women and Afro-Americans and to link industrial production to government needs. The requirements of the War left the USA as the strongest industrial producer in the world, thanks to innovation and technical advancements. The federal government now also had a stronger bureaucracy to implement its wishes.

2 EQUAL RIGHTS AND BLACK MIGRATION

SOURCE 5.1 Some of the black soldiers of the 369ᵗʰ Infantry (15ᵗʰ N.Y.) who won the Croix de Guerre for gallantry in northern France

Whilst immigrants and women were recognised for their war efforts, black soldiers had had to serve in segregated regiments usually doing menial tasks. Of those who fought, many received awards from the French government, but none from their own. The War had raised expectations of greater equality for Afro-Americans. As one black veteran said, 'I'm glad I went. I done my part and I'm going to fight right here till UNCLE SAM does his'. The flow of black workers from the South to the North increased after 1915, many settling in Chicago. Wartime demands for labour provided them with jobs, better pay and raised expectations. But by 1919 resentment amongst white workers and competition for scarce housing led to rioting in 25 cities across the country. The Chicago riots, lasting five days, were the most violent with shootings and lynchings.

3 THE RED SCARE

The defeat of Germany did not end hate and intolerance towards those with different and potentially threatening beliefs. The menace of the 'Hun' was replaced by the supposed menace of communism. The Bolshevik Revolution in 1917 (which had overthrown the Tsar) and the THIRD INTERNATIONAL in 1919 (which pledged its members to revolution throughout the world) revived fears of radical violence in the USA. A series of bombings in the summer of 1919 induced a reaction led by the Attorney General A. Mitchell Palmer to order wholesale arrests and jailing of both aliens and citizens, without any legal process. Homes were entered without search warrants and property removed or destroyed. The Department of Justice also sent propaganda to newspapers, which excited public opinion against radicals. After the dramatic seizure of 6000 suspected radicals in New York in January 1920 and an unproven threat of revolution in May, lawyers and politicians began to realise how Mitchell Palmer was abusing his power, and by the summer the hysteria was over.

The legacy of the Great War

4 THE INFLUENZA PANDEMIC

First reported at an army camp in Kansas, in March 1918, the influenza virus spread rapidly – into American cities, into the American army in France, and then across the world during 1918 and 1919. It was estimated that 40 million people died, including large numbers of the young and old. In the USA there were 700,000 deaths, from an illness that started like a cold but then could kill swiftly, and had no cure. It seemed as uncontrollable as the war in Europe and as difficult to end.

5 THE FAILURE TO JOIN THE LEAGUE OF NATIONS

Congress rejected President Wilson's ideal of a world free of war, when it refused to sign the Treaty of Versailles and join the League of Nations. Wilson's illness and lack of political skills played their part in his failure to persuade Congress, but this refusal was symbolic of the USA's unwillingness to realise that its post-war power was needed within such an international organisation.

FOCUS ROUTE

Make notes to answer the following questions.

1 What were America's global interests?
2 What were the major challenges to America's interests?
3 What international problems did the conference and treaties of the 1920s try to solve?
4 What were the strengths and weaknesses of each attempt from the USA's perspective?
5 How successful had the USA been in achieving its foreign policy aims by 1932?
6 Mark key events and policies on your Focus Route chart from page 72.

B How did the policy of 'independent internationalism' support American global interests, 1920–32?

■ 5B Which direction?

Its economic investments through trade, financing, overseas bases and in foreign industries meant that it had to be involved overseas to protect them.

It did not want to see another major war because of the disruption it would cause to trade and domestic stability.

After 1919 the USA tried to follow a policy of 'independent internationalism', which meant active involvement with other nations, but also an insistence on freedom of action to protect national interests. The aim was to create a world order in which the USA could prosper. Because of this desire to have the best of both worlds, foreign policy emphasised:

- preventing another war by controlling the arms race
- maintaining America's economic supremacy.

To achieve this the USA would therefore have to be involved in three main areas: Europe, the Far East and Latin America. The specific problems the USA faced can be seen in Chart 5C.

■ 5C Foreign policy problems

■ Learning trouble spot

When did a president start work?
Remember that presidential elections are held every four years in November, but until 1933 the new president did not take up the post until 4 March of the next year. The Twentieth Amendment of 1933 changed this to 20 January. The presidency dates given throughout this book are those of the election year, not the year of formally taking office.

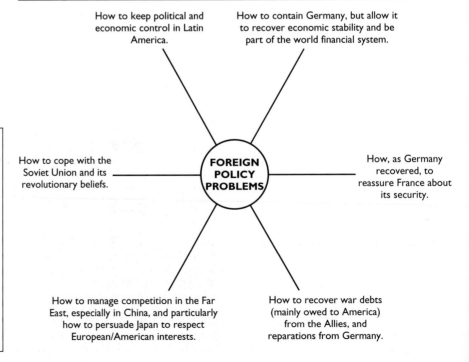

How to keep political and economic control in Latin America.

How to contain Germany, but allow it to recover economic stability and be part of the world financial system.

How to cope with the Soviet Union and its revolutionary beliefs.

FOREIGN POLICY PROBLEMS

How, as Germany recovered, to reassure France about its security.

How to manage competition in the Far East, especially in China, and particularly how to persuade Japan to respect European/American interests.

How to recover war debts (mainly owed to America) from the Allies, and reparations from Germany.

Who made foreign policy?

Policy was formally made by the president who appointed a secretary of state. Both men (there was no female secretary of state until 1997) had to take into account the wishes and demands of Congress, and also of popular opinion. After Wilson was defeated in 1920 all the presidents until 1932 were Republicans. The Republican Party believed in limited government, giving more opportunities to state, local and individual interests. They believed in giving aid to corporations, including via tax cuts, to encourage consideration of public interests.

The presidents, 1920–32

SOURCE 5.2 Warren Harding (left) elected in 1920, who died in office in 1923, with his Vice-President, Calvin Coolidge who went on to become president, winning the election of 1924

SOURCE 5.3 Herbert Hoover, president from 1928 to 1932

Did conferences and treaties resolve America's worries about foreign involvement?

So the USA pursued a policy of 'independent internationalism', although Chart 5B (page 74) shows you the contradictions. It avoided isolationism through trading involvement, the spread of American culture (music, films, industrial methods) and through initiating international action. These included:

- conferences on arms control in which the USA took the lead
- active support for an 'open-door' trading policy for China
- the refusal to recognise any anti-democratic communist regime
- offers of humanitarian aid for the famines suffered in the Soviet Union in 1923
- the recovery of war debts, since the USA was owed the most.

1 The Washington Conference, 1921–22

SOURCE 5.4 American Secretary of State Charles E. Hughes (second left) and the French Foreign Minister Ariste Briand (third left) at the Washington Conference, 1921

THE SECRETARIES OF STATE

1921–25 Charles E. Hughes
1925–29 Frank B. Kellogg
1929–33 Henry L. Stimson
1933–44 Cordell Hull

76

INTERNATIONALISM OR ISOLATIONISM – DID THE USA PURSUE AN INCONSISTENT FOREIGN POLICY, 1920–39?

In 1921 nine major powers (America, Britain, Japan, France, Italy, China, Portugal, Belgium and the Netherlands) met to discuss the arms race, particularly the build up of navies. They all realised that arms production was wasteful to economies needing to repay debts, and that arms competition led to war – 1914 was too recent a reminder of that. The USA was particularly anxious to control Japan. So in what has been described as one of the most stunning speeches in diplomatic history, Charles E. Hughes proposed deliberately destroying ships. For the USA it meant the destruction of 30 ships, with equivalent numbers for other nations, and, in total, more tonnage of shipping than all the admirals of the world had sunk in centuries. The conference then passed three treaties:

 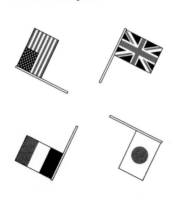 

- **The Five Power Treaty** – limited the tonnage of American, British, Japanese, French and Italian navies.

- **The Four Power Treaty** – ended the Anglo–Japanese alliance and instead offered consultation by America, Britain, Japan and France in the event of an Asian crisis.

- **The Nine Power Treaty** – the five major powers plus China, Portugal, Belgium and the Netherlands established 'open-door' principles as international law, whilst recognising Japan's particular interest in Manchuria.

The Conference was generally regarded as a success. Although tensions between competing countries remained, the rest of the decade stayed peaceful and the signatories abided by the agreements. The Conference certainly recognised Japan as a major power and kept it within international systems for the rest of the decade.

2 The Dawes Plan, 1924
This American-created plan prodded other nations into dealing with the problem of reparations. It proposed reducing Germany's annual reparations payments (which totalled $33 billion) so that the payments were, in future, related to the level of Germany's financial recovery.

ACTIVITY

Defaulting on war debts angered the American people. What would they have replied to each of the three arguments put forward in Chart 5D?

■ 5D Debt repayments by the Allies and Germany were a constant source of friction

3 The Locarno Pact, 1925

In this pact Germany, France and Belgium guaranteed each other's boundaries.

4 The Kellogg–Briand Pact (also known as the Pact of Paris), 1928

French mistrust of Germany had not ended in 1918 or with the Locarno Pact. The 62 signatories of this international pact pledged to settle disputes peacefully. War should only be resorted to for self-defence. However, without the power of sanctions the agreement was, in effect, meaningless.

By 1929 the world seemed to be more stable and the USA was certainly flourishing economically. The USA produced half the world's industrial goods. It was the major creditor nation, the major exporter and an investor across the globe. It had wealth and stability and there had been no further war. But then came the worst financial crisis of the twentieth century, the Wall Street Crash in New York in October 1929 (see Chapter 6 pages 100–3 for more details). The Crash led to the collapse of American banks, made people less willing to invest and resulted in the mistrust of government economic policy. The Crash was primarily responsible for increased tariffs against imports and the resentment over unpaid foreign debts. Its effects spread throughout Europe, Asia and Latin America. It was like the wash from a speedboat and no one knew how to deal with its wake. Apart from its financial impact, it also had a major impact on confidence. This was not just the confidence of investors, but also of peoples and politicians who wanted stability for themselves and their countries.

■ 5E The US economy: tariffs and exports 1917–41 (from US Bureau of Census)

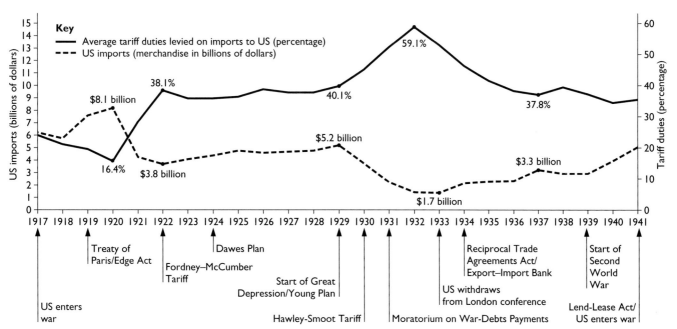

ACTIVITY

Using Chart 5E answer the following questions:

1 What specific changes were there to tariff duties during these years?

2 What was happening to export levels at the same time?

3 Why do you think these changes made the economy unstable?

4 Which world events also affected this pattern?

Why did Asia become a threat to peace?

By the 1930s Japan, which had been treated as one of the major world powers in the 1920s, was anxious to assert its power more widely in Asia. Japan had few natural resources and needed raw materials, mainland markets for its products and naval protection for its trading if it was to feel secure. Japan had strong ties with America, being America's third largest customer but, at the same time, the Japanese government knew that China was a rival for American support. Another complication was that many Japanese resented the racially motivated restrictions on Japanese immigration to the USA.

■ 5F Map of Manchuria

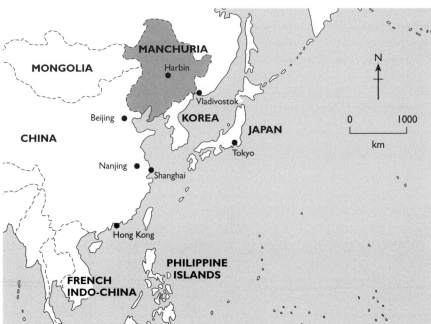

In 1931 in an attempt to solve its geopolitical problems, Japan invaded Manchuria and renamed it Manchuko. It was a first step to both more economic security and to satisfying a militarist group in the government. Manchuria provided coal, iron, timber and farm produce. It provided more space for Japanese settlement from the overcrowded islands, as well as acting as a buffer against any possible Soviet invasion.

The League of Nations condemned the invasion of Manchuria, but took no action. The USA responded by issuing the Stimson Doctrine (Stimson was the secretary of state), which refused to recognise Japan's control of Manchuria. Japan then attacked the important port of Shanghai. The USA was alarmed at this continuing aggression and began to fear that Japan might ally with the Soviet Union, a nation still mistrusted by America. Might Japan and the USSR block and harm American interests in the Far East?

Stimson therefore threatened that if Japan did not keep the Nine Power Treaty (which allowed an open-door trading policy with China), then the USA would not keep to the restrictions on naval size agreed in the Five Power Treaty. War was becoming a possibility, but at this point President Hoover and Stimson reached stalemate. The President refused to challenge Japan further by threatening other retaliation. He hoped that leaving things as they were would deter further aggression. He thought that Japan might be fearful of being crushed between the Soviet Union's ambitions for expansion and the resistance of China against further attacks. However, there was a strengthening of nationalistic feeling and anti-Americanism in Japan. Here, as elsewhere, the economic failures after 1929 had ended confidence in American money and treaties.

SOURCE 5.5 Cartoon on the Kellogg Pact, 1932, entitled 'The Open Door'; the easy destruction of Manchuria, with its gateway to the riches of China, was a practice for further aggression by Japan

ACTIVITY

Study Source 5.5. This contemporary cartoon shows a grinning Japanese soldier attacking the helpless teddy bear figure of the Kellogg Pact at the gates of Manchuria.

1 What are the typical features of the soldier (look out for them in later representations)?
2 Do you think you are supposed to sympathise with Japan's attack? What are the reasons for your opinion?
3 Identify the reasons for Japan's attack on Manchuria. Are these reflected in the cartoon?

FOCUS ROUTE

Make notes on the benefits to the USA brought about by the 'good neighbour' policy, using the following headings:

- economic
- geographic
- political.

C Getting involved – being a 'good neighbour' in Latin America

One effect of the Japanese invasion of Manchuria in 1931 was to revive criticism of the USA as an imperial power in Latin America. The USA may have contributed social benefits to the area (road-building, new schools, tariff reform, generous loans), but its involvement had also been for American gain. The USA was too deeply involved economically in Latin America to withdraw (with as much as $3.5 billion invested) and too conscious of the need to maintain geographical security to let other countries become powerful in the area. The solution was President Franklin D. Roosevelt's 'Good Neighbour' policy with its idea of 'give them a share'.

■ 5G How to be a 'good neighbour' (when you're big and powerful)

Remove military occupations.

Support strong leaders, with training if necessary.

End the Platt Amendment of 1901, which gave the USA the right to intervene in Cuban affairs.

Respect international treaties regarding non-intervention in other states' affairs.

Give more support for economic development so that Latin America would become less dependent on Germany, Italy and Japan.

Initiate a policy of Pan-Americanisation, i.e. a community of North, Central and South American states, setting out policies of non-intervention by one nation in the affairs of another.

Such policies were aided by the influence of American culture, through music and films. In turn Latin America, through immigrants and its more exotic culture, influenced American tastes.

But even good neighbours have arguments:

- America's strong-arm tactics in supporting dictators went undiminished. Somoza in Nicaragua, Trujillo in the Dominican Republic and Batista in Cuba were favoured as leaders prepared to support American interests so long as the USA was not too concerned about their often corrupt and brutal methods of acquiring and keeping power.
- Mexico was the nearest and probably richest of America's neighbours. Its interest in maintaining its unique culture and keeping control of natural resources had been encouraged in 1934 by President Cardenas' pledge of 'Mexico for the Mexicans'. The practical result of this was strikes against US corporations for higher wages by oil workers in 1937. When these demands were refused President Cardenas nationalised the oil companies' properties. The American responses of economic retaliation and diplomatic pressure were met by the threat of Mexico buying Japanese and German goods, and even of oil sales to Hitler. By 1940 the international situation (war in Europe and discontent in the Pacific) forced the Americans to make a compensation settlement and to give control of the Mexican oil fields to a nationalised company, PEMEX.

80

INTERNATIONALISM OR ISOLATIONISM – DID THE USA PURSUE AN INCONSISTENT FOREIGN POLICY, 1920–39?

FOCUS ROUTE

1 Note down the factor that the historian LaFeber identifies in Source 5.6 as influencing American foreign policy at this time.

2 As you work through Section D find evidence to support this factor.

3 What other factors would you identify as dictating foreign policy and its actions? (Consider the ambitions of individuals, the economic needs of nations, the desire to avoid another war.)

■ 5H The growing use of force in Europe and Asia 1933–39

1933	Hitler made Chancellor of Germany Japan leaves the League of Nations
1934	Japan declares Amau Doctrine setting out its sphere of interest in East Asia
1935	Germany announces re-armament Italy invades Abyssinia (Ethiopia)
1936	German occupation of Rhineland Beginning of Spanish Civil War Italy announces Rome–Berlin Axis Japan signs anti-Comintern (communist) pact with Germany
1937	Sino-Japanese War
1938	*Kristallnacht* in Germany *Anschluss* – the union of Germany and Austria Germany invades Sudetenland Munich Conference
1939	Occupation of Czechoslovakia and Poland by Germany Franco's victory in Spanish Civil War Nazi–Soviet non-aggression Pact Britain and France declare war on Germany

D Did the USA retreat into isolationism in the 1930s?

By 1932 American 'independent internationalism' was fading. There was a widespread desire for isolationism. A sense of 'let them get on with it' prevailed and many ordinary Americans were reluctant to face unpleasant realities abroad. This was the result of:

- more aggressive methods being used by some nations, particularly Germany, Italy and Japan, to realise their ambitions
- the sense of 'never again' still lingering from the First World War, making Americans reluctant to consider re-arming
- the ending of mass immigration after 1924, reinforcing beliefs that Americans could be successful on their own, without outside help, and without giving help to others
- the Crash of 1929 which, in weakening world economies, made economic and political stability more desirable
- President Hoover focusing more on how to cope with the Depression in the USA, than with foreign events.

However, isolationism was not as easy to achieve as many people had hoped – see Source 5.6.

SOURCE 5.6 W. LaFeber, *The American Age*, 2nd edn, 1994, p.385

It was, after all, tough for Americans to deny themselves overseas markets while they suffered from a crushing economic depression. Needs at home dictated policies abroad.

War debts

Europe's economic problems were made worse by the continuing need to make war debt repayments to the USA. As the effects of the Depression spread, reducing production and creating high levels of unemployment, European nations were unable to continue repayments. President Hoover halted them in 1931, when only $2.6 billion had been repaid, out of the $9.9 billion that was owed. This caused anger within America and led to the passing of the Johnson Act of 1934, which forbade the granting of government loans to foreign governments who were in default on debts owed to the USA. This was to have serious implications for Britain and France in 1939.

Aggression in Europe and Asia

Chart 5H shows the growing use of force in Europe and Asia to settle disputes and to acquire more land. The American reaction to all of these events was muted. It used neither economic sanctions nor military nor moral ones to control or diminish the actions of Hitler, Mussolini, Franco or General Tojo. Could the USA have made a difference? There is no simple answer. The 1930s was a period fraught with complex issues: ambitious and ruthless dictators; public fears about unemployment; and the momentum of events unfolding. The President, Franklin D. Roosevelt (FDR), was anxious not to jeopardise domestic recovery from the Depression, and was constrained by his perception that the American public and politicians might be opposed to more interventionist policies.

The threat of war on two fronts

The USA barely reacted when the Japanese sank the *Panay*, an American gunboat on the Yangtze in December 1937. The Japanese apologised, claiming that it was an accident. By 1938 Japan had declared a 'New Order' in Asia, with Japan as the dominant power. In response the USA decided to increase the US navy, fortify its Pacific bases and end a trade treaty with Japan, thus indicating its continuing support for China. Yet it was also anxious, as the situation in

Europe advanced towards war, to avoid military entanglements on both western and eastern fronts.

Relations with the USSR

The desire to trade with the USSR, as the world's largest nation, was made difficult by its anti-democratic political stance. America's theoretical and active concern for the principles of freedom and democracy were very different from Soviet ideas about collective action and production. Yet recovery from the Depression required sales of industrial products, and the USSR was a major purchaser of farm equipment. In 1933 the USA recognised the USSR as a legal state. The first ambassador, William Bullitt, was an advisor to FDR and pro-Soviet, but within two years he returned disillusioned and angry at what he saw as Moscow's continuing desire for world revolution. However, there were also geopolitical considerations. The USA did not want the USSR to become an ally of Japan as the two nations might expand their power in the Pacific at a great cost to American trade. So the relationship with the Soviet Union continued, but it was one of caution, mistrust and a lack of concern for each other's welfare or for peace.

Problems at home

In March 1933 Franklin D. Roosevelt began his first presidency, pledging to deal with the domestic crisis of the Depression. There was considerable opposition to involvement abroad. Congress reflected ordinary American's feelings, including the desire for isolation from others' troubles. Paramount was the fear of the USA losing its freedom of action if it had to fight abroad again. The Conservatives and the Republicans feared higher taxes and a more powerful executive, whilst the Liberals feared that war would leave domestic problems unsolved. Congress had refused to ratify joining the League of Nations or joining the World Court in 1935. It passed Neutrality Acts in 1935, 1936 and 1937.

The Neutrality Acts

1935 – If there was a war then the USA would not supply arms to either side.

1936 – No loans could be made to belligerents.

1937 – Warring countries could only purchase arms from the USA if they were paid for and taken away by the purchaser (the 'cash and carry' principle). The USA would remain neutral with regard to the Spanish Civil War (although Germany and Italy were supporting the fascist challenge of Franco against the elected republican government). Americans were not to travel on the ships of belligerent nations (to avoid a repeat of the *Lusitania* situation).

Moving away from isolationism

Despite the popular desire for isolation, Secretary of State Hull believed in the importance of world trade as a force for both peace and reviving the USA's economy. He realised the damaging effects of high tariffs. In 1934 he introduced:

The Reciprocal Trade Act – reduced tariffs by 50 per cent by special agreements with 'most favoured' nations.

The Export–Import Bank – a government agency set up to give loans to foreigners wanting to buy American goods.

Industrial leaders also tended to be sympathetic to Europe. Large companies like General Electric, IBM and Standard Oil invested there, and refused FDR's requests in 1938 for a moral embargo on fascism. They wanted low tariffs and world trade as priorities.

By 1939 the president could no longer ignore the worsening situation in the world. Although he had supported the Appeasement policies of Britain and France towards Germany and Italy, it was clear from Germany's increasing threats to occupy Czechoslovakia that the policy was ineffectual and despised by Hitler. The USA had to move away from the limitations of the Neutrality

ACTIVITY

American policy towards Europe changed during the 1930s. Identify the turning points which caused that change.

82

INTERNATIONALISM OR ISOLATIONISM – DID THE USA PURSUE AN INCONSISTENT FOREIGN POLICY, 1920–39?

FIRESIDE CHATS

Roosevelt's fireside chats began a week after he became president, in March 1933. These messages were broadcast on the radio evey Sunday, with an estimated 60 million Americans tuning in. Roosevelt used them to explain to people what he was doing and why he was doing it. Radio had never been used in this way before.

Acts, which could result in aid being denied to victims of German aggression; victims with whom most Americans had sympathy. FDR used his annual State of the Union message on 4 January 1939 to raise awareness in a language and tone familiar from his radio fireside chats (see Source 5.7).

SOURCE 5.7 Franklin D. Roosevelt's State of the Union message, 4 January 1939

… There comes a time in the affairs of men when they must prepare to defend not their homes alone but the tenets of faith and humanity on which their churches, their governments and their very civilization are founded. The defense of religion, of democracy, and of good faith among nations is all the same fight. To save one we must now make up our minds to save all … We have learned that when we deliberately try to legislate neutrality, our neutrality laws may operate unevenly and unfairly … We ought not to let that happen anymore.

He was supported by Cordell Hull, who declared that it was 'just plain chuckle-headed' to keep the Neutrality Acts. Congress refused to cancel the arms embargo, but it did not stop FDR secretly sending 500 bombers to France with the rationale that 'our frontier is now the Rhine'. In fact, in 1938 the president had acquired funds to build up the air force. Congress did, however, refuse the proposal of Senator Ludlow that there should be a national referendum before any declaration of war. This would seriously handicap presidential power at a time of crisis. At the same time Mussolini and Hitler were rejecting American diplomatic moves to restrain their aggression. The German invasion of Poland in September 1939 and the subsequent declarations of war by Britain and France against Germany, forced more radical and overt action. By November Congress had agreed to the 'cash and carry' principle for arms sales and FDR had the means to aid those who were America's natural allies in the defence of democratic values against fascism.

SOURCE 5.8 *Laocoon*, by Clifford Kennedy Berryman, 1938. This cartoon was based on the Greek story of Laocoon who, with his two sons, was crushed to death by sea serpents because he had offended his master, the god Apollo. Here the powerful serpent of isolationism crushes American opinion and makes it difficult to make a rational decision

ACTIVITY

1 What can you deduce from the cartoon (Source 5.8) about contemporary views on foreign policy?
2 Why did the coils of the serpent prove to be less powerful than they seemed?

DISCUSS

1 To what extent had isolationism broken down by 1939?
2 What were the key factors which had kept it going?
3 What were the key factors working against isolationism?

Jewish refugees

On the night of 9 November 1938 many German city streets were covered in glass, not as the result of a bomb or air attack, but because of a deliberate, government-inspired attack on Jewish shops and homes. Two nights previously a young German Jewish refugee in Paris had shot and killed a German diplomat. *Kristallnacht* ('Crystal Night' or the 'Night of the Broken Glass') was the reprisal. Synagogues were burned, 20,000 Jews arrested as criminals and an unknown number killed. An 'atonement fine' was levied on all Jews and a few weeks later all Jewish assets were confiscated.

In 1933 America had warned Germany about its treatment of Jews. By 1938 many people outside Germany were aware of the reality of Hitler's determination to annihilate the Jewish race. The actions of *Kristallnacht* were a dramatic demonstration of Hitler's fanatical desire to 'purify' the German race. Jews were deemed inferior and to be removed. Although FDR recalled the American ambassador and allowed Jews to stay longer in America than permitted, he took little other direct action. The National Origins Act of 1924 set government immigration policy, and did not recognise 'refugees', i.e. those likely to become 'a public charge'. Jews were only allowed to leave Germany (if they could get a visa) with the equivalent of $4 and would be paupers wherever they arrived. The Depression had made immigrants unwelcome, and the anti-semitism of some Europeans had been brought to America. Between 1933 and 1941 it is estimated that only an average of 8500 Jews a year were allowed to settle in America (although these did include the physicist Albert Einstein, the composer Kurt Weill and the architect Walter Gropius). This official indifference to the suffering of German Jews continued throughout the Second World War.

TALKING POINTS

1 Until the superpower years of 1945 onwards, presidents gained more prestige and better chances of re-election from solving domestic crises rather than foreign ones. Do you think that is still true today?
2 What swayed the American voters in the last presidential election?

E Review: Internationalism or isolationism – did the USA pursue an inconsistent foreign policy, 1920–39?

Foreign policy decision-making required co-operation – the president made the policy and Congress had the ultimate power to declare war. However, if the president belonged to one political party and a different party held the majority in Congress then decision-making could be confused and competitive.

SOURCE 5.9 The American historian, Norman A. Graebner, writing in 1970 (quoted in D. Merrill and T. Paterson, *Major Problems in American Foreign Relations*, Vol. II, 5th edn, 2000, pp.36–9)

Isolationism and internationalism had more in common than the conflicting rhetoric of the twenties would suggest. Americans – even the isolationists – had no desire to escape the world of commerce and investment. Businessmen, isolationists and internationalists alike, demanded that their government sustain their privileged economic position everywhere on the globe. And because a stable world environment would best serve the needs of Americans, many citizens insisted that the country accept the moral responsibility for the peace, provided that the responsibility entail no specific obligation for the defense of any foreign country or region. These limited, and generally conflicting, objectives established the bounds of popular national policy. The successive Republican administrations of the twenties, satisfied the demands of nationalists who believed in 'America First'. The repeated involvements of the United States in the cause of peace delighted those internationalists who believed that the nations should serve, not merely the needs of its own citizens, but the needs of humanity everywhere. United States' policies varied from narrow nationalism to limited internationalism, all designed to serve the specific interests of trade and investment as well as the general interest in peace.

ACTIVITY

1 Why does the author of Source 5.9 argue that internationalism and isolationism were not incompatible?
2 Why could both internationalists and isolationists be satisfied by America's foreign policy between the wars?
3 What were the limitations on America's moral responsibility?
4 If you have completed the Focus Route from page 72 look back at your completed chart. Do you agree with Graebner (Source 5.9) that 'United States' policies varied from narrow nationalism to limited internationalism'?

ACTIVITY

Create an argument between two individuals or groups with passionately opposing views about the USA's role in the world between 1920 and 1939. Use these statements and questions as a guide:
- Which was more important – domestic security or international peace?
- Had the USA learnt the 'right' lessons from the First World War?
- Was it America's fault that the initiatives to control armaments in the 1920s were not maintained?
- Economic policy was too dominant and short-sighted.
- Public opinion was too dominant and too uninformed.
- The USA should have taken a moral or military or economic stand (or all three) against aggression.

ACTIVITY

Using your notes, personal study and discussion ideas answer the following essay title:

Did the USA pursue an inconsistent foreign policy, 1920–39?

You will need to identify those aspects of the policy that appear inconsistent and those that do not. Identify the justifications for consistency and inconsistency.

The essay title implies that the policy was inconsistent. Before you begin writing you will need to decide what you think, and, most importantly, have the evidence to support your opinion.

KEY POINTS FROM CHAPTER 5

Internationalism or isolationism – did the USA pursue an inconsistent foreign policy, 1920–39?

1 After the First World War there were powerful domestic forces and needs pushing America towards isolationism.

2 The USA refused to sign the Treaty of Versailles or join the League of Nations, symbolising its fear of entanglement in overseas conflicts.

3 The USA attempted, by treaties and conferences in the 1920s, to create a peaceful and prosperous world. These showed signs of success during this period.

4 The Wall Street Crash in 1929 and the resulting Depression encouraged inward-looking policies and also created friction with Europe over debt repayments.

5 In the 1930s American protests at aggression by Germany and Japan were not supported by economic and industrial sanctions or penalties.

6 A policy of neutrality became a passive response to aggression, but events in Europe made maintaining this policy impossible.

7 The Second World War demonstrated the failure of American attempts to be isolationist or neutral. Other nations, by their aggression or appeasement, contributed to this failure.

8 Relations with Latin America improved and were to be especially useful in the Second World War.

9 Despite the popular appeal of isolationism, the USA was never likely to retreat entirely from world affairs because of the growth of its industry and trade. These required the USA to continue to play a part in world affairs.

6

The twenties – Jazz Age or Depression Blues?

CHAPTER OVERVIEW

SOURCE 6.1 Enjoying the benefits of expanding industrialisation. This is Revere Beach near Boston in the 1920s. Visitors travelled by car and had money and time to enjoy the nearby amusement arcades as well as the sea

FOCUS ROUTE

How should we remember the twenties? For the successes of the Jazz Age or for the failures of the Depression Blues? As you work through this chapter collect evidence to complete your own copy of this table. There will be measurable evidence, such as statistics, and evidence that relates to quality of life, such as entertainment.

Jazz Age	Depression Blues	Other evidence or suggested ways of naming the era

SOURCE 6.2 An unbelievable sight before 1929. The impact of the Crash and increasing unemployment reduced respectable men to having to queue for cheap meals

SOURCE 6.3 A typical scene at Small's Paradise Club in Harlem, in 1929

The years from 1920 to 1932 have been given many names – an age of jazz and an age of affluence were positive ones. More negative were an age of irresponsibility, of anxiety and the oddly named age of normalcy. Another – the 'Roaring Twenties' – suggests something loud and exciting. These names appear to contradict each other. The twenties began with good things including the continuing inventiveness of American technology, the wealth and opportunities from industrial manufacturing and a greater acceptance of the role of women beyond the home. However, there were also negatives – the treatment of black Americans as second-class citizens, the economic problems of farmers, the difficulties of poor working conditions and powerful employers, and anger against immigrants, supposed revolutionaries and those who challenged traditional beliefs. This chapter will examine these contradictions – wealth and poverty, excitement and routine – and how the USA responded to the immense challenge of the Wall Street Crash of 1929.

A The American dream (pp. 87–89)

B Cars, Capone, the Teapot Dome and all that jazz – was this an age of affluence? (pp. 89–94)

C Xenophobia, fundamentalism and conservatism – was this an age of intolerance? (pp. 94–99)

D Why did the Wall Street Crash become the Depression? (pp. 100–03)

E Who was to blame? (pp. 104–06)

F Review: The twenties – Jazz Age or Depression Blues? (pp. 106–07)

DISCUSS

Look carefully at the details in Sources 6.1–6.3. What can you learn from them about the 1920s?

TALKING POINT

How many reasons can you suggest to explain why different historians put forward different interpretations of the twenties?

FOCUS ROUTE

1 What were:
  a) the economic
  b) the social changes
  that promised a better life during
  this period?
2 What were the hints that a better
  life might come at a price?

A The American dream

'If I get to Paris I won't need any more, and if I don't get to Paris I won't need any more either.' The speaker was a young, handsome airman discussing his five sandwiches and one day's worth of tinned rations (see Source 6.4). He was about to set off on the first solo, non-stop, 3610 mile flight from New York to Paris. Charles Lindbergh did succeed; in 33½ hours. In the National Air and Space Museum in Washington DC you can see his plane suspended from the ceiling, and marvel that such flimsiness could ever cross the Atlantic. To Americans his flight was a wonderful example of the best of their national character – individualism, self-reliance and hard work. It was also a marvellous example of American technology as it was only 24 years since the Wright brothers had made the first flight for twelve seconds over a North Carolina beach.

Why was a better life possible?

An inevitable reaction to war was to look for, and even expect, a better life afterwards. Otherwise why was it worth fighting? The twenties were no different. Not only were there expectations, but there were also real possibilities for a better life. Why? In terms of economic development and its effects it seemed that the First World War had released an energy and an ambition to succeed that exceeded that of any other nation in the world.

SOURCE 6.5 H. Evans, *The American Century*, 1998, p.182

Optimism, like everything else in America was mass-produced ... Such was the exuberance of the people, manifested in spectacular bursts of invention and productivity, so fervent the cause of scientific management, so prodigious the stock of investment capital ...

The presidents of the decade – Warren Harding, Calvin Coolidge and Herbert Hoover – brought varying levels of skill to the job. All were Republicans and reflected their party's confidence in the future, and especially a reliance on the success of business and industry. After the necessary government controls during the War, presidents and Congress were anxious for a more *laissez-faire* approach, with a clear separation between business and government. However, this policy ignored, and also created, problems both for industry and finance (reflected in the 1929 Crash), and also for ordinary working Americans.

SOURCE 6.4 Charles Lindbergh standing in front of *The Spirit of St Louis*, the aeroplane he piloted across the Atlantic in 1927

■ 6A Reasons for optimism

The industrial power of the USA had been expanded by the war, with the government's encouragement.

The mass production of standardised products was possible because of abundant raw materials and cheap energy sources. Mass production and mass markets meant cheaper consumer goods. This was an area in which the USA was unique.

The population of 1890 had doubled to 123 million by 1920 and, for the first time, the urban population was larger than the rural one. Now 52 per cent of the population lived in towns where industrial manufacturing produced more national wealth than farming.

City populations increased and as land around cities became cheaper and transport links improved, the beginning of suburbs and homes for more workers were encouraged.

The USA had no war debts to pay. It was a creditor nation lending to others and earning interest on its loans.

There were no major disagreements between the political parties on economic policies.

Effective management techniques and efficient working practices continued to be developed.

Technological developments were encouraged to counteract worker shortages.

Workers' wages rose as production doubled between 1919 and 1929. New industries developed, for example, in light metals and chemical engineering.

Wider use of birth control methods reduced family sizes allowing more income to be spent on consumer goods and entertainment. Continuing improvements in diet and cleanliness resulted in better health and longer life for most of the population.

ACTIVITY

Read the extracts from presidential speeches in Sources 6.6–6.8. Identify the ideas that Presidents Harding, Coolidge and Hoover had about how the USA should be governed.

SOURCE 6.7 Calvin Coolidge (president 1923–28), quoted in H. Evans, *The American Century*, 1998, p.182

The man who builds a factory, builds a temple. And the man who works there worships there.

SOURCE 6.6 Warren Harding (president 1921–23), quoted in H. Evans, *The American Century*, 1998, p.180

America's present need is not heroics, but healing; not nostrums, but normalcy*; not revolution but restoration; not agitation but adjustment; not surgery but serenity; not the dramatic, but the dispassionate; not experiment, but equipoise; not submergence in internationality, but sustainment in triumphant nationality.
*NB it is probable that Harding meant to say normality not normalcy.

SOURCE 6.8 Herbert Hoover speaking in 1928, the year of his election as president, quoted in J. Lorence, *Enduring Voices*, 2000, pp.193–94

Even if government conduct of business could give us more efficiency instead of less efficiency, the fundamental objection to it would remain unaltered and unabated. It would destroy political equality. It would increase rather than decrease abuse and corruption. It would stifle initiative and innovation. It would undermine the development of leadership. It would cramp and cripple the mental and spiritual energies of our people. It would extinguish equality and opportunity. It would dry up the spirit of liberty and progress ... One of the great problems of government is to determine to what extent the government shall regulate and control commerce and industry and how much it shall leave alone. No system is perfect ... It is just as important that business keep out of government as that government keep out of business ... By adherence to the principles of decentralized self-government, ordered liberty, equal opportunity, and freedom of the individual, our American experiment in human welfare has yielded a degree of well-being unparalleled in all the world. It has come nearer to the abolition of poverty, to the abolition of fear of want than humanity has ever reached before.

What were the threats to a better life?

In 1929 two sociologists, Robert S. Lynd and Helen Merrell Lynd published a book on the Indiana town of Muncie. They saw it as an example of typical American urban life, and so called their book *Middletown*. It is still recognised as an important piece of sociological research. Two extracts from this book are given in Source 6.9.

ACTIVITY

Read Source 6.9 and make notes on the following questions:

1 What did people want?
2 What were their worries?
3 What were the possible threats to American affluence?
4 Why, according to Source 6.9, was American society less stable than it appeared?

SOURCE 6.9 R. S. Lynd and H. Merrell Lynd, *Middletown: A Study in American Culture*, 1929

Extract 1
For both working and business class no other accompaniment of getting a living approaches in importance the money received for their work. It is more this future, instrumental aspect of work, rather than the intrinsic satisfactions involved, that keeps Middletown working so hard ... The diffusion of new urgent occasions for spending money in every sector of living is exhibited by such new tools and services commonly used in Middletown today, but either unknown or little used in the nineties ... In the home ... in spending leisure time ... In education ... Under these circumstances, why shouldn't money be important to people in Middletown? ... One leading Middletown businessman summed up this trend ... 'Next to the doctor we think of the banker to help us and to guide us in our wants and worries today'.

Extract 2
In less than four decades, business class and working class, bosses and bossed, have been caught up by Industry, this new trait in the city's culture that is shaping the pattern of the whole of living. According to its needs, large numbers of people anxious to get their living are periodically stopped by the recurrent phenomenon of 'bad times' when the machines stop running, workers are 'laid off' by the hundreds, salesmen sell less, bankers call in loans, 'credit freezes', and many Middletown families may take their children from school, move into cheaper homes, cut down on food, and do without many of the countless things they desire ... The working class is mystified by the whole fateful business. Many of them say, for instance, that they went to the polls and voted for Coolidge in

November 1924, after being assured daily by the local papers that 'A vote for Coolidge is a vote for prosperity and your job'; puzzle as to why 'times' did not improve after the overwhelming victory of Coolidge.

SOURCE 6.10 M. Johnson, *Reading the American Past*, Vol. II, 2nd edn, 2002, p.119

During the 1920s complacency became an article of faith among many comfortable Americans. Things were as they should be, business was good, America was strong and God was in His heaven. Republican presidents explained the logic of contentment that appealed to many voters. Beneath the gaze of the satisfied, however, other Americans felt disorientated and dissatisfied by the economic, political and racial status quo. For them, complacency was a problem, rather than a result of all the problems being solved.

FOCUS ROUTE

As you read Sections B and C identify how and why:

1 Some citizens benefited from government policies and attitudes.
2 Some citizens were ignored or mistreated.

B

Cars, Capone, the Teapot Dome and all that jazz – was this an age of affluence?

What did people aspire to?

Part of the 'American Dream' was to be comfortable, secure and able to keep on improving your life. The ideal home in the 1920s would be recognised by its bathroom. Here you would have an enamel bathtub, toilet and washbasin, unlimited hot water and privacy. Bliss for the aspiring householder seeking the 'American Dream'. And how was it possible? Through mass production, mass marketing and an expectation that things could only get better – so keep on spending.

■ **6B The American Dream**

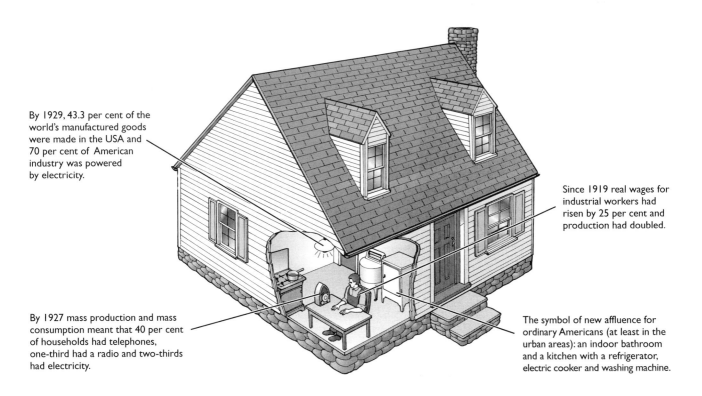

By 1929, 43.3 per cent of the world's manufactured goods were made in the USA and 70 per cent of American industry was powered by electricity.

Since 1919 real wages for industrial workers had risen by 25 per cent and production had doubled.

By 1927 mass production and mass consumption meant that 40 per cent of households had telephones, one-third had a radio and two-thirds had electricity.

The symbol of new affluence for ordinary Americans (at least in the urban areas): an indoor bathroom and a kitchen with a refrigerator, electric cooker and washing machine.

SOURCE 6.11 The assembly line at a Ford plant

By the mid-1920s the Ford assembly lines were producing one car every 24 seconds. There were 25 million new cars on the road, many bought using new credit schemes – buy now, pay later. Their impact was immense: they enabled workers to live in suburbs; farmers to travel further than their local store for supplies; reduced the need for small local churches and schools; and encouraged the idea of distance travel with diners and 'tourist courts' (motels) along main roads. They had an unanticipated environmental effect too, with discarded tyres and wrecks, contaminated streams and exhaust fumes fouling the air. They were to have an impact on future American foreign policy with the demand for cheap oil. And cars were the decade's status symbol – the symbol of affluence, of sex (no chaperones in cars), of speed and of freedom.

SOURCE 6.12 Built, in only fourteen months, of steel, limestone, brick, concrete and glass, at 443.2 metres the Empire State Building was to remain the tallest building in the world for 42 years

How did the organisation of business contribute to affluence?

Large corporations, rather than small family-owned businesses, continued to dominate the economy after the First World War. It was a period of mergers as OLIGOPOLIES came to the fore. There was continuing development in using efficient management techniques. Business schools, such as the one at Harvard, became popular for training professional managers. Money was spent on research. The time and motion ideas used at the Ford plants were a model for others. Trading abroad was encouraged, both for selling goods and in setting up production plants. General Electric had factories in Latin America, China, Japan and Australia. Ford had factories across the British Empire. This meant cheaper production costs and easier access to raw materials, for example, livestock in Argentina and rubber in Malaya.

The largest companies also practised 'welfare capitalism', providing benefits such as pensions and vacations for their workers. However, this was also an attempt to keep unions out of factories. Unions found it difficult to compete with company schemes and union membership fell, as did the number of strikes. However, only the largest firms were able to operate such schemes so the majority of American workers were not affected and nobody, in any kind of company, had job security.

How did people know what to buy?

Visualise a typical twenties' scene; eating your Kellogg's cornflakes for breakfast and enjoying toast from your General Electric toaster, dressed in ready-made clothes, you drive to work in your black Model T Ford, watch Charlie Chaplin or Rudolph Valentino at the local movie house and return to your suburban home to read the *Saturday Evening Post* or the *Readers' Digest* by electric light, or listen to music and commercials on the radio.

What were you doing? Exactly the same thing as thousands of other Americans across the continent, because mass production, transportation and mass advertising encouraged you to spend, but not necessarily to save. How had you paid for these goods and entertainment? Either through the higher wages paid in the 1920s or by relying on credit.

Did you notice that these are all branded goods, not just any cereal or newspaper? The 1920s saw the advent of advertising linked to the new theories of self, initiated by Freud. He argued that the unconscious mind shaped behaviour. Advertisers, like Edward Bernays and Bruce Barton, appealed to social aspirations and personal insecurities to sell more goods. They highlighted socially unacceptable conditions, such as 'ashtray breath' and body odour, then offered the 'right' products as a cure-all. People no longer spent money to acquire necessities. Spending was for pleasure. Advertisers therefore learned how to control public taste and develop consumer spending and they had a willing audience. Americans with a steady income enjoyed being mass consumers.

And all that jazz!

Business profits and increased pay packets were not just spent on domestic appliances and cars. The entertainment industry provided new experiences that changed social attitudes and behaviour in the USA and around the world. This was the era of the flapper, the Hollywood star, the baseball game, the jazz band in Harlem. It was the end of chaperoning unmarried couples and the beginning of the acceptance of birth control. Freedom was no longer just a political idea (as with the abolition of slavery or the principles of the Progressives and social reform), but a chance to make individual choices. Such changes challenged the traditional patterns that had been inherited from small town rural America, but were proving less relevant in urban, industrial life.

Jazz was not only a style of music, but also a symbol of a new way of living. As music it was a mix of ragtime, blues and African rhythms which gave instrumentalists, nearly always black, the opportunity to improvise. It was associated with smoky clubs and speakeasies (saloons selling illegal drink), with spontaneity and a new atmosphere of permissiveness amongst the young.

SOURCE 6.13 Duke Ellington leading his jazz band. Notice the instruments in the orchestra and you may be able to imagine the sort of sounds that would be made. Duke Ellington's most famous tune was *Take the 'A' Train*

ACTIVITY

You can hear the difference in music styles if you listen to recordings of a Sousa march and then Louis Armstrong playing his trumpet. How would you move to each of those? How does the music make you feel?

It was no coincidence that 'jazz' became slang for sexual intercourse. The music played, for example, by Louis Armstrong and Duke Ellington, and sung by Billie Holliday and Bessie Smith, also led to an appreciation of black culture. It seemed to have an honesty and a vitality that was missing from traditional white music. The music was part of the Harlem Renaissance, when that northern area of New York City became the centre for a surge in black artistic creativity.

One of America's most successful novelists of the time, F. Scott Fitzgerald, the author of *The Great Gatsby* and *Tender is the Night*, called the twenties the Jazz Age. Despite the image of the Jazz Age, many white novelists and poets felt a sense of futility at how life seemed to be dominated by business and materialism. Many, like Ernest Hemingway and T. S. Eliot, moved to Europe, especially to Paris, to live a less conservative and a freer lifestyle that was not governed by material consumption and monetary success. Instead life was for pleasure and excess. Yet even Fitzgerald realised the cost, writing in *Echoes of the Jazz Age* in 1931, 'It was borrowed time anyway – the whole upper-tenth of the nation living with the insouciance of grand dukes and the casualness of chorus girls'. So much of it was to end with the Wall Street Crash.

What problems did this affluence create?

1 Prohibition

Many people, led by the Anti-Saloon League, Church groups and Progressive reformers, saw alcoholic drink as a weakening influence on American behaviour and health. Yet at the same time, brewers expanded the number of saloons and, to make them more profitable, permitted gambling. To anti-drink campaigners this only increased the evils of drink. They argued that America needed sober workers, as this would reduce absenteeism and accidents at work, and increase productivity. The Eighteenth Amendment passed in 1919 prohibited the manufacture, sale and transportation of intoxicating liquors. Soft drink manufacturers were delighted! Popular ideas about the virtue of self-help were reinforced by the supposed self-control required for abstaining from drink. The Amendment was expected to reform society for the better, and when combined with an education campaign, eventually eliminate drunkenness from American life.

Did prohibition work?

It certainly reduced the quantity of alcoholic drink sold in the 1920s to about one-third of previous levels, and even after the Amendment was repealed in 1933 consumption of alcohol was slow to rise. But the unpopularity of prohibition with the majority of the urban population meant that it was gradually ignored. Illicit drinks, with names like Jackass Brandy and Yack Yack Bourbon, were made in unreliable strengths, creating an industry earning $2 billion a year for bootleggers (makers and suppliers of illegal liquor). The Congressional Committee reporting in 1931 on the enforcement of prohibition outlined the changes in society since 1918 (see Source 6.14).

SOURCE 6.14 The Congressional Committee on the enforcement of prohibition, 1931

There is a mass of information before us as to a general prevalence of drinking in homes, in clubs, and in hotels; of drinking parties given and attended by persons of high standing and respectability; of drinking by tourists at winter and summer resorts; and of drinking in connection with public dinners and at conventions ... much allowance must be made for the effect of new standards and independence and individual self-assertion, changed ideas as to conduct generally, and the greater emphasis on freedom and the quest for excitement since the War ... It is evident that, taking the country as a whole, people of wealth, business men and professional men and their families, and, perhaps, the higher paid workingmen and their families, are drinking in large numbers in quite frank disregard of the declared policy of the National Prohibition Act ...

2 Crime

One of the other problems was, undoubtedly, crime. A society anxious to do well and show its success included those who were less fussy about how they made their wealth. The Eighteenth Amendment of 1919 prohibiting the manufacture and sale of alcohol was an easy target for illegal wealth creation. The source of illegal liquor was often via criminals. Al Capone ('You can do more with a kind word and a gun, than with a kind word alone.') was the nation's most famous criminal. At 26 he was the leader of the Big One syndicate, and having already openly killed a fellow gangster (though eyewitnesses managed to forget what they had seen) was willing to use violence to enforce his gangland authority. In the 1929 St Valentine's Day massacre his men killed seven of the rival Bugs Moran gang, but no convictions resulted. He was the controller of illegal drink and vice provision in Chicago, reputedly with an income of $60 million a year. Using intimidation, bribery and violence he ensured that not only rival gangsters, but also local politicians and police were kept at a distance. His explanation reflects the double standards of the time:

'Everybody calls me a racketeer. I call myself a businessman. When I sell liquor, it's called bootlegging. When my patrons serve it on a silver tray on Lake Shore Drive, it's called hospitality.'

Capone managed to evade any serious criminal charge; finally being jailed for tax evasion by a federal court in 1931. He died of syphilis in 1947.

3 Corruption

The Teapot Dome scandal

The Teapot Dome scandal was the most famous example of corruption at the highest level of politics. President Warren Harding was a genial, small-town senator ill-suited for the demands of the presidency and content to delegate power to friends and cronies. He is reported to have said, 'I am a man of limited talents. I don't seem to grasp that I am president'. One minister and crony, Albert Fall, the secretary of the interior, took over $300,000 in loans and bribes to allow two oil speculators to get leases on naval oil reserves in Teapot Dome, Wyoming and in California. It took six years for the investigation to find sufficient evidence for conviction. Fall was jailed for a year and fined $100,000. 'Teapot Dome' became the symbol of 1920s corruption in government.

DISCUSS

Do you think that the 'Jazz Age' is an appropriate description for the 1920s based on your study so far? Do you have any alternative titles?

SOURCE 6.15 *Juggernaut*, by Clifford Kennedy Berryman, 1924

The Attorney-General, Harry M. Daugherty, was also investigated for malpractices, but a jury failed to convict him. A pattern emerged of government support for those already successful or wealthy. The government reduced taxes on corporations and wealthy individuals in 1921. The following year tariffs were raised (making imported goods more expensive) by the Fordney-McCumber Tariff Act. Agencies created to monitor business practice, such as the Federal Trade Commission co-operated with businesses rather than regulating them. At the same time the Supreme Court, under Chief Justice William Taft (the former president), protected business from anti-trust legislation and ruled against labour unions in their attempts to organise strikes.

FOCUS ROUTE

Continue your notes from the Focus Route on page 89.

C Xenophobia, fundamentalism and conservatism – was this an age of intolerance?

People might have had higher material expectations, but many still wanted to retain traditional values of thrift, hard work and the importance of home and family. At the same time a more materialistic culture was being encouraged by movies, advertisements and mass circulation magazines. It is not surprising that there were confusing reactions.

Who was American?

1 Immigrants
In May 1920 an Italian shoemaker, Nicola Sacco, and an Italian fish peddler, Bartolomeo Vanzetti, were arrested and charged with robbery and murder in Massachusetts. Armed when arrested, but with little other evidence against them, they were found guilty, called 'those anarchist bastards' by the judge and sentenced to the electric chair. Supporters protested that they were innocent and had been caught up in an atmosphere of intolerance and anti-radical prejudice because of their origins and political views. A new trial was rejected

SOURCE 6.16 A prison guard sits with Bartolomeo Vanzetti (left) and Nicola Sacco, who were convicted of murder

and the two were executed in August 1927. Just before his death Vanzetti said, 'If it had not been for these thing, I might have live out my life among scorning men. I might have die, unmarked, unknown, a failure. Now we are not a failure … Never in our full life can we hope to do such work for tolerance, for justice, for man's understanding of man, as now we do by accident.'

Fifty years later the governor of Massachusetts accepted that they had not had a fair trial, and exonerated them.

The fate of the two men symbolised the antipathy felt towards foreigners after the First World War. Immigrants were the most obvious recipients of this. By 1924 Congress had brought in strict quotas for the numbers and the origin of acceptable immigrants. As Senator Parish of Texas said in Congress in 1921:

'Our country is a self-sustaining country. It has taught the principles of real democracy to all the nations of the earth; its flag has been the synonym of progress, prosperity, and the preservation of the rights of the individual, and there can be nothing so dangerous as for us to allow the undesirable foreign element to poison our civilization and thereby threaten the safety of the institutions that our forebears have established for us … Now is the time to … keep from our shores forever those who are not in sympathy with the American ideals'.

Since 1880 the USA had absorbed 23 million immigrants, although some returned to their native countries after making money or being unable to settle. Many were Roman Catholics or Jews from southern and eastern Europe. They brought new languages, cultures and standards to the USA, but for many white Protestant Americans, descended from the earliest settlers, this mass of newcomers were seen as 'indigestible lumps in the national stomach'. A belief in 'nativism' developed, valuing only those born in the USA. The uncertainties of the post-war world and the fears of radicalism derived from the Russian revolution of 1917 led to attempts to stop further immigration. Literacy tests were already used as a screening device and further legislation followed:

1921 – Number of immigrants limited to three per cent of each national group as counted in the Census of 1910.

1924 – National Origins Act reduced immigration to two per cent of each nationality as in the Census of 1890, when numbers from southern and eastern Europe were low.

1927 – A maximum of 150,000 immigrants per year were permitted, and none were permitted from Japan or China. This soured relations with Asia and roused anti-American feelings in Japan.

There were fewer restrictions on Puerto Ricans and Mexicans, until unemployment, especially after 1930, made them unwelcome and forced many to return home. The quotas were to have repercussions for Jews trying to escape from Nazi persecution in the late 1930s. The legislation did, however, dramatically reduce the number of immigrants, and it was not until 1965 that a non-discriminatory immigration law was passed.

2 Black migrants

Another form of internal immigration had been the great migration of black Southerners to the North, especially to industrial centres like Chicago and Detroit. The boll weevil infestation of 1914 and frequent flooding had made cotton farming less profitable. At the same time agents from the large industries, family members who had already moved north, and cheap railroad fares gave incentives to move. In 1910 the black population in Chicago was 44,000. By 1930 it was 234,000. Migrants hoped to improve their lives with more and better paid work and to join family and friends. Was it worth it? Certainly there was more work and higher wages, churches provided a community focus, as did music groups, and organisations were created to support new arrivals. Communities set up businesses for themselves – newspapers, funeral directors, saving and loan companies and drugstores. But there was no end to deliberate or insidious segregation, with separate housing, violence between black and white workers and discrimination on the grounds of skin colour.

The 1920s did see the beginning of the movement to raise pride in African heritage. Marcus Garvey, born in Jamaica, created the Universal Negro Improvement Association (UNIA). He argued for separatism from white culture and lives, and for black Americans to abandon the USA for a new life in Africa:

'I saw before me a new world of black men, not peons, serfs, dogs and slaves, but a nation of sturdy men making their impression upon civilization and causing a new light to dawn upon the human race … We believe in the purity of both races … It is a vicious and dangerous doctrine of social equality to urge,

SOURCE 6.17 A black family moving north with all their possessions

BIRTH OF A NATION AND THE KKK

The film *Birth of a Nation* directed by D.W. Griffith was the first film of the modern movie industry. It was full of stereotypes – the faithful 'darkie' (black slave), threatening mulattos (people of mixed parentage), good white Southerners and greedy YANKEES coming to take the riches of the South. It was also hugely popular, and insidiously racist.

Arguing for the importance of white supremacy and patriotism, the white-cloaked and hooded members of the KKK, using a flaming cross as their symbol, and singing songs like *Onward Christian Soldiers*, claimed to be protecting the true America; the peoples of the Nordic race. The Imperial Wizard Hiram W. Evans spoke of confusion in thought and opinion, which had led to moral breakdown and economic distress; topics familiar to many ordinary Americans in both rural and urban areas. Un-Americans were those who were unbelievers, bootleggers, those guilty of marital infidelity, criminals and the corrupt. The KKK focused on harassing immigrants, blacks, Jews and Roman Catholics for being un-American, using the same methods as in the past: intimidation, arson, and physical violence including lynching. Unlike the 1870s they also gained some political power as their membership rose to 4 million. However, the restrictions on immigration weakened their appeal and the organisation collapsed in 1927 amid accusations of corruption and internal rivalry. But the atmosphere of bigotry and hatred was less easy to disperse, and the government took no role in easing such social tensions.

as certain colored leaders do, that black and white should get on together, for that would destroy the racial purity of both. We believe that black people should have a country of their own where they should be given the fullest possible opportunity to develop politically, socially and industrially.' (in M. Johnson, *Reading the American Past*, 2nd edn, 2002, pp.130–34)

Although he had some success setting up black business he was deported to the West Indies after being convicted of mail fraud. However, the Depression ended any hopes of black workers improving their status. Survival had to matter more than political rights. His ideas about black pride influenced the founders of the Nation of Islam or Black Muslims and were revived in the 1960s with the Black Power organisation.

3 The revival of the Ku Klux Klan

SOURCE 6.18 A Klan initiation ceremony. The attitude to non-white, non-Protestant, non-Americans was best shown by the revival of the Ku Klux Klan. Having been an anti-Reconstruction group in the 1860s and 1870s, its beliefs were reactivated by the film *Birth of a Nation* in 1915

TALKING POINT

In Chapter 1 you considered the role that government could and should play in integrating former slaves into society as equal citizens. The revival of the KKK suggests that too little had been done for black citizens and for other minority groups. What do you think the government should have been doing to mitigate the influence of the KKK? Unhappily no government took on these bullies until the 1960s.

Why was religious fundamentalism popular?

Darwin's theory of evolution stated that humans and primates shared a common ancestor, but teaching this theory was banned in Tennessee and other states because it contradicted the story of the Creation in the Bible. Fundamentalists believed in the literal truth of the Bible. A challenge to the ban was made in 1925 in the Scopes trial, nicknamed the 'monkey trial'. A high school biology teacher, John T. Scopes, challenged the Tennessee law, which banned the teaching of evolution in schools. The case, taking place in a sweltering courtroom, attracted national attention, and was notable for the clash between the two lawyers: Clarence Darrow and William Jennings Bryan, the politician, three-time presidential candidate and fundamentalist. Bryan insisted that Eve came from Adam's rib and that God had created the world in six days, but was not prepared to say that the days were 24 hours long. Darrow tried to present scientific evidence that disproved such beliefs. It took the jury eight minutes to return a verdict that Scopes was guilty of violating a state law and that the state law was constitutionally sound. Scopes was subsequently fined. The press mocked the illogicality of Bryan's faith, but the law remained for 30 years.

In an age where some Protestants were seeking to retain and enhance traditional values they would not tolerate arguments that challenged the literal interpretation of the Bible. Fundamental Protestants rejected such ideas and created their own churches, encouraging revival meetings and open-air preaching. Their concerns were linked to the apparent declining standards of morality, because of mass entertainment and advertising, and the greater secularisation of society.

Why did unions struggle?

SOURCE 6.19 Reinhold Niebuhr writes in his diary about life in the auto factories of Detroit, the home of the Ford Motor Company (in M. Johnson, *Reading the American Past*, Vol. II, 2nd edn, 2002, pp.123–26)

1925 – So artificial is life that these factories are like a strange world to me ... The foundry interested me particularly. The heat was terrific. The men seemed weary. Here manual labor is a drudgery and toil is slavery. The men cannot possibly find any satisfaction in their work. They simply work to make a living. Their sweat and their dull pain are part of the price paid for the fine cars we all run.

And why did he think that conditions were so bad?

A city which is built around a productive process and which gives only casual thought and incidental attention to its human problems is really a kind of hell ... Modern industry, particularly American industry, is not Christian. The economic forces which move it are hardly qualified at a single point by really ethical considerations.

He was particularly critical of Henry Ford, who caused unemployment to thousands by closing his auto works for six months when he changed production from the Model T to the new Model A.

Naive gentlemen with a genius for mechanics suddenly become the arbiters over the lives and fortunes of hundreds of thousands. Their moral pretensions are credulously accepted at full value. No one bothers to ask whether an industry which can maintain a cash reserve of a quarter of a billion ought not to make some provision for its unemployed ...

Wages had risen 21 per cent between 1923 and 1929. Surely workers would be happy? Credit, particularly for buying cars, was popular, even if it meant 'a dollar down and a dollar forever'. So popular was credit that lending to purchasers was the tenth largest business by 1929. Radios, costing around $75, were among the other popular desirables. Were unions needed when there were such signs of prosperity?

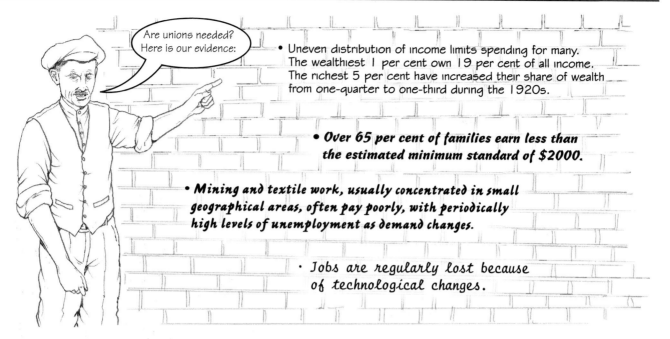

Are unions needed?
Here is our evidence:

• Uneven distribution of income limits spending for many. The wealthiest 1 per cent own 19 per cent of all income. The richest 5 per cent have increased their share of wealth from one-quarter to one-third during the 1920s.

• *Over 65 per cent of families earn less than the estimated minimum standard of $2000.*

• *Mining and textile work, usually concentrated in small geographical areas, often pay poorly, with periodically high levels of unemployment as demand changes.*

· *Jobs are regularly lost because of technological changes.*

Yet unions struggled to recruit and keep their members. Employers insisted on open shops (i.e. with union membership a choice not a condition of employment), and this became known as the 'American Plan' of employment. The large industries that offered 'welfare capitalism' with profit-sharing, pensions, bonus and health programmes undermined the necessity for unions. Yet there were also so-called 'yellow dog' contracts which forbade union membership, and intimidation and violence were used to discourage union involvement. In 1923 the senior and long-serving AFL union leader Samuel Gompers died, and his successor was more restrained in his opposition to industrial practices. The confrontations led by the radical Wobblies, or Industrial Workers of the World, were regarded as typical of all potential union behaviour and too much like that of revolutionaries. So using the courts in 1922 and 1923, the government banned strikes by railroad workers and miners because they were organised by unions. Unions were not able to stop the changes in demand that reduced workforces or threatened job security. What could unions offer in such circumstances? Not enough, was the opinion of many workers, and membership declined from 5 million in 1920, to 3.5 million in 1929.

ACTIVITY

Can you solve the problem?

1 What is the problem outlined here? You may need to read this several times – it needs thinking through carefully!
'Mass production made mass consumption a necessity. Workers' incomes were rising, but not at a rate that kept pace with the nation's growing industrial output. Without broadly distributive purchasing power, the engines of mass production would have no outlet and would eventually fall idle.' (in D. Kennedy, *Freedom from Fear*, 1999, p.21)

2 There were five possible solutions:
   a) Raise wages
   b) Cut back on production
   c) Sell more abroad
   d) Get more people into employment
   e) Lower the price of goods.
   List the advantages and disadvantages of each of these solutions.

3 What impacts would be difficult to predict?

4 Which solution would you choose if you were the secretary of the Treasury?

5 Which would you choose if you were a factory worker?

FOCUS ROUTE

1 What have you read already that makes you think that the economy might have problems (e.g. difference in incomes, using credit)?
2 What was the immediate impact of the Wall Street Crash in 1929? Who was most affected at this stage?
3 What was the impact by 1931? Who was affected by then?

D Why did the Wall Street Crash become the Depression?

'We have more cars, more bathtubs, oil furnaces, silk stockings, bank accounts than any other people on Earth ... I have no fears for the future of our country. It is bright with hope.' (Hoover's Inaugural Address in March 1929.)

How did the USA get from that to this?

SOURCE 6.20 If you lost your job, as many did as the effects of the Wall Street Crash spread, you could end up homeless. Many homeless unemployed lived in shanty towns like this one, nicknamed 'Hoovervilles' after President Hoover who seemed unable to solve the economic problems

■ 6D Underlying problems in the economy

1 The demand for new houses slowed down and a decline in construction began. This meant less need for building materials and construction workers.

2 The enthusiastic purchase of cars and consumer goods slowed down. Companies had large stocks to sell and so, not needing more goods, laid off workers. Unemployed workers were not consumers.

3 Farmers had prospered during the First World War, but soon lost their expanded markets abroad. Farm incomes totalled $22 billion in 1919, but by 1928 had fallen to $8 billion. As demand, and therefore prices, fell so did farmers' incomes and they found it difficult to repay loans on land or to buy new equipment.

4 The unequal distribution of wealth had made the wealthy even richer, but much of their expenditure was on their lifestyles or on stock market speculation, not on manufactured goods. The rich could not make up for the lack of purchases by the newly unemployed.

5 Businesses had kept prices high and increased their profits, but not paid higher wages. There was too little spare money around to buy goods and revive the economy.

6 High tariffs made exporting to the USA less worthwhile for foreign companies, so they bought fewer American goods in return, adding to the decline in consumer sales.

7 The payment of reparations by Germany to the Allies relied on loans from the USA to restart their industry and provide income. The Crash and subsequent Depression reduced these loans, so Germany could not pay its reparations, and the Allies were therefore unable to use these reparation payments to repay their war debts to the American banks.

HOW TO SPECULATE TO ACCUMULATE

The gamble involved in buying shares is that you speculate (i.e. make a bet) on whether a particular stock will rise or fall. If it rises in value on the stock market you can sell your shares and receive more money than you had paid to buy the shares (accumulate). If the shares fall in value, and you want to sell the shares, you would receive less money than you had paid for them originally. The 'trick' is to buy shares when they are cheap and sell when they are worth more, so that you can make a profit.

When the economy is booming you can be sure of never losing any money, as shares will just continue to increase in value as companies make higher profits. Or can you be sure? A popular way to buy shares in the USA at the time was to buy 'on the margin', in effect buying on credit. This meant that you only paid a part of the cost of the share (perhaps as little as 25 per cent) and you could be required at a later date to pay the balance. However, you hoped that as stocks rose in value, that rise would pay your outstanding balance. Buying 'on the margin' allowed you to spread your risks by buying shares from more than one company, providing all the stocks did not lose value at the same time. If they did, you might have to repay the balance on all of them without having first made a profit.

TALKING POINTS

1 How do people behave in a panic? What were the options if you had lost all your savings?

2 As you read on in this chapter and the next, note how people were able to control their situation, and what happened when they were not.

ACTIVITY

Which of the points in Chart 6D would reduce:
a) sales of US goods
b) the number of workers employed by manufacturers?

What was the Wall Street Crash?

Industry is valued by its 'stock' – its total worth. The stock is divided into shares, which can be bought and sold on the stock market. Shareholders are entitled to a share of the profits of the company. Share values rise and fall according to the profits of the company in which they are invested. During the 1920s buying shares became popular. It was a form of gambling. But it seemed a safe way to gamble as the economy was doing well, the nation seemed prosperous and trade was booming.

There were warning signs of economic problems if people chose to note them. Unfortunately, no one in the 1920s had them in a neat chart like Chart 6D!

The Crash that could never happen

More Americans had started to dabble in buying shares, with about ten per cent of all households involved by the end of the decade. In 1928 and 1929 stock prices rose rapidly making shares more valuable. There was some concern about the level of speculation, but it was also seen as a symbol of American prosperity. However, from September 1929 there was an increase in the number of shares being sold. The value of stocks was reduced, so more investors wanted to sell before the value of their shares became too low.

On Black Thursday, 24 October, panic began and 12,894,650 shares were traded (the highest total previously recorded was less than 4 million).

The panic continued on 25 October and 28 October.

On Tuesday 29, Black Tuesday, the market in the sale of shares collapsed. A total of 16,410,030 shares were traded.

What did this mean to you if you were an investor (or were you now a loser)?

If you had bought 'on the margin' you tried to sell your shares in order to raise money to pay your 'on the margin' balance. But by Black Tuesday everyone was trying to do the same thing at the same time. Over four days the value of your shares dropped too rapidly for you to make profits, or even to have the cash from selling them to use to pay back your balance.

So how could you pay your 'on the margin' balance, which you still had to pay even though your stock was worthless now? You had to pay your debt from whatever money you had saved or whatever you had to sell – your business, your land, your house, your car, your tools. You were not the only one losing money. It was reputed that the Rockefeller family lost four-fifths of its fortune, that Winston Churchill lost $500,000 and the banker J. P. Morgan Junior as much as $60 million.

If you were using your savings to pay your debts you went to your bank. The banks in turn wanted borrowers to pay back their loans in order to be able to give cash to depositors. If the borrower (such as a manufacturing company who had borrowed to buy new machinery, or an investor who had borrowed to invest in shares) could not pay, the bank had no money, was forced to close and the depositor lost their savings. Businesses and manufacturers who had borrowed for expansion were now in debt. If they could not sell goods or services, they could not repay their debts or pay wages. A vicious downward spiral had begun.

ACTIVITY

Draw a diagram, in the form of a downward spiral, to show how the Crash of October 1929 led to the Depression. Include events and the government's attempts to stop the economic crisis.

SOURCE 6.21 Investors waiting to withdraw their savings from their local bank. As banks began to fail, lacking the cash to pay their depositors, you probably wished that you had kept your money under the proverbial mattress, instead of entrusting it to the bank vault. Unfortunately savings were not in the vault as they had been lent to investors and manufacturers

How did the government respond to the Crash?

Andrew Mellon, the wealthy Secretary to the Treasury, saw the Crash as a valuable blip in the economic system. If companies were forced to close, then the money invested in them was 'liquidated' and could be used to invest in new, more profitable and more worthwhile industries and ventures. This liquidation would, according to Mellon, 'purge the rottenness out of the system. High costs of living and high living will come down. People will work harder, have a moral life. Values will be adjusted, and enterprising people will pick up the wrecks from the less competent people'. So Mellon's advice to President Hoover was to do nothing – the system would sort itself out, as it had always done. Hoover, who had seen the effectiveness of voluntary action during the First World War, believed that that alone would be sufficient to help the unemployed. He did take some action, but they were the wrong things too quickly and the right things too late and too incompletely.

ACTIVITY

1 Use Chart 6E, on page 103, to answer the following questions. How did the Crash and subsequent Depression change:
   a) industry
   b) farming
   c) ordinary lives?
2 Why were these changes so frightening to so many people?

■ 6E The reality of the Depression

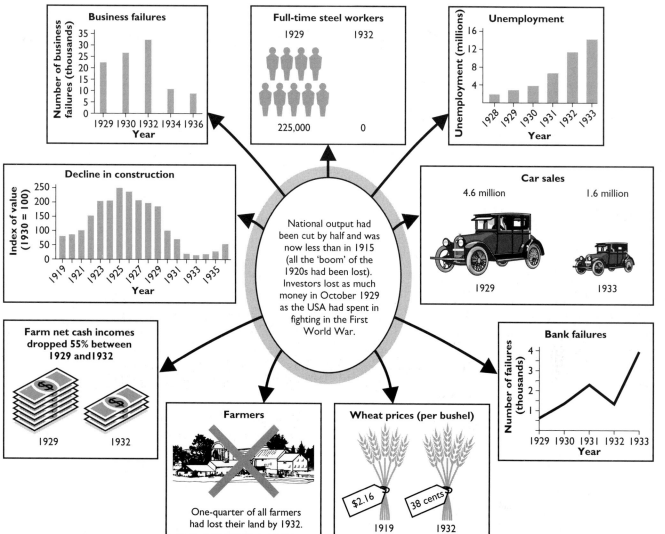

Business failures
Number of business failures (thousands) / Year: 1929 1930 1932 1934 1936

Full-time steel workers
1929   1932
225,000   0

Unemployment
Unemployment (millions) / Year: 1928 1929 1930 1931 1932 1933

Decline in construction
Index of value (1930 = 100) / Year: 1919 1921 1923 1925 1927 1929 1931 1933 1935

National output had been cut by half and was now less than in 1915 (all the 'boom' of the 1920s had been lost). Investors lost as much money in October 1929 as the USA had spent in fighting in the First World War.

Car sales
4.6 million   1.6 million
1929   1933

Farm net cash incomes dropped 55% between 1929 and 1932
1929   1932

Farmers
One-quarter of all farmers had lost their land by 1932.

Wheat prices (per bushel)
$2.16   38 cents
1919   1932

Bank failures
Number of failures (thousands) / Year: 1929 1930 1931 1932 1933

ACTIVITY

Explain why each item in Chart 6F either helped or hindered recovery from the Crash.

■ 6F The government responses to the Crash

THE RIGHT THINGS

1   The Reconstruction Finance Corporation was set up in 1932 to loan money to private corporations via:
    a) Glass–Seagall Act to offer a wider range of community loans
    b) Federal Home Loan Bank Act to encourage banks to offer cheaper home mortgages.
2   1932 Emergency Relief and Construction Act – gave relief money to states for federal and local public works.

President Hoover

THE WRONG THINGS

1   Interest rates were raised in 1931. This made borrowing more expensive and so reduced the amount of money available for spending, just when more spending was needed.
2   The Hawley–Smoot Act of 1930 raised import duties by one-third despite letters of protest from a thousand economists. If foreign countries could not sell profitably in the USA they could not earn enough dollars to repay war debts to American bankers.
3   Hoover was anxious to keep a balanced federal budget (as much coming in as being spent). By 1931 he wanted to decrease federal spending, and though he permitted some increase in public work projects he rejected relief bills proposed by Congress. How could people cope without some government relief? At the same time the Revenue Act of 1932 increased corporate and income taxes. How could industry expand and take on more workers when they had to pay more taxes? How could people spend when more of their earnings were being used to pay taxes?

E Who was to blame?

■ 6G Who was to blame?

The workers

Many businessmen argued that workers were the main cause of the Depression. They were accused of being reckless with their earnings, too willing to gamble on the stock market for easy profits and too spendthrift in their willingness to buy on credit.

The unions

The failure of unions to increase their membership had weakened their collective bargaining power. Little had been done to raise wages, especially for the poorest workers, or to raise awareness about inequalities.

Businessmen

In 1932 a Senate investigation into Wall Street, encouraged by the president, found evidence of bond price rigging and excessive bonus payments. In the early 1930s stories of teachers working without pay, and even fainting in schools for lack of food, contrasted sharply with those of executives being paid large salaries and bonuses and then avoiding paying income tax. The Crash ended the idea that financiers had the secret of how to create and maintain national prosperity.

Capitalists

Why were shoe factories closed down when people needed shoes? Why were crops allowed to rot and animals slaughtered and their carcasses discarded when people were hungry? How could there be breadlines when there were grain silos full of wheat? How was it 'democratic' to have people suffering so much? People were asking if the government valued individual human dignity. Some economists did put forward novel solutions. John Maynard Keynes (see biography box) argued that as more money was needed for people to spend, the government should lower taxes and provide employment through public works.

> **John Maynard Keynes (1883–1946)**
> An English economist who had been critical of the financial aspects of the Versailles Treaty, Keynes argued for a DEFICIT BUDGET. This meant that a government would be spending more than it was receiving in taxes. It was how governments had to behave in wartime, but post-war governments had all striven to have balanced budgets. Keynes thought that in a financial crisis like this one you had to take risks; you must 'get across the crevasse before it is dark'.

Europe

If European nations had paid their war debts to American banks then the banks would be more secure. If Europeans could have sorted out their own problems in 1914 there would have been no need for the USA to enter the First World War.

President Hoover

Hoover had much experience as an effective administrator of relief programmes during and after the First World War. What he was much less effective at was initiating such programmes, and responding in a flexible and compassionate way to individuals. He did accept that government had a responsibility in an economic crisis, but he gave support to the financial structure rather than to individuals. He feared that federal relief would weaken the essence of the American character – its self-sufficiency and individualism – and people would no longer rely on themselves and their community to succeed. Therefore his emphasis was on voluntary help for those in need, and the funding of institutions to help the needy. It was insufficient. By the time of his defeat in the 1932 election, Hoover was one of the most unpopular of presidents. His name was used mockingly – a 'Hoover blanket' was newspaper used by the homeless to keep warm; 'Hoovervilles' (see Source 6.20) were shanty towns made of old packing cases, scrap metal and wrecked cars, created in urban open spaces by the homeless; and a 'Hoover flag' was an empty pocket turned inside out. Recent historians have been less critical of Hoover than his contemporaries. Here is one historian's sympathetic assessment of Hoover's last year, 'He kept up a punishing regimen of rising at six and working without interruption until nearly midnight. His clothes were dishevelled, his hair rumpled, eyes bloodshot, complexion ashen … Never temperamentally suited to the pelting and abuse of the political arena, a man naturally diffident and inordinately self-protective, Hoover was painfully bruised by blows from both the left and the right. As early as 1919 he had conceded that "I do not … have the mental attitude or the politician's manner … and above all I am too sensitive to political mud."' (in D. Kennedy, *Freedom from Fear*, 1999, p.94)

> **DISCUSS**
>
> In the election of 1932, against Franklin D. Roosevelt, Hoover won only six states, all in the north-east corner of the USA. Does this seem a fair verdict on Hoover's administration? It could be argued that there was such a unique set of circumstances in 1929–32 that all those with the responsibility to resolve the Depression were at a loss as to how to resolve it.

BONUS EXPEDITIONARY FORCE

Whether from character, inappropriate experience, or lack of insight, Hoover was unable to offer the practical and confidence-building measures that were so desperately needed. His reaction to the Bonus Expeditionary Force protest was typical of his lack of political flair. Veterans of the First World War were hoping that Congress would vote to pay bonuses for their war service, to help them through the Depression, although they were not due to be paid until 1945. Fifteen thousand mainly unemployed men calling themselves the Bonus Expeditionary Force (BEF) arrived in the capital to lobby Congress. They camped and marched around the Congress building until Hoover and the Senate rejected the bill, whereupon most of them, bitterly disappointed, returned home. However, a few thousand stayed on in a shanty town. Hoover refused to meet them and, more seriously, allowed a confrontation to develop by demanding that the protesters depart. Army forces, including tanks, led by General MacArthur and Major Eisenhower, were brought in. The BEF retaliated with stones, and the police with firing and tear gas. The army cleared the site. MacArthur claimed that the BEF were revolutionaries whilst the government said they were communists, but no evidence was found. Rather they seemed to reflect the despair and hopelessness of ordinary people that was gripping the nation.

SOURCE 6.22 Veterans of the First World War camp outside the Capitol waiting for the Congress vote on their bonuses, June 1932

F Review: the twenties – Jazz Age or Depression Blues?

The events of the 1920s had challenged American ideas about freedom, especially freedom of the individual. Dissent was seen as dangerous and to be curtailed, hence the popularity of the KKK and Red Scare attacks (see page 73) on radicals. Yet this was also an era of accepted social change. The relaxation in traditional expectations of women's behaviour, the availability of contraception, the decline in family size and the greater acceptability of divorce were now familiar in urban areas. The range and availability of consumer goods altered people's images of a comfortable life. Jazz and new literature portrayed a more experimental and casual age. New influences, from areas like Harlem, and dramatic urban buildings like skyscrapers, suggested a dynamic and progressive decade. So there was a conflict between 'Americanisation' with its desire for a more homogenous national culture and the excitement and diversity portrayed through music, the automobiles and the open road. In the next decade there were three factors with the potential to limit individual freedom:

1 The *laissez-faire* attitude of the Republican governments to business had allowed practices and structures to flourish that were not beneficial to the nation.
2 The worldwide impact of the Crash meant that in the future Americans were to be affected by, and would affect, other nations' problems.
3 The scale of unemployment and suffering experienced after the Crash was reducing people's choices about how to live their lives.

■ **Learning trouble spot**

The complete picture

As you complete this activity, you will probably have doubts about what to include and what to ignore, and about what is most appropriate for each category. Such doubts are essential. Events in the past did not happen in order to fit into neat textbook exercises. As a historian you are trying to find useful links to explain events. There will always be events that will not fit the pattern you are trying to establish. You should not ignore them. They may, for example, help to explain another 'story' that was happening. Most importantly they help you realise the immense complexity of trying to explain human behaviour and interaction.

ACTIVITY

1 Sum up the nature of the period 1920–32 by completing your own copy of this table with evidence of either continuities or changes.

Topic	Normalcy/Continuities	Novelty/Changes
Family		
Employment		
Industry		
Farming		

2 Was this the Jazz Age or the decade of the Depression Blues – or would you give the period 1920–32 another name, e.g. an age of anxiety, of affluence, of normalcy, of assurance, of intolerance?

3 You are presenting an overview of the 1920s for a programme on 31 December 1929. You are basing the programme around ten key images, with explanatory text.
   a) What ten images would you choose to be the framework of your programme?
   b) What is the justification for your choices?
   c) What would be the title of your programme?
   d) Discuss your choices in groups.

KEY POINTS FROM CHAPTER 6

The twenties – Jazz Age or Depression Blues?

1 The vitality of the 1920s was reflected in changing lifestyles for the young and for women, and in an appreciation of black culture.

2 There was nostalgia in the 1920s for an imagined and better past, at the same time as an excitement about the present.

3 The irrationality of the 1920s was reflected in the attitudes to science by fundamentalists, and by the reaction to immigrants and other minority groups.

4 The productivity boom, particularly in consumer goods, masked the insecure employment status of many workers, which led them to be cautious about spending by the end of the decade.

5 The problems of agriculture after the First World War were deeply entrenched and threatened to make life even harder for farmers.

6 The weakening of the power of unions diminished their ability to demand stable employment and improve wages and conditions.

7 The presidencies of Harding, Coolidge and Hoover were business and *laissez-faire* oriented, without being rigorous in protecting all aspects of the national economy.

8 The Wall Street Crash and its effects were unprecedented in American history.

9 The Depression that followed seemed uncontrollable, and threatened the stability of ordinary lives.

10 Whoever won the presidential election in 1932 would have to solve a multitude of problems, with no obvious available solutions.

7

America in the 1930s – did the New Deal end the Depression?

CHAPTER OVERVIEW

ACTIVITY

Sources 7.1–7.5 outline the story of the New Deal.

1 Briefly note down what you see or read in each one.
2 What do these sources tell you about:
   a) why the New Deal was needed
   b) what actions were taken
   c) how successful it was?
3 What else do you need to know to understand the story of the New Deal?
4 At the end of this chapter you will be asked to return to this Activity.

SOURCE 7.1 Written by a British Labour Party activist, Mary Agnes Hamilton, who was visiting the USA in 1931–32 for a cross-country lecture tour (in M.A. Hamilton, *In America Today*)

Nowhere, in New York or any other city, can one escape from the visible presence of those who with perhaps unconscious cruelty are called 'the idle'. At every street corner, and wherever taxi or car has to pause, men try to sell one apples, oranges, or picture papers ... On a fine day men will press on one gardenias at fifteen cents apiece; on any day, rows of them will line every relatively open space, eager to shine one's shoes.

SOURCE 7.2 Dorothea Lange's photo of 'milling about people' – a family on a dusty road in the Midwest in 1938

SOURCE 7.3 *Construction of a Dam*, a mural by William Gropper, 1937: a project and illustration funded by the PWA

SOURCE 7.4 Extract from a letter written by journalist Lorena Hickok, 6 June 1934 from Florence, Alabama

Out of nearly 70,000 families on relief in Tennessee, probably 30,000 or more live in small towns or in the country … Table land. Thin soil. Terrible housing. Illiteracy. Evidence of prolonged under-nourishment. No knowledge of how to live decently or farm profitably if they had decent land … with standards of living so low that, once on relief, they are quite willing to stay there for the rest of their lives. It's a mess.

SOURCE 7.5 Poster explaining social security benefit, from the Social Security Board, 1935

DISCUSS

What criteria would you use to gauge the success or failure of the New Deal? Would success mean the total removal of economic problems?

By 1932 Americans were puzzled and fearful at the way their nation was changing. A decade of possibilities was being replaced with one that appeared to be an economic catastrophe. Ordinary people were losing their homes, their jobs and their security. These were despairing times. The election of a new president, Franklin Delano Roosevelt, was to be the starting point for a radical change in American economy and society. His programmes, known as the New Deal, would regulate the financial structure, introduce social welfare benefits, and provide support for workers in an unprecedented way. They involved the mass of the population in the recovery from the Depression and created a unity of interest and purpose, which was to be used again in the demands of the Second World War after 1941. The long- and short-term impact and its successes and failures have been much debated.

This chapter will look at the problems facing the new president and outline the different programmes of the New Deal, from 1933–34 and 1935–37. You will be able to make judgements on the New Deal and on the importance of President Franklin D. Roosevelt as its initiator and persuader.

A A depressed nation, 1932–33 (pp. 110–13)

B The first New Deal – did it provide relief and start recovery? (pp. 114–21)

C The second New Deal – did it complete recovery and start reform? (pp. 121–26)

D New Deal or Raw Deal? (pp. 126–31)

E What were Roosevelt's strengths and weaknesses in pursuing the New Deal? (pp. 131–32)

F Review: Did the New Deal end the Depression? (pp. 132–35)

ACTIVITY

You are a young person soon to leave college in 1933. You have been asked to write an article of 300 words about your and your friends' concerns in the winter of 1932–33. Use Sources 7.6–7.14 as evidence of what was happening in America and how it was affecting ordinary people.

A A depressed nation, 1932–33

A depressed nation can suffer the same symptoms as a depressed person – panic, hopelessness about the future, constant apprehension and an inability to actively change the situation. The Crash had first surprised and then ruined many lives, and there was no leader who was able to provide effective solutions. By 1932 hope and optimism were gone and the winter of 1932–33 was one of quiet desperation for many, and militant anger for some. The political hiatus between November's election and the March inauguration had probably never seemed so long to the American people. Hoover was still president but both he and Congress were short of ideas and energy. They had little political power to change the worsening situation. Roosevelt was not yet formally president. He was unwilling to be infected with Hoover's unpopularity by working alongside him in the interregnum. It was a winter of stagnation and increasing misery for:

* the unemployed
* the homeless and those threatened with eviction
* banks struggling to keep reserves as depositors panicked and withdrew their savings
* manufacturers who could not see where their new markets would come from
* farmers struggling with diminished incomes because of the low prices paid for their produce.

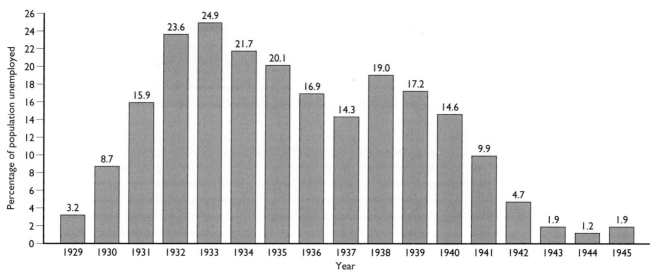

SOURCE 7.6 Unemployment, 1929–45

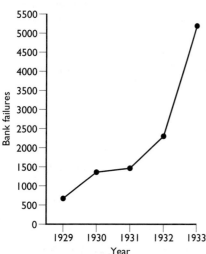

SOURCE 7.7 US bank failures, 1929–33

SOURCE 7.8 The Parks family (husband, wife and three children) of Iowa were interviewed about how they coped during the Depression (in R. Maidment and M. Dawson, *The USA in the Twentieth Century*, 2nd edn, 1999, pp.102–04). Claud Park suffered ill-health after working in the paint section of a foundry and could only get irregular work. This meant that his weekly wage varied from $5 to $25 a week. The family had already borrowed from relatives, and had to give up an insurance policy

By December 1932 the situation had become desperate. The temperature was below zero, and there was little fuel or food left. As the Parks owed a coal bill of $40 and a grocery bill of $25, they expected credit to be discontinued at any time … they could see no alternative except to apply for relief; yet they both felt that they would be 'disgraced', [but] Claud got 'scared about the kids' and thought 'we can't let the kids starve just because we are proud'. The next morning … he went to the courthouse to make application for relief. When he arrived at the courthouse he couldn't go in. 'I must have walked around the block over a dozen times …'. Finally he got up sufficient courage to make his application.

SOURCE 7.9 An unemployed miner and his family in West Virginia show the hopelessness and poverty of the Depression

SOURCE 7.10 The American historian, William E. Leuchtenburg describes the 'Winter of Despair' (in *Franklin D. Roosevelt and the New Deal*, 1963, p.25)

In February 1933 ... In the Blue Ridge, miners smashed company store windows and storekeepers were given the choice of handing out food or having it seized. Unemployed workers in Detroit invaded self-service groceries in groups, filled their baskets, and left without paying. In Iowa leagues of the unemployed enlisted jobless gas and light workers to tap gas and electricity lines. In Des Moines, workers boarded streetcars in groups of ten or twenty and told the cowed conductors to 'charge the fares to the mayor'. In Chicago, a group of fifty-five was charged with dismantling an entire four-storey building and carrying it away brick by brick.

SOURCE 7.11 Emil Loriks was a state senator in South Dakota from 1927 to 1934. Here he describes the reaction of farmers to farm sales when neighbours were forced to sell their farms because of the drop in agricultural prices (quoted in S. Terkel, *Hard Times*, 1970, p.227)

Oh, the militancy then! At Milbank, during a farm sale, they had a sheriff and sixteen deputies. One of them got a little trigger-happy. It was a mistake. The boys disarmed him so fast, he didn't know what happened. They just yanked the belts off 'em, didn't even unbuckle 'em. They took their guns away from 'em. After that we didn't have much trouble stopping sales ... Deputies would come along with whole fleets of trucks and guns [to enforce farm sales]. One lone farmer had planks across the road. They ordered him to remove them. They came out with guns. He said, 'Go ahead and shoot, but there isn't one of you S.O.B.s getting out of here alive.' There were about fifteen hundred farmers there in the woods. The trucks didn't get through. It was close in spirit to the American revolution.

SOURCE 7.12 Written by British Labour Party activist Mary Agnes Hamilton who was visiting the USA in 1931–32 for a cross-country lecture tour (in M. A. Hamilton, *In America Today*)

The American people, unfamiliar with suffering, with none of that long history of catastrophe and calamity behind it which makes the experience of European nations, is outraged and baffled by misfortune. Depression blocks its view; it cannot see round it. Misled in the onset by leaders who assured it, in every soothing term and tone, that reverse was to last but a little while; that it was the preliminary to recovery; that American institutions were immune to the ills that had laid the countries of the rest of the world upon their backs; that prosperity was native to the soil of the Union, and all that was needed was to wait till the clouds, blown up by the wickedness of other lands, rolled by, as they were bound to do, and that speedily; the nation now suffers from a despair of any and every kind of leadership ... The defeatism that has been so lamentably evidenced in Congress is not peculiar to Congressmen, any more than is the crude individualism of their reaction. It lies alike a pall over the spirit of the nation ... to that restoration of confidence for which everybody pleads, which everybody sees as necessary. But how to break it nobody knows.

SOURCE 7.13 Larry Van Dusen remembers his craftsman father and the strains of unemployment, in S. Terkel, *Hard Times*, 1986, p.107

One of the most common things – and it certainly happened to me – was this feeling of your father's failure. That somehow he hadn't beaten the rap ... Remember too, the shock, the confusion, the hurt that many kids felt about their fathers not being able to provide for them. This reflected itself very often in bitter quarrels between father and son ... My father led a rough life; he drank. During the Depression, he drank more. There was more conflict in the home. A lot of fathers – mine among them – had a habit of taking off. They'd go to Chicago to look for work. To Topeka. This left the family at home, waiting and hoping that the old man would find something. And there was always the Saturday night ordeal as to whether or not the old man would get home with his pay-check. Everything was sharpened and hurt more by the Depression.

SOURCE 7.14 From R. S. Lynd and H. Lynd's *Middletown: A Study in American Culture*, 1929 (see page 88)

... the great knife of depression had cut down impartially through the entire population cleaving open lives and hopes of rich as well as poor. The experience has been more nearly universal than any prolonged recent emotional experience in the city's history.

ACTIVITY

Listen to songs of the period, such as *Brother Can You Spare a Dime* and *We Sure Got Hard Times Now*. To what extent can you regard songs as historical evidence?

■ Learning trouble spot

Oral history

How reliable is oral history? If you have ever played Chinese Whispers, or had to recount a conversation to someone, you have probably realised how hard it is to remember exactly what was said. If you have ever recounted an event in your life you will probably realise how much you have missed out, and how much you may have, unwittingly, changed. Would your parent or brother/sister tell exactly the same story? Oral history is spoken memory. There are several examples of oral history in this book. Think about their strengths and limitations in interpreting the story of twentieth-century America.

FOCUS ROUTE

1 What personal qualities did Roosevelt bring to the presidency?
2 What were his principal ideas?

DISCUSS

By what criteria would Americans decide if Roosevelt had been a successful president? For example, did he have to end the Depression or only alleviate it?

The inauguration of Franklin Delano Roosevelt

In August 1932 Franklin Delano Roosevelt, governor of the state of New York, accepted the Democratic Party's nomination as their presidential candidate in the November election against Herbert Hoover. One phrase in his acceptance speech was later picked out by a journalist; the phrase was 'a new deal'.

Born in 1882 to wealthy parents in New York state, Roosevelt was an only child. After the death of his father, he was looked after by his mother, who remained an important part of his life until her death in 1941. He trained as a lawyer before entering state politics, becoming Assistant Secretary to the Navy during the First World War. In 1905 he married Eleanor, a niece of Theodore Roosevelt, and they had six children, one of whom died in infancy. In 1921 Roosevelt contracted polio, for which there was no cure at the time. Permanently disabled, he surprised many by his determination, with the help of Eleanor, his mother and his friends, to recreate a normal life. Many observers believed this experience of pain contributed to his warmth to others, particularly the distressed and worried. Roosevelt had recognised that depression could lead to passivity and uncertainty. In recovering from polio he had demonstrated determination and courage, and showed graceful acceptance of his disability.

To many in 1932, Roosevelt did not seem a very strong candidate. He seemed sensible and decent but also indecisive, lacking in conviction and without clear policies. However, his infectious smile, warm voice, relaxed demeanour and obvious pleasure in meeting people, were in total contrast to Hoover's restraint and defeatist manner. He also radiated assurance about the value of what he was doing. A recent assessment asserts, 'In Washington, Roosevelt was a master of the art of personal political persuasion ... He could "stroke the hand" and massage the ego of the most disgruntled cabinet member. He could flatter and assuage the most surly and self-important congressional leader.' (from A. Badger, *The New Deal: Depression Years, 1933–40*, 1989, p.8)

SOURCE 7.15 FDR as governor of New York in 1930. Because of an agreement made with photographers, which they respected from 1933 onwards, Roosevelt was never shown struggling with his disability, which left him unable to walk without leg braces and support from others. Much later, when a memorial was being created to him in Washington, there were protests by disability-awareness groups that he should be portrayed more truthfully as someone who had successfully coped with the limitations on his physical life. After much debate the memorial did include a statue of Roosevelt in a wheelchair

ACTIVITY

Personal research
To get a flavour of the early thirties:
• Listen out for the popular songs after 1933 including *Happy Days are Here Again, Whistle While You Work*, and, released six days after the inauguration, *There's a New Day Comin'*.
• Watch the cartoons of Donald Duck and Mickey Mouse, the films *King Kong* and *The Thin Man*.
• Read F. Scott Fitzgerald's *Tender is the Night* and John Steinbeck's *Grapes of Wrath*.
Do they convey a sense of depression and gritty realism or do they suggest hope and escapism?

DISCUSS

A Washington journalist said of Hoover that he 'can calculate wavelengths, but cannot see color ... He can understand vibrations but cannot hear tone'.
How does this description explain the difference between Hoover and Roosevelt?

Whilst Roosevelt had refused to support Hoover's economic suggestions in the last days of his presidency, he had not been idle. He gathered around him a group of advisors, mainly from universities, who became known as his 'Brain Trust'. Roosevelt never claimed to have extensive economic knowledge, but he was receptive to the ideas of others. Raymond Moley, Rexford Tugwell, Basil O'Connor, and Adolf Berle argued about ideas, drafted speeches, talked to economists and fed Roosevelt with a stimulating range of possibilities. He, and they, gradually consolidated their principal ideas:

• They accepted that this was an age of large corporations and that there should be co-operation between business and government.
• They rejected the extremes of socialist and *lassez-faire* solutions.
• There was a general distrust of financiers and speculators who did not have the interests of the nation as a focus for their activities.
• Initially there was support for a balanced budget.
• There was a need to reform the structures of business and how they were regulated by government.

They, and he, read widely. Their influences included the ideas of Dewey ('learn by doing'), of progressives like Jane Addams with her interest in missionary social gospel ideas (that the lives of the poor should be both morally and materially improved), and of Woodrow Wilson and his ideas of moral responsibility. In a campaign speech in San Francisco in 1932 Roosevelt hinted at his ideas (see Source 7.16).

SOURCE 7.16 One of Roosevelt's campaign speeches, San Francisco, 1932 (in M. Johnson, *Reading the American Past*, 2nd edn, 2002, pp.138–39)

Every man has a right to live; and that means that he also has the right to make a comfortable living ... We have no actual famine or dearth; our industrial and agricultural mechanisms can produce enough and to spare ... Every man has a right to his own property; which means a right to be assured, to the fullest extent attainable, in the safety of his savings ... If, in accord with this principle, we must restrict the operations of the speculator, the manipulator, even the financier, I believe we accept the restriction as necessary, not to hamper individualism but to protect it ... We know that liberty to do anything which deprives others of those elemental rights is outside the protection of any compact; and that the Government in this regard is the maintenance of a balance ...

SOURCE 7.17 Roosevelt became president in March 1933. His Inaugural Address on 4 March 1933 set the tone for the years to come

So, first of all, let me assert my firm belief that the only thing we have to fear is fear itself – nameless, unreasoning, unjustified terror which paralyzes needed efforts to convert retreat into advance. In every dark hour of our national life a leadership of frankness and vigor has met with that understanding and support of the people themselves which is essential to victory.

Such a comforting speech (Source 7.17) was desperately needed. The banking system seemed on the verge of collapse. The pace of bank failures increased during the winter. In February 1933 Detroit's banks collapsed. Michigan and Maryland extended bank holidays to try to curb the demand from depositors. On 1 March Kentucky, Tennessee, California, Louisiana, Alabama and Oklahoma all closed their banks. On Inauguration Day 38 states closed their banks and the rest had restricted business.

B The first New Deal – did it provide relief and start recovery?

The Hundred Days

The Hundred Days is the name given to the 73rd session of Congress, which was dominated by Democrats and progressive Republicans. It met from 9 March to 16 June. In that short time it passed fifteen bills, an exceptional burst of legislative activity, and set the future direction of the first part of the New Deal, from 1933 to 1934. It was also the time when Roosevelt and his advisors had to consolidate ideas into concrete proposals. They became the symbol of its energy, commitment, flexibility, and of Roosevelt's particular character. However, it was unclear in March 1933 how much Roosevelt could do to revive and reinvigorate the nation or how the nation would respond.

What was achieved during the Hundred Days?

The first week of the Hundred Days

Sunday 5 March
A four-day banking holiday has been declared as well as a halt to all transactions in gold.

Wednesday 8 March
Roosevelt's first press conference. Realising the importance of the press Roosevelt has announced that there will be twice weekly conferences (compared to Hoover who had one a year). He also said that there is no need to submit written questions in advance and that he can be quoted on factual matters. He will also give 'off the record' background comments directly to reporters.

Thursday 9 March
Congress were called to a special session where the Emergency Banking Act was passed. This will allow banks to open on 13 March under government supervision.

Friday 10 March
Congress were informed of plans to cut $500 million from the federal budget as an emergency economy, and to introduce a Beef-Wine Revenue Act, which will finally end prohibition.

Sunday 12 March
The first fireside chat by a president was broadcast today. Roosevelt told us that it was safe to return our savings to the banks. I felt reassured by his words.

Monday 13 March
The fireside chat seems to have worked! When the banks reopened more money was invested than withdrawn, even though no cash has been available now for more than one week.

■ 7A The gold standard

WHAT WAS THE GOLD STANDARD?
It was an agreement between the major trading nations of the nineteenth century to stabilise their currencies.
In 1871, the leaders of the industrial nations agreed that gold would be a measure of their national wealth. They would only issue paper money and coins to the value of the amount of gold that they, as a nation, possessed. The cost of an ounce of gold had a fixed price, in dollars, which was agreed by all the signatories to the International Gold Standard.
For this system to work each nation needed:
• a central bank (e.g. the Bank of England, the Federal Reserve Bank)
• a single unit of value (e.g. the dollar)
• a government monopoly on the issuing of notes
• the ability to be able to restrict the supply of new notes if gold reserves declined.

In the USA the Gold Standard Act of 1900 stated that all paper money must be backed by gold.

WHY DID IT STOP BEING EFFECTIVE?
• The First World War had made balanced trading difficult as nations spent more money than they had in their treasuries and still had debts to pay off.
• Some stability was re-established through the 1920s until destroyed by the Wall Street Crash.
• In 1931 Britain came 'off' the Gold Standard because it wanted to keep its paper money at its existing value, even though it did not have enough gold, at the price that gold was set at, to balance gold reserves with notes in circulation. Many other industrialised countries also came

'off' at the same time. The USA came 'off' in April 1933.
• It was realised that there was international economic instability so the London Conference was held in July 1933 to try to recreate a system of global economic balance.
• However, President Roosevelt, unlike his predecessor, Hoover, believed that America's Depression problems could only be solved at home. He announced a devaluation of the dollar and the conference collapsed as it was unable to decide on an internationally agreed value for gold.
• There was now no longer a fixed exchange rate for currencies. This at a time when most industrialised nations were suffering from the effects of the Depression and there were ambitious and militant politicians seeking to expand their nations by aggressive military action.

On 19 April Roosevelt abandoned the gold standard, forcing a decline in the value of the dollar and an increase in the price of goods and stocks. The hope was that with more dollars around people would spend more, production would rise, more jobs would be created and unemployment would end. What happened? People did not spend! The effects of the Crash had discouraged investors and small savers alike from taking risks. So the government had to recognise that besides creating more money it also had to ensure that it was used. People had to be encouraged to spend and the government had to get a better balance between prices and wages. Part of the key to this was to ensure that unions were effective in stopping wage reductions, since the lower the wages the less money workers would have available for spending. On 20 June 1934 the Gold Reserve Act required all gold to be impounded in banks of the Federal Reserve. The price of an ounce of gold was set at $35.

What were the New Deal programmes?

'The New Deal erected an institutional scaffolding designed to provide unprecedented stability and predictability for the American economy' (D. Kennedy, *Freedom from Fear*, 1999, p.376).

Speaking in 1932 Roosevelt gave a clue about the way he would do things, 'The country needs, and unless I mistake its temper, the country demands, bold, persistent experimentation. It is common sense to take a method and try it. If it fails, admit it frankly and try another. But above all, try something.' The aims of the first part of the New Deal were:

- to relieve human suffering
- to promote economic recovery.

These aims were to be achieved by:

- correcting the financial crisis
- offering initial short-term relief to the unemployed
- recognising that under-consumption was more of a problem than over-production
- promoting industrial recovery by increased government spending and by co-operative agreements between government, industry and unions
- raising the prices of farm and manufactured goods to reduce production, thereby reducing supply and making the goods produced more valuable.

There was also a less well-defined aim – implicit in Roosevelt as a person and in his administration – to restore hope and energy to Americans as individuals. This could not have a defined strategy. It relied on the results of the new legislation and on the creation of a new attitude within the nation.

FOCUS ROUTE

1 Copy and complete this table, noting how each of the measures of the first New Deal benefited different parts of the American economy.

How the first New Deal programmes helped the nation				
Act, date	Agriculture	Manufacturing	Finance	Employment

2 How do you think these programmes changed people's attitudes and expectations?

The first New Deal (ALPHABET AGENCY) programmes (Chart 7B) were either replaced by the second New Deal of 1936–37 or ended with the changed demands of the Second World War. A few, particularly ones regulating finance, designed to avoid the extremes of 1929, continue today.

1933

AGRICULTURAL ADJUSTMENT ACT (AAA)

Purpose: Used farm subsidies to regulate farm production.

Comment: Disbanded after the Second World War.

FARM CREDIT ACT

Purpose: Provided short- and medium-term loans to enable farmers struggling with low incomes to keep their homes and land by refinancing their mortgages.

Comment: It removed the fear of losing both home and employment. It gave security for the future to enable farmers to take advantage of other government agricultural programmes to raise production.

CIVILIAN CONSERVATION CORPS (CCC)

Purpose: Provided work for young men aged 18–25, paying $30 a month, of which $25 had to be sent to their families. Stayed in camps, organised on military lines, and worked on regional environmental projects, such as national parks where they built trails, recreation facilities and access roads.

Comment: Disbanded in 1942.

FEDERAL EMERGENCY RELIEF AGENCY (FERA)

Purpose: Families were paid relief benefits for taking work organised by the government, with $500 million given to states and local governments.

Comment: Suspended in 1935, because the Works Progress Administration (see page 123) projects started and financial aid was given as a result of the unemployment insurance of the Social Security Act of 1937.

TENNESSEE VALLEY AUTHORITY (TVA)

Purpose: Regional planning of a deprived area, with hydro-electricity production, environmental conservation, flood control and educational and health projects. Involved the states of Virginia, North Carolina, Tennessee, Georgia, Alabama, Mississippi and Kentucky.

Comment: Still in operation, though criticised for its unanticipated environmental impact.

NATIONAL INDUSTRIAL RECOVERY ACT (NIRA), INCLUDING THE NATIONAL RECOVERY ADMINISTRATION (NRA)

Purpose: Attempted to establish national economic planning by devising and running a series of codes for industries. The codes were to control production, prices, labour relations and trading practices. Run by General Hugh Johnson.

Comment: The NRA was ruled unconstitutional by the Supreme Court in 1935 and came to an end.

PUBLIC WORKS ADMINISTRATION (PWA)

Purpose: Run by Harold Ickes, this programme financed 34,000 federal, state and local projects costing a total of $6 billion – a large source of employment. Major involvement in housing, energy supplies and conservation. Included the Civil Works Administration, run by Harry Hopkins.

Comment: Discontinued in 1939, as it had not had sufficient success in reducing unemployment or promoting private investment, but it was valued for other achievements. It promoted Roosevelt's belief in work relief rather than cash subsidies through the dole. It gave over 4 million unemployed people paid work on useful local projects and helped to raise morale and create optimism that the Depression could come to an end.

BANKING ACT (GLASS–SEAGALL BANKING ACT)

Purpose: Prohibited commercial banks from selling stock or financing corporations. Created the Federal Deposit Insurance Corporation (FDIC), which guaranteed savings deposits up to $2500 (later raised to $5000, and now at $100,000). Protected the ordinary depositor from loss of savings.

Comment: It separated investment banks from commercial banks so that investors' money could no longer be used for speculative ventures on the stock market. The guaranteeing of individual deposits diminished the fear that investors might lose all their savings through the misuse of their funds by the bank.

1934

FEDERAL COMMUNICATIONS COMMISSION (FCC)

Purpose: Agency to regulate wired and wireless communications, later to regulate television as well. Part of a programme of government regulation of new enterprises.

Comment: Continues today.

FEDERAL HOUSING ADMINISTRATION (FHA)

Purpose: Federal guarantees of private mortgages, with reduced down payments from 30 per cent to 10 per cent, and extended repayment time from 20 to 30 years. Enabled more Americans to purchase their own homes.

Comment: Continues today.

SECURITIES AND EXCHANGE COMMISSION (SEC)

Purpose: Regulatory agency for trading in stocks and bonds to comply with federal laws.

Comment: Continues today.

How did the programmes ease the Depression?

The Agricultural Adjustment Act (AAA)

The AAA was a recognition of the problems of farmers. Its aim was to get prices for farm goods back to those of their 'golden age' during 1910–14. In order to achieve this there were voluntary cut-backs in production, reducing the quantity of food available so that prices rose. There were seven basic commodities involved including wheat, cotton, tobacco and most controversially, pig-rearing. Over 6 million pigs had to be slaughtered, 'before they could reach the full hogness of their hogdom', at a time when there was hunger in many rural families. The Act was also passed too late to stop spring planting and so acres of crops had to be ploughed under. Initially the plan was successful, with farm incomes rising 58 per cent between 1932 and 1935. Although the Supreme Court ruled it to be unconstitutional in 1936, it was revived and a similar act was passed in 1938, as part of the second New Deal. However, the Act did have two important negative effects. Firstly, it speeded up agricultural production, changing it from family-run businesses to large commercial enterprises. Secondly, landowners, especially in the South, in reducing their production, also ended the contracts of sharecroppers and tenants, both black and white. An unexpectedly large group, already amongst the poorest in the nation, were now likely to be both unemployed and homeless.

The Tennessee Valley Authority (TVA)

Roosevelt's personal interest in the provision of electricity in the Tennessee Valley had been encouraged by a visit to Muscle Shoals, Alabama. At a time when local people had only wood burning stoves and kerosene lamps, public utility companies there had been blocking schemes to extend the use of the dam for the production of electricity. The plans for the TVA were intended to regenerate an area of long-established poverty. By 1936 nine dams were built or under construction, with more planned. They provided cheap hydro-electricity, and much more: they opened up rivers for navigation; fostered soil conservation and forestry; encouraged experiments with fertilisers; stimulated new industries to come to the region; and, most importantly, provided jobs and revived self-respect. Harry Hopkins sent Lorena Hickok, a journalist, to report back. She wrote about the TVA in Alabama (see Source 7.18).

SOURCE 7.18 Lorena Hickok's report on the TVA in Alabama, 6 June 1934

A Promised Land, bathed in golden sunlight, is rising out of the grey shadows of want and squalor and wretchedness down here in the Tennessee Valley these days. Ten thousand men are at work, building with timber and steel and concrete the New Deal's most magnificent project, creating an empire with potentialities so tremendous and so dazzling that they make one gasp . . . Thousands of them are residents of the Valley, working five-and-a-half hours a day, five days a week for a really LIVING wage . . . and in their leisure time they are studying – farming, trades, the art of preparing themselves for the fuller lives they are to lead in the Promised Land. You are probably saying, 'Oh, come down to earth!' But that's the way the Tennessee Valley affects one these days . . . My guess is that whatever they do or don't do about rural rehabilitation down in Tennessee, in another decade you won't know this country. And the best part of it is that here the Government will have control. There's a chance to create a new kind of industrial life, with decent wages, decent housing. Gosh, what possibilities! . . . 'Oh, I haven't heard anybody say anything about the Depression for three months', remarked a taxicab driver in Knoxville . . . 'Business is three times as good as it was a year ago. You ought to see the crowds at the ballgames.'

ACTIVITY

Compare Source 7.18 with Source 7.4 (page 109). How useful is this comparison in assessing the effects of the TVA?

DISCUSS

What impressed Lorena Hickok (Source 7.18)? What did she think was important? If you were a long-term resident of the area, what do you think would be important to you as an individual?

SOURCE 7.19 The Blue Eagle was the symbol of the NRA and was displayed by participating businesses

The National Recovery Administration (NRA)

The National Recovery Administration is seen as the central part of this first New Deal. Its aim was to:

- reduce competition by the implementation of codes to set wages and prices, and so hopefully stabilise business
- provide more jobs, paid at an acceptable rate, through these controls.

Management, labour and government met to create codes for each industry. All the codes had a standard 40-hour working week and a minimum weekly wage of $12–$13. There was also a ban on children under sixteen working. The Blue Eagle, and its motto of 'We Do Our Part' was the symbol of compliance. It was initially popular, with 2 million signing the pledge; a reaction to a positive attempt to solve the Depression crisis. However, by 1935 business confidence was returning and the codes were seen as too restrictive. It is probable that this stage of the Depression needed more goods to be bought rather than restrictions on over-production. The NRA continued until 1935 when the Supreme Court declared it unconstitutional. There was no attempt to revive it. Source 7.20 provides a recent criticism.

SOURCE 7.20 D. M. Kennedy, *Freedom from Fear,* 1999, p.184

The Blue Eagle was meant to symbolize unity and mutuality, and it no doubt did for a season, but Johnson's ubiquitous 'badge of honor' also clearly signified the poverty of the New Deal imagination and the meagreness of the methods it could bring to bear at this time against the Depression. Reduced to this kind of incantation and exhortation for which they had flayed Hoover, the New Dealers stood revealed in late 1933 as something less than the bold innovators and aggressive workers of government power that legend later portrayed.

The NRA did demonstrate the government's desire for economic stability and the typical New Deal desire to try something, anything, to move the nation out of the Depression. What continued was the standardisation of working practices, as well as government support for workers through the principle of collective bargaining. So an assessment of its value has to be made on both a short- and long-term basis.

The Public Works Administration (PWA)

The PWA funded a federal theatre project, federal writers' project and federal music project. Not only did these create jobs, but they also provided entertainment, inspired creativity and demonstrated American culture to a wider audience. The interest in factual knowledge about the state of the nation encouraged documentary recordings. The Farm Security Administration commissioned photographs, notably those of Dorothea Lange (see Source 7.2, page 108) and Paul Taylor. There were accusations that such projects were amateurish and a waste of public money. Others thought that there was an overly left-wing bias in much of the work. However, at a time when totalitarian regimes in Germany and the Soviet Union were controlling the arts, these projects remained free of censorship or overt propaganda.

The PWA had a budget of $3.3 billion to create work, preferably permanent rather than 'make-do' work. There was, for example, major road building, like the Skyline Drive in the Shenandoah National Park and the subways in Chicago. In the winter of 1933 Harry Hopkins, who had always favoured work relief rather then dole payments, introduced the Civil Works Administration (CWA) to speed up getting the unemployed into work. It provided 4.2 million people with proper paid work, at a rate of 40–60 cents an hour, doing light construction and maintenance, upgrading roads, laying sewers and improving schools and hospitals. The CWA lasted for five months and meant that millions were able to cope through the winter, as they waited for the economy to improve. It was, however, the end of the relief element of the New Deal as Roosevelt feared that people might develop too great a reliance on the government as an employer.

SOURCE 7.21 Construction of the giant Triborough bridge in New York. This project was financed with a PWA grant of $44,200,000

DISCUSS

Which **two** of the effects of the New Deal shown in Chart 7C do you think were the most significant?

■ 7C Why were the Hundred Days important?

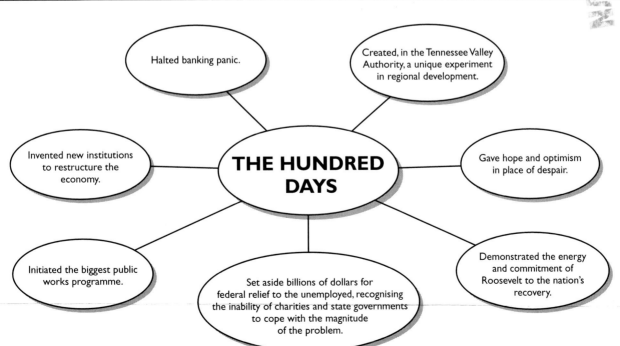

Halted banking panic.

Created, in the Tennessee Valley Authority, a unique experiment in regional development.

Invented new institutions to restructure the economy.

THE HUNDRED DAYS

Gave hope and optimism in place of despair.

Initiated the biggest public works programme.

Set aside billions of dollars for federal relief to the unemployed, recognising the inability of charities and state governments to cope with the magnitude of the problem.

Demonstrated the energy and commitment of Roosevelt to the nation's recovery.

Who were the New Deal activists?

FOCUS ROUTE

Read Source 7.16 again (page 113).

1 In his speech Roosevelt identified the following needs:
   a) the rights of the ordinary person
   b) the safety of savings
   c) restrictions on manipulators of finance
   d) the protection of individualism
   e) the need for the government to provide a balance between freedom and restrictions.
   What did Roosevelt do in the first Hundred Days to address each of these concerns?
2 What did he and his administration do during the rest of the first New Deal, to 1934, to address these concerns?

Harold Ickes (1874–1952) and Harry Hopkins (1890–1946)
Harold Ickes (right) was secretary to the interior, ran the Public Works Administration (PWA) and was Hopkins' boss. He was slow to spend the $3 billion allocated for the PWA by Congress, much to Hopkins' frustration. Harry Hopkins ran the Civil Works Administration (CWA) in 1933–34 using PWA funds. In the Second New Deal he also ran the Works Progress Administration (WPA). Hopkins, was 'a chain-smoking, hollow-eyed pauper-thin social worker, a tough-talking, big-hearted blend of the sardonic and the sentimental' (D. Kennedy, *Freedom from Fear*, 1999, p.145). He disliked means-testing recognising how humiliated it made people feel. In 1932 he reminded Lorena Hickok, a journalist working for him, that on her exploratory assignments for him, '… when you talk with them don't ever forget that but for the grace of God, you, I, any of our friends might be in their shoes'. He was not afraid to talk bluntly to Roosevelt and was one of his closest advisors during the Depression. The president relied on his advice during the Second World War, providing a room for him in the White House.

Frances Perkins (1882–1965)
Frances Perkins, secretary of labor from 1933–45. She was the first woman Cabinet member, and had particular responsibility for the Fair Labor Standards Act (see page 123).

Eleanor Roosevelt (1884–1962)
This photograph shows Eleanor Roosevelt visiting an Afro-American day nursery, funded by the Works Progress Administration (see page 123), in Des Moines, Iowa. The President's wife was especially interested in the concerns of the black community and of women. She actively worked for justice and equity for black Americans, both on New Deal programmes, and by supporting an anti-lynching law (which Southern senators blocked). She encouraged FDR to meet black leaders and tried to respond to their concerns, often addressing black audiences.
She was actively involved with Hopkins in trying to ensure that women were able to work on federal projects, and that they received equal pay for equal work. She also encouraged the appointment of female administrators for New Deal programmes. Eleanor Roosevelt seemed to have little reward for her efforts, but she was much admired, her support was valued, and she represented the New Deal values of reform and social justice.

General Hugh Johnson (1882–1942)
General Hugh Johnson led the
National Recovery Administration
(NRA) from 1933 until his dismissal in
1934. His character did little to make
such a complicated system work. One
historian described him as negotiating
with 'his own particular blend of
bluster, bombast, Bourbon and
baloney'. Another as 'Melodramatic in
his temperament, mercurial in his
moods, ingeniously profane in his
speech, Johnson could weep at opera,
vilify his enemies, chew out his
underlings, and rhapsodize about the
virtues of the NRA with equal
flamboyance'.

FOCUS ROUTE

Make notes on the following questions.

1 What further measures were taken
   to end the Depression?
2 Where was reform, as opposed to
   relief, needed?
3 Had life for ordinary Americans
   improved by 1941?

The grassroot activists

Those who were involved in putting the ideas and laws of the New Deal into
practice knew that they were working on something that was different. Joe
Marcus was in his early twenties when he went to work on a Harry Hopkins
project (see Source 7.22).

SOURCE 7.22 Joe Marcus comments on a Harry Hopkins project, in S. Terkel, *Hard
Times*, 1970, pp. 265–67

*The New Deal was a young man's world ... Given a chance as a youngster to try
out ideas, I learned a fantastic amount. The challenge itself was great. It was the
idea of being asked big questions ... The climate was exciting. You were part of a
society that was on the move. You were involved in something that could make a
difference. Laws could be changed. So could the condition of the people ... We
weren't thinking of remaking society. That wasn't it. I didn't buy this dream
stuff. What was happening was a complete change in social attitudes at the
central government level. The question was: How can you do it within this
system?*

C ## The second New Deal – did it complete recovery and start reform?

The first New Deal programmes raised expectations from those on the left and
anger from those on the right. Roosevelt had to choose a path away from the
middle ground and opted for more social and economic reform in 1935. He
went on to have an easy win in the 1936 presidential election, losing only two
out of the 48 states. But it was clear that many problems still remained and
Roosevelt recognised these in his second Inaugural Address in January 1936
(Source 7.23).

SOURCE 7.23 Roosevelt's second Inaugural Address, January 1936

*In spite of our efforts and in spite of all our talk, we have not weeded out the
over-privileged, and we have not effectively lifted up the under-privileged. We do
not destroy ambition, nor do we seek to divide our wealth into equal shares – we
do assert that the ambition of the individual to obtain for him and his a proper
life is an ambition to be preferred to the appetite for great wealth and great power.*

Here was a new focus: less on business needs, and more on reforming areas
that affected ordinary people – unions able to fight for their members' needs,
financial security in old age, cheap electricity – as well as the continuing fight
to reduce the still high levels of unemployment. Roosevelt also recognised that
he had to say whose side he was on, 'I should like it said of my first
Administration that in it the forces of selfishness and lust for power met their
match. I should like to have it said of the second Administration that in it these
forces met their master'.

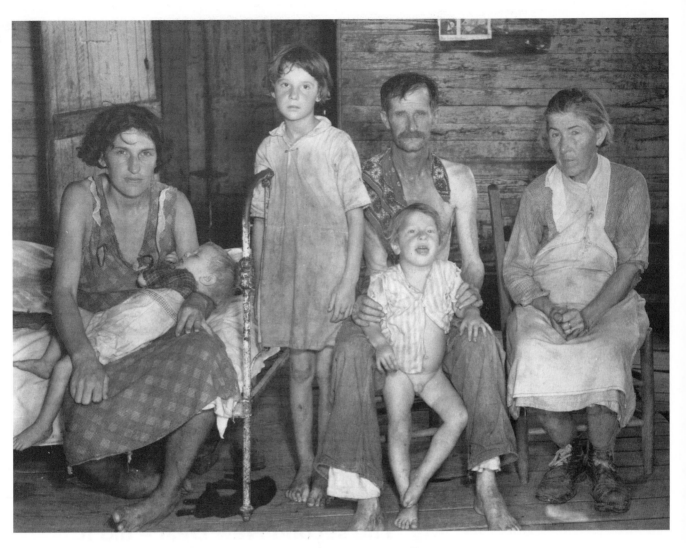

SOURCE 7.24 Photo of a cotton farm family. From James Agee and Walker Evans, *Let Us Now Praise Famous Men*, 1939

Was reform necessary?

It had become evident during the first New Deal that there were two groups in society who needed government help; the rural 'hidden poor' and poorly paid workers. The rural 'hidden poor' had been exposed by the Tennessee Valley Authority projects, Source 7.24 shows poorly paid workers.

In 1936, photographer Walker Evans and journalist James Agee toured cotton farms in the South run by white tenant farmers. Their book, *Let Us Now Praise Famous Men* (see Source 7.24), published as a result of their tour was starkly honest and demonstrated to new audiences the harsh realities of life for these poor families. Both black and white citizens struggled to have the most basic housing and education. Even those in work faced problems as violence and intimidation were used against union members. Armed thugs were hired and the police supported employers. The methods were exposed by a 1936 Senate sub-committee enquiring into industrial unions. They found that intimidation, spying on union member activities and violence were all common.

DISCUSS

1 Who do you think Roosevelt meant were the 'forces of selfishness and lust for power'?
2 Who do you think might be less enthusiastic about the New Deal programmes of 1933–34? What did they fear losing? Look back at those who benefited from the 1920s.

■ **7D Major legislation of the second New Deal, 1935–38**

1935

NATIONAL LABOR RELATIONS ACT, ALSO KNOWN AS THE WAGNER ACT, WHICH SET UP THE NATIONAL LABOR RELATIONS BOARD (NLRB)

Purpose: Strengthened the power of labour unions by allowing collective bargaining.

Comment: Created a way of peacefully solving labour disputes without resorting to violence, which had characterised employment disagreements in the past.

WORKS PROGRESS ADMINISTRATION (WPA)

Purpose: Established work relief programmes funding a vast range of projects directed at different areas, including the Federal Art Project (FAP). Run by Harry Hopkins.

Comment: Ran for eight years and employed 8.5 million people, using local officials to administer the projects.

NATIONAL YOUTH ADMINISTRATION (NYA)

Purpose: Established by the WPA to encourage the education and training of young people.

Comment: Disbanded during the Second World War.

RURAL ELECTRIFICATION ADMINISTRATION (REA)

Purpose: Gave loans for cheap rural electricity in areas where there was no public utility supply. It was the government's commitment to bring electricity to rural areas, through the setting up of an agency to aid farm co-operatives. These were eligible for low-cost federal loans to pay for the installation of power lines.

Comment: The Act was very successful – in 1935 only 10 per cent of farms had electricity, by 1940 it was 40 per cent and by 1950 90 per cent. America's vast landscapes were being conquered by a new kind of unity.

SOCIAL SECURITY ACT (SSA)

Purpose: Created guaranteed retirement payments for over-65s, set up federal insurance for the unemployed, and provided additional assistance for the disabled, for public health and for dependent women and children.

Comment: Continues today.

1937

FARM SECURITY ADMINISTRATION (FSA)

Purpose: Gave guaranteed loans to small farmers and tenants to buy small properties or to rehabilitate farms. This enabled more farmers to stay on their farms.

Comment: Maintained migrant labour camps for agricultural workers as part of its remit that no one should be excluded from its benefits.

1938

FAIR LABOR STANDARDS ACT

Purpose: Set a minimum wage of 40 cents an hour and a maximum working week of 40 hours for businesses involved in interstate commerce, and particularly for workers not in unions. It raised the wages of 12 million workers by 1940. The system was a model for the future. It was opposed by Southern conservatives on the grounds of excessive government interference with business. They also feared that Southern industry, with its traditional low wage structure, would lose its competitiveness.

Comment: It gave the benefits of a shorter working week and a minimum hourly wage by statute, rather than by union negotiation. This was the last New Deal reform to become law.

NATIONAL HOUSING ACT

Purpose: Established the United States Housing Authority and set up housing projects for low income families.

Comment: Encouraged house building and home ownership, but was also discriminatory against black Americans and inadvertently promoted suburban over inner-city housing.

How did the second New Deal help the nation?

National Labor Relations Act (Wagner Act)

This Act set up the National Labor Relations Board which:

- presided over labour/management relations
- enabled unions to have collective bargaining rights with federal support.

If the majority of workers wanted a union then the company had to agree and negotiate with the workers over wages, hours and working conditions. It established union membership as a right and revitalised the labour movement (especially in areas of mass production – cars, aluminium, rubber, mining). Elections for union representatives had to be supervised and complaints about employer's unfair work practices had to be heard, although it was not until 1946 that workers could bring charges against employers for unfair work practices. It was the first time that the pressure and authority of the federal government was used to encourage and support workers' rights, and to give recognition to the legitimacy of union organisations.

Union membership rose from 3.7 million in 1935, to 8.5 million in 1940. However, this increase was not achieved without further violence, notably by the Ford company and the Republic Steel Company. A protest at the latter's Chicago plant in 1937 ended with the deaths of ten demonstrators, all shot in the back by police. Companies found the new union method of protest through peaceful sit-down strikes much harder to deal with.

Social Security Act, 1935

The USA was the only industrial nation not to have a national welfare system to protect the vulnerable. Despite this, critics said the SSA was another step away from the traditional American values of self-reliance and individualism. Others thought that the provisions were insufficient. The old age pension did not start until 1942 and payments varied from $10–$85 per month. It did not include certain occupations including farmers and domestic servants, many of whom were black and female. The unemployment insurance was for the future, not those currently unemployed. All contributors had to pay the same rate, regardless of income. Economists said that it took money out of circulation just at the time when the economy was beginning to recover. However, Roosevelt did not want benefits to be a hand-out, but rather to be 'earned'. He had established the principle that the federal government had a responsibility for social welfare.

How did the New Deal change the landscape?

Federal Art Project (FAP)

SOURCE 7.25 *The New Deal* painted by Conrad A. Albrizio. Painted in 1934 and dedicated to President Roosevelt, this mural was placed in the Leonardo Da Vinci Art School in New York. It was typical of the large-scale work of the time, funded by the FAP, most with themes reflecting the changes that ordinary people were experiencing. Notice the image of Roosevelt comforting a despairing worker, and the types of work that surround this central image of reassurance

It was felt that artists had as much right to practise their skills as other workers under the WPA programmes. The Federal Writers' Project recorded more than 10,000 life stories from different occupation and ethnic groups.

Rural electrification

'I just turned on the light and kept looking at Paw. It was the first time I'd really seen after dark.' Cars and machinery had eased the working life of farmers, now electricity eased that of their wives. Electricity brought washing machines (instead of tubs over fires), irons which were lighter and easily heated, pumps to raise water, refrigerators so that fresh produce could be stored, and radios to hear about national events. Electric light replaced kerosene lamps so people could read and write at night, and children could study more easily. Electric milking machines eased a daily chore often performed by children.

The Tennessee Valley Authority, the Civilian Conservation Corps, the Civil Works Administration and the Works Progress Administration all initiated projects that were visible improvements. National park facilities, public buildings, roads, schools and hospitals benefited from projects designed to ease unemployment.

Native Americans

SOURCE 7.26 John Collier, standing behind Harold Ickes, secretary to the interior, with a group of Flathead (Salish) Indian (Native American) chiefs. Ickes is signing a constitution providing for Indian self-rule, 1935

Native Americans, neglected since the beginning of the century, also benefited from the New Deal. John Collier, appointed as Commissioner for Indian Affairs, was responsible for the Indian Reorganization Act of 1934. It ended the Dawes Severalty Act, which had put Native American affairs under the control of the government, and gave Native Americans self-rule for their tribal areas. Native Americans were to develop their land as they chose, have better education facilities on the reservation and recreate their cultural/economic lifestyles. Years of neglect were difficult to end and Native Americans, although given more autonomy, remained poorer than most citizens for the remainder of the century.

Why had the Depression not ended by 1939?

In 1933 unemployment was 13 million, in 1937, 7.7 million and by 1939, 10 million. However, in 1929 it had been less than 1 million.

Did the New Deal fail? Historians struggle to give one answer, just as they struggle to give one over-riding explanation for the severity and length of the Depression. The Depression and the New Deal did expose the depth of the

SOURCE 7.27 A. Badger, *The New Deal: Depression Years, 1933–40*, 1989, p.311

... the ultimate constraint that circumscribed the New Deal's achievements: the underlying conservative response of the people themselves to the Depression. Middle-income Americans may have more sympathy with the poor and the jobless in the 1930s than before or after. Workers may have exhibited greater class solidarity in those years. But more striking is the pervasive and persistent commitment to self-help, individual liberty, localism and business-oriented individualism.

DISCUSS

At both local and Congressional level there was a conservative response to tackling the Depression. What were people trying to protect, and trying to avoid?

problem of poverty, especially the 'old poor' – those who had always been ill-paid, -housed, -clothed, -fed and -educated. The New Deal did tackle such previously ignored problems. However, it also had to fight the heritage of previous policies and *laissez-faire* attitudes. Another factor was that the New Deal demanded too much from the federal government. The bureaucratic organisation of information-gathering and implementation necessary to carry out, in full, the proposed policies and ambitions, simply did not exist. There was also no general recognition that for some policies, like social welfare ones, intervention from 'big government' in Washington was necessary. Without this intervention the implementation of these policies was down to local officials, power elites and interest groups, who were not as committed to New Deal policies as their initiators.

Keynes, the influential economist, author of the widely regarded book, *The General Theory of Employment Interest and Money*, argued that massive government expenditure was the only way to bring the Depression to an end, even though it meant deficit spending and an unbalanced budget. Although by 1937 Roosevelt felt unable politically to continue with an unbalanced budget, the result of his withdrawal of federal funds from projects was an immediate rise in unemployment. The nation had still not recovered and full employment only returned with the massive government expenditure necessary during the Second World War.

Did it matter that there was no complete recovery?

The fact that the New Deal did not solve all of America's problems did not end Roosevelt's popularity. He won an unprecedented third presidential term in November 1940 (and again during the Second World War in 1944). However, the sense of revolution that had been around in 1932 had disappeared and Americans were less likely to be radical in their attitudes or expectations. The failure to end the Depression was important primarily for individuals: the long-term unemployed who would become more depressed at their restricted life; those who did not benefit from the new legislation (the workers excluded from the Social Security Act, for example); and those who were forced to leave their homes to search for work, with all the accompanying problems of family stress and disruption.

D New Deal or Raw Deal?

FOCUS ROUTE

Who were the losers of the New Deal? Complete your own copy of this table to identify the range of ways some Americans were 'losers' of the New Deal.

Group	Advantages of the New Deal	Disadvantages of the New Deal
Long-term unemployed		
Afro-American migrants		
Dust Bowl migrants		
Mexican migrants		
Women		

I The long-term unemployed

The New Deal probably eased poverty for many, however in 1939, 17 per cent of the population were still unemployed, compared to 3.5 per cent in 1929. The long-term problems of 'old poverty' inherited by the Roosevelt administration, were particularly difficult to solve. (Look back to Larry Van Dusen's evidence in Source 7.13, page 112). It was only with the demands of war production that there was full employment by 1943 and, by 1945, a need for more workers.

The unemployed also saw actions like the Agricultural Adjustment Administration production cutbacks as wasteful and immoral. The slaughtering of 6 million pigs in 1933 and the ploughing under of 10.4 million acres of cotton contrasted sharply with the reality of the under-nourished, ill-clothed unemployed. At the same time petty crime, begging and prostitution increased. As divorce was too expensive the number of desertions, usually by husbands, increased, and by 1940 it was estimated that 1.5 million men had left home.

2 Afro-American migrants

New Deal programmes were often indifferent to meeting the needs of black Americans, as in the exclusion of domestic workers (a major area of black female employment) from the Social Security Act. There was also discrimination against them shown by the Federal Housing Administration's refusal to give mortgages for black families in traditionally white neighbourhoods. There was racial segregation in the Civilian Conservation Corps and in the Tennessee Valley Authority projects. Sharecroppers, many of them black Americans, suffered particularly badly as farms went out of production and farmers reduced the number of labourers required. Around 200,000 were displaced by the Agricultural Adjustment Administration's programme and forced to travel to towns for work at a time when jobs were scarce and prejudice still strong. More black workers were unemployed than white. Such discrimination affected their health – black American life expectancy was ten years less than that of white Americans living in the same area. Lynching increased, with twenty deaths in 1930 and 24 in 1934. Overall, there was little attempt to change the patterns of racism in the USA. The president relied on Southern white Democrats for support in Congress and refused, for example, to support an anti-lynching bill.

However, not all New Deal programmes were discriminatory. The Works Progress Administration was particularly known for being 'colour-blind', with 1 million black Americans working for it by 1939.

Black industrial workers also benefited from the constitution of the Congress of Industrial Organizations (CIO), which prohibited its constituent unions from discrimination on the grounds of race. Such statements and actions made it difficult to return to old patterns of segregation. They gave an optimism that organised self-help was possible. There were hints of change. One success was in 1935 with the last challenge to Reconstruction legislation: the GROVEY V. TOWNSEND case. The same year the Supreme Court ruled against Alabama's use of all white juries. The SCOTTSBORO CASE – nine young black men accused of raping two white women in a freight train in Alabama – aroused much comment about fair trials and racial prejudice.

Black voters had traditionally supported the Republican Party as the party of emancipation. The New Deal programmes passed by a Democratic president and Congress changed that allegiance. While programmes might be affected by discrimination at a local level, it was not the intent of the administration. Roosevelt had stated, 'We are going to make a country in which no one is left out'. Therefore, black voters began to vote for the Democrat Party; this support was rewarded in the 1960s by the Texan Democrat president, Lyndon B. Johnson. Migration to the northern industrial cities was also beginning to alter the political balance, particularly in Chicago, Cleveland and Detroit. In the north about 88 per cent of the black population lived in cities, whereas in the South 68 per cent lived on the land in 1930.

3 Dust Bowl migrants

The lands of the central region of Oklahoma, Kansas, Arkansas, Texas and Missouri were unsuitable for intensive cultivation. By the early thirties the top soil was thin and easily blown away in oppressive dust storms. In desperation 80,000 farmers and their families left their arid farms and travelled, like many before them, to the west, particularly to California. They were not just farmers, but anyone connected to agriculture – retailers, salesmen, professionals with no one to teach and no one to bank for. Most went to the San Joaquin valley to find work, but there was little available on a regular basis and there was

TALKING POINT

A different kind of 'loser'?
One of the criticisms of Roosevelt is that his focus on domestic recovery allowed the totalitarian regimes of Germany, Italy and Japan to continue their aggression unchecked. The USA chose to take no active role in forcing change until it was too late for negotiation. Roosevelt's refusal to be involved in the World Economic Conference in London in July 1933 had set America's attitude, 'The sound internal economic system of a nation is a greater factor in its well-being than the price of currency in changing terms of the currency of other nations.' was his message to Congress. Do you think the following assessment by a modern historian is justified?
'The Depression had helped to reinforce an isolationism of the spirit, a kind of moral numbness, that checked American humanitarianism as tightly as political isolationism straitjacketed American diplomacy.' (D. Kennedy, *Freedom from Fear: The American People in Depression and War, 1929–45*, 1999, p.415)

competition with Hispanic migrants for the same unskilled harvest picking jobs. With little union support, the Okies, as they became known, had poor working and living conditions. It was through documentary writing and photographs, especially by Dorothea Lange (Source 7.2, page 108) and James Agee (Source 7.24, page 122), that their plight and helplessness was revealed. John Steinbeck's novel, *The Grapes of Wrath*, about the migrant Joad family, provided another vivid picture of typical suffering. Eventually over a third of the Okies, finding no better fortune in the west, returned to the eastern plains.

4 Mexican migrants

Mexican migrants working in the south and west as far as Texas and Colorado were unable to benefit from New Deal relief programmes if they were not US citizens. Resentment was directed at them for taking work and there were frequent calls for their deportation. Sometimes their active involvement in unions was another reason for repatriation.

5 Women

The harshness of the Depression forced many women into work when none was available for the men in their families. Usually this work was paid at a lower rate than that paid to men, and often in areas not covered by the NRA codes, such as laundry work. However, the traditional areas of women's work, including clerical and service industries, were among the quickest to recover from the Depression. The continuing expansion in the use of machinery meant that more unskilled workers, as opposed to craft workers or those with manual strength, were needed. In the Second World War women were to prove even more effectively how they could cope in previously male-dominated manufacturing areas, such as ship-building. Yet there was still the prevailing sense that women worked only for 'pin money' whereas men were the rightful breadwinners. Many organisations refused to let married women work, and the American Federation of Labour (AFL) also opposed this. Women like Eleanor Roosevelt and Frances Perkins drew attention to the discrepancies (see page 120). The administration itself did employ more women, even at a senior level, such as judges and ambassadors.

Who were the critics?

1 Ordinary people

The critics included ordinary people who felt their hard work was being undermined.

SOURCE 7.28 Minnie Hardin, a farmer, wrote to Eleanor Roosevelt, in 1936 (quoted in M. Johnson, *Reading the American Past*, 2nd edn, 2002, pp.150–52)

We have always had a shiftless, never-do-well people whose one and only aim in life is to live without work … We cannot help those who will not try to help themselves and if they do try, a square deal is all they need, and by the way that is all the country needs or has ever needed: a square deal for all and then, let each paddle their own canoe, or sink … several women have fainted while at work and at the same time we couldn't go up or down the road without stumbling over some of the reliefers, moping around carrying dirt from one side of the road to the other and back again, or else asleep … You people who have plenty of this world's goods and whose money comes easy, have no ideas of the heart-breaking toil and self-denial which is the lot of the working people who are trying to make an honest living, and then have to shoulder all these unjust burdens seems like the last straw … The crookedness, selfishness, greed and graft of the crooked politicians is making one gigantic racket of the New Deal, and it is making this a nation of dead-beats and beggars and if it continues the people who work will soon be nothing but slaves for the pampered poverty rats and I am afraid that these human parasites are going to become a menace to the country unless they are disenfranchised …

FOCUS ROUTE

Make notes on the following questions.

1   What were the main criticisms of the New Deal?
2   How valid were the criticisms, given the ulterior motives of some critics?

TALKING POINT

During the New Deal period many Americans wrote personal letters, like the one in Source 7.28, to the president and his wife. What might we learn from them about the writers and about their views of the president?

2 The American Liberty League

Formed in 1934 from disaffected Democrats, the American Liberty League also argued that the welfare payments were too generous and took away the American virtue of individualism and self-reliance. They joined others who felt that the essential American spirit of enterprise was being lost by federal regulation, including former President Hoover who believed that the government was interfering and controlling too many aspects of national life – the economy, banking, union membership, employers' rights.

SOURCE 7.29 A cartoon of July 1935, entitled *Gulliver's Travels*, showing Uncle Sam as Gulliver (from Jonathan Swift's novel, *Gulliver's Travels*) tied down, not by Lilliputians, but by the New Dealers and their new policies

3 The Supreme Court

Many critics, especially Republicans, felt that Roosevelt had over-extended the power of the executive. Americans had always been concerned, since the writing of their Constitution, that the 'over-mighty state' could destroy individualism. The Supreme Court with its nine judges appointed for life began to question the extent of power given to the executive (the president). By the end of 1936 it had ruled against seven out of nine New Deal cases, including the Agricultural Adjustment Administration and the National Recovery Administration. Having already denied states the right to set minimum wages, it now also denied the federal government this right.

4 Huey Long

Huey Long, Governor of Louisiana, one of the poorest states in the USA, felt there had been too little help for the poor. He created the Share Our Wealth Society, with its aims of: limiting personal fortunes; a minimum income no less than one-third of the average; regulation of working hours; an old age pension for those over 60; the storing (not the destruction) of agricultural surplus;

payment to war veterans and the disabled; equal opportunities in education and training for all children; and taxes on the highest earners to pay for these reforms. In 1935 when Long made these demands, unemployment was still around 17 million. His demagogic style was attractive to those feeling disadvantaged by the American distribution of wealth, and by mid-1935 his society had 7 million members.

5 Dr Francis Townsend

Dr Francis Townsend of California proposed the Old Age Revolving Plan, whereby the government would pay monthly pensions of $200 to all citizens over the age of 60, provided that they spent it in that month. The plan was financially impossible, but it drew attention to the problems of a group ignored by other New Deal programmes.

6 Historians

'Economically the New Deal had been opportunistic in the grand manner.' (J. M. Burns, *Roosevelt: The Lion and the Fox*, 1956, p.322)

More recent critics of the New Deal have argued that its successes were accidental. Despite its almost mythical status as the saviour of a depressed nation it was not a coherent plan. The historian David Kennedy asks if there was any unity of purpose given that the administration 'tinkered' with contradictions:

- with inflation and price controls
- with deficit spending and a balanced budget
- with farm acreage reduction and land reclamation
- with the promise of consumption and the intimidation of investment.

'That accusation has echoed repeatedly in assessments that stress the New Deal's mongrel intellectual pedigree, its improbably plural constituent base, its political pragmatism, its abundant promiscuity, inconsistencies, contradictions, inconstancies and failures.' (D. Kennedy, *Freedom from Fear: The American People in Depression and War, 1929–45*, 1999, pp.364–65)

Did the critics have an impact?

1 The popularity of the ideas of Long and Townsend could not be ignored, especially that of Long who was a potential presidential candidate in 1936. However, his assassination in September 1935 ended that threat to Roosevelt's easy re-election. Yet his Share Our Wealth Society's ideas, and those of Townsend, influenced Roosevelt's thinking in the second New Deal, as did the criticisms of liberals such as the respected Supreme Court Justice Louis Brandeis and the influential judge Felix Frankfurter who argued that Roosevelt was too cosy with big business. They said society needed reforms, and governments should recognise that, not just show concern for business security. The second New Deal legislation on Social Security, Rural Electrification, Farm Security Administration and the Fair Labor Standards Act were practical responses to this disquiet.

2 Black Americans put up increasing resistance to their unequal treatment. The NAACP, led by Charles H. Houston and Thurgood Marshall, challenged university entry discrimination. The Harlem Tenants' Association challenged rent increases and evictions based on racial prejudice. Retailers who refused to employ black staff were boycotted with the 'Don't Buy Where You Can't Work' slogan. Roosevelt hired black advisors. Mary McLeod Bethune was one of the most prominent. Not only a friend of Eleanor Roosevelt she was also the Director of the Division of Negro Affairs for the NYA. There was a growing sense that, although legal challenges were useful, more direct self-help action was needed, yet the idea lacked a strong leader to drive it forward.

3 The criticism about deficit financing led to Roosevelt cutting back government programmes in 1937 and the Federal Reserve tightened credit, so that borrowing money was more expensive. Within a year industrial

ACTIVITY

Write a short paragraph to demonstrate your understanding of David Kennedy's argument.

DISCUSS

Which of the criticisms of the New Deal, if any, do you have most sympathy with?

production had fallen by one-third and 4 million people had lost their jobs. By April 1938 Roosevelt had reacted by asking Congress for $3.75 billion for relief. It was clearly too early to aim for a balanced budget and the Depression continued for another two years, until rescued by the demands of the war machine.

4 Roosevelt's exasperated reaction to the rejection by the Supreme Court of several New Deal programmes was to attempt to increase the number of federal and Supreme Court judges. It was handled clumsily and vigorously challenged as 'court packing'. It reinforced the idea of a dictatorial president. In the end the plan proved unnecessary as one dissenting judge became a supporter of New Deal legislation and the retirement of others brought more sympathetic judges onto the bench.

■ **Learning trouble spot**

Whose perspective?
One of the difficulties in studying the USA is appreciating what a vast country it is. Decisions made in Washington DC could seem very distant to someone in the hills of Dakota or the deserts of Arizona. Understanding local differences and interests requires local research, and often that has either not been carried out, or not been widely published. A textbook like this one with its broad, overview perspective cannot give regional and local nuances and opinions. Yet they were there, and they were important to individuals and communities, especially in a nation with a traditional fear of 'over-mighty' central government.

 What were Roosevelt's strengths and weaknesses in pursuing the New Deal?

SOURCE 7.30 R. Hofstadter, *The American Political Tradition*, 1974

At the heart of the New Deal there was not a philosophy but a temperament.

SOURCE 7.31 J. M. Burns, *Roosevelt: The Lion and the Fox*, Vol. I, 1956, pp.403–04

Roosevelt, in a sense, was captive to himself as well as to his political environment. He was captive to his habit of mediating among pressures rather than reshaping them, of responding eclectically to all the people around him, of balancing warring groups and leaders against one another, of improvising with brilliance and gusto. Impatient of theory, insatiably curious about people and their ideas, sensitively attuned to the play of forces around him, he lacked that burning and almost fanatic conviction that great leadership demands. Roosevelt was less a great creative leader than a skilful manipulator and a brilliant interpreter ... when its solution demanded a union of intellectual comprehension and unified and continuing strategic action, Roosevelt saw his efforts turn to dust as in the case of court packing. He was always a superb tactician, and sometimes a courageous leader, but he failed to achieve that combination of tactical skill and strategic planning that represents the acme of political leadership.

SOURCE 7.32 D. Kennedy, *Freedom from Fear*, 1999, p.365

Unarguably Roosevelt sought to enlarge the national state as the principle instrument of the security and stability that he hoped to impart to American life ... Much of the security that the New Deal threaded into the fabric of American society was often stitched with a remarkably delicate hand, not simply imposed by the fist of an imperious state.

ACTIVITY

The New Deal has become a much researched topic especially since the Second World War and again in the 1980s.

1 Identify the common opinions in the descriptions of Roosevelt in Sources 7.30–7.35.
2 In which areas is he criticised?
3 How might the skills Roosevelt possessed, identified here, help in ending the Depression?
4 Which three aspects of his political skills are you particularly impressed by?

SOURCE 7.33 E. Foner, *The Story of American Freedom*, 2000, pp.203–04

Along with being a consummate politician, Roosevelt was a master of political rhetoric. The first president to employ the radio to bring his message directly into American homes, he was particularly adept at appealing to traditional values in support of new departures ... he transformed 'liberalism' from a shorthand for weak government and laissez-faire economics into belief in an activist, socially conscious state, an alternative both to socialism and to unregulated capitalism. He also reclaimed the word 'freedom' from conservatives and made it a rallying cry for the New Deal.

SOURCE 7.34 A. Badger, *The New Deal: Depression Years, 1933–40*, 1989, p.8

In Washington, Roosevelt ... could flatter and assuage the most surly and self-important congressional leader. But critics complained that he failed to use the full power of his charismatic authority. He compromised too much. He allowed himself to be the prisoner first of southern conservatives, then of isolationist public opinion. He sore tried the patience of congressional leaders by sudden and pre-emptory demands for legislation on which he had not consulted them ... He could be immensely considerate and loyal to close political associates. Yet he could be petty, vindictive, and cruel ... in the interests of whim or his own personal political advantage.

SOURCE 7.35 Harold Ickes, Secretary of the Interior, 1933–45 (in J. M. Burns, *Roosevelt: the Lion and the Fox*, Vol. I, 1956, p.374)

*You are a wonderful person but you are one of the most difficult men to work with that I have ever known' Ickes blurted out on one occasion.
'Because I get too hard at times?' Roosevelt asked.
'No, you are never too hard but you won't talk frankly even with people who are loyal to you and of whose loyalty you are fully convinced. You keep your cards close up against your belly ...'*

F **Review: Did the New Deal end the Depression?**

DISCUSS

1 Before you start working through this Review, go back to the Activity at the beginning of the Chapter Overview where you were asked to describe and assess the New Deal (page 108). Were your answers to questions 1–3 accurate? Discuss your answers with a partner or in a small group.

2 Make some instinctive (rather than carefully reasoned) judgements on the following points. (Discussion will be more useful than writing as you will have to justify your opinions to your possibly sceptical group!)

   a) What is your opinion about the New Deal?

   b) What do you think of Roosevelt as a president?

SOURCE 7.36 Poster advertising *Top Hat*, starring the most famous of dancing partners, Fred Astaire and Ginger Rogers, with music by the most popular composer of the thirties, Irving Berlin

■ 7E What the New Deal was not

✘ a coherent programme of relief and recovery
✘ an attempt to redistribute wealth
✘ an attempt to make the USA socialist or fascist
✘ a dictatorship
✘ a rigid adherence to maintaining a balanced budget
✘ a programme that was concerned about the depressions in the rest of the world and their political impact (though it was interested in economic effects)
✘ a dramatic and radical solution, but a conservative one, or a set of improvisations, some of which were contradictory
✘ the abandonment of capitalism or the rejection of enterprise and industrialisation. The USA did not become socialist or fascist. It was the reshuffling of cards, not a new game that was being played. Yet it did change America nonetheless.

■ 7F What were the realities behind the New Deal policies?

1 The era of economic growth, the norm since the mid-nineteenth century, had ended.
2 The private sector, left to itself could never generate or sustain sufficient employment and investment to sustain the modern economic needs of the USA.
3 Structural reform of the economy was needed and change was not just necessary, but essential.
4 The USA was self-sufficient and satisfied with economic isolationism (as it was in the 1930s with foreign policy isolationism).
5 '...Roosevelt's most important single idea – the idea that government had positive responsibility for the general welfare. Not that government itself must do everything, but that everything practicable must be done ... government must insure that something *is* done' (J. M. Burns, *Roosevelt: the Lion and the Fox,* Vol. I, 1956, p.476)

POPULAR CULTURE

Were there any bright moments amidst the gloom of the Depression? By 1940, with radios in 30 million homes, one daytime favourite was the soap opera, sponsored by soap manufacturers, with the following successful recipe, '12 minutes of dialogue, add predicament, villainy and female suffering in equal measures, throw in a dash of nobility, sprinkle with tears, season with organ music, cover with a rich announcer voice and serve five times a week'. Over 60 per cent of families went to the movies every week and, as drive-in cinemas were opened, that pleasure was combined with car ownership. It was the age of 'talkies', of the first Walt Disney cartoons such as *The Three Little Pigs* and those featuring Mickey Mouse, of the comedies of the Marx Brothers, gangster and horror films and the Busby Berkeley musicals with ridiculous stories and wonderful synchronised dancing. The most popular film was *Gone With the Wind,* the romantic Civil War epic of Rhett Butler and Scarlett O'Hara, and the flight from Atlanta as General Sherman's troops advanced. Spectator sports attracted thousands, as cars transported people for leisure, rather than in their search for work.

Did the New Deal extend or constrain freedom?

It has been argued that the New Deal was part of the humanistic movement that started with the Enlightenment in the eighteenth century: the belief that it was right to make people's lives on earth better. Roosevelt indicated his belief in this, speaking in June 1936:

'Governments can err, presidents do make mistakes, but the immortal Dante tells us that divine justice weighs the sins of the cold-blooded and sins of the warm-hearted in different scales. Better the occasional faults of a Government that lives in a spirit of charity than the constant omission of a Government frozen in the ice of its own indifference.'

Freedom can mean both 'being able to *do* something (such as change your job, get an education, vote without restrictions), or to be free *of* something, such as despair or poverty. The New Deal did not free those suffering from the unequal distribution of wealth, or those suffering racial prejudice. It did recognise an 'American standard of living'. In the 1930s this meant jobs, reasonable wages, employment rights and security for all. For the first time freedom was linked with economic security and equality, and not just the right to vote.

TALKING POINT

When politicians and leaders make mistakes, does the intent (cold-blooded or warm-hearted) behind their wrong-doing or mistakes make a difference to how you judge them?

SOURCE 7.37 'Oh the old gray mare, she ain't what she used to be', by C. K. Berryman, 26 December 1943. The weary New Deal donkey is allowed to rest as war preparations take priority

Was it all worthwhile?

The demands of war from 1941 overtook those of domestic reform (see Source 7.38), and finally solved the problem of unemployment. It seemed to prove dramatically that, as Keynes had argued, deficit financing was the only way to end a depression. War demanded total effort for success and there would have to be whole-hearted financial commitment.

SOURCE 7.38   Before and after the New Deal, 1929–41

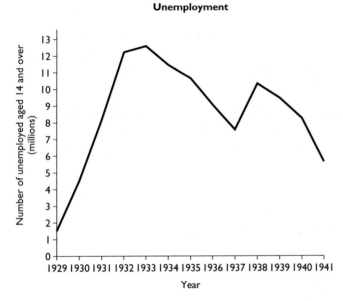

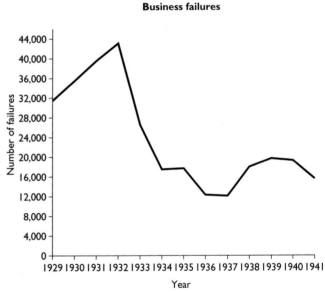

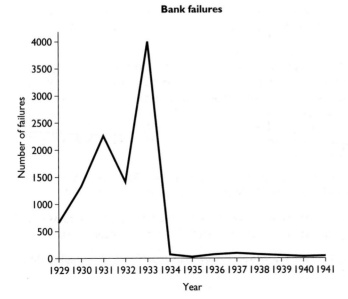

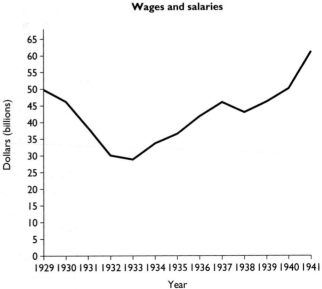

KEY POINTS FROM CHAPTER 7

America in the 1930s – did the New Deal end the Depression?

1 Franklin D. Roosevelt continued the expansion of presidential power started by Theodore Roosevelt and Woodrow Wilson, with centralised decision making in the White House.

2 The New Deal was inclusive and wide ranging in its provisions of direct relief for the needs of one-third of the population between 1933 and 1939.

3 Federal government would now intervene in the national economy if the private sector was not able to guarantee economic security.

4 The regulation of the stock markets and financial power became centred in Washington because of the start of the Federal Reserve System.

5 The New Deal continued the Progressive ideals of order and regularity for the good of the majority.

6 The New Deal laid the foundations for the post-war welfare state (although it was never as extensive as in Europe).

7 There was a recognition that poverty was a structural economic problem, not the fault of the individual. Poverty would not necessarily end with full employment.

8 The Democratic Party changed its popular base to include organised labour, black Americans, women, unemployed, second-generation immigrants, and the middle class who saw their property protected. It became a broad coalition of different group interests.

9 The New Deal promoted union membership at the same time as allowing the continuing development of large corporations.

10 There is continuing argument as to whether the New Deal was conservative or radical, but it was undoubtedly pragmatic and practical.

11 The New Deal programmes were proactive in meeting the immediate needs of 1933. They were reactive to problems identified during subsequent years.

12 Only the coming of world war ended the continuing problem of unemployment.

8

From neutrality to the bomb – was this America's 'good war'?

CHAPTER OVERVIEW

ACTIVITY

What do the images in Sources 8.1–8.3 tell you about:

a) the way the Second World War was fought

b) the impact of the war on ordinary Americans?

SOURCE 8.1 D-Day, 6 June 1944. American soldiers leave their landing craft to wade, under German fire, to the Normandy beach. The landing on the northern French coast was the beginning of the Allied march on Berlin and the end of the Nazi regime

SOURCE 8.2 The Japanese city of Hiroshima after the USA exploded the first atom bomb on 6 August 1945. No warning was given. Every brick building within a mile of the blast disappeared. An estimated 80,000 people died instantly, rising to 140,000 dead by the end of the year. Three days later a second bomb was dropped on Nagasaki, killing 36,000 people. Japan formally surrendered on 14 August

SOURCE 8.3 A poster by J. Howard Miller entitled *We Can Do It!*. Did all American women look like this? Rosie the Riveter became the symbol of war work and the role that women could play, especially working in traditionally male occupations. This poster was produced for the War Production Co-ordinating Committee in 1942 to encourage women to volunteer for war work

In 1939 the USA resisted any military involvement in the conflict in Europe. However, as Hitler's army overran continental Europe in 1940, there was a growing sense that the USA was vulnerable, especially if Britain was invaded. By mid-1941 there were German challenges to American shipping in the Atlantic. Was this war in all but name? The decision to enter the war was made for America by Japan, with its attack on America's Pacific fleet base at Pearl Harbor, Hawaii, in December 1941. The USA immediately declared war on Japan. As Japan had a defensive treaty with Germany, a declaration of war by Germany on the USA soon followed.

This chapter will look at how American neutrality was forced to an end by the pressure of events, at the American contribution to the Allies' victory in Europe and at whether this can be considered to be America's 'good war'. In abandoning neutrality, the USA had to mobilise its domestic resources as much as its military ones. It succeeded, achieving military victories on two fronts and with its land undamaged. The war also revitalised industry and brought beneficial technological change, increasing affluence and improvements in civil rights. Perhaps, above all, there was a sense of fighting a war for a just cause. Cumulatively these developments led many Americans to see the Second World War as a 'good war'. Were they right?

A Keeping neutral, 1939–41? (pp. 138–45)

B How significant was the American contribution to victory in Europe, 1941–45? (pp. 146–47)

C Did the bomb win the war in the Pacific? (pp. 148–52)

D How did the Home Front win the war? (pp. 153–58)

E Planning the peace (pp. 159–61)

F Review: Was this America's 'good war'? (pp. 161–65)

TALKING POINT

Can any war be 'good'? Can you suggest any examples of 'good wars'?

138

FROM NEUTRALITY TO THE BOMB – WAS THIS AMERICA'S 'GOOD WAR'?

FOCUS ROUTE

Make notes on the following questions using pages 138–45.

1 Why did the USA remain neutral in 1939?
2 What were the Neutrality Acts and why did they constrain the president?
3 In what ways was the USA practising 'biased neutrality'?
4 Who benefited from this form of neutrality and in what ways?
5 How did Roosevelt prepare the USA for war?

A   Keeping neutral, 1939–41?

How did the USA respond to fascist aggression?

SOURCE 8.4 *Increasing Pressure*, a cartoon by David Low, 1938, showing the gradual and insistent build up of Nazi control over nations in Europe

FOCUS ROUTE

1 Whilst you work through Section A, mark on your own version of the following timeline the events which moved the USA from neutrality to war.

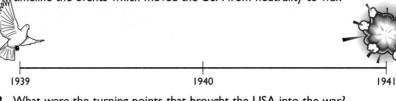

1939   1940   1941

2 What were the turning points that brought the USA into the war?

During the early- and mid-thirties the USA behaved like most other Western democracies – they hoped that the danger of war would either eventually dissipate of its own accord or would be resolved if dictators' demands were appeased. The sense of 'never again' that grew after the First World War was confirmed when the Nye Committee of 1934 (which enquired into the role of bankers and munitions manufacturers in 1917–18) found evidence that the nation had been pushed towards war by these interests. The Depression also made Americans look inward rather than face the complexities of European politics. The Neutrality Acts (see page 81) were the result. There was no sense in the USA of a desire or a need for war.

Roosevelt, always pragmatic, wanted to keep more flexibility of action, but he recognised the strength of the Americans' desire to keep out of involvement. He had sufficient information to know of Hitler's treatment of German Jews and of Poles being forced into slave labour. Yet his concern, as illustrated by his New Deal programmes, was to keep the nation together. Critics argue that he underestimated public support for opposing Germany and that he was too

SOURCE 8.5 'Come on in ... I used to know your daddy', published in *New York Daily News*, 1936

ACTIVITY

Study the cartoon in Source 8.5.

1 Who are the two characters and what do they represent?
2 Who is 'your daddy'?
3 What would Americans in the 1930s understand about this cartoon?
4 What alternative title could it be given?

TALKING POINT

Appeasement has long been reviled as a cowardly policy against dictatorships. Why do you think that is so, given the popularity of the policy in the 1930s? Were there any justifications for appeasement in the 1930s?

cautious, but it can also be argued that the nation was militarily, economically and emotionally unprepared for war. Gallup polls in 1937 told him so, as did the fact that the Ludlow Amendment was nearly passed. This would have made a declaration of war only possible with the consent of a public referendum, unless America was attacked on its own territory. Such an amendment would have removed from the president and Congress any freedom of manoeuvre or ability to react speedily to events.

The German invasion of Poland in September 1939 finally ended Roosevelt's impartiality as he recognised the danger of German domination. In October 1939 Congress passed the Declaration of Panama. It warned warring nations to stay away from the coast of North and South America. Within the USA as a whole there was less concern and the 'Phoney War' of the winter of 1939 seemed to indicate that there was no real threat. However, the Battle of Britain between the German Luftwaffe and the RAF in the summer of 1940 changed attitudes.

■ 8A Effects of the Battle of Britain

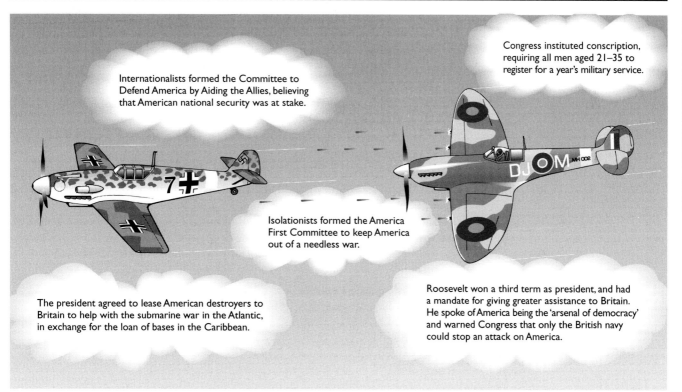

Internationalists formed the Committee to Defend America by Aiding the Allies, believing that American national security was at stake.

Congress instituted conscription, requiring all men aged 21–35 to register for a year's military service.

Isolationists formed the America First Committee to keep America out of a needless war.

The president agreed to lease American destroyers to Britain to help with the submarine war in the Atlantic, in exchange for the loan of bases in the Caribbean.

Roosevelt won a third term as president, and had a mandate for giving greater assistance to Britain. He spoke of America being the 'arsenal of democracy' and warned Congress that only the British navy could stop an attack on America.

SOURCE 8.6 Roosevelt's message to Congress, 6 January 1941

We look forward to a world founded upon four essential human freedoms. The first is freedom of speech and expression – everywhere in the world. The second is freedom of every person to worship God in his own way – everywhere in the world. The third is freedom from want ... everywhere in the world. The fourth is freedom from fear ... anywhere in the world.

WAR BONDS

The war eventually cost $304 billion, of which 45 per cent was paid through current taxation. Of the rest, $50 billion came from the sale of war bonds. This was a voluntary scheme, whereby individuals bought small denomination bonds, with the revenue going to the Treasury, which promised that the money would be repaid.

The president's speech on 6 January 1941 (see Source 8.6) clearly alerted Americans to the possibility of war and the reasons for which it would be fought. The 'four freedoms' were traditional American values, which contrasted sharply with fascism. Any new war would be fought for good moral reasons, not for conquest and glory. The illustrator Norman Rockwell, working for the popular *Saturday Evening Post,* produced four paintings about these freedoms (Source 8.7). They portrayed ordinary Americans, doing ordinary things, in their homes and communities. Their popularity led the government to reproduce them as posters and advertisements for War Bonds – the major way in which everyone could be involved in paying for the war.

FROM NEUTRALITY TO THE BOMB – WAS THIS AMERICA'S 'GOOD WAR'?

140

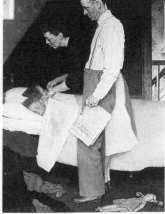

SOURCE 8.7 *The Four Freedoms*, by Norman Rockwell, 1943 (from left to right: freedom of speech; freedom of worship; freedom from want; freedom from fear)

ACTIVITY

1 Describe one of the posters in Source 8.7 in detail.
2 What emotions might it stimulate?
3 Who do you think it was intended to influence?

From biased neutrality to war – the events of 1941

On 11 March 1941 Congress agreed to the Lend-Lease Bill. This allowed the president, by executive order, to 'lend, lease, or otherwise dispose of' arms and supplies to any country whose defence was vital to the USA. Congress allocated $7 billion. Isolationists objected, claiming that, just like the Agricultural Adjustment Administration's policy of ploughing up crops, this policy would 'plow under every fourth American boy'.

Although the RAF had been superior in the Battle of Britain, America was still concerned at the threat created by the possibility of a German invasion of Britain. Secret military consultations had begun between the USA and Britain. Continuing throughout the war, they were a source of stability and co-operation between these two allies. America agreed to send patrols with convoys across the Atlantic. Roosevelt had also changed the definition of the Western Hemisphere, i.e. the area of the Atlantic that the USA would protect. It now included Greenland and Iceland, and further threatened German shipping and navy. Such changes increased the risk of war. This risk was accelerated by an invasion, a meeting and an attack.

1 The invasion

Germany invaded the USSR on 22 June 1941. By the winter they were close to Moscow, had surrounded Leningrad and were heading towards Stalingrad. Churchill and Roosevelt recognised the danger. If Hitler neutralised the threat from the Soviet Union on his eastern front, then expansion toward the Atlantic would follow. Both Britain and America offered aid to the USSR.

2 The meeting

After Roosevelt and Churchill's meeting, the Atlantic Charter, a joint Anglo-American communiqué, setting out a vision of a post-war world, was published on 14 August. See Chart 8B.

SOURCE 8.8 Franklin D. Roosevelt and Winston Churchill, the British Prime Minister, meet for the first time off the Canadian coast in August 1941

■ 8B The Atlantic Charter

○		○
○		○
○	Uphold the 'four freedoms'.	○
○	Ban aggression and require the disarmament of aggressor nations.	○
○	Give self-determination to liberated nations.	○
○	Advocate the formation of a new international organisation (to be the United Nations).	○
○	Pledge the freedom of the seas.	○
○		○

Why was the Atlantic Charter important?

- It was the beginning of the 'special relationship' between the USA and Britain.
- It was the beginning of a personal and political friendship between the two leaders that lasted throughout the war. They are reputed to have conversed every day.
- It set out plans for a new world order based on democratic principles.
- It recognised Stalin as a partner and promised to continue sending supplies to the USSR. The Americans provided 13 million pairs of shoes for the Soviet army.
- Roosevelt thought that the American public would still not support war, but achieving the Charter aims would be impossible without involvement in warfare. Churchill told his War Cabinet on his return, 'The president has said that he would wage war, but not declare it', and that he would look for an 'incident' which would justify formal hostilities. It was expected that the 'incident' would be in the Atlantic. Instead it came in the Pacific, four months later.
- The USA was already expressing concerns about the continuation of imperialism by Britain, France and the Netherlands once the war was over.

142

FROM NEUTRALITY TO THE BOMB – WAS THIS AMERICA'S 'GOOD WAR'?

ACTIVITY

President Roosevelt has been described as a 'silent accomplice' of Hitler and, in contrast, as a soldier of democracy.

1 What evidence is there to support these two descriptions of Roosevelt before December 1941?
2 Which description do you think is the more accurate?

FOCUS ROUTE

Make notes on the following questions.

1 Why did Japan behave aggressively towards its neighbours?
2 What internal forces dictated Japanese policy?
3 What actions by the USA antagonised Japan?
4 What reactions did it expect, and what actually happened as a result of its aggression?

SOURCE 8.10 Roosevelt addresses Congress, 8 December 1941

Always will we remember the character of the onslaught against us. No matter how long it may take us to overcome this premeditated invasion, the American people in their righteous mind will win through to absolute victory. I believe I interpret the will of Congress and of the people when I assert that we will not only defend ourselves to the uttermost, but will make very certain that this form of treachery shall never endanger us again ... With confidence in our armed forces – with the unbounded determination of our people – we will gain the inevitable triumph, so help us God. I ask that the Congress declare that since the unprovoked and dastardly attack by Japan on Sunday December 7, a state of war has existed between the United States and the Japanese Empire.

3 The attack

In September 1941 America claimed that one of its ships, the *Greer*, supposedly carrying only mail and passengers, had been attacked. In fact the *Greer* had been in deliberate pursuit of a German submarine (U-boat). The incident allowed Roosevelt to order the navy to sink any U-boat on sight, and to provide escorts for merchant shipping. Incidents continued throughout October, so that by November there was a state of undeclared war, though the USA claimed to be acting only in a defensive capacity. This remained the situation until early December.

How did Japan surprise the USA?

SOURCE 8.9 The battleship *Arizona* blazing in Pearl Harbor, 7 December 1941

A Japanese fleet sailed for Hawaii on 2 December 1941. On Sunday, 7 December just before 8.00 a.m., without any warning, its planes began a two-hour air attack on the USA's main Pacific base at Pearl Harbor. Japan hoped that in that time it would be able to take unassailable control of the western Pacific and create the economic superiority it wanted.

The plan nearly worked. The attack sank and disabled nineteen ships, destroyed 150 planes at nearby Hickham Field airbase and killed 2400 Americans, most of them sailors. The same day the Japanese attacked the Philippines, Guam, Midway Island, Hong Kong and the Malay Peninsula. However:

a) the most important ships, the aircraft carriers, were at sea on a training exercise and could not be located by the planes
b) the planes did not attack the onshore factories and oil tanks that supplied the fleet, and were essential for its maintenance
c) the Japanese fatally underestimated the reaction of America. The unprovoked attack 'had silenced America's debate on neutrality, and a suddenly unified and vengeful nation prepared for the struggle.' (G. Tindall and D. Shi, *America: A Narrative History*, 5th edn, 1999, p.318)

The next day Roosevelt addressed Congress about 'a date which will live in infamy'. He noted that the two governments had been in negotiation as the fleet was sailing, even up to one hour before the attack started.

Did the USA provoke war with Japan?

ACTIVITY

Using a map of the western Pacific, note the geopolitical strengths of Japan, China and the USSR in that region. Think about ports, access to the sea, neighbours, resources, population.

SOURCE 8.11 The diplomat John Paton Davies describing the USA/Japan/China triangle (quoted in W. LaFeber, *The American Age: US Foreign Policy at Home and Abroad*, 2nd edn, 1994, p.405)

Japan was the actor, China the acted upon. And the US was the self-appointed referee who judged by subjective rules and called fouls without penalties, until just before the end of the contest. This provoked the actor into a suicidal attempt to kill the referee.

■ 8C Steps to protecting Japanese interests

Japan was a small group of four islands, which saw itself as over-populated and desperately short of raw materials, such as oil, coal and rubber, for industrial production. These were the steps Japan took to strengthen its national power.

STEP 1, 1932

In 1932 Japan took control of Manchuria with its rich resources.

STEP 2, 1937

Extended its control into China. In 1937 the Sino-Japanese war started. Largely ignored by the rest of the world, and unchallenged by the League of Nations, the conflict between Japan and China remained a regional affair. By 1941 Japan controlled the coast and nearly half the population of China, but the Chinese refused to surrender. Jiang Jieshi (Chang Kai-Shek) of the Nationalists and Mao Zedung (Mao Tse-Tung) of the Communists allied together to defend their country. America supplied aid to them to protect its own trading interests.

STEP 3, 1940

Created the Greater Asia Co-Prosperity Sphere in the Pacific – a copy of the American model of hegemony (leadership of a group of states by one state) in Latin America. This directly challenged American interests and ignored the demands for independence being made by countries controlled by European nations – French Indo-China, Dutch East Indies and the British Malay Peninsula.

STEP 4, 1940–41

Protected its borders with the Tripartite Pact with Germany and Italy in 1940. Each would declare war on any state that attacked one of the others. Japan also agreed a non-aggression pact with the USSR in April 1941. German successes in Europe in 1940 gave Japan new opportunities. France and the Netherlands were conquered and Britain distracted, thus European imperial possessions, with their rich natural resources, were exposed. Together with the American protectorate of the Philippines, they became a target for Japan's expansion. In July 1941, Japan took over French Indo-China.

144

FROM NEUTRALITY TO THE BOMB – WAS THIS AMERICA'S 'GOOD WAR'?

ACTIVITY

1 What qualities did Grew (Source 8.12) recognise in the Japanese that were important to understanding their attitude?

2 How would these attitudes affect their behaviour towards the USA?

3 What risks did the USA run if it ignored the Japanese character?

4 How reliable, or not, do you think Grew's opinion was? (Consider his diplomatic position, his probable expertise and how that might influence his thinking, and how easy it might be for an American to understand the Japanese character.)

SOURCE 8.12 The US ambassador to Japan, Joseph Grew, offering his assessment of Japan, its character and its likely reactions to threats or sanctions aimed at curtailing aggression, in 1939

Statisticians have proved to their own satisfaction ... that Japan can be defeated by economic pressure from without. But the statisticians generally fail to include the psychological factors in their estimates. Japan is a nation of hardy warriors still inculcated with the samurai do-or-die spirit which has by tradition and inheritance become ingrained in the race ... To await the hoped-for discrediting in Japan of the Japanese army and Japanese military system is to await the millennium. The Japanese army is no protuberance like the tail of a dog which may be cut off to prevent the tail from wagging the dog: it is inextricably bound up with the fabric of the entire nation ...

A treatyless situation plus an embargo would exasperate the Japanese to a point where anything could happen, even serious incidents which could inflame the American people beyond endurance and which might call for war. The Japanese are so constituted and are now in such a mood and temper that sanctions, far from intimidating, would almost certainly bring retaliation, which, in turn, would lead to counter-retaliation. Japan would not stop to weigh ultimate consequences ... I think that our dignity and our power in themselves counsel moderation, forbearance and the use of every reasonable means of conciliation without the sacrifice of principle ... In our own interests, particularly our commercial and cultural interests, we should approach this problem from a realistic and constructive standpoint.

American interests

During the 1930s trade and economic issues dictated America's policy toward Japan. After the invasion of Manchuria in 1932 there was a growing awareness of the aggressive and nationalist ambitions of Japan in the Pacific. However, as in Europe, the USA adopted an attitude of neutrality, and even appeasement, although this made it harder to avoid war as Japan's aggression increased. The economic sanctions the USA applied were not sufficient to deter further aggression.

While Roosevelt concentrated on directing policy and strategy in Europe, relations with Japan were left to the Secretary of State Cordell Hull, working with new Japanese ambassador, Kichisaburo Namura. By 1941 Hull had two choices:

1 to support China more completely against Japan, which would result in military intervention

2 to impose economic sanctions on Japan which bought 80 per cent of its oil from American suppliers.

■ 8D The US reaction to the seizure of French Indo-China

The stick
Sanctions – starting with less important goods in 1940 and then by September 1941 barring access to American petroleum and scrap iron, freezing Japanese assets in American banks, and putting an embargo on trade.

The carrot
At the same time there was the promise of better relations if agreement could be reached over China; America wanted to continue an open-door trading policy.

145

FROM NEUTRALITY TO THE BOMB – WAS THIS AMERICA'S 'GOOD WAR'?

Did Roosevelt deliberately sacrifice Pearl Harbor?

The stunning surprise of the attack has raised questions about how it was possible. Right-wing historians have accused Roosevelt of deliberately withholding information about the Japanese attack from the commander at Pearl Harbor, knowing that the shock of the attack would justify war. Others disagree, suggesting that, although there is evidence of the mishandling of information, there was no deliberate withholding of crucial warnings on 7 December. There is little evidence that Roosevelt would have deliberately put the Pacific fleet at such a risk. He knew by November that war was inevitable, but delay was favoured more than incitement.

Did the stick work?

Sanctions would have left Japan with only two years' supply of oil reserves. The Prime Minister, Prince Fumimaro Konoye, and the Emperor tried to reach some settlement with the USA, but failed. This led to the toppling of Japan's moderate government by the military faction. Konoye was replaced as prime minister by the War Minister Hideki Tojo. Now war was almost inevitable unless there were major American concessions.

Did the carrot work?

Both sides refused to make concessions and, whilst the talking continued, war preparations accelerated in Japan. The Japanese military assumed that the USA did not want a war, but dared not risk relying on this assumption knowing that the American-ruled Philippines acted as a barrier between Japan and Indo-China. Their only hope of defeating the USA, or of it agreeing to a ceasefire, was to have quick, overwhelming successes in the Pacific, before the USA could get its war production working.

Did the US government know of Japan's plans?

American officials knew that a war was imminent. Unknown to the Japanese, they were able to intercept and read their diplomatic Purple Codes and knew in December 1941 that an attack was planned. It was assumed that the Philippines were the likely target. No one expected the first attack to be 5000 miles from Japan or that the Pacific fleet in Pearl Harbor would be the target.

Why was the USA at war on two fronts in December 1941?

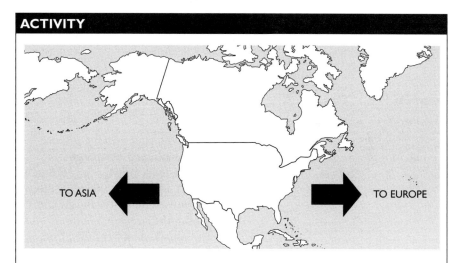

TO ASIA

TO EUROPE

1 Where on this map would you place the following reasons, a–i, explaining why the USA was fighting on two fronts? Some reasons may apply to fighting both enemies.
   a) The surprise Japanese attack on Pearl Harbor gave the USA no choice but to declare war.
   b) The Tripartite Pact meant that Germany and Italy would aid Japan.
   c) The situation in Europe was worsening, especially as submarine warfare in the Atlantic was increasing.
   d) Britain was requesting more aid.
   e) American public opinion was more prepared for war in order to restore democracy and freedom.
   f) Roosevelt's beliefs about fighting fascism (the 'four freedoms') were influential.
   g) Pearl Harbor not only angered Americans, but also roused latent racist feelings toward Japan.
   h) Internationalism was stronger in Congress than isolationism.
   i) The USA's determination to force Japan to withdraw from China would never be acceptable to the Japanese, and China was too weak against the Japanese army.
2 Are there any others you would add?

How much difference would fighting on two fronts make to the USA? What would be required of its army, navy and air force? What would be required of its civilians? How do you think Americans might have responded to this crisis?

Did the reasons for the USA going to war in 1941 make the Second World War a 'good war'? List the arguments for and against.

FOCUS ROUTE

1 List the contributions made by the USA to victory in Europe.
2 How would you describe the significance of the USA's contribution:
   a) essential
   b) valuable
   c) marginal
   d) your own answer?
   Justify your answer.

B How significant was the American contribution to victory in Europe, 1941–45?

DISCUSS

What criteria could you use to assess the significance of America's contribution to the war effort?

Why were the Allies victorious?

a) The diplomatic strategy

The alliance between the USA, USSR and Britain was remarkable given the strong and self-willed leaders of each nation. Meetings between the Allied leaders dictated the course of the war, particularly discussion of the opening of a second front in Europe to relieve the German attack on the USSR.

■ 8E The Allied Conferences

Date	Place	Those involved	Outcomes
August 1941	Newfoundland	Roosevelt, Churchill	Britain requesting aid, Atlantic Charter agreed.
January 1942	Washington DC	Roosevelt, Molotov the Soviet Foreign Minister	Offer of a second front in Europe. Powers to have regional superiority.
January 1943	Casablanca	Roosevelt, Churchill	Postpone cross-Channel invasion. Planned invasion of Sicily. Allies would demand unconditional surrender of Axis powers.
November 1943	Tehran	Roosevelt, Churchill, Stalin	Planned invasion of France. Stalin to join war against Japan when Germany was defeated. Agreement to create international organisation for peace after the war.
September 1944	Quebec	Roosevelt, Churchill	Post-war Germany to be divided or de-industrialised.
October 1944	Moscow	Stalin, Churchill	Areas of Allied influence after the war.

b) The military strategy

America's entry into the war brought massive numbers of American weapons, transport, aeroplanes and ships. However, it still took three years before the Allied powers took over Berlin and VE Day could be celebrated across Europe on 8 May 1945.

The Allied victory resulted from:

1 Russia's three great obstacles to any invader:

   • the courage and determination of the Soviet people, with their belief in their motherland and their willingness to use a 'scorched earth' policy in order to win
   • the vastness of the country, which made supplying the invading German army difficult
   • the Soviet winter, as the siege of Leningrad (St Petersburg) and defence of Stalingrad (Volgograd) show.

2 Stalin's ruthlessness and determination for victory for the USSR.

3 The Allied strategy to defeat Germany in North Africa and then open a second front via Sicily and Italy. These battles against a weaker German army gave the USA more time to gear up its industrial production and to train its soldiers.

4 American industrial production. The demands of being the 'arsenal of democracy' meant that industrial production rose by 90 per cent and agricultural production by twenty per cent. By 1945 the USA had produced more than twice the war supplies of Germany, Italy and Japan combined.

5 The advantages of cracking the Enigma Code. Enigma was a cipher machine

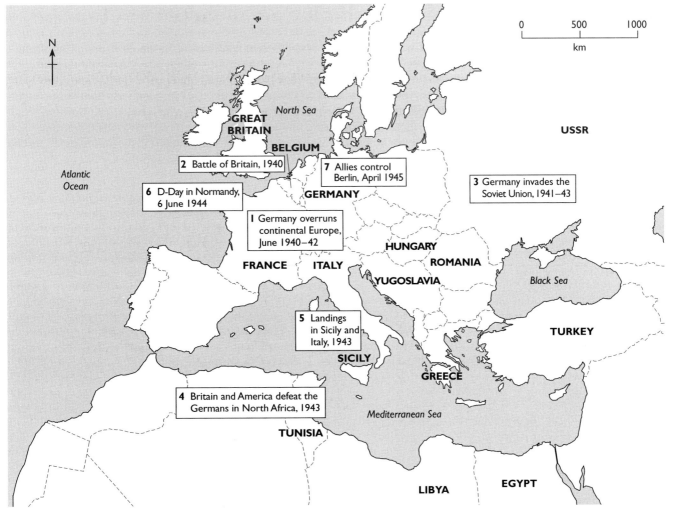

Map of Europe showing:

- **GREAT BRITAIN**
- **2** Battle of Britain, 1940
- **7** Allies control Berlin, April 1945
- **3** Germany invades the Soviet Union, 1941–43
- **6** D-Day in Normandy, 6 June 1944
- **1** Germany overruns continental Europe, June 1940–42
- **5** Landings in Sicily and Italy, 1943
- **4** Britain and America defeat the Germans in North Africa, 1943
- *North Sea*, **BELGIUM**, **GERMANY**, **USSR**, **HUNGARY**, **ROMANIA**, **FRANCE**, **ITALY**, **YUGOSLAVIA**, *Black Sea*, **TURKEY**, **SICILY**, **GREECE**, *Mediterranean Sea*, **TUNISIA**, **LIBYA**, **EGYPT**, *Atlantic Ocean*

Scale: 0 – 500 – 1000 km

that looked like a typewriter. It was used by the German forces to encode their messages, by a method they thought was unbreakable. It was – until 1940. The staff of Bletchley Park, near Milton Keynes, broke the code in Operation Ultra. The knowledge gained gave the Allies an awesome advantage over German plans, troop and supply movements.

6 Operation Overlord was the invasion of north-west Europe on what became known as D-Day – 6 June 1944. This meant that Hitler's troops were stretched across Europe from the USSR to the Channel. If the invasion had failed, it would have taken another year to prepare a second attempt. In that time more German troops could have been sent to the Soviet Union, and Germany's new V-1 and V-2 missiles could have been further developed for attacks against Britain. The American Dwight D. Eisenhower was Supreme Allied Commander of Overlord. On D-Day an Allied army of 156,000 men mainly from the USA (73,000 troops), Britain and Canada, with over 5000 ships, 50,000 vehicles and air force support landed on the five assault beaches in Normandy – Utah, Omaha, Gold, Juno and Sword. The landings, onto mined beaches and under German machine gun fire, resulted in an estimated 10,000 Allied casualties (2500 dead and the others wounded or missing) on the day. Of these 2000 casualties fell during the American landing on Omaha beach. This initial assault was followed by weeks of hard fighting by the Allied armies across the French countryside, before the liberation of Paris by the Americans on 25 August. The war continued until May 1945, with fierce German resistance in the Ardennes region of Belgium in December, but it was clear that the Allies were going to win. As Soviet troops took over Berlin in April 1945 Hitler committed suicide in his bunker.

ACTIVITY

'In terms of the US contribution to the Allied victory, the Second World War can be seen as America's "good war".' What evidence is there for and against this statement?

148

FROM NEUTRALITY TO THE BOMB – WAS THIS AMERICA'S 'GOOD WAR'?

FOCUS ROUTE

As you work through Section C, make notes to answer the following questions:

1 Identify the military demands of fighting against Japan.
2 How did racism affect the conduct of the war?
3 What advantages did the USA have for gaining victory?

C Did the bomb win the war in the Pacific?

The war in the Pacific was different from that in Europe because of the strong racial revulsion felt by each side toward the other. The Japanese regarded themselves as both a genetically and morally pure race: the Yamoto. They believed and practised creeds of physical purity and high spiritual values and were trained to believe in the code of Bushido, which stated that bravery, self-sacrifice and death were honourable, whilst surrender was dishonourable. To them the Americans were degenerate, greedy, materialistic and individualistic. They portrayed them with horns, fangs and claws, and Roosevelt as a blue-faced demon.

SOURCE 8.13   A poster produced by the War Production Board 1942–43, with the slogan 'Remember Pearl Harbor ... work – fight – sacrifice.'

SOURCE 8.14   Peggy Terry, from rural Kentucky, quoted in S. Terkel, *The Good War*, 1984, pp.110–11

We were very patriotic and understood that the Nazis were someone who would have to be stopped ... With the Japanese ... we were just ready to wipe them out. They sure as heck didn't look like us. They were yellow little creatures that smiled when they bombed our boys ... In all the movies that we saw, the Germans were always tall and handsome. There'd be one meanie, a little short dumpy bad Nazi. But the main characters were good-lookin' and they looked like us. The Japanese were all evil ...

To the Americans the Japanese were inferior, sub-human and irrational. They were portrayed as apes, monkeys, buck-toothed and of small-stature. Descriptions of them were usually prefaced with the word 'yellow' and their brutality was a consistent theme in US propaganda. The Japanese application of Bushido to the treatment of prisoners won them a reputation for cruelty and inhumanity that too easily matched the racist stereotypes. They ignored the Geneva Convention on the treatment of prisoners and the Bataan March, after the capture of the Philippines in 1942, became notorious. Forced to march over 104 kilometres, more than 10,000 American and Filipino prisoners died on the route from ill-treatment and starvation. To the USA it became the symbol of Japanese brutality toward prisoners of war and local people.

TALKING POINT

Is it justifiable to distort the characteristics of another nation or people as part of wartime propaganda?

■ 8G War in the Pacific

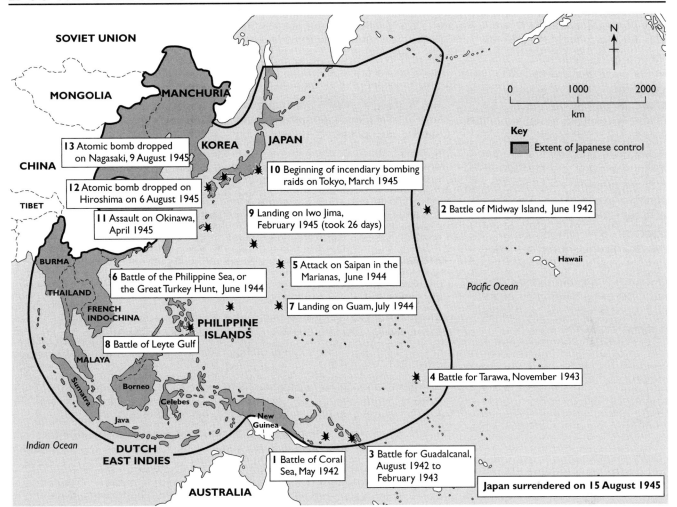

13 Atomic bomb dropped on Nagasaki, 9 August 1945

12 Atomic bomb dropped on Hiroshima on 6 August 1945

11 Assault on Okinawa, April 1945

10 Beginning of incendiary bombing raids on Tokyo, March 1945

9 Landing on Iwo Jima, February 1945 (took 26 days)

2 Battle of Midway Island, June 1942

6 Battle of the Philippine Sea, or the Great Turkey Hunt, June 1944

5 Attack on Saipan in the Marianas, June 1944

7 Landing on Guam, July 1944

8 Battle of Leyte Gulf

4 Battle for Tarawa, November 1943

1 Battle of Coral Sea, May 1942

3 Battle for Guadalcanal, August 1942 to February 1943

Japan surrendered on 15 August 1945

Key
■ Extent of Japanese control

SOVIET UNION, MONGOLIA, MANCHURIA, CHINA, TIBET, KOREA, JAPAN, BURMA, THAILAND, FRENCH INDO-CHINA, PHILIPPINE ISLANDS, MALAYA, Sumatra, Borneo, Celebes, Java, New Guinea, DUTCH EAST INDIES, AUSTRALIA, Hawaii, Pacific Ocean, Indian Ocean

0   1000   2000
km

SOURCE 8.15 Although not publicised at the time, this was a war of great brutality on both sides. The first picture of a dead American soldier was not published until 1943. The Japanese refusal to surrender meant that they would fight to their death, and kill as many of the enemy as possible. The favoured American weapon for island fighting was the flamethrower, shown here. This was used to destroy vegetation where the enemy might be hiding and to set fire to, and thus block, cave entrances. Fighting on the Pacific islands meant temperatures of 100°F and 100 per cent humidity – you would sweat as you stood still even without your weaponry and uniform. You would be unsure when you would have the next drink of water – dehydration and heat exhaustion killed more soldiers than bullets. There were endemic diseases – malaria, typhus and dengue fever

150

FROM NEUTRALITY TO THE BOMB – WAS THIS AMERICA'S 'GOOD WAR'?

SOURCE 8.16   A letter from John Conroy from the naval hospital in San Francisco, 24 December 1942, to his parents, quoted in M. Johnson, *Reading the American Past*, Vol. II, 2nd edn, 2002, p.165

…You keep asking so I'll tell you. I have been shell-shocked and bomb-shocked … I've been living the life of a savage … So many of my platoon were wiped out … it's hard to sleep without seeing them die all over again. Our living conditions on Guadalcanal had been so bad – little food or hope – fighting and dying every day – four hours sleep out of 72 – the medicos here optimistically say I'll pay for it for the rest of my life. My bayonet and shrapnel cuts are all healed up, however … none of us will be completely cured for years … I can't stand to walk much. The sudden beat of a drum or any sharp resonant noise has a nerve-ripping effect on us. Ah, well, let's not think, but just be happy that we'll be together soon.

SOURCE 8.17   From Allen Spach, somewhere in the Pacific, to his father in February 1943. He was part of an island landing which was attacked by Japanese planes and the navy

My health is as well as can be expected as most of us boys in the original outfit that left the States together about [CENSORED] of us are still here. The others are replacements. The missing have either been killed, wounded or from other various sources, mainly malaria fever … Left to do or die we fought hard with one purpose in mind to do, kill every slant-eyed bastard within range of rifle fire or the bayonet, which was the only thing left to stop their charge. We were on the front line for 110 days before we could drop back for a shave, wash up … We have had to face artillery, both naval and field, mortar bombings, sometimes three or four times a day, also at night, flamethrowers, hand grenades, tanks, booby traps, land mines, everything I guess except gas. The most common headache caused by machine gun fire, snipers, rifle fire, and facing sabres, bayonet fighting, the last most feared of all … The average age of the boys was 21 … God bless the whole world and I'm looking forward to the days when Italy and Germany are licked so that the whole might of the Allied nations can be thrown in to crush Japan and the swines that are her sons, fighting to rule the white race.

SOURCE 8.18   Beginning of the cockpit manual read by kamikaze pilots

Transcend life and death. When you eliminate all thoughts about life and death, you will be able to totally disregard your earthly life. This will enable you to concentrate your attention on eradicating the enemy with unwavering determination, meanwhile reinforcing your excellence in flight skills.

And at the moment of attack:

Remember when diving into the enemy to shout at the top of your lungs: 'Hissatsu' (Sink without fail). At that moment, all the cherry blossoms at the Yasukini shrine in Tokyo will smile brightly at you … At the very moment of impact: do your best. Every deity and the spirits of your dead comrades are watching you intently. Just before the collision it is essential that you do not shut your eyes for a moment so as not to miss the target. Many have crashed into the target with wide-open eyes. They will tell you what fun they had … You can clearly see the muzzles of the enemy's guns. You feel that you are suddenly floating in the air. At that moment, you see your mother's face. She is not smiling or crying … You view all that you experienced in your twenty-odd years of life in rapid succession … only delightful memories come back to you … Then you are no more.

ACTIVITY

Use Sources 8.15–8.18 to make notes on the following questions:

1 What were the problems of fighting in the Pacific war?
2 What did Americans think of their enemy?
3 Why might the USA think that Japan would never surrender?
4 What do you think the parents of US soldiers, and anyone who read their letters, would feel about:
   a) the value of the war
   b) the Japanese?
5 How might the war have changed soldiers' hopes for the future?

KAMIKAZE ATTACKS

Of all attacks these were the most feared by American sailors. As the Americans captured more islands their supply fleets grew larger. Not only did they need food and armaments, but also ships with the equipment for building air fields, hospitals, bridges and ports. It was estimated that every fighting soldier needed nineteen more to support him. Japanese kamikaze pilots would deliberately crash their planes into these ships. During the capture of Okinawa in April 1945, supply ships faced kamikaze attacks by up to 300 planes. Although many were shot down, they damaged over 350 ships and killed nearly 5000 sailors. Ironically, they also damaged the Japanese air force. Every attack meant one less pilot to fight, one less pilot to train others, one less pilot to attack more effective targets.

DISCUSS

From 1941 to 1945 there was also a large British army fighting Japanese forces in India and Burma. Their war ended on VJ Day, when Japan surrendered, several months after VE Day marked the end of the war in Europe. Soldiers in this army felt that they were the 'Forgotten Army' – why do you think they were forgotten?

151

FROM NEUTRALITY TO THE BOMB – WAS THIS AMERICA'S 'GOOD WAR'?

FOCUS ROUTE

1 Why was the atom bomb a different kind of weapon?
2 Summarise the arguments for using this weapon.
3 Summarise the arguments against its use.
4 If you had been involved in the decision-making, which argument would you have found most persuasive?

Was the use of the atom bomb justified?

The Manhattan Project

On 16 July 1945 an atomic bomb codenamed 'Trinity' was exploded above the New Mexico desert. The scientists gathered there saw it as the successful completion of five years' work. But the scientific director, Robert Oppenheimer, recognised that it would change the world. He quoted from the Hindu text, the *Bhagavad Gita*, 'If the radiance of a thousand suns were to burst at once in the sky, that would be like the splendour of the Mighty One ... I am become death. The shatterer of worlds'.

The Manhattan Project began with the ideas of Albert Einstein, the eminent German refugee physicist, in 1939. He suggested that a new and powerful bomb could be created from the atom of uranium ore. Work started on the Manhattan Project the following year with American and British scientists. Roosevelt had already decided not to tell Stalin, seeing it already as a possible bargaining counter for the peace settlement. Roosevelt died suddenly in April 1945. His successor, Vice-President Harry Truman, knew nothing about the project until he was sworn in as the next president.

Should the bomb be used?

President Truman

It seems to me the most terrible thing ever discovered, but it can be made useful.

Paul Tibbetts (pilot of the *Enola Gay*, which dropped the bomb on Hiroshima)

We're going to kill a lot of people, but by God we're going to save a lot of lives. We won't have to invade Japan.

Charles Sweeney (pilot of the plane which dropped the atom bomb on Nagasaki)

I saw these beautiful young men who were being slaughtered by an evil, evil military force. There was no question in my mind that President Truman made the right decision.

A Lawyer

Remember 'jus in bello' – the rules governing the conduct of war. They state that the casualties inflicted and the methods used must be proportionate to the ends being pursued.

General George Marshall

The only conventional way to end the war is to invade the islands of Kyushu and Honshu. We estimate that each invasion will result in at least a quarter of a million American casualties.

An American code breaker

I know from our intercepts that Prince Konoye has asked to see Stalin about ending the war. We know that the Japanese ambassador in Moscow, Naotake Sato, has warned the Japanese Foreign Minister, Shigenori Togo, that Japan must face the reality that they have lost the war. However, Togo warns him that Japan is not ready to surrender unconditionally.

An American expert on Japan

The Japanese will never surrender if they have to give up their emperor whom they regard as a god. Do we know if the Japanese military, who are directing the war, will agree to any negotiations for peace? How long are we going to wait for the Japanese to negotiate?

Survivor of the attack on American ships in Pearl Harbor

The Japs attacked us without warning and killed so many of my friends. We were helpless. They deserve the same.

Mother of American prisoner of war

I hate the Japs. We have heard of their cruel and inhuman treatment of prisoners. That is probably happening to my son. They deserve to be bombed until they surrender and I get my son back.

Secretary of War Henry Stimson

The Russians were granted concessions at the conference in Yalta if they entered the war against Japan and we cannot retract them. They will help us end the war more quickly and save American lives.

Chief of Staff to Presidents Roosevelt and Truman, Admiral William D. Leahy

The lethal possibility of atomic warfare in the future is frightening. My own feeling was that in being the first to use it, we had adopted an ethical standard common to the barbarians of the Dark Ages. I was not taught to make war in that fashion, and wars cannot be won by destroying women and children.

Deputy Director of the Office of Naval Intelligence, Ellis Zacharias

Just when the Japanese were ready to capitulate, we went ahead and introduced to the world the most devastating weapon it had ever seen and, in effect, gave the go-ahead to Russia to swarm over Eastern Asia ... It was the wrong decision. It was wrong on strategic grounds. And it was wrong on humanitarian grounds.

Brigadier General Carter Clarke (the military intelligence officer who prepared summaries for Truman of the intercepted Japanese cables)

We didn't need to do it, and we knew we didn't need to do it, and they knew we didn't need to do it. We used them as an experiment for two atomic bombs.

152

FROM NEUTRALITY TO THE BOMB – WAS THIS AMERICA'S 'GOOD WAR'?

ACTIVITY

1 Use the evidence on page 151 to list the arguments for and against using the nuclear bomb in 1945.
2 Why were the conclusions expressed by the US Strategic Bombing Survey group (Source 8.19) less valued at the time the decision was made in 1945?
3 What was the concern of the scientists of the Franck Report (8.20)?

ACTIVITY

Did the victory in the Pacific and the way it was achieved make this a 'good war'? List the arguments for and against.

SOURCE 8.19 The report of the US Strategic Bombing Survey Group, July 1946, assigned to study the effects of air attacks on Japan

Based on detailed investigation of all the facts and supported by the testimony of the surviving Japanese leaders involved, it is the Survey's opinion that certainly prior to 31 December 1945 and in all probability prior to 1 November 1945, Japan would have surrendered even if the atomic bombs had not been dropped, even if Russia had not entered the war, and even if no invasion had been planned or contemplated.

SOURCE 8.20 The Franck Report, written in June 1945, by a group of scientists involved in the Manhattan Project at the University of Chicago

... If the United States would be the first to release this new means of indiscriminate destruction upon mankind, she would sacrifice public support throughout the world, precipitate the race of armaments and prejudice the possibility of reaching an international agreement on the future control of weapons ... we urge that the use of nuclear weapons in this war be considered a problem of long-range national policy rather than military expediency, and that this policy be directed primarily to the achievement of an agreement permitting an effective international control of the means of nuclear warfare.

Two atom bombs were dropped – on Hiroshima on 6 August and on Nagasaki on 9 August. No warnings were given. Neither city was primarily a military target. The bombs killed more than 100,000 people instantly, with at least that number dying later from radiation poisoning.

Japan offered to surrender on 10 August. The USA accepted, provided that the Emperor was subject to the Allies, and appeared to suggest that he would be able to retain his position. After much debate in Japan the terms were accepted on 14 August. The war against Japan had ended.

■ **Learning trouble spot**

Historiography

Historiography is the study of how interpretations of the past change over time, and what causes them to do so. In the aftermath of the Second World War and with the evidence of the destructive capacity of the atom bomb in photographs and memories, the consensus of historians was that the bomb was justified to save lives and end the war quickly.

By the 1960s and the peak of the Cold War, with the Cuban missile crisis of 1963, the opinion that it had been used to intimidate the Soviets and keep them out of the Pacific grew stronger. At this time the bomb was seen as the real beginning of the Cold War.

By the 1990s the opinion was that the possible casualties from continuing the war had been exaggerated and too little had been done diplomatically to establish peace with Japan, which was clearly defeated by the summer of 1945.

All the interpretations reflect the interests of their time, as well as new sources for analysis.

SOURCE 8.21 *Keep these hands off*, a government poster published in 1945

SOURCE 8.22 *Junk Rally*, a poster published in 1942

Roosevelt had asked that everyone be involved in helping the war effort and collecting scrap was a community activity, in which even children could participate. Initially there was little guidance for volunteers from Washington, and it was not clear what the priorities were. The two posters shown in Sources 8.21 and 8.22 were found in the collection of a woman from Massachusetts who ran a wartime Red Cross bandage wrapping centre, and displayed the posters to encourage the volunteers who worked there.

SOURCE 8.23 *This is Nazi brutality*, painted by Ben Shahn in 1942 and published by the government. After the shooting of two Nazi officials, the Czech town of Lidice had been obliterated by the Nazis. All the Czech men were killed and the women and children sent to concentrations camps. The cruelty was the symbol of the reality of German occupation

SOURCE 8.24 'This world cannot exist half slave and half free'. This poster echoed Lincoln's words about slavery. The image of freedom was a common one in wartime propaganda, contrasting with slavery created by fascist regimes, such as the use of slave labour and the treatment of Jews by the Germans and of prisoners by the Japanese

The whole US population was affected by the rationing of butter, meat, sugar and petrol, etc. and a speed restriction of 35 mph to conserve fuel. People acted on their own initiative by creating 'Victory Gardens' and canning excess produce – 'eat what you can and can what you can't'. Clothing styles were restricted – there were only six colours of shoes, three of which were brown, for example. The federal government also set up the Office of Price Administration to fix ceiling prices on commodities, control rents and set up national rationing schemes. Women were encouraged to sign the Home Front Pledge stating that they would pay no more than the ceiling price. Inevitably, there were black markets and objections from businesses who preferred market prices, rather than controlled ones.

With simple and direct language Roosevelt used his fireside chats to explain to the public that their help with the war effort was needed, at a time when the war in the Pacific was going badly (see Source 8.25).

SOURCE 8.25   A radio broadcast by FDR, April 1942

Not all of us can have the privilege of fighting our enemies in distant parts of the world … But there is one front and one battle where everyone in the United States – every man, woman and child – is in action, and will be privileged to remain in action throughout this war. That front is right here at home, in our daily lives, in our daily tasks. Here at home everyone will have the privilege of making whatever self-denial is necessary, not only to supply our fighting men, but to keep the economic structure of our country fortified and secure during the war and after the war.

How was industry organised for war?

The government also had to control industrial production and to this end a number of measures were taken:

1 The War Production Board, established in January 1942, had the remit of changing production priorities to the needs of the military. Silk ribbon factories now made silk parachutes, and car factories made tanks and planes.
2 The War Management Commission, set up in 1942, had to recruit workers where they were needed most.
3 New industries were created particularly for synthetic materials, such as rubber. Research into improving military weapons, such as radar and the atom bomb, would also have peacetime uses.
4 In order to keep industry profitable, government contracts guaranteed profits and a web of interdependence created a triangle of military needs, government contracts and business production.
5 Agriculture became more mechanised as farm workers were needed for fighting. It was to be the end of the family-run farm, as more and more were bought up by co-operatives or became part of large agri-business units.
6 Labour unions continued to increase their membership. In 1941 they had agreed to a no-strike/no lock-out pledge with employers, to aid war production. The National War Labor Board (NWLB) banned closed shops. After a series of strikes in 1943, especially in the mines, the War Labor Disputes Act enforced a 30-day cooling-off period before a strike and authorised the NWLB to settle disputes.

Were these measures successful?

- In 1940, 6000 planes were built, in 1942, 47,000 and in 1943, 85,000.

- Between 1940 and 1945 the US produced 86,333 tanks and 12.5 million rifles.

- In the shipyards 107 aircraft carriers and 35 million tons of merchant shipping were produced.

- The female workforce increased by between 6 and 8 million due to the demands of war work.

- By 1945 the USA had produced more than twice the war supplies of Germany, Italy and Japan combined.

DISCUSS

What two reasons did Roosevelt give for civilian involvement?

How did the war affect women?

SOURCE 8.26 Women train workers *c.* 1942

SOURCE 8.27 Afro-American women welders, New Britain, Connecticut, 1943

Sources 8.26 and 8.27 are two classic images of the way American women responded to the shortage of male industrial workers. Before 1941 women had been thought unsuitable for such work and often had to give up paid work on marriage. Now, after a few weeks' training, many were doing semi-skilled jobs – crane operators, tool makers, shell loaders, aircraft makers and lumberjacks. The main recruitment targets were young women and those with older children, as there was little organised childcare for women in factories. There were, of course, variations in response across the USA. As well as industrial work an estimated 350,000 women joined uniformed groups such as the Women's Army Auxiliary Corps, the Marine Corps Women's Reserve and the Navy Nurse Corps.

SOURCE 8.28 A poster entitled *Answers to women's questions about war work*, 1943

156

FROM NEUTRALITY TO THE BOMB – WAS THIS AMERICA'S 'GOOD WAR'?

SOURCE 8.29 *Longing Won't Bring Him Back Sooner ... Get a War Job*, by Lawrence Wilbur, 1944

SOURCE 8.30 *Soldiers Without Guns*, a poster published in 1943

ACTIVITY

Study the posters shown in Sources 8.28–8.30 and Rosie the Riveter in Source 8.3 (page 137), and then make notes to answer the following questions.

1 What emotion is being appealed to in each poster?
2 What impression of the work is being presented? (Clean, difficult, skilful, etc.)
3 Do you think that women would have found these images attractive? Explain your answer.

It was not clear what would happen after the war ended. Would women want to, and be allowed to, keep the same jobs? A slogan for a vacuum cleaner advertisement expressed the more likely post-war image, 'You're fighting for a little house of your own, and a husband to meet every night at the door. You're fighting for the right to bring up your children without the shadow of fear'. It did not give much optimism for dramatic social change in the role of women. But some women had welcomed the changes that the war had brought, both at the beginning and for its long-term effects (see Source 8.31).

SOURCE 8.31 Dellie Hahne from Los Angeles, quoted in S. Terkel, *The Good War*, 1984, pp.117 and 122

While my conscience told me that war was a terrible thing, bloodshed and misery, there was an excitement in the air ... Suddenly, single women were of tremendous importance. It was hammered at us through the newspapers and magazines and radio. A young woman had a chance to meet hundreds of men in the course of one or two weeks, more than she would in her entire lifetime, because of the war. I became a nurses' aid, working in the hospital. Six or eight weeks of Red Cross training. The uniform made us special people.
... There was one good thing came out of it. I had friends whose mothers went out to work in factories. For the first time in their lives, they worked outside the home. They realized that they were capable of doing something more than cook a meal ... 'Cause they had a taste of freedom, they had a taste of making their own money, a taste of spending their own money, making their own decisions. I think the beginning of the women's movement had its seeds right there in World War Two.

DISCUSS

1 Was Rosie the Riveter to be only a war emblem who would be back pushing a vacuum cleaner when the war ended?
2 What factors would determine the future for women?

Did the war change the lives of black Americans?

Many black Americans could only too easily see the war as a white man's war. As one black student said to his tutor, 'The Army Jim Crows [slang for segregation] us. The navy lets us serve only as mess men. The Red Cross refuses our blood. Employers and labor unions shut us out. Lynchings continue. We are disenfranchised, Jim Crowed, spat upon. What more could Hitler do than that!'

The army kept units segregated, and few black soldiers were permitted to fight. They worked in the stores, loaded ammunition and kept the supply trucks running. The air force would not accept black candidates and fights between white and black servicemen were not uncommon. The double-V sign became the symbol of victory against enemies on the battlefield and against racism at home. It became more difficult to justify fighting a war for freedom from fascism whilst still restricting freedom for ordinary black Americans.

157

FROM NEUTRALITY TO THE BOMB – WAS THIS AMERICA'S 'GOOD WAR'?

SOURCE 8.33 *United We Win*, a poster from 1943. This was the picture that the government wanted of an integrated and committed society

SOURCE 8.32 Timuel Black lived in Detroit and joined the army in 1943. He and his fellow Northern blacks felt a little superior to less well-educated Southern blacks serving with them. This was as nothing to the way white soldiers viewed them (quoted in S. Terkel, *The Good War*, 1984, p.279)

We were shipped overseas. On board, blacks had their quarters and the whites had theirs. We didn't associate with one another. Different mess halls, different everything … We stayed in Wales, getting ready for the invasion [of Normandy in 1944]. Black soldiers and white soldiers could not go to the same town. The ordinary British were absolutely amazed, looking at these two armies. I guess they hadn't thought about their two armies, too; the colonial and the regular. But they were chagrined by this racial situation, which they'd never seen. White soldiers would say, 'Don't have anything to do with those niggers. They have tails, they howl at night', all kinds of funny stories. Very often if we got into fights, the British guys and gals would be on our side.

The general movement of workers meant a growing concentration of black migrants in some northern cities such as Chicago, Detroit and Cleveland. This gave them increased political power as a group, and new opportunities to use their vote. It created cultural communities that encouraged activists. During the war the membership of the NAACP (see page 17) rose from 50,000 to 450,000. The Congress of Racial Equality (CORE) was formed. The idea of peaceful protest, like the sit-down strikes in factories, was appealing as a method to desegregate cinemas and restaurants in the north. One such non-violent protest was planned by Asa Philip Randolph, head of the Brotherhood of Sleeping Car Porters, an all-black union of rail workers. He objected to segregation in both the military and the defence industries. He proposed to get 10,000 black workers to march down Pennsylvania Avenue in front of the White House in July 1941. The number of potential marchers had risen to 100,000 by May and the government was becoming worried. A week before the march, Randolph met the president. Randolph refused to call off the march unless the president acted. Roosevelt's reluctant response was to issue Executive Order 8802. It demanded that employers make defence jobs available, 'without discrimination, because of race, creed, color or national origin'. A Fair Employment Practices Committee was formed to investigate complaints and compel action. It had some success and by 1944 1 million black workers had jobs in manufacturing. It was the beginning of the end of traditional 'slave' jobs. As one black woman said, 'My sister always said that Hitler was the one that got us out of the white folks' kitchen'.

However, the tensions over jobs and housing continued. In 1943 there were 250 racially-motivated conflicts in 47 different cities. The worst was in Detroit where 25 black and nine white people were killed. Yet the government remained muted in its response. Some of its leaders held racist beliefs and the excuse was always that the war had to come first.

SOURCE 8.34 D. Kennedy, *Freedom from Fear*, 1999, p.768

Coming at a moment that was kindled with opportunities for economic betterment and social mobility, Executive Order 8802 fanned the rising flame of black militancy and initiated a chain of events that would eventually end segregation once and for all, and open up a new era for African-Americans.

SOURCE 8.35 Alan Brinkley 'The Legacies of World War II' in R. Griffith and P. Baker (eds.), *Major Problems in American History Since 1945*, 2nd edn, 2001, pp.31–2

And yet it would be a mistake to exaggerate the impact of the war on the willingness of Americans to confront the nation's 'race problem'. For the war did not simply inspire those who believed in racial equality to reconsider the nation's customs and institutions. It also inspired those who did not defend white supremacy with renewed ardour. Among white Americans, and among white Southerners in particular, there were many who considered the war not a challenge [but] rather a confirmation of their commitment to preserving the old racial order. To them democracy meant their right to order their society as they pleased and to sustain the customs and institutions they had always known … World War II changed America's racial geography economically, spatially, and ideologically. It ensured that the system of segregation and oppression that had enjoyed a dismal stability for more than half a century would never be entirely stable again. But it ensured, too, that the defenders of that system would confront the new challenges to it with a continued and even strengthened commitment.

GUNNAR MYRDAL'S *AN AMERICAN DILEMMA*

One of the influences for change was an account of the USA's racial past, present and future. *An American Dilemma* was written in 1944, by a Swedish social scientist, Gunnar Myrdal, for the Carnegie Foundation. Myrdal admired American ideals – the belief in equality, justice, equal opportunity and freedom, but said these beliefs were in contradiction to the racial inequality in America. Having identified what was a national problem, Myrdal's suggestion was for planned peaceful change in which the federal government would take the lead. By 1945 liberal thinkers and politicians had begun to make the 'race problem' a key issue to resolve in the post-war world. At the same time the war, both through work and military service, had given black Americans more economic and political power to make stronger demands. The war was to be a watershed in civil rights.

The internment of the Nisei

One group who were prohibited from involvement in the war effort were Japanese-Americans. After the attack on Pearl Harbor Roosevelt, under military and political pressure, issued Executive Order 9066, which enabled the military to insist on the removal of all Japanese-Americans living on the west coast. There were nearly 120,000 of whom two-thirds were Nisei, or American-born citizens. They were given 72 hours' notice to leave their homes and, with only one suitcase, were moved into isolated camps where they lived in barrack-like cabins surrounded by barbed wire and watch towers. There were ten camps in total – one in Arkansas and the others in the western states. Homes, businesses and friends were left behind for two years. After a time, Japanese-Americans were allowed limited freedom of movement if they swore an oath of loyalty to the USA. An all-Japanese army unit was created which fought in Italy.

The legality of internment was challenged in the courts, in 1943, in the Korematsu case, but rejected by the Supreme Court. The Court and Congress refused to acknowledge that the decisions were based on racial prejudice. In 1983, a federal judge finally accepted that racist views had led to internment, and in 1988 Congress did offer an apology to each of the camp's survivors and a payment of $20,000.

What impact did the war have on American society?

1 War demands forced the population to travel across the continent, living and working in new areas, creating a 'melting pot', which also involved those fighting in different parts of the world.
2 To many 'wartime was more interesting than peace' because it gave a focus to lives and signalled the end of the Depression.
3 Returning soldiers had to cope with families who had learned to live without them. Often friends had moved away. Many soldiers had experienced brutality that was difficult to describe, and felt that they had lost their youth.
4 The number of marriages and babies born increased both during and after the war.
5 The massive increase in industrial production led to post-war affluence and a demand for open markets across the world.
6 The war brought an end to unemployment problems.
7 Wartime demands had extended the power of the federal government, and of the president. The military/industrial/government links were to remain.
8 Black Americans had demonstrated the power of mass action, and now had the beginnings of economic and political power.
9 The G.I. (US soldier) Bill of Rights, passed in 1944, gave living allowances and paid tuition fees for returning soldiers to study for a degree or extend their skills. Over 1 million men enrolled in 1946 and higher education qualifications became the key to upward social and economic mobility.

ACTIVITY

Did changes on the Home Front demonstrate that American citizens had a 'good war'? List the arguments for and against.

FOCUS ROUTE

1 Copy and complete the following table to show the problems that existed as a result of the end of the Second World War, and the proposed solutions to these problems.

Problems that needed to be resolved	Proposed solutions to these problems

2 Which problems were left for later?

All the Allies were interested in their post-war spheres of influence. In October 1944 Stalin and Churchill agreed that Romania and Bulgaria were to be Soviet spheres of influence and Greece was to be a British sphere of influence, with them sharing authority in Hungary and Yugoslavia. Poland at the end of the war had two governments – one in exile in London accepted by the USA and Britain and the other in Lublin which was pro-communist. (It was hoped that the two governments would work together, but after the war Poland soon became a Communist satellite state.) Germany was to be divided into four zones shared between the powers (now including France) and Berlin, the capital, was to be similarly divided.

Civilians had been targets in this war in an unprecedented way. Not only were people killed but survivors lost homes, possessions, jobs and security. Thousands of refugees, including many children, were tramping the roads of central Europe as the war ended. Assistance for them was a post-war priority.

What were the plans for international co-operation?

The United Nations, 1944
The details of the United Nations were discussed at Dumbarton Oaks, a mansion in the north-west of Washington DC. The USSR, Britain, China and the USA devised a charter, with a security council dominated by the five permanent powers (France was included) and a less powerful general assembly of all of the world's nations. The first meeting was held in San Francisco in April 1945.

The International Monetary Fund and the World Bank
Held in the hills of New Hampshire at Bretton Woods on 22 July 1944, a meeting of capitalist economies (the USSR did not attend) tried to create a stable post-war global trading order. It approved the idea of Henry Morgenthau, the American Secretary to the Treasury, of fixing currencies to the dollar. The meeting set up two institutions:

- The International Monetary Fund (IMF) was to assure that every nation's currency was freely convertible into that of its trading partners. It could also lend money to those nations temporarily short of foreign reserves. In return, it could insist that the borrower change its economic and trade policies. The USA provided half the $10 billion capital needed to start the fund.
- The International Bank for Reconstruction and Development, or the World Bank, would finance long-term programmes, especially ones beyond the scope of a nation's private bankers.

The Yalta Conference

SOURCE 8.36 The last meeting between the three great wartime leaders at Yalta in February 1945. They arranged a further meeting at Potsdam after Germany's defeat, but Roosevelt died in April. Here at Yalta he looks unwell and tired. Behind the three leaders stand their main foreign advisors, (from the left) Eden, Stettinius and Molotov

Military planning had to contain political ambitions as well. The position of troops at the end of the war might be important in determining political boundaries. Stalin and Roosevelt had different political beliefs and systems. They had started the war from different bases and for different reasons. At the Yalta Conference the following points were decided:

- Germany would pay some reparations, particularly to the USSR.
- The United Nations would be a universal organisation, with the major powers as permanent members of the Security Council possessing the power of veto.
- The USSR guaranteed 'friendly' governments on the borders of Eastern Europe and would permit 'free elections' in Poland.
- The USSR would enter the war against Japan three months after the end of the German war and would gain Asian territories in exchange.
- The next meeting would be after Germany's surrender and would be a series of peace conferences, not a re-run of the drama of Versailles in 1919.

SOURCE 8.37 Harry Truman being sworn in as President, 12 April 1945

161

FROM NEUTRALITY TO THE BOMB – WAS THIS AMERICA'S 'GOOD WAR'?

Counter factual history

Counter factual history is the debate about 'what if…'. Discussing what did **not** happen can be a way of assessing the importance and reasons for what did. For example:
What if the bomb had not been dropped on Hiroshima?
What if Roosevelt had been alive for the Potsdam peace conference?

ACTIVITY

Do the plans for peace justify the description of the Second World War as a 'good war'? List the arguments for and against.

On 12 April 1945 Roosevelt died. Eleanor Roosevelt told Vice-President Truman the news. He asked her, 'Is there anything I can do for you?' She replied, 'Is there anything we can do for you? You are the one who is in trouble now'. Later when he spoke to the press for the first time Truman said, 'Boys if you ever pray, pray for me now. I don't know whether you fellows ever had a load of hay fall on you, but when they told me yesterday what had happened, I felt like the Moon, the stars and all the planets had fallen on me'. Truman had virtually no foreign policy experience and had had little contact with Roosevelt since the election. Suddenly he was faced with negotiating the end of wars against two enemies, and dealing with coalition partners who were much more experienced and confident than he was.

SOURCE 8.38   Averell Harriman (quoted in S. Terkel, *The Good War*, 1984, pp.300–31) was an emissary of Roosevelt to Britain and the USSR during the war. He suggested that Roosevelt was very realistic about Stalin and knew that Stalin

… would never surrender. We became convinced that, regardless of Stalin's awful brutality and his reign of terror, he was a great war leader. Without Stalin, they never would have held.

He also felt the post-war world would have been different if Roosevelt had lived,

I think Stalin was sort of afraid of Roosevelt. Whenever Roosevelt spoke, he sort of watched him with a certain awe. He was afraid of Roosevelt's influence in the world. If FDR had lived, the Cold War wouldn't have developed the way it did, because Stalin would have tried to get along with Roosevelt.

 ## Review: Was this America's 'good war'?

SOURCE 8.39   E. Foner, *The Story of American Freedom*, 2000, p.219

World War II came to be remembered as the Good War, a time of national unity in pursuit of indisputably good goals.

SOURCE 8.40   D. Kennedy, *Freedom from Fear*, 1999, p.857

Small wonder that America chooses to think of it as the good war. It was a war that had brought them as far as imagination could reach, and beyond, from the ordeal of the Great Depression, and had opened apparently infinite vistas to the future. The huge expenditure clinched the Keynesian doctrine that government spending could underwrite prosperity and inaugurated a quarter-century of the most robust economic growth in the nation's history – an era of the very greatest expectations.

SOURCE 8.41   The American historian David Kennedy published *Freedom from Fear* in 1999. This quote is adapted from pp.852–58. He was critical of America's role, arguing that:

1 the USA was slow to realise the menace of Hitler
2 it provoked Japan into war
3 it fought with greater bestiality in the Pacific than was ever admitted
4 racism, against black Americans, against the Japanese and against minorities was not challenged by political leaders
5 the Japanese war was prolonged because of a rigid demand for unconditional surrender
6 the atom bomb was used against civilians when Japan was ready to surrender.

On the other hand economic success was immense (from p.856)

… they alone among warring peoples had prospered, emerging unscathed at home while 405,399 American soldiers, sailors, marines and airmen had died. These men were dignified in death by their service, but they represented proportionally fewer military casualties than in any other major belligerent country. Beyond the war's dead and wounded and their families, few Americans had been touched by the staggering sacrifices and unspeakable anguish that the war had visited upon millions of other people around the globe.

162

FROM NEUTRALITY TO THE BOMB – WAS THIS AMERICA'S 'GOOD WAR?'

SOURCE 8.42 Alan Brinkley 'The Legacies of World War II' in R. Griffith and P. Baker (eds.), *Major Problems in American History Since 1945*, 2nd edn, 2001, p.27

The war ended the Depression and made the nation rich again. It created expectations of abundance that would survive for more than a generation. And it removed what had in the 1930s been deep doubts about the ability of the capitalist economy ever again to experience substantial growth …
Alone among the major nations, the United States faced the future in 1945 with an intact and thriving industrial economy poised to sustain a long period of prosperity and growth. Gross National Product in the war years rose from $91 billion to $166 billion; 15 million new jobs were created, and the most enduring problem of the Depression – massive unemployment – came to an end; industrial production doubled; personal incomes rose (depending on location) by as much as 200 per cent.

SOURCE 8.43 Comparative statistics of the number of deaths, and the size of armies in the Second World War, from H. Evans, *The American Century*, 1998, p.385

	Deaths in combat	**Military force**	**Civilian deaths**
USA	290,500	16 million	less than 10
USSR	14.5 million	20 million	7.5 million
Britain	500,500	8 million	70,000
Germany	2.8 million	10 million	2.3 million
Japan	1.5 million	6 million	670,000

N.B. The British military figures include Commonwealth troops, particularly from Canada, Australia and India.

By the end of the war the USA had half the world's manufacturing capacity and generated half of its electricity, owned two-thirds of the world's gold stocks, had the largest merchant fleet and a near monopoly on aerospace and electronics industries. And it was, for the moment, the only nation with the atom bomb. To Americans the war had been fought for the principles of freedom and to protect democracy across the world. The 'four freedoms' of 1941 were still the guide to ordinary Americans, but industrialists and politicians could see other gains from victory.

SOURCE 8.44 Statistics to show the wartime economic boom

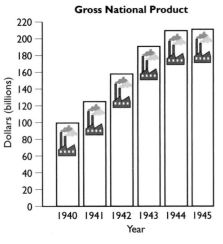

Gross National Product

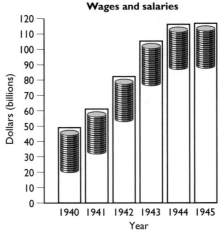

Wages and salaries

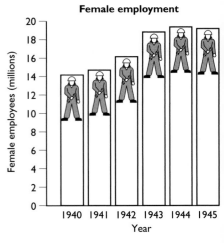

Female employment

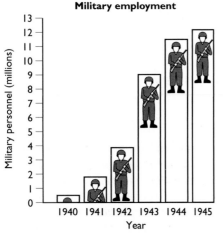

Military employment

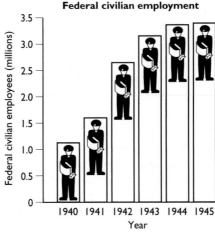

Federal civilian employment

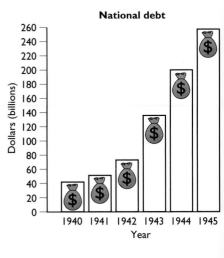

National debt

163

FROM NEUTRALITY TO THE BOMB – WAS THIS AMERICA'S 'GOOD WAR'?

ACTIVITY

1 Use Sources 8.40–8.50 to identify why the Second World War was, or was not, America's 'good war'.
2 Collate these points together with your answers to the 'good war' Activity at the end of each section in this chapter (pages 145, 152, 158 and 161).
3 What general conclusion do you come to about whether this was America's 'good war'?

SOURCE 8.47   Dellie Hahne, in S. Terkel, *The Good War*, 1984, p.166

The good war? That infuriates me. Yeah, the ideas of World War Two being called a good war is a horrible thing. I think of all the atrocities. I think of a madman who had all this power. I think of the destruction of the Jews, the misery, the horrendous suffering in the concentration camps. In 1971 I visited Dachau [a concentration camp in Germany]. I could not believe what I saw ... I know it had to be stopped and we stopped it. But I don't feel proud, because we were so devious ... If we'd only had a different approach, that's all I'm asking for. If you have to live through a war, be truthful. Maybe you have to get people to fight a war, maybe you have to lie to them ...

SOURCE 8.49   John Abbott, a Californian, remembering the war, in S. Terkel, *The Good War*, 1984, p.166

We were ready for a war. We'd had a long Depression. People needed a change and a war promised to make things different. Get off those bread lines. Build another bomber for peace. They just changed the slogans. That was the most popular war we ever had. People sang, danced, drank – whoopee, the war.

SOURCE 8.45   General William Buster who fought against the Japanese in North Africa, Italy and Normandy. Quoted in S. Terkel, *The Good War*, 1984, p.197

The dedication and patriotism of the American people that was evident in World War Two just wasn't there in the others [i.e. Korea, Vietnam]. If people know there's a good reason for what they're doing, they're enthusiastic about it. But when they have doubts, it's difficult ... I'm certainly not war-like. I always think, blessed be the peacemakers. But somebody's gotta take care of the peacemakers while they're makin' peace.

SOURCE 8.46   Admiral Gene Larocque served in the Pacific and then worked for the Department of Defense in the Pentagon. Quoted in S. Terkel, *The Good War*, 1984, p.193

World War Two has warped our view of how we look at things today. We see things in terms of that war, which in a sense was a good war. But the twisted memory of it encourages the men of my generation to be willing, almost eager, to use military force anywhere in the world. For about twenty years after the war, I couldn't look at any film on World War Two. It brought back memories that I didn't want to keep around. I hated to see how they glorified war ... I hate it when they say, 'He gave his life for his country'. Nobody gives their life for anything. We steal the lives of those kids. We take it away from them. They don't die for the honor and glory of their country. We kill them.

SOURCE 8.48   A soldier, Robert Rasmus, quoted in S. Terkel, *The Good War*, 1984, pp.39, 41–2, 48

When I went in the army, I'd never been outside the states of Wisconsin, Indiana, and Michigan ... Of course I was absolutely bowled over by Europe, the castles, the cathedrals, the Alps. It was wonderment. I was preoccupied with staying alive and doing my job, but it seemed, out of the corner of my eye, I was constantly fascinated with the beauty of the German forests and the medieval bell towers. At nineteen you're seeing life with fresh eyes ... We've seen a little of the war now ... We've sent out patrols and captured prisoners ... It was still fun and dramatics. When the truck took us from Cologne south through Bonn, for me it was, 'Hey, Beethoven's birthplace!' ... We were in rolling hills and great forests ... I could almost hear Wagnerian music. I was pulled in two directions: 'Gee, I don't want to get killed'. And, 'Boy, this is gorgeous country' ... World War Two ... affected me in many ways ever since. I think my judgement of people is more circumspect. I know it's made me less ready to fall into the trap of judging people by their style or appearance. In a short period of time, I had the most tremendous experiences of all of life: of fear, of jubilance, of misery, of hope, of comradeship, and of endless excitement, the theatrics of it.

SOURCE 8.50   Alex Shulman was a Jewish doctor who landed on D-Day and then crossed Germany with the American troops. He visited the concentration camp at Buchenwald c. April 1945. Quoted in S. Terkel, *The Good War*, 1984, p.287

Americans have never known what war really is. No matter how much they saw it on television or pictures or magazines. Because there is one feature they never appreciated: the smell. When you go through a village and you suddenly get this horrible smell ... You look out and see these bloated bodies ... You see bloated horses and cows and the smell of death. It's not discriminating, they all smell the same. Maybe if Americans had known even that, they'd be more concerned about the peace ... I'm glad I participated. I felt that whatever little I did was something. My job was to save lives. I was asked, 'How could you take care of those Germans? Doesn't that bother you?' Oh, I started looking at them at first as Germans and Nazis. Then I started looking at them as victims. Especially at the end, when I saw the kids and the old men. Could I blame the kid for what his parents or the Nazi leaders did? It was a terrible, mixed feeling.

How did the Second World War change US foreign policy?

■ 8H US foreign policy was changed for the rest of the twentieth century because of the Second World War

In 1945 America was on the victorious side, it had suffered fewer casualties than the other countries involved in the war and was the richest nation in the world.

It had fully committed itself to the defence of democracy, in opposition to totalitarianism.

It was no longer an isolationist nation.

It contained contradictory feelings towards the Soviets. Without Soviet help the war may have been lost, but the USSR was a communist state. These tensions eventually culminated in the Cold War.

What sort of post-war world would it or could it be? Had America been changed enough to tackle the commitments and involvements in other nations' foreign affairs, that were necessitated by post-war problems?

SOURCE 8.51   R. Schulzinger, *US Diplomacy since 1900*, 4th edn, 1998, p.200

At the end of the war, Americans' hopes exceeded the ability of any nations to realize them. The real sense of obligation former coalition partners had to America could not mask equally strong feelings of envy and fear for the future.

SOURCE 8.52   E. Foner, *The Story of American Freedom*, 2000, p.233

Whether in the guise of universal free enterprise or a global New Deal, the war had produced an imperial vision of America's role in the post-war world, a vision so inextricably tied to the promise of economic abundance.

ACTIVITY

Was the Second World War a 'good war' for the USA? Write an essay arguing for and against this view.

There are numerous topics to choose from, but take care to select ones that reflect political, economic and social change. You could choose from, for example: military events, making the peace, working on the Home Front, war aims, the experience of fighting, the challenges to racial inequality, the benefits for women, Roosevelt's leadership, the impact of the war on those fighting or those at home.

In the final paragraph give your opinion, but remember, it must be based on evidence. Of course, when you have completed Section Three of this book you may want to change that opinion. You will have, by then, a more informed and longer-term view of the war and its impact on the second half of the twentieth century.

1 American industrial production played a major part in the Allied victory in the Second World War, the most destructive war in history.

2 The war established America's global pre-eminence as a military and economic power, and one of the world's two superpowers.

3 It was unclear how the relations between a communist USSR and a democratic USA would develop after the war alliance ended.

4 It was the beginning of the end of the pre-war empires of Britain, France and the Netherlands.

5 The American continent was untouched by physical destruction.

6 It brought an end to the Depression.

7 It continued the expansion of the powers of the federal government and the continuation of the liberal consensus started by the New Deal.

8 Women and black Americans had been essential to the war effort, but did not have equal rights in society.

9 The war had enhanced the power of big corporations and had embedded a government/military/industrial co-dependency that would be hard to end.

10 War production encouraged population growth, social mobility, and the development of the Sun Belt – the states of the south-west from Texas to California.

11 The impact of being the first country ever to use nuclear weapons was, as yet, unknown.

Section 2 Review: Prosperity, collapse, destruction and victory, 1920–45

ACTIVITY

Write at least three bullet points for each theme to summarise how each one developed between 1920 and 1945. The pictures on these two pages will get you started, but remember they only tell you part of the story.

By 1919 the key developments in American history, identified at the beginning of Section 2 (page 70) were:

- growing wealth created by industrialisation
- the emergence of the USA as a reluctant international power
- the slow progress to civil rights for minorities
- the increase in presidential authority and changing use of executive power.

SOURCE 1 Withdrawing savings, 1932. The Crash of 1929 meant that debts, made by buying shares and having to sell them at a loss, had to be paid. Depositers queued at banks to withdraw their savings to make the payments

SOURCE 2 Hiroshima, 1945. The first atom bomb was dropped on Hiroshima, Japan in August 1945. It was a deliberate act of war against a nation without a similar weapon, to force the Japanese government to accept unconditional surrender

SOURCE 3 Black migrants. This family are travelling with all their belongings to what they hope will be a better life in the northern states. Most migrants like these left farming in the south for industry or domestic work in the north

SOURCE 4 Yalta Conference, February 1945. The Second World War required the full commitment of the nations involved. Here, the three leaders of the western Allies – Churchill, Roosevelt, and Stalin – meet to discuss the end of the war and its aftermath

The most powerful nation, 1945–92

The end of the Second World War had made two nations – the **USA** and the **USSR** – into superpowers. Other nations who had fought in the war had lost empires, industrial capacity or governments. However, a new conflict – the Cold War – emerged between these two superpowers.

The challenges facing the **USA** between 1945 and 1992 were:

- **How to react to the territorial ambitions of the USSR in Europe and Asia.**
- **How to contain the spread of communism.**
- **How to extend their own ideology, democracy and free market capitalism to other countries.**
- **How to create a more just and equal society, especially for black Americans and other minority groups.**

How would you expect these challenges to guide America's policies and actions? For example:

Why might they want to get a man on the moon?

What might happen if the USA got too involved in its battles against communism?

SOURCE 1 American astronauts on the Moon

SOURCE 2 American soldiers awaiting evacuation from the Vietnamese jungle

Was there more to the American Dream than simply buying more 'stuff'?

SOURCE 3 A large shopping mall

Could the Americans really trust their leaders in this new and dangerous world? Would the law apply equally to everyone?

SOURCE 4 President Nixon departing from the White House in August 1974 after the threat to impeach him because of the Watergate scandal

9

Why did the Cold War begin, 1945–49?

CHAPTER OVERVIEW

SOURCE 9.1 Was this where the Cold War started? Russian soldiers fly the Soviet flag over a defeated Berlin, May 1945. Stalin's determination to reach the German capital first had succeeded. Churchill feared the consequences of this victory, but had been unable to persuade American military leaders that if they failed to reach Berlin first, their more leisurely crossing of Germany would have immeasurable political results

SOURCE 9.2 General George Marshall's words to Congress at the end of the Second World War

The peace can only be maintained by the strong ...

The end of the Second World War brought peace; of a kind, and not for long. Another war – the Cold War – gradually developed and became a reality from 1949 to 1992. This was not a war fought with grand battles and mass armies and fleets. It was a war fought across the world with a range of weapons – military, economic, cultural and political, including even space satellites.

This chapter will focus on the beginning of the Cold War in Europe between 1945 and 1949. World peace was expected in 1945. Nuclear annihilation seemed possible by 1949. The tensions of trying to establish a peace became part of an ideological battle between the two superpowers which had been created by the war. The USA waved the flag of democracy. The USSR waved the flag of communism. By 1949 neither nation would compromise. Historical debate still continues as to who was to blame, or rather who should take more of the blame.

A Why did the end of the Second World War create tension between the Allies? (pp.171–75)

B Why was there a Cold War by 1949? (pp. 175–83)

C Review: Why did the Cold War begin, 1945–49? (pp. 183–84)

DISCUSS

What reasons can you suggest for the outbreak of the Cold War?

1945	Yalta Conference
	Roosevelt dies and is succeeded by Harry Truman
	First meeting of the United Nations in San Francisco
	Germany surrenders
	Potsdam Conference, with Attlee replacing Churchill as British prime minister
	Nuclear bombs dropped by USA on Hiroshima and Nagasaki
	Japan surrenders
	Vietnam declares independence
1946	Kennan's telegraph on 'containment'
	Churchill's Iron Curtain speech
	Philippines granted independence
1947	Truman Doctrine
	Marshall Plan
	House Committee on Un-American Activities investigates communism in Hollywood
	Communists take power in Hungary
	National Security Act creates new presidential advisors
1948	Berlin Airlift
	Communists take power in Czechoslovakia
	Truman recognises the new state of Israel
1949	NATO created
	USSR explodes atomic bomb
	Communists led by Mao Zedong seize control in China

FOCUS ROUTE

Note your answers to the following questions:

1 What were the factors which increased tension between the USA and the Soviet Union?
2 Why was Germany important in the development towards the Cold War?
3 What did the USA want to keep, and fear to lose?
4 What did the USSR want to keep, and fear to lose?

A # Why did the end of the Second World War create tension between the Allies?

Why was settling the peace so difficult?

The Potsdam Conference

The leaders of the wartime coalition, Stalin, Roosevelt and Churchill, had had a wary respect for one another. Roosevelt certainly believed that he could work with Stalin and moderate some of his demands and suspicions. The suddenness of Roosevelt's death, and Truman's foreign policy inexperience created stresses at a crucial time. Sources 9.4 and 9.5 detail two historians' opinions of Truman.

SOURCE 9.3 The Potsdam Conference held outside Berlin in July 1945. Stalin represented the Soviet Union as he had throughout the war. Truman represented the USA, but had been president only since April. Attlee, representing Britain, had been prime minister since the Labour Party had come to power only one week earlier. However, Attlee had been deputy prime minister throughout the war and was familiar with past actions and future plans. The Conference was called to discuss the results of the defeat of Germany, and the anticipated defeat of Japan. It was the first, and only, time that the three leaders met together

DISCUSS

What do Sources 9.4 and 9.5 suggest were Truman's strengths and weaknesses in dealing with foreign policy?

SOURCE 9.4 P. Johnson, *A History of the American People*, 1997, p.690

No one who reads Truman's diaries, and studies his voluminous papers with care, can be in doubt that he was outspoken, at times vituperative, a volcano of wrath – though a quickly subsiding one – a good hater, a typical hot-blooded American of his time, but also decent, generous, thoughtful, prudent, and cautious when it came to the point, a constitutionalist and a thorough democrat, and a natural leader too.

SOURCE 9.5 J. Patterson, *Grand Expectations*, 1996, p.97

In his foreign policy Truman is best described ... as a patriotic, conscientious, and largely colorless man whose fate it was to cope, sometimes imaginatively and sometimes imprudently, with some of the most difficult policy problems in American history.

The end of the war left a power vacuum with the defeat of the German Axis powers and of Japan. The war also brought to an end the empires of Britain, France, Germany and the Netherlands. The world was now to be led by the two superpowers of the USA and the Soviet Union. Only they had the resources to impose their power on the world. It was a unique opportunity to shape a new world, and to learn the lessons of the Versailles settlement of 1919.

The Potsdam Conference of July 1945 made the following decisions:

- the complete disarmament of Germany
- the dismantling of all Nazi institutions and laws
- a war crimes trial (held in Nuremberg in 1946)
- that reparations be taken by each power from the German occupation zone it controlled
- the unconditional surrender of Japan.

What were America's aims at the end of the war?

Those planning the peace were influenced by the First World War, and a wish to avoid acts that would have economic consequences, like heavy reparations and war debts. As an Allied power the USA wanted:

- the end of totalitarianism
- the end of global economic depression
- the end of war.

For the good of its own people the USA wanted:

- the management of world affairs by the 'Four Policemen' – the USSR, China, Britain and the USA, together with the United Nations
- self-determination for liberated countries
- gradual and orderly de-colonisation
- an expansion in American economic spheres of influence
- open-door policy and lower tariffs to enable easier expansion of American trade into Europe.

DISCUSS

In the Economic Bill of Rights outlined by Roosevelt in his State of the Union Address in January 1944 he stated that every American had the right to a decent job, sufficient food, shelter, clothing, and financial security in illness, unemployment and old age. How would any of the points above contribute to this aim?

Why was Germany important in the early development of the Cold War?

Why was Germany important in the early development of the Cold War?

■ 9B Post-war Europe

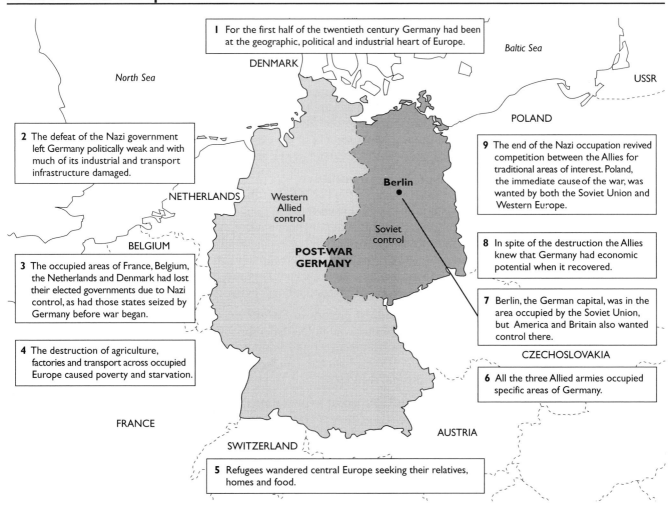

1 For the first half of the twentieth century Germany had been at the geographic, political and industrial heart of Europe.

North Sea

DENMARK

Baltic Sea

USSR

POLAND

2 The defeat of the Nazi government left Germany politically weak and with much of its industrial and transport infrastructure damaged.

NETHERLANDS

Western Allied control

Berlin

Soviet control

POST-WAR GERMANY

9 The end of the Nazi occupation revived competition between the Allies for traditional areas of interest. Poland, the immediate cause of the war, was wanted by both the Soviet Union and Western Europe.

BELGIUM

3 The occupied areas of France, Belgium, the Netherlands and Denmark had lost their elected governments due to Nazi control, as had those states seized by Germany before war began.

8 In spite of the destruction the Allies knew that Germany had economic potential when it recovered.

7 Berlin, the German capital, was in the area occupied by the Soviet Union, but America and Britain also wanted control there.

CZECHOSLOVAKIA

4 The destruction of agriculture, factories and transport across occupied Europe caused poverty and starvation.

6 All the three Allied armies occupied specific areas of Germany.

FRANCE

AUSTRIA

SWITZERLAND

5 Refugees wandered central Europe seeking their relatives, homes and food.

■ 9C The lessons of the war

America believed that the war had taught that:

- appeasement was an unsuccessful policy option against aggression

- Americans did not want to return to the economic worries of the Depression

- the war had provided prosperity, social stability and optimism

- American beliefs in democracy and freedom had been proved right and should be promoted across the globe

- the Soviet Union wanted total control over territories in which America also had an interest, especially Germany.

The Soviet Union believed that the war had taught that:

- it needed to protect its land borders, in Eastern Europe, in Asia and along its southern Middle Eastern frontiers

- it needed German reparations to repair the damage to its industry and agriculture

- America and Britain might ally against Soviet interests as they had appeared to do during the war.

Why did relations become cooler by 1946?

a) Economic needs of the Soviet Union

In the months after Potsdam goodwill was strained and suspicions increased. The USA had cancelled the Lend-Lease scheme (see page 140) immediately after the Japanese war ended in August 1945, but without warning its recipients, which included Britain and the Soviet Union. It shocked both countries. The USA had already stalled on a request from the Soviet Union in 1945 for $6 billion for post-war reconstruction. To the Soviet Union the cancelling of the Lend-Lease scheme underlined both American economic superiority and an American desire to use its economic strength against other nations, as well as ignoring the contribution of the Soviet army to victory. It meant that the Soviet Union had to rely on reparations from Germany, Eastern Europe and Manchuria, at the expense of ignoring American fears of Soviet expansion and domination in Europe.

b) Spheres of influence

This in turn led the USSR to fear that the USA might interfere in areas where the Soviet Union needed to feel secure. There developed competition over 'spheres of influence' – where a nation had military, territorial or economic control. The Soviet Union was deeply anxious to protect its land border. The USA and Britain were not prepared to give up their influence in their German zones and in Western Europe. They saw Stalin as another potential Hitler, intent on territorial aggression to defend his nation's security.

c) Communist parties in Europe

They were small but influential, especially in France and Italy. As Europe struggled with recovery and social unrest it was feared that such parties might request Soviet Union aid. The threat of this in Greece, in 1948, was the stimulus for the Marshall Plan.

d) America's 'great expectations'

The success of the war had deepened Americans' belief in democracy. It brought out the beliefs of manifest destiny – God was on America's side. So, to a natural satisfaction in victory was added an almost messianic belief that America was right.

e) Ideology

An ideology is a scheme of ideas that are the basis of a political or economic system. The American ideology was that of democratic capitalism. Private enterprise was the way in which wealth was produced, distributed and owned, and shared with the workers. For Americans such an economic system best represented the ideal of freedom. The Soviet ideology was that of communism. Here the means of production, distribution and exchange are shared by all, according to need not wealth.

■ Learning trouble spot

Ideologies

Question: What have Cinderella and the Cold War got in common?
Answer: They are both stories of 'good' versus 'evil'.
Cinderella was the good sister who had evil step-sisters and a step-mother. But her goodness and beauty shone through the hardship and grime and she married the handsome prince and lived happily ever after, as people always do in fairy stories. Surely the Cold War was not a fairy story? Not at all if you look at the photographs and read the documents later in this book about Korea, Vietnam and Latin America. So what is the link? Just as 'good' Cinderella triumphed, so the USA believed that their 'good' ideology of capitalist democracy should, and would, be triumphant in the post-war world. Cinderella had the help of a fairy godmother. The USA had the help of immense resources and industrial capacity. Their 'magic' could be used in many ways. In the period from 1949 to 1992 it was used to defeat the 'evil' ideology of communism. Just as in fairy stories, there was a tendency to see the world in black and white, good and evil – 'you're with me or you're against me'. Such attitudes make diplomacy, compromise, co-operation or negotiation difficult. As you study this period, look out for those times when less fairy tale and more realism would have been helpful, especially for innocent civilians.

ACTIVITY

List the reasons you have identified so far for the outbreak of the Cold War.

■ Learning trouble spot

Geopolitics Reminder

This is the term given to the importance of the geographical location of a country. Nations have different elements that make them successful and wealthy: the climate; raw materials; the fertility of the land; access to trade routes to buy necessities and sell products. The USA had immense reserves of raw materials, a varied climate and a varied landmass that made it possible to grow a wide range of useful crops. Japan lacked sufficient raw materials, such as coal and iron, to become industrially powerful, and sought to change that perceived weakness. These matters affect a nation's prosperity.

But where a country is 'placed' in relation to possible enemies and allies also matters. If a country went to war how many fronts would it have to fight on? How many borders would it have to defend? Could it move troops quickly from one front to another? Were its common boundaries with strong or weak states, and were those states in competition with it for raw materials or access to the sea? Did it have to defend itself on land as well as at sea? How easy was it for an enemy to invade and cross its landmass? Obviously the development of air power and bombs changed the importance of some of these factors, but they still remain important considerations.

Look at these questions again and think of answers in relation to the USA and the Soviet Union during the Second World War.

When you are analysing Cold War events remember to include geopolitics as part of your assessment.

FOCUS ROUTE

As you work through Section B make notes on the following questions.

1 What did the USA fear in the immediate post-war period?
2 What evidence was there to justify these fears?
3 How far was the evidence misunderstood or incomplete?

B Why was there a Cold War by 1949?

What were the building blocks of American policy towards the Soviet Union, 1946–49?

The Landscape – The Iron Curtain

SOURCE 9.6 Churchill speaking at Fulton, Missouri on 9 March 1946 at Truman's invitation. Churchill, leader of the Conservative Party though no longer prime minister, introduced one of the most evocative phrases of the Cold War – the 'Iron Curtain'

SOURCE 9.7 Winston Churchill speaking in Missouri, 9 March 1946, quoted in D. Merrill and T. Paterson, *Major Problems in American Foreign Relations,* Vol. II, 5th edn, 2000, pp.212–14

A shadow has fallen upon the scenes so lately lighted by the Allied victory. Nobody knows what the Soviet Russia and its communist international organisation intends to do in the immediate future, or what are the limits, if any, to their expansive and proselytizing tendencies ... We understand the Russian need to feel secure on her western frontiers from all renewal of German aggression ...

From Stettin in the Baltic to Trieste in the Adriatic, an Iron Curtain has descended across the continent. Behind that line lie all the capitals of the ancient states of Central and Eastern Europe ... all these famous cities and the populations around them lie in the Soviet sphere and all are subject, in one form or another, not only to Soviet influence but to a very high and increasing measure of control from Moscow ... What is needed is a settlement ... From what I have seen of our Russian friends and allies during the war, I am convinced that there is nothing they admire so much as strength, and there is nothing for which they have less respect than for military weakness.

Churchill went on to warn of the possible expansion of the Soviet Union across the world. He said that the 'iron' division used border barriers, watch towers, troops and restrictions on travel to keep the Eastern European populations under Soviet control. Typically governments were communist, free speech was restricted, secret police used intimidation and imprisonment to control people, and industry and agriculture were taken over by the state. Churchill's image of a 'curtain' was to become almost a reality with the building of the Berlin Wall in 1961, to physically divide East and West Berlin. The speech added to American fears that Soviet consolidation of territory in Eastern Europe was a direct threat to American security.

ACTIVITY

Read Source 9.7 and answer the following questions.

1 What does the phrase 'expansive and proselytizing tendencies' mean with reference to the Soviet Union?
2 Why was Churchill impressed by the Soviets during the war?
3 How effective do you think the image of an Iron Curtain is?

■ 9D The Iron Curtain division of Europe, with Soviet-controlled Eastern Europe separated from American-Allied Western Europe

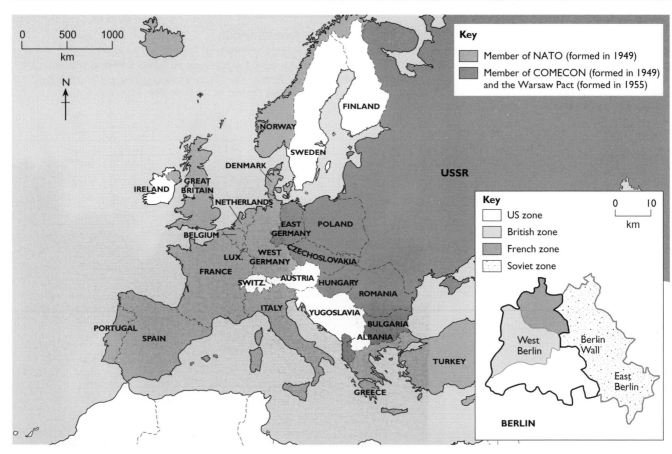

1 Copy and complete the table below to record how each of the 'Building Blocks' of American policy, described on pages 177–81, either increased or decreased tensions between the superpowers.

Building block	Increased tensions	Decreased tensions
Containment		
The Truman Doctrine		
The Marshall Plan		
The division of Germany and Berlin		
The creation of NATO		
NSC-68		
The nuclear bomb		

2 Was it the intention of US politicians to increase tensions with the Soviet Union, or did this happen accidentally?

SOURCE 9.8 George Kennan, the Moscow-based diplomat who wrote the influential 'Long Telegram' advocating the policy of containment

1 Why did Kennan (Source 9.9) think that the Kremlin was fearful of the West?
2 How did he think that the Soviets would seek security in general?
3 How would they seek security from their fear of the USA?
4 Why should the USA be worried about Soviet power?

The Building Blocks
1 Containment

On 22 February 1946, an American diplomat in Moscow sent a telegram to the State Department in Washington. This 'Long Telegram' was to become the most famous telegram of the second half of the twentieth century. The sender was a career diplomat, George Kennan. He went on to write an article in the influential journal *Foreign Affairs*, writing as Mr X, setting out his views to a different audience of general readers as well as policy specialists. He outlined his ideas about the motivation behind Soviet behaviour.

SOURCE 9.9 An extract from the 'Long Telegram', quoted in D. Merrill and T. Patterson, *Major Problems in American Foreign Relations*, Vol. II, 5th edn, 2000, pp.210–12

At bottom of Kremlin's neurotic view of world affairs is traditional and instinctive Russian sense of insecurity. Originally, this was insecurity of a peaceful agricultural people trying to live on vast exposed plain in neighbourhood of fierce nomadic peoples. To this was added, as Russia came into contact with economically advanced West, fear of more competent, more powerful, more highly organised societies in that area. ... Russian rulers have invariably sensed that their rule was relatively archaic in form, fragile and artificial in its psychological foundation, unable to stand comparison or contact with political systems of Western countries. For this reason they have always feared foreign penetration, feared direct contact between Western world and their own, feared what would happen if Russians learned truth about world without or if foreigners learnt truth about world within. And they had learned to seek security only in patient but deadly struggle for total destruction of rival power, never in compacts and compromises with it.

... we have here a political force committed fanatically to the belief that with US there can be no permanent modus vivendi *[accommodation of a disagreement], that it is desirable and necessary that the internal harmony of our [American] society be disrupted, our traditional way of life be destroyed, the international authority of our state be broken, if Soviet power is to be secure. This political force has complete power of disposition over energies of one of the world's greatest peoples and resources of world's richest national territory, and is borne along by deep and powerful currents of Russian nationalism. In addition, it has an elaborate and far flung apparatus for exertion of its influence in other countries ...*

Kennan's view of the Soviet Union was widely accepted, and he was recalled to Washington to work for the State Department Policy Planning Staff. His ideas were accepted as the definitive view of Soviet intent and behaviour. The policy of 'containment' was devised. To Kennan it was 'a long-term, patient but firm, and vigilant containment of Russian expansionist tendencies'. Such a sustained policy could halt Soviet aggression through politics and diplomacy. However, the policy developed into a more aggressive, militarist one that challenged the Soviet Union on a global basis and was totally opposed to any possibility of communist influence or expansion of territory. Kennan was later critical of the way his opinion had been used to justify the excesses of anti-communism.

2 The Truman Doctrine

On 12 March 1947, the president spoke to Congress. He asked for aid for Greece and Turkey. Britain was no longer able to support the anti-communists in the Greek civil war and it was feared that Stalin would support communist guerrillas there. Truman portrayed to Congress how the possible victory of the communist forces in the eastern Mediterranean could open the door to Soviet domination in the Middle East. His threat, exaggerated as it was, persuaded Congress to approve $400 million for aid. It ended the policy of post-war cutbacks in foreign spending and suggested a new level of intensity in the conflict with the Soviet Union. Truman had established a national consensus that fighting communism was the purpose of the policy of containment. Notice that all the world is included in his promise (see Source 9.10). Were there to be no limits to American geographic and financial support?

SOURCE 9.10   The Truman Doctrine, 12 March 1947, in R. Griffith and P. Baker, *Major Problems in American History Since 1945*, 2nd edn, 2001, pp.87–8

At the present moment in world history nearly every nation must choose between alternative ways of life. The choice is often not a free one.

One way of life is based upon the will of the majority, and is distinguished by free institutions, representative government, free elections, guarantees of individual liberty, freedom of speech and religion, and freedom from political oppression. The second way of life is based upon the will of a minority forcibly imposed upon the majority. It relies upon terror and oppression, a controlled press and radio, fixed elections, and the suppression of personal freedoms.

I believe that it must be the policy of the United States to support free peoples who are resisting attempted subjugation by armed minorities or by outside pressures.

I believe that we must assist free peoples to work out their own destinies in their own way.

I believe that our help should be primarily through economic and financial aid which is essential to economic stability and orderly political processes.

ACTIVITY

Read Source 9.10 and answer the following questions.

1 How does Truman describe the realities of communism?

2 How is the American system different?

3 What justification do you think Truman has for giving such sweeping support for those who want 'freedom'?

■ **Learning trouble spot**

Telling all of the story at once

One of the frustrating, but also interesting, aspects of studying the past is that you cannot know all the stories at the same time. The 1940s became a time of anti-communist reaction and fears of Soviet spying for the Americans. That story is told in Chapter 11. For the moment you are looking at the story of foreign relations, but remember that for the USSR, just as for the USA and other states, there were other influential events going on within their countries. For example: the Soviet Union demonstrated its scientific knowledge by testing its first atom bomb in 1949; China was in the middle of a political revolution which would make it a communist state; and Britain was creating a new social welfare system whilst coping with the severe economic effects of the Second World War, as well as trying to be a Great Power.

SOURCE 9.11 Poster advertising the Marshall Plan

SOURCE 9.12 Photo taken in 1950 of (from left to right): W. Averell Harriman, Special Assistant to the President; Secretary of Defense, George C. Marshall, 1947–49 (Secretary of State at the time of the Marshall Plan); President Harry S. Truman; Dean G. Acheson, Secretary of State, 1949–53

SOURCE 9.13 In June 1947 George Marshall, the secretary of state, announced the Marshall Plan, in D. Merrill, and T. Patterson, *Major Problems in American Foreign Relations*, Vol. II, 5th edn, 2000, p.223

Congress finds that the existing situation in Europe endangers the establishment of a lasting peace, the general welfare and national interest of the United States, and the attainment of the objectives of the United Nations. The restoration or maintenance in European countries of principles of individual liberty, free institutions, and genuine independence rests largely on the establishment of sound economic conditions, stable international economic relationships, and the achievement by the countries of Europe of a healthy economy independent of extraordinary assistance. The accomplishment of these objectives calls for a plan of European recovery, open to all nations which co-operate in such a plan, based upon a strong production effort, the expansion of foreign trade, the creation and maintenance of internal financial stability, and the development of economic co-operation ... Our policy is directed not against any country or doctrine but against hunger, poverty, desperation and chaos.

The Plan required self-help and mutual co-operation from its recipients. It was not just a gift from the USA, but a starting point to help Western Europe recover from the economic rigours of the war, rigours made worse by an appalling winter in 1946–47. It has been acknowledged as one of the most generous and positive achievements of the post-war world. Marshall was not only a highly respected soldier, but also an excellent administrator. The Plan gave over $12 billion over four years to sixteen countries. It enabled European industrial production to rise by 64 per cent and opened up international trade. It was particularly successful in reviving the economy of Western Germany. It ended the threat of communist parties gaining political control there, and quickly restored industrial self-sufficiency. Being part of the Plan required countries to exchange financial information and work towards eliminating trade barriers.

However, to the Soviet Union the message of the Marshall Plan seemed to be 'You too can be like us'. The unspoken message was that being like the USA was better than being like the Soviet Union. Therefore, the Plan was seen as a lure to get at its Eastern European states, and Moscow refused to let Czechoslovakia, Hungary and Poland join. Again, suspicion of the other side's motives prevented co-operation and stiffened the Iron Curtain. Perhaps they

SOURCE 9.14 The Berlin Airlift

were right. The *New York Times* journalist Michael Hoffman, believed that the Plan was also designed to persuade Europeans of the value of American mass production and consumption, 'They learned that this is the land of full shelves and bulging shops, made possible by high productivity and good wages, and that its prosperity may be emulated elsewhere by those who will work towards it'. (Quoted in 'You too can be like us' by David Ellwood, *History Today*, October 1998, p.34.)

4 Defending the division of Germany and Berlin

In June 1948 the USA, Britain and France fused their German areas of occupation, including those in Berlin, into one, in order to encourage the political unity of Berlin. Fearing the impact of this, the Soviets imposed a blockade on all road, rail and river traffic to West Berlin. The only way into West Berlin was by air, so for eleven months the US and British air forces flew in food and fuel, in the Berlin Airlift. The Soviets were forced to accept the continuation of Western occupation in the city. In 1949 the areas of Western occupation became the Federal Republic of Germany. The Soviet Union later formed their zone into the German Democratic Republic.

5 The creation of NATO

In April 1949 the North Atlantic Treaty Organization (NATO) was established. It was a military alliance of most of Western Europe with North America. Dean Acheson (secretary of state, 1949–53) accepted that European nations could not easily pursue economic recovery (which would benefit American trade) if they feared being attacked again. The Soviet Union had not demobilised its army, and had vastly more troops available for rapid deployment in Europe. It was clear that a military force to oppose and contain these forces was needed. The twelve founding nations of NATO – the USA, Britain, Canada, France, Italy, Portugal, Belgium, the Netherlands, Luxembourg, Denmark, Norway and Iceland – agreed that an armed attack on one was an armed attack on all. Later Greece, Turkey and West Germany joined. The USA, then and now, provided the major share of weapons and money (with an initial $1.3 billion), and five US army divisions were based in Germany (where they still are). With fewer troops available than the Soviets, the NATO force relied more heavily on nuclear weapons, many sited in Europe. The NATO agreement tied the USA to the defence of Europe, and hence to international affairs. Together with the Marshall Plan and the Truman Doctrine the USA was demonstrating its determination to defend capitalism and Western democracy.

In response, the Soviet Union created its own military alliance in the Warsaw Pact of Eastern European states, in 1955. It can be argued that NATO was the major force for peace in Europe during the Cold War. However, others argue that it increased Soviet fears about its security with the threat of aggression so close to its borders. Parallel organisations were founded in Asia (SEATO – Southeast Asia Treaty Organisation – in 1954) and the Middle East (CENTO – Central Treaty Organisation – in 1959). The creation of NATO finally confirmed that a Cold War was now in existence.

6 NSC-68

The Second World War had made military planners realise the need for a more integrated military system. Such a system would need an institution to co-ordinate it with the nation's diplomatic strategy. In 1947 the National Security Act was passed. It established:

- the Department of Defense covering the army, navy and air force
- the Central Intelligence Agency (CIA) to co-ordinate intelligence-gathering across the government
- the National Security Council, headed by an advisor, who counselled the president on all security matters.

In 1949 Paul Nitze, the head of the Policy Planning Staff, wrote a statement of national defence policy. Known as NSC-68 it advocated a massive expansion of US spending on military power – from $13 billion to $45 billion per annum. Why? Because Nitze deemed that the Soviet Union sought 'to impose its absolute authority over the rest of the world'. Neither appeasement nor isolation were regarded as possible policies. The document was accepted in 1950. It was proof that the Americans were prepared to win the Cold War, regardless of the cost. It was also accepted that it was to be a military, and not a diplomatic, confrontation.

7 The nuclear bomb

The USA was the only nation with the atom bomb. The Soviet Union had the knowledge to build one, thanks to wartime spying, but did not do so until 1949. Two bombs had already been dropped and although there was much protest about Hiroshima and Nagasaki, it was not clear under what circumstances the USA would use them again. As a result of the Soviet success in developing an atomic bomb, Truman, with Acheson's urging (but not that of Kennan who called for restraint), approved the development of the much more powerful hydrogen bomb.

ACTIVITY

Steering a course for the future, 1945–49

You are Captain Truman of the good ship *The USA*, steering a course for the future in 1945. Your maps are out of date (the world has never been organised like this before) and your compass relies on a belief in democracy and a free world, and the desire to maintain the benefits of the Second World War.

You are well aware of your responsibilities. On your desk you have a notice that says 'The buck stops here'. You have little experience of directing your mighty ship, but are anxious to do well and impress those around you.

What difficulties will you face at sea? A sea-faring captain could face rocks above and below the surface, whirlpools, unsafe harbours, unfriendly foreign ships, even pirates, as well as different advice about the best course to be steered. The captain needs to choose the right course and stay on it. To do this, accurate information about the safety of foreign waters and the right weapons to deal with a crisis are needed. The captain also needs to be able to cope and react to the unexpected and unpredictable.

To complete this Activity you will need to use the material you have studied so far.

1 Why was it difficult for Truman to lead the USA in the immediate post-war period?
2 What was his 'compass' of beliefs?
3 What were the 'rocks' and 'whirlpools' between 1945 and 1949?
4 What weapons did he have (both military and economic)?
5 What 'course' did he choose with regard to American relations with the Soviet Union?
6 Was he a good captain? (Did the USA have to fight another war; did it remain secure and wealthy; was it the best course in the circumstances; did his 'voyage' lead to more difficulties?)
7 The Cold War started during Truman's presidency. Was he responsible for it beginning?

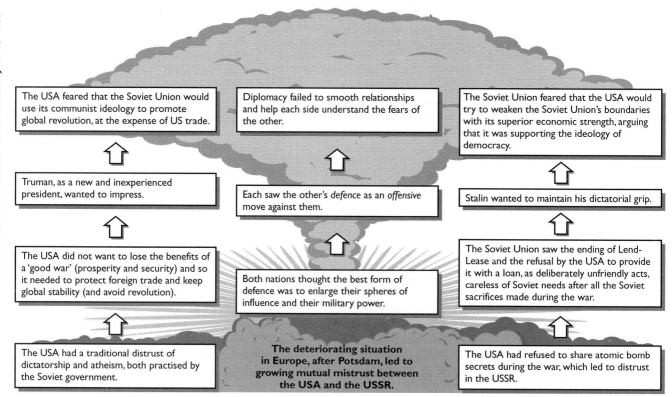

The USA feared that the Soviet Union would use its communist ideology to promote global revolution, at the expense of US trade.

Diplomacy failed to smooth relationships and help each side understand the fears of the other.

The Soviet Union feared that the USA would try to weaken the Soviet Union's boundaries with its superior economic strength, arguing that it was supporting the ideology of democracy.

Truman, as a new and inexperienced president, wanted to impress.

Each saw the other's *defence* as an *offensive* move against them.

Stalin wanted to maintain his dictatorial grip.

The USA did not want to lose the benefits of a 'good war' (prosperity and security) and so it needed to protect foreign trade and keep global stability (and avoid revolution).

Both nations thought the best form of defence was to enlarge their spheres of influence and their military power.

The Soviet Union saw the ending of Lend-Lease and the refusal by the USA to provide it with a loan, as deliberately unfriendly acts, careless of Soviet needs after all the Soviet sacrifices made during the war.

The USA had a traditional distrust of dictatorship and atheism, both practised by the Soviet government.

The deteriorating situation in Europe, after Potsdam, led to growing mutual mistrust between the USA and the USSR.

The USA had refused to share atomic bomb secrets during the war, which led to distrust in the USSR.

■ Learning trouble spot

Capital cities

Sometimes as a way of shorthand, writers will use the name of a capital city in place of the name of the country. So Moscow will be used to represent the Soviet Union, Washington DC to represent the USA, London to represent Britain, and so on. You may find it useful to check your geographical knowledge of capital cities as a result.

Who was to blame for the Cold War?

Opinion on this debate has varied over time, partly because of the benefit of hindsight and because of the release of more documents and disclosures of the decision-making process. Opinions can also change according to the political climate. There was, for instance, no way during the rabid anti-communist atmosphere of the USA in the 1950s that anyone would have been listened to if they had blamed the USA for starting the Cold War.

For the first ten years of the Cold War, Western historians tended to blame the Soviet Union because:

- it was an atheistic dictatorship, and as such, alien to American ideas of freedom
- the Soviet Union aggressively challenged America's desire to spread democracy
- communism had, as its intent, world revolution
- the USSR's geographical interests were a threat to areas of the world that the USA was interested in – Europe, Indo-China, the Middle East
- Soviet interests and behaviour were a threat to American security.

Revisionist historians from the 1960s blamed the USA because:

- the West failed to understand the depth and intensity of the Soviet Union's fear of another German attack
- Soviet domination of Eastern Europe was inevitable in 1945 because of Soviet military control, and had been discussed between Stalin and Churchill in 1944, so there was little point in making an issue of it
- Stalin's foreign policy was more cautious than the USA would accept, especially as the USA did not recognise the post-war economic and ethnic problems of the Soviet Union
- the USA, by its actions during and immediately after the war, increased Stalin's sense of national insecurity
- the USA had over-grand expectations of its world role after 1945, based on its military success and economic abundance.

Yet another set of historians argue that both sides contributed to the development of the Cold War and both could have managed the crises less dangerously (see Sources 9.15 and 9.16).

SOURCE 9.15   J. Patterson, *Grand Expectations*, 1996, p.91

America's leaders frequently whipped up Cold War fears that were grossly exaggerated, thereby frightening its allies on occasions and deepening divisions at home ... Whether the Cold War could have been managed much less dangerously however, is doubtful given the often crude diplomacy of Stalin and his successors and given the refusal of American policy makers to retreat from the grand expectations about the nature of the post-war world.

SOURCE 9.16   E. Hobsbawm, *Age of Extremes – the Short History of the Twentieth Century, 1914–91*, 1994, p.234

... while the USA was worried about the danger of a possible Soviet world supremacy some time in the future, Moscow was worried about the actual hegemony of the USA now, over all parts of the globe not actually occupied by the Red Army. It would not take much to turn an exhausted and impoverished USSR into yet another client region of the US economy ... Intransigence was the logical tactic.

We have to analyse decisions and explain attitudes in order to decide who, if anyone, was most to blame for the development of the Cold War. Nations had to make choices between alternatives. The choices may have been based on inadequate knowledge and unrealistic fears at a time when the reactions of others were unpredictable. Think of Truman sailing his ship (Activity, page 181). Once the Cold War was a reality no one knew how China, the Third World of non-aligned nations, the new nations of the Middle East and former colonies, and states controlled by the Soviet Union, might behave. The world of 1950 was a more dangerous place than the post-war world of 1945.

ACTIVITY

Weigh up the evidence. Do you think that one side was more responsible than the other for the development of the Cold War?

Review: Why did the Cold War begin, 1945–49?

SOURCE 9.17   R. D. Schulzinger, *US Diplomacy since 1900*, 4th edn, 1998, p.12

America imbued the Soviets with awesome powers and detected evil intentions toward world domination. World politics became a 'great game' for pre-eminence ... The stakes, however, rose steeply after the development of nuclear weapons ... When around 1960, both the US and Soviet Union acquired the capacity to destroy life in each other's countries, the rivalry took on a grisly aspect.

SOURCE 9.18   J. Patterson, *Grand Expectations*, 1996, p.135

This was the uniquely difficult and bi-polar world that arose after World War Two: two very different societies and cultures found themselves face-to-face in a world of awesome weaponry.

DISCUSS

'No war is inevitable until it starts' (A. J. P. Taylor).
Do you think that this statement is true about the Cold War? What would the USA and the Soviet Union need to have done, or not done, to avoid it? Could any other country have stopped it and, if not, why not?

ACTIVITY

The historian Eric Hobsbawm, in his survey of the twentieth century, *Age of Extremes*, describes the Cold War as an ideological tennis match. The two players were the USA and the Soviet Union, both anxious to win.

1 What 'balls' (issues) were being hit between the two?
2 How powerful were the respective 'rackets' (sources of political power)?
3 How did the players' strengths differ?
4 What did each side fear would happen if they lost a game?
5 What might happen if they lost the match?

KEY POINTS FROM CHAPTER 9   **Why did the Cold War begin, 1945–49?**

1 The Cold War was a bi-polar confrontation between the USA and the USSR, which lasted from 1949 to 1992.

2 The Soviet Union feared the USA's present power in 1945, and the USA feared the Soviet Union's future power.

3 Ideological differences were thought to be irreconcilable by 1949.

4 The division of Germany and the sharing of the capital of Berlin caused continual friction.

5 The USA used its economic strength through the Marshall Plan, and its military strength, through NATO, to keep Western Europe allied to American interests.

6 The American superiority of nuclear weapons was equalised by the Soviet Union's ability to build and test one successfully in 1949.

7 Historians still debate who was to blame for starting the Cold War.

10

Fighting the Cold War – how successful was the USA, 1950–68?

After 1950 the Cold War became a worldwide conflict. The two superpowers challenged each other across the world – most famously in Korea, Cuba and Vietnam. There were also confrontations in the Middle East, in Africa and in Latin America, but at no time did the two powers directly face each other. Nuclear weapons were never used, except as threats and for negotiation.

The chapter title uses the word 'successful'. For the USA success meant the establishment of their political belief in democracy, their economic belief in maintaining the production of wealth and their social beliefs in the goodness of American culture. Achieving such 'success' needed military backing and the whole-hearted support of the American people, so patterns of spending and national expectations were established that lasted until the disaster of Vietnam forced a change in the 1960s.

This chapter concentrates on the Korean War, on Eisenhower's diplomatic battles, on Kennedy's confrontation over missiles in Cuba, and the defeat and disillusionment of Vietnam. By 1968, many Americans did not think that the Cold War had been a 'good war', but had it been a successful one?

■ 10A Timeline 1950–68

1950	Beginning of the Korean War
1951	USA and Japan sign Mutual Security Pact
1952	USA and Israel defence agreement
	Truman defeated by Eisenhower in presidential election
	Britain tests A-bomb
	USA tests first H-(hydrogen)bomb
1953	Korean War ends
	Soviet Union tests H-bomb
1954	Southeast Asia collective defence treaty to protect South Vietnam
1955	Soviet Union creates Warsaw Pact as opposition to NATO
1956	Suez crisis
	Soviet Union crushes revolution in Hungary
	Eisenhower wins second term as president
1957	UN creates International Atomic Energy Authority
	Britain tests H-bomb
	Soviet Union launches first inter-continental ballistic missile and puts Sputnik into space
1958	Crisis in Lebanon involves American troops

1959	Alaska and Hawaii become forty-ninth and fiftieth states of the USA
1960	France tests A-bomb
	Kennedy beats Nixon in presidential election
1961	Berlin Wall built
1962	Cuban crisis
1963	Nuclear weapons on US navy Polaris submarines
	Treaty banning atmospheric nuclear testing
	Kennedy assassinated
	Johnson becomes president
1964	China tests A-bomb
1965	Operation Rolling Thunder increases bombing of Vietnam
	Beginning of anti-war protests
1966	France withdraws from NATO
1967	Six Days War in Middle East is won by Israel
1968	Tet Offensive in Vietnam demonstrates Viet Cong strength
	Johnson refuses to stand for second term as anti-war protests increase
	Beginning of peace talks for Vietnam in Paris
	Nixon elected president

A Was the Korean War a success in the ideological battle? (pp. 186–88)

B Could a MAD world be a safe world? (pp. 189–92)

C Why did the Cuban crisis frighten the world, 1960–62? (pp. 192–96)

D Why was the Vietnam War so disastrous for the USA, 1945–73? (pp. 196–208)

E Review: How successful was the USA in fighting the Cold War, 1950–68? (pp. 208–09)

186

FIGHTING THE COLD WAR – HOW SUCCESSFUL WAS THE USA, 1950–68?

■ Learning trouble spot

Limited war

To the Americans limited war meant war in one place and without the use of nuclear weapons. It was the type of war that the American military were prepared for, and was the model of Second World War warfare. However, such a model became less common as Cold War fighting took place against unpredictable enemies who preferred guerrilla tactics over fighting set-piece battles with heavy tanks and artillery.

SOURCE 10.1 Mao Zedong (Mao Tse-Tung), the leader of the communist revolution in China

A Was the Korean War a success in the ideological battle?

The Cold War comes to Asia

America's concern about Korea began in China. In 1947 China was plunged into a civil war that had been brewing for years. Mao Zedong (Mao Tse-Tung) led the Communist Party against the ruling Nationalists, led by Jiang Jieshi (Chiang Kai-shek). The latter, though corrupt and inefficient, had the support of the USA. By 1949, the communists, who had much peasant support, were successful and the Nationalists fled to the island of Taiwan (Formosa), where they remain in power today.

The new Chinese government seized American property in China and allied, unsurprisingly, with its communist neighbour, the Soviet Union. As the USA felt that they had 'lost' China and saw Mao as a puppet of Stalin, China had to become part of the policy of containment (see page 177). The USA decided that the best way to 'contain' or restrict Chinese expansion was to develop Japan as its major Pacific ally. Japan was still occupied by the USA in the post-war period, but industrial growth was encouraged and military bases developed on its islands. The Cold War had come to Asia and the next stop would be Korea.

Why Korea?

In 1945 at Yalta, Korea had been divided at its 38th Parallel. The North was ruled by the communist government of Kim Il-Sung, supported by the Soviets who trained the North Korean army. In the South the USA supported Syngman Rhee and provided military assistance. On 25 June 1950 the North Korean army suddenly invaded the South. Stalin had approved the action, expecting little American reaction, but he had not promised Soviet military help.

Truman and Acheson reacted quickly, prompted by memories of Japanese and German aggression and appeasement in the 1930s. They persuaded the United Nations to pass a resolution condemning North Korea as an aggressor and calling for collective security action. The resolution was passed as the Soviet Union was not there to exercise its Security Council veto. The result was a three-year-long Korean war. Supposedly it was a war fought to restore South Korean freedom, but in reality it was the first proxy war where other countries' disputes were used as a battleground for the Cold War. While it was theoretically a UN operation, the USA provided 90 per cent of the soldiers.

■ Learning trouble spot

Chinese spelling

The traditional form of Chinese spelling is known as the Wade-Giles system. After 1976 the Chinese government used the 'pinyin' translations. This meant that Peking became Beijing, and Mao Tse-Tung became Mao Zedong. This book uses this later spelling style, but includes the Wade-Giles style in brackets the first time a familiar word is used.

1 June 1950 – North Korea crossed the 38th Parallel to invade South Korea. Truman demanded action by the UN, which agreed to send a peacekeeping force to restore the border.

2 Three days later Truman ordered American troops to Korea under the command of General Douglas MacArthur. The American fleet was ordered to patrol the waters between Taiwan and China, as it was feared that China would take advantage of the war to invade Taiwan.

3 In September, South Korean and American soldiers were pushed back to the small area around Pusan, and almost out of the country.

4 MacArthur, in a daring operation, by-passed the North Korean army and landed troops at Inchon, on 15 September. Seoul, the South Korean capital, was liberated by the Americans and the North Koreans were pushed back to the 38th Parallel.

5 Truman declared that the aim was not just to contain North Korea in its own territory, but to reunite Korea by force – to 'roll back' communism. American troops could therefore cross the 38th Parallel.

6 American planes attacked bridges on the Yalu River, the boundary between Korea and China. The USA was warned by China not to bomb their links with Korea.

7 MacArthur, wanting to assert American power, ignored the warnings and sent troops close to the Yalu River. Two days later the Americans were attacked by tens of thousands of Chinese troops in night-time assaults and hand-to-hand fighting. Within a month the Americans were forced south to the 38th Parallel. There were heavy American casualties in the bitter cold, and many were taken prisoner.

8 Truman gave up the attempt to unify Korea.

9 July 1951 – Armistice talks began, with most discussion focused on the repatriation of prisoners of war (POWs).

10 The war continued for another two years. Over 40 per cent of American casualties were in this period. A reporter said to a marine, 'If I were God, what would you want for Christmas?' The marine replied, 'Give me tomorrow'.

11 July 1953 – An armistice was signed at Panmunjom. The new Soviet government (Stalin had died in March) encouraged a settlement. POWs, who included Koreans from both sides, were given a choice of whether to stay in the land of their captivity or to return home.

Key

— — — Farthest US advance, Oct.– Nov. 1950

- - - - - Farthest North Korean advance, Sept. 1950

USSR

Vladivostok

CHINA

MANCHURIA

R. Yalu

Chosan

Sinuiju

Hyesanjin

Chongjin

Iwon

Sea of Japan

NORTH KOREA

Wonson

Pyongyang

Armistice Line 7 July 1953

38th Parallel

Kaesong

Panmunjom

Inchon

Seoul

Chunchon

R. Nakong

Taejon

Pohang

Kunsan

Taegu

Yellow Sea

SOUTH KOREA

Pusan

JAPAN

0 ———— 300

km

SOURCE 10.2 General MacArthur

The results of the Korean War

1 The 38th Parallel remained the border with a DEMILITARISED ZONE between the two countries. A communist government controlled the North and a democratic one controlled the South.

2 Over 54,000 American soldiers died and 11,000 were held as POWs. Nearly 5 million Koreans and Chinese died and 120,000 were held as POWs.

3 Much of North Korea suffered damage to crops, transport and factories.

4 Truman had defended South Korea from aggression and demonstrated more resolve than the Chinese and North Koreans had expected, but the USA failed to unify Korea in spite of their military superiority.

When Truman gave up the attempt to unify Korea, General MacArthur demanded an attack on China to smash communism. He suggested that Truman was being an appeaser. Truman's response was to fire him for insubordination, even though the General was a hero to many Americans. Truman was clear about the reason for his decision, 'I fired [MacArthur] because he wouldn't respect the authority of the president. I didn't fire him because he was a dumb son of a bitch, although he was, but that's not against the law for generals. If it was, a half to three-quarters of them would be in jail' (in M. Miller, *Plain Speaking: an Oral Biography of Harry S. Truman*, 1974).

188

FIGHTING THE COLD WAR – HOW SUCCESSFUL WAS THE USA, 1950–68?

SOURCE 10.3 The Korean War Memorial, Washington DC, with nineteen stainless steel statues of soldiers, dressed for combat in the cold of Korea, representing all the military units and ethnic groups involved. The war had initial public support in 1950, but support dwindled as the stalemate continued. It was not until 1995 that this memorial to the war was erected

Did the Korean War have any impact on American foreign policy?

1 It set the pattern for US foreign policy for the rest of the decade and made clear that the Cold War was now a global fight against communism. It brought the Cold War to the Pacific and to Asia.

2 Truman could argue that the USA had won because they had stopped the aggressive expansion of communist rule and had shown the value of the policy of containment.

3 Executive power increased as troops were sent without Congress being asked to declare war. Truman argued that as commander in chief he had sufficient authority. It was the beginning of an 'imperial' style of presidency which was to last for twenty years. The president decided on foreign policy without Congressional involvement.

4 The policy of NSC-68 was implemented (see page 181) with an expansion in troop numbers and overseas military bases. Defence expenditure rose from $13 billion in 1950 to $50 billion by 1953. Bases were established in Saudi Arabia, Spain and elsewhere, but with little regard for the political beliefs of those countries (Spain had a fascist government, Saudi Arabia had an autocratic monarchy, for example). It was sufficient that they were anti-communist. It was the continuation of the wartime military-industrial complex (see page 191) which was to dominate defence spending for decades.

5 Truman's apparent threat to use nuclear weapons in 1952 led to worldwide protest. It raised the question of whether such weapons could ever be used.

ACTIVITY

Was the Korean War a victory for American ideology or had the US merely been given 'a fig leaf of legitimacy' to justify its policy of containment?

1 What do you think the 'fig leaf' was?

2 Find two pieces of evidence for each argument and explain how they support that argument.

WHY WAS THE THIRD WORLD USED AS A BATTLEGROUND FOR THE COLD WAR?

Many Third World countries (e.g. India, Egypt, Indonesia, Ghana) refused to take sides in the Cold War, declaring themselves non-aligned. They wanted to control their own resources and pursue their own political ideals. At the same time, many were poor and in need of assistance to exploit their resources. Some looked to the USSR for this aid.

Many in the USA therefore saw the Third World as an uncontrollable threat – to American political control of a region, to American trade, to getting a return on investments and aid, and to the containment of communism. The USA therefore believed that the USSR could be countered in the Third World by promoting the American model of modern industrialisation driven by private enterprise. Such a model would provide wealth and the pleasures of the American way of life, typified by Hollywood movies, Coca-Cola and denim jeans. Propaganda through films, magazines, exhibitions and radio showed an America to be admired and emulated.

B Could a MAD world be a safe world?

MAD is the acronym for Mutually Assured Destruction
or 'You drop a bomb on me and I'll drop one on you.'

In the opinion of the historian Eric Hobsbawm (in *Age of Extremes – the Short History of the Twentieth Century, 1914–91*, 1994, p.234), 'Both sides ... committed themselves to an insane race to mutual destruction and to the sort of nuclear generals and nuclear intellectuals whose profession required them not to notice this insanity'.

Truman had won the presidential election in 1948, against the predictions of opinion polls. He was unable to stand in 1952 because of the Twenty-Second Amendment and the successful candidate was Dwight D. Eisenhower, a Republican, former soldier and the commander of D-Day in Normandy. His vice-president was Richard Nixon. Nixon lost the 1960 presidential election but finally won in 1968.

FOCUS ROUTE

1 Using the information on pages 190–92, complete your own copy of the table below.
2 Did Eisenhower reduce or increase Cold War tensions?
3 How successful were Eisenhower's policies in fighting the Cold War?

Eisenhower's policies and actions	Cooled tensions or raised the temperature?	Success or failure in terms of US objectives?

ACTIVITY

Select from Chart 10C one example of both the USA and the USSR increasing the arms race and in each example explain how the other country reacted.

■ 10C The Arms Race

1945
It started with the building of nuclear bombs in Los Alamos.

1953
The USA detonated the first hydrogen bomb (H-bomb). The Soviet Union also tested an H-bomb.

1954
A US test destroyed the Pacific island of Bikini. The explosion was seven times as powerful as that over Hiroshima.

1957
The Soviet Union fired the first Inter-continental Ballistic Missile (ICBM) and sent the first satellite, *Sputnik*, into space.

The USA reacted by building more ICBMs and Intermediate-Range Ballistic Missiles (IRBMs) to be launched from Polaris submarines.

The USA had a nuclear stockpile of 5543 weapons.

The Soviet Union had 650 weapons.

1958
The USA launched its first satellite, *Explorer I*, and the National Aeronautics and Space Administration (NASA) was created.
B-52 long-range bombers were available in the USA.
US IRBMs in Europe were targeted at the Soviet Union.

190

FIGHTING THE COLD WAR – HOW SUCCESSFUL WAS THE USA, 1950–68?

By 1960, in spite of public fears of the USA being behind in the arms race, it actually was ahead with a combination of B-52s, ICBMs and Submarine-Launched Ballistic Missiles (SLBMs). There were attempts to slow down the race, but neither side would agree to a nuclear test ban or to arms control treaties that required inspections to check for compliance. Winston Churchill said that a 'balance of terror' had replaced the pre-war 'balance of power'. In spite of this awesome amount of potential destruction no nuclear bomb was detonated in anger or retaliation. As Eisenhower said of a nuclear war, 'you might as well go out and shoot everyone you see and then shoot yourself'.

Did Eisenhower cool the Cold War?

■ 10D Eisenhower's foreign policy assumptions

The Soviet Union would pursue an aggressive foreign policy.

Aggression had to be met with similar aggression.

Technology had an important military role.

Third World nationalism could be ignored.

SOURCE 10.4 President Eisenhower (right) and his secretary of state, John Foster Dulles. The two men worked closely together

The federal budget should be balanced.

The 'domino' theory, that if one country fell to communism then others would fall.

It was better to stop a problem getting worse by limited means rather than just ignoring the problem.

SOURCE 10.5 M. B. Norton, et al., *A People and a Nation*, 6th edn, 2001, p.838

Partisan Democrats promoted an image of Eisenhower as a bumbling, passive, aging hero. Granted, Eisenhower did not always stay abreast of issues because he chose to delegate authority to others, and he seemed stuck in tired views just when the international system was becoming more fluid. Without doubt, though, the president commanded the policy-making process and tamed the more hawkish proposals of Vice-President Richard Nixon and Secretary of State John Foster Dulles.

SOURCE 10.6 M. B. Norton, et al., *A People and a Nation*, 6th edn, 2001, p.838

Few Cold War warriors rivalled Dulles' impassioned anti-communism, often expressed in biblical terms ... Though polished and articulate, Dulles impressed people as arrogant, stubborn, and hectoring – and averse to compromise, an essential ingredient in successful diplomacy.

SOURCE 10.7 In this cartoon by Herblock, which appeared in *The Washington Post* in 1956, Dulles, the secretary of state, dressed as Superman, demonstrates 'brinkmanship' to Uncle Sam (the USA). The caption reads, 'Don't Be Afraid – I Can Always Pull You Back'. The threat of military action was supposed to be sufficient to stop the actual use of it. This policy was effective in stopping the Korean War, when a nuclear attack was hinted at, and against Chinese threats to Indo-China (the present Vietnam, Laos and Cambodia) in 1954

Eisenhower's Cold War policies

a) The New Look

This was the reliance on superior air power and nuclear weapons for use in limited wars, thus making a saving on the cost of conventional forces (prompted by the experiences of Korea). It was also known as 'more bangs for the buck' or 'more rubble for the rouble', as it was presumed that the threat of nuclear weapons would be sufficient to deter aggression. The difficulty came when the nuclear threat could not be carried out because of regional risks, possible retaliation or public opposition. Ground forces would then have to be used. This was to be the situation in Vietnam.

b) 'Massive retaliation'

This meant the nuclear destruction of the Soviet Union or China if either took action deemed to be aggressive. It was presumed that this threat would deter the Soviets. Chinese reaction was less predictable.

c) CIA

Devised as an intelligence-collecting body in 1947 and headed by John Dulles' brother Allen, it undertook anti-communist activities and covert (secret) operations. They were, by their very intent, difficult to control. The CIA secretly helped Muhammad Reza Pahlavi become Shah of Iran in place of the Nationalist premier Muhammad Massadegh in 1953. This gave America an ally next to the Soviet border and provided American oil companies with generous concessions. However, the unjustified intervention created latent hostility in Iran towards the USA.

The CIA also supported a coup in Guatemala in 1954 against the elected President Jacoba Arbenz Guzman, partly because he had challenged excessive land ownership by the American-owned United Fruit Company. It failed to overthrow President Sukarno in Indonesia whom the US thought was too tolerant of communism in his country.

d) Third World

US policy was to:

- offer aid for economic development
- become involved in internal political change or even try to initiate it, and to insist on support for anti-communist policies.

e) Eisenhower Doctrine, 1957

This stipulated that the USA would intervene in the Middle East if any government threatened by a communist takeover asked for help.

f) Arms control

In 1955 Eisenhower proposed 'Open Skies' whereby the USA and the Soviet Union would allow aerial surveillance to check disarmament. It was dismissed by Krushchev (see Source 10.8) as just another form of spying. In 1958 both nations did agree to suspend nuclear tests, especially as the fall-out from above-ground tests was causing much public concern.

g) Summit meetings

Meetings were held between leaders in the belief that face-to-face discussions could be more productive than those between officials. They were held in Geneva in 1955 and proposed for Paris in 1960. Just before this meeting the Soviet Union shot down a U-2 American spy-plane and captured the pilot, Gary Powers. Eisenhower was forced to admit the plane's intent and Khrushchev refused to attend the summit.

h) Military-industrial complex

One of the results of the Second World War had been the establishment of strong links between the military, the producers of weapons and the government. These links were accelerated by the Cold War policies of Truman and Eisenhower. However, in his farewell address, Eisenhower warned of the risk of too much military spending, not just because it made for an unbalanced federal budget, but also because of the power it gave to manufacturers. Eisenhower feared the influence of these unelected individuals and companies on government decisions. During the 1960s the cost of the global containment policy continued to rise and Eisenhower's concerns were seen to be justified.

i) Hungary

In 1956 Khrushchev began a policy of relaxing the controls Stalin had imposed on Eastern Europe. However, when moderate communists in Hungary, led by Imre Nagy, threatened to leave the Warsaw Pact, Khrushchev sent in tanks to quell the rebellion. Nagy was removed and shot, and a more acceptable leader, Janos Kadar, took over. In spite of appeals by the rebels the US government did not intervene. A more moderate government in Hungary might have helped the USA 'contain' the Soviet Union, but the risks of intervention were thought to be too high.

j) Suez

In July 1956, the Egyptian leader Gamal Nasser took control of the Suez Canal, the important trade waterway which gave a quicker route from the Mediterranean to the Indian Ocean. He planned to use the tolls from the Canal to pay for the new Aswan Dam. Britain and France were particularly angered and with Israel's help invaded the Canal Zone. They were not supported by the USA who forced them to withdraw by the use of financial sanctions. However, as Nasser's Egypt had Soviet help, the Middle East became another area of Cold War tension.

k) Quemoy and Matsu

These two islands, very close to the Chinese mainland, were governed by Taiwan. In 1954 China began shelling them. However, an American threat of further action was enough to end the shelling and the dispute about ownership was shelved. It was a clear example of the policy of containment being successfully used against China.

l) Berlin

SOURCE 10.8 Nikita Khrushchev, Soviet leader 1958–64, speaking about his threat to end the occupation of Berlin by the USA, Britain and France in 1959. Eisenhower avoided a military challenge and the threat gradually faded. It is possible that personal contact between the leaders had made compromise easier.

192

FIGHTING THE COLD WAR – HOW SUCCESSFUL WAS THE USA, 1950–68?

DISCUSS

Before you analyse Eisenhower's foreign policy, think how the Cold War could have been 'cooled' or 'heated up'. What kinds of actions might reduce tensions and what might increase them?

DID FOREIGN AID AND INTERVENTION WORK?

'Sometimes' and 'for a while' are probably the best answers. The newly independent countries often saw American attitudes as paternalistic ('we know best'), racially biased and dismissive of nationalistic feelings. Ironically, the USA did not see Third World nationalism as similar to America's fight for independence in 1776, but rather as a direct path to communist takeover. Security fears overrode gaining allies in areas close to communist controlled areas. Neutrality was not trusted; the USA wanted active, not passive support.

■ **Learning trouble spot**

When was the book written?

The effectiveness of Presidents Truman and Eisenhower as political leaders has been reassessed in the last decade. Truman now tends to be blamed more for over-reacting to and misunderstanding the Soviet Union and thus increasing Cold War tensions. Eisenhower is now more highly regarded because of his apparent calmness and subtle manipulation of actions, allowing Dulles to be regarded as the harsher policy maker. Assessments of any leaders depend on a combination of factors, for example evidence available about their intent, seeing what the long-term effects of their policies have been, and information from new sources. The death of the principal character or an important witness to events can release new material. So when you look at a history book, check when it was written. The author will have been limited by the evidence available, influenced by the events at the time of writing and by their own memories of events. Reading more than one biography or assessment helps build up the 'true' picture.

C Why did the Cuban crisis frighten the world, 1960–62?

FOCUS ROUTE

1 How did Kennedy make the world a more dangerous place before the Cuban missile crisis?
2 Did the USA benefit from the Cuban crisis?
3 In what ways was the world a safer place after the Cuban missile crisis?

John Fitzgerald Kennedy (1917–63)

The first Catholic and the youngest president, Democrat John Fitzgerald Kennedy offered hope, excitement and a determination to make the USA the winner in all the races – arms, space, missiles. His vigour and charm were attractive; though, ironically, later studies have shown how much he depended on medication for recurrent digestive and back problems. Kennedy, the son of a wealthy and politically active father (Joseph Kennedy had been ambassador to Britain) was a sharp contrast to the apparent quiet cosiness of Eisenhower, and to his more abrasive, less attractive opponent, Richard Nixon. The result of the 1960 election was, however, very close – 34,227,096 (JFK) to 34,108,546 (RN) in the popular vote.

ACTIVITY

1 Good guy or bad guy? Sort the policies described in the diagram below according to whether they were 'good guy' policies to fight communism or 'bad guy' policies.
2 What impact was it hoped that each of these policies would have?
3 Why might each policy not work as the US intended?
4 Which of these types of policy was likely to be more significant in the Cold War?

■ 10E   Kennedy's Cold War strategy

'Let every nation know that we shall pay any price, bear any burden, meet any hardship, support any friend, oppose any foe to assure the survival and success of liberty' (Kennedy's Inaugural Speech, January 1961).

PEACE CORPS

Established in 1961. Young people volunteered to work in poor areas of the world, teaching English, improving water supplies and providing basic medical care. It had both an idealistic intent and a Cold War one. The hope was that American generosity and practical involvement in Third World countries would deter them from looking to communist states for aid.

FOOD FOR PEACE

Under the guidance of the State Department, surplus agricultural products were given to Third World countries.

ALLIANCE FOR PROGRESS

A programme for Latin America, which gave money for food, medicine and education. As with similar programmes, it did not solve basic economic and social problems. Handouts and piecemeal help were not sufficient and could prevent countries from taking responsibility for their own improvement. Countries also saw these activities as meddling in their affairs especially when the political intent of the USA was realised.

MILITARY BUILD-UP

Kennedy promised to create a flexible military response to any threat, from nuclear to guerrilla. The military budget increased by fifteen per cent in 1961, and there was an increase in the number of nuclear weapons available.

BERLIN WALL

In 1961 the Soviet Union built a concrete and barbed wire barricade to stop East Berliners leaving for the political and economic freedoms of the Western sector. Kennedy reasserted, in his visit to the Wall in 1962, that the world should be free, but he did not challenge the Soviets further.

BAN ON ATMOSPHERIC TESTING

Kennedy increased the number of nuclear weapons, but at the same time he set up the Arms Control and Disarmament Agency and signed the Limited Test Ban Treaty with the Soviet Union in 1963. This banned nuclear testing in the atmosphere, under water and in space.

SPACE PROGRAMME

The NASA budget was increased to meet Kennedy's promises to put a man on the Moon before the end of the decade. In April 1961 the Russian Yuri Gagarin won the race to be the first man in space. One month later the first American, Alan Shephard, flew into space. The race was the public face of Cold War competition. On 20 July 1969, NASA, after spending $25 billion, landed the first American on the Moon – Neil Armstrong. It was a demonstration of American organisation, optimism and technological expertise. The Soviet Union never copied the feat.

COUNTER-INSURGENCY

Kennedy wanted to be able to make a more flexible response to communist challenges. The Green Berets were formed to fight against guerrillas and in small-scale attacks. They also protected American economic advisors and helped to train local military and police forces.

CIA

Continued to act against regimes that appeared to be opposed to US interests and might ally with communists. In the Congo, the Premier, Patrice Lumumba, was murdered with CIA support in 1961, because he had formed links with the Soviet Union. In Brazil, the CIA organised opposition to the election of the President Joao Goulart, who had land reform policies which affected US companies. When this failed they encouraged a successful military coup against him in 1964.

SOURCE 10.9   President Kennedy looking across the Berlin Wall to East Berlin, June 1963

Was the Cuban missile crisis a victory for the USA?

SOURCE 10.10 In the centre, shaking hands, are Gamal Nasser of Egypt (left) and Fidel Castro, meeting in New York; two of the Third World leaders who most angered the USA because of their pro-Soviet support and anti-American declarations

Kennedy saw Cuba as a menacing communist satellite on America's doorstep (Cuba is only 56 kilometres from Florida). Before 1959, Cuba was ruled by Fulgencio Batista, an ally of the USA, whose corrupt regime had encouraged American business, tourists and organised crime. In 1959 Nationalists, led by Fidel Castro, overthrew Batista. Eisenhower's reaction was to request a CIA plan to overthrow the new government. This was an illegal act. Neither then nor subsequently has there been any attempt at negotiation or at any other aim than a forceful end to Castro's rule. Kennedy inherited and approved the plan – an invasion by Cuban exiles and Americans, which took place in the Bay of Pigs on 17 April 1961. It was a total failure. Most of the invaders were captured, the planned assassination of Castro never happened and the Cubans did not rise up in support of the invaders. Castro went on with his programme of health, education and land reforms. The invasion only made him more willing to look to the Soviet Union for assistance.

Next America created Operation Mongoose – involving disruption to Cuba's trade, more raids and another attempt at assassination – Kennedy's desire to end the Castro regime. The result was a crisis which brought the world close to nuclear war.

SOURCE 10.11 Spy-plane photographs taken on 23 October 1962, of Soviet missile sites being constructed on Cuba

■ 10F   The sixteen days of brinkmanship, October 1962

195

FIGHTING THE COLD WAR – HOW SUCCESSFUL WAS THE USA, 1950–68?

14 October	15 October	16 October	17 October
American U-2 spy planes take photos of missile sites in Cuba.		First meeting of the EXCOM – a committee of military figures and politicians in the White House – to consider US reactions.	

18 October	19 October	20 October	21 October
Meeting between Kennedy and Andrei Gromyko, Soviet foreign minister: Kennedy: The Soviet Union is behaving in a hostile manner in Cuba. Gromyko: No, only offering Cuba defence help. More missile site preparations photographed.	US military chiefs argue for a military solution. Kennedy fears that any attack on Cuba would result in a 'tit-for-tat' attack on Berlin and the inevitable result would be the use of nuclear weapons.		

22 October	23 October	24 October	25 October
Kennedy makes a TV broadcast about the Cuban missiles. He imposes a blockade around Cuba and gives an ultimatum for the immediate withdrawal of the missiles by the Soviet Union, warning that if conflict was not avoided it would be a war 'where the fruits of victory would be as ashes in our mouths'.	Kennedy forbids boarding of Soviet ships in international waters as that would be too proactive. Intelligence received that the missiles could be ready for fighting by 25 or 26 October.	Soviet freighters en route to Cuba and due to arrive in seven days. Three had missile onboard. Soviet nuclear armed submarines in the Caribbean. Kennedy and advisors discuss their next move. Later that day news comes that Soviet ships had slowed and some had turned back.	At the UN, the US Ambassador Adlai Stevenson, challenges the Soviet ambassador that the USSR had placed missiles on Cuba. The Soviet ambassador denies the accusation and Stevenson produces the reconnaissance photographs in front of the General Assembly, proving Soviet activity on the island. However, the missiles on Cuba were now ready and could be fired with only five hours' notice.

26 October	27 October	28 October	29 October
	A U-2 spy plane is shot down over Cuba and the pilot killed. The military demands an invasion in reprisal, as the ultimatum does not seem to be effective.	Khrushchev agrees to remove the missiles if the USA promises not to invade Cuba. There is also a secret agreement that the USA will remove its missiles from Turkey. Kennedy agrees. The crisis is over.	

DISCUSS

Was Cuba 'a thorn in the flesh' or 'a dagger in the heart'? These were two descriptions used by Senator William Fulbright of Arkansas, chairman of the Foreign Relations Committee. Which is the more appropriate phrase?

ACTIVITY

How far could you say that the Cuban crisis had shown that the USA was successful in fighting the Cold War? Make notes of events and your assessment of success in terms of short-term achievements.

Why was the crisis so serious?

1 The USA did not know that there were already missiles on Cuba being prepared for firing. Evidence suggests that Cuba would have fired them had the USA invaded the island.
2 The USA did not know that the Soviet commander in Cuba had been given permission for a pre-emptive nuclear strike if the USA invaded.
3 Khrushchev had little inside knowledge of American thinking or plans. He only knew of possible American plans for an invasion of Cuba because a journalist's comments were overheard in a Moscow bar. He did not realise how much pressure Kennedy was under from his generals to invade Cuba.
4 If nuclear weapons were used, no one knew how the war they would create would end, but everyone feared the worst.

Was the world a safer place by 1963?

The misunderstandings and poor communications of the Cuban crisis led to a 'hot line' being installed between the Soviet and American leaders, so that confrontation could be less public. Compromise was more possible in private; less so under the glare of television cameras. Television had brought the crisis into people's living rooms and heightened the sense of imminent catastrophe. It also highlighted the risk of nuclear war and encouraged political protests against these weapons.

196

FIGHTING THE COLD WAR – HOW SUCCESSFUL WAS THE USA, 1950–68?

SOURCE 10.12   President Kennedy with his wife Jackie, beginning their motorcade through the Dallas streets on a re-election visit on 22 November

Minutes after the photo in Source 10.12 was taken, Kennedy was shot dead. The USA and much of the rest of the world was stunned.

Kennedy's apparent triumph over Cuba had been brief. The shock of Kennedy's death prevented negative assessments of his policies for many years. However, recent interpretations have been more critical of his style and the little he delivered of the promises he made. In contrast, both Eisenhower and Johnson have become more highly regarded.

 D   # Why was the Vietnam War so disastrous for the USA, 1945–73?

FOCUS ROUTE

As you work through Section D, make notes on the following questions:
1 **a)** What were the North Vietnamese fighting for?
   b) What were the South Vietnamese fighting for?
   c) What was the USA fighting for?
2 What advantages did the USA have in fighting the Viet Cong?
3 What advantages did the Viet Cong have?
4 Who was ultimately successful and why?
5 How successful was the USA in fighting the Cold War through Vietnam?

■ **Learning trouble spot**

The order of events

This section on Vietnam covers a different period from the other sections in this chapter. All topics need to be put in the context of their past. This book so far has not discussed the end of imperialism after the Second World War, or the rise of nationalism that caused it. It would be difficult to understand the drama and intensity of Vietnam without knowing how the story started. This section also continues beyond 1968 because the Vietnam War did not reach its painful conclusion until the peace treaty in 1973. To stop the story in 1968 would make it too disjointed. When you read Chapter 13, on the USA after 1968, try to keep in mind the on-going problem of Vietnam.

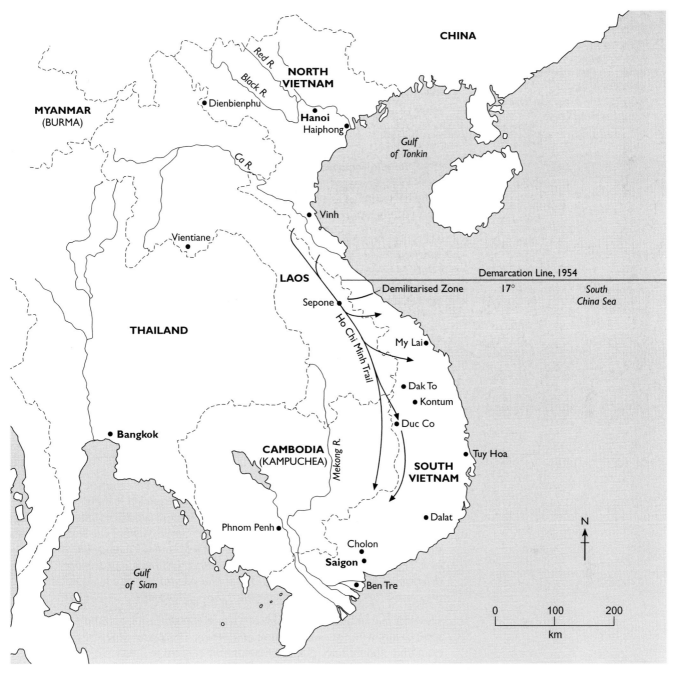

SOURCE 10.13   Map of Vietnam

Ho Chi Minh (1890–1969)
Born in poverty in Indo-China, Ho Chi
Minh moved to France in 1917. Here he
began his lifelong involvement with the
international Communist movement,
founding the Indo-China Communist
Party in 1930. During the Second World
War he formed a resistance force – the
Viet Minh – against the Japanese,
receiving secret support from the USA.
In 1945 he proclaimed the Democratic
Republic of Vietnam in Hanoi, and led
his forces against the French and, later,
the Americans. He died before Vietnam
became independent, but Saigon was
renamed Ho Chi Minh City in his
honour.

FOCUS ROUTE

1 Why did the USA have an interest in Indo-China in 1945?
2 Why was that interest challenged by the Vietnamese?
3 Why did the American interest continue after 1954?

How did the USA become involved in Indo-China, 1945–60?

At the end of the Second World War the USA had to choose between its mistrust of the Soviet Union and China, and one of its founding principles, anti-colonisation. The USA had fought Britain in 1776 to be free of colonisation, and believed that other countries had the right to choose to be independent. Before 1941, and its occupation by Japan, Indo-China had been under French colonial control.

In 1945:

- the Vietnamese wanted independence
- the French wanted the country back for economic reasons
- the USA wanted a strong France to withstand communism, both in Europe and in this area of Asia.

Therefore France was allowed to re-establish its control in Indo-China, with American aid. This decision simply provoked Ho Chi Minh, leader of the Viet Minh, to begin the fight for independence.

SOURCE 10.14 Using the language of the American and French Declarations of Independence, the Viet Minh sought land reform and independence

The Vietnamese Declaration of Independence, 1945

All men are created equal. They are endowed by their Creator with certain inalienable rights, among these are life, liberty and the Pursuit of Happiness. This immortal statement was made in the Declaration of Independence of the United States of America in 1776. In a broader sense, this means: All the peoples on the earth are equal from birth, all the people have a right to live, be happy and free. The Declaration of the French Revolution made in 1791 on the Rights of Man and the Citizen also states, 'All men are born free and with equal rights ...'

Nevertheless, for more than eighty years, the French imperialists, abusing the standard of Liberty, Equality and Fraternity, have violated our Fatherland and oppressed our fellow-citizens. They have acted contrary to the ideals of humanity and justice. ... we, members of the Provisional Government of the Democratic Republic of Vietnam, solemnly declare to the world that Vietnam has the right to be a free and independent country ... The entire Vietnamese people are determined to mobilize all their physical and mental strength to sacrifice their lives and property in order to safeguard their independence and liberty.

The USA feared that, as Ho Chi Minh was a communist, he would naturally want to ally with the Soviet Union and China. Therefore, America gave France economic and military aid, but Eisenhower refused to intervene directly. In 1954 the Viet Minh's siege of Dien Bien Phu led to the French surrender. The Geneva Accord drawn up in 1954:

- recognised French withdrawal from the area
- partitioned Vietnam at the 17th Parallel, between North and South governments
- required free elections to be held in two years
- recognised Laos and Cambodia as neutral states.

But the USA was fighting the Cold War and determined to contain communist expansion. Eisenhower feared that the collapse of one Asian state would lead to the collapse of many. If Ho Chi Minh won the election in 1956 he would run all Vietnam as a communist state. So the USA:

- refused to sign the Geneva Accord
- gave military support to Ngo Dinh Diem, the leader of South Vietnam
- agreed with his decision to postpone the elections
- ignored his persecution of opponents
- set up a military mission of 1000 'advisors' (not combat troops) in Saigon.

Unfortunately for the Americans Diem was unpopular and ineffective.
This was the situation that President Kennedy inherited in 1960.

199

FIGHTING THE COLD WAR – HOW SUCCESSFUL WAS THE USA, 1950–68?

FOCUS ROUTE

1 What were the factors that persuaded the USA into its initial military involvement in Vietnam?
2 What were the factors which escalated that involvement?

The Americanisation of Vietnam, 1960–65

1 The decisions of President Kennedy

In his Inaugural Speech, Kennedy had promised that the USA would support freedom around the world. It was a grandly generous promise which, if carried out, would cost the USA much in money and military involvements.

■ 10G The pressures on Kennedy

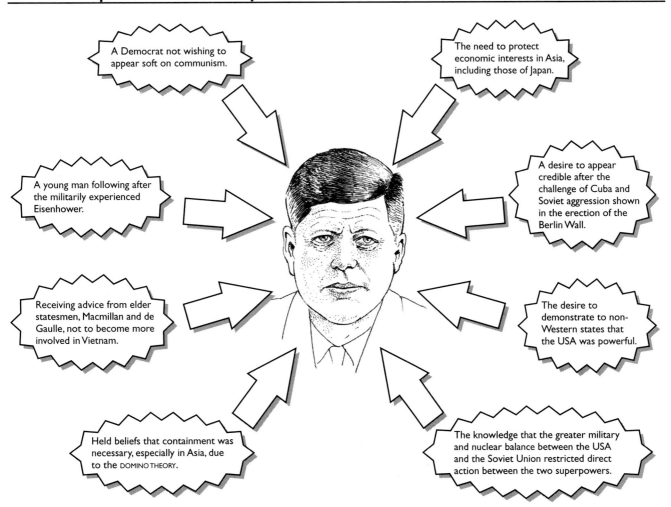

A Democrat not wishing to appear soft on communism.

The need to protect economic interests in Asia, including those of Japan.

A young man following after the militarily experienced Eisenhower.

A desire to appear credible after the challenge of Cuba and Soviet aggression shown in the erection of the Berlin Wall.

Receiving advice from elder statesmen, Macmillan and de Gaulle, not to become more involved in Vietnam.

The desire to demonstrate to non-Western states that the USA was powerful.

Held beliefs that containment was necessary, especially in Asia, due to the DOMINO THEORY.

The knowledge that the greater military and nuclear balance between the USA and the Soviet Union restricted direct action between the two superpowers.

Kennedy decided:

- to try to create a more flexible policy, using economic aid, encouraging nation-building, and backing this up with counter-insurgency forces (the Green Berets) against guerrilla forces
- to continue to support Diem and the South Vietnam Army (ARVN) by dollar aid and air support
- to send more military 'advisors' and equipment under project 'Beef-up'.

Did it work?

- The Diem regime continued to be corrupt and unpopular, especially amongst landless peasants.
- The Viet Cong (a group of guerrilla fighters) continued to pursue their independence campaign, creating the National Liberation Front in South Vietnam.
- The 15,000 advisors failed to improve the ARVN.
- The CIA gave covert encouragement to the ARVN to get rid of Diem.

On 1 November 1963 Diem was assassinated. On 22 November 1963 Kennedy was assassinated. There is no evidence that the two assassinations were linked.

DISCUSS

1 What were Johnson's choices?
2 What persuaded him to make the decisions that he did?

2 The decisions of President Johnson

When Johnson became president after Kennedy's assassination in 1963 there were 16,000 advisors in Vietnam. 'Advisors' included soldiers, but none on active service. When his presidency ended in 1968 there were 500,000 soldiers there and, six months earlier, he had turned down a request for 200,000 more. 'It was as if we were trying to build a house with a bulldozer and a wrecking crane' (unknown US official).

By 1964, Johnson's choices were limited. He was inexperienced in foreign affairs and relied on the expertise of Robert McNamara, his secretary of defense, and McGeorge Bundy, his national security advisor. He was being urged that only a full-scale military force could stop the collapse of the South Vietnamese government. In the summer of 1964, American patrols in the Gulf of Tonkin, off the North Vietnamese coast, claimed to be have been fired on. Johnson was able to go to Congress to request a response. They passed a resolution, known as the Gulf of Tonkin Resolution, that the president was authorised to, 'take all necessary measures to repel any armed attack against the forces of the US and to prevent further aggression'. It meant that the president, without any further consultation or permission from Congress, could use force to conduct his foreign policy. He could, in effect, wage war without formal approval from Congress. This resolution was not revoked until June 1970, therefore only the president directed the war.

'The greatest single error that America has made in its national history?' This was the comment of George Ball, under-secretary of state, at the 21 July 1965 meeting in the White House to decide whether to escalate the war. Ball had warned that 'once on the tiger's back, we cannot be sure of picking the place to dismount'.

In July 1965 the Joint Chiefs of Staff asked for 100,000 soldiers to be sent to Vietnam. They argued that their attacks so far had been limited and only more force would have an impact. Secretary of Defense Robert McNamara argued that US credibility was at stake and that the USA was committed to support South Vietnam.

SOURCE 10.15   A transcript of the 21 July 1965 White House meeting, which lasted all day (from M. Johnson, *Reading the American Past*, 2nd edn, 2002, pp.453–54)

Morning of the 21 July

The President: ... is there another course in the national interest, some course that is better than the one McNamara proposes? We know that it is dangerous and perilous, but the big question is, can it be avoided?
Ball: There is no course that will allow us to cut our losses. If we get bogged down, our cost might be substantially greater. The pressure to create a larger war would be inevitable ...
The President: ... We haven't always been right. We have no mortgage on victory. Right now, I am concerned that we have very little alternatives to what we are doing. I want another meeting, more meetings before we take any definitive action ...

Afternoon of the 21 July

Ball: We cannot hope to win, Mr President. The war will be long and protracted. The most we can hope for is a messy conclusion. There remains a great danger of intrusion by the Chinese ... I am concerned about world opinion. If we could win in a year's time, and win decisively, world opinion will be alright. However, if the war is long and protracted, as I believe it will be, then we will suffer because the world's greatest power cannot defeat guerrillas. Then there is the problem of national politics. Every great captain in history was not afraid to make a tactical withdrawal if conditions were unfavourable to him. The enemy cannot be seen in Vietnam. He is indigenous to the country. I truly have serious doubts that an army of Westerners can successfully fight Orientals in an Asian jungle.
The President: This is important. Can Westerners, in the absence of accurate intelligence, successfully fight Asians in jungle rice paddies? ...

Ball: I think that we all have underestimated the seriousness of this situation ... I think that a long protracted war will disclose our weakness, not our strength. The least harmful way to cut losses in SVN [South Vietnam] is to let the government decide it doesn't want us to stay there. Therefore, we should put proposals to the GVN [government of South Vietnam] that they can't accept. Then, we move to a neutralist position. I have no illusions that after we were asked to leave South Vietnam, that country would soon come under Hanoi control ...

The President: But George, wouldn't all these countries say that Uncle Sam was a paper tiger, wouldn't we lose credibility breaking the word of three presidents, if we did as you have proposed? It would seem to be an irresponsible blow. But I gather you don't think so?

Ball: No, sir. The worse blow would be that the mightiest power on earth is unable to defeat a handful of guerrillas.

SOURCE 10.16   An extract from *In Retrospect*, 1995, the memoirs of Robert McNamara

We of the Kennedy and Johnson administrations who participated in the decisions on Vietnam acted according to what we thought were the principles and traditions of this nation. We made our decisions in the light of those values. Yet we were wrong, terribly wrong ... Looking back I clearly erred by not forcing – then or later, in either Saigon or Washington – a knock-down, drag-out debate over the loose assumptions, unasked questions, and thin analysis underlying our military strategy in Vietnam.

SOURCE 10.17   Protest also came from politicians who questioned American motives and policy. The views of Senator William Fulbright, chairman of the Senate Foreign Relations Committee. From the *Congressional Record CXII*, 17 May 1966

The attitude above all others which I feel sure is no longer valid is the arrogance of power, the tendency of great nations to equate power with virtue and major responsibilities with a universal mission ... I do not question the power of our weapons and the efficiency of our logistics ... What I question is the ability of the United States, or France or any other Western nation, to go into a small, alien undeveloped Asian nation and create stability where there is chaos, the will to fight where there is defeatism, democracy where there is no tradition of it and honest government where corruption is almost a way of life ... The cause of our difficulties in southeast Asia is not a deficiency of power but an excess of the wrong kind of power which results in a feeling of impotence when it fails to achieve its desired ends ... We are trying to remake Vietnamese society, a task which certainly cannot be accomplished by force and which probably cannot be accomplished by any means available to outsiders. The objective may be desirable, but it is not feasible ...

SOURCE 10.18   The beginning of the president's speech to the Johns Hopkins University in Baltimore, on 7 April 1965 (quoted in M. Johnson, *Reading the American Past*, 2nd edn, 2002, pp.449–50)

Why must a nation hazard its ease, its interest, and its power for the sake of people so far away? We fight because we must fight if we are to live in a world where every country can shape its own destiny, and only in such a world will our own freedom be finally secure. This kind of world will never be built by bombs and bullets. Yet the infirmities of man are such that force must often precede reason and the waste of war, the works of peace. We wish that it were not so. But we must deal with the world as it is, if it is ever to be as we wish ...

Why are we in South Vietnam? We are there because we have a promise to keep. Since 1954 every American president has offered support to the people of South Vietnam. We have helped to build, and we have helped to defend. Thus, over many years, we have made a national pledge to help South Vietnam defend its independence. And I intend to keep that promise.

We are also there to defend world order ... To leave Vietnam to its fate would shake the confidence of all these people in the value of an American commitment and in the value of an American word. The result would be increased unrest and instability, and even wider war.

ACTIVITY

Using Source 10.15:

1 What were Ball's objections to escalating the war in Vietnam?

2 Why do you think a guerrilla army would be so difficult for Americans to fight against?

3 On what points did the president agree with him?

4 Where did the president have his doubts?

Using Source 10.16:

5 Where does McNamara think he failed in the decision-making over Vietnam?

Using Sources 10.15 and 10.17:

6 Where do Fulbright and Ball agree about the probable impact of escalating the war?

7 What does Fulbright mean by 'the arrogance of power'?

Using Sources 10.18 and 10.19:

8 Why do you think President Johnson agreed to increase the number of troops?

202

FIGHTING THE COLD WAR – HOW SUCCESSFUL WAS THE USA, 1950–68?

SOURCE 10.19 President Johnson's greatest interest was his Great Society programme to alleviate poverty in America. Yet he realised the risks in putting those interests first (in D. Kearn, *Lyndon Johnson and The American Dream*, 1976, pp.251–52)

ACTIVITY

1 What does Source 10.19 tell you about Johnson's beliefs?
2 What was his dilemma?

If I left the woman I really love – the Great Society – in order to get involved with that bitch of a war on the other side of the world, then I would lose everything at home. All my programs. All my hopes to feed the hungry and shelter the homeless ... But if I left that war and let the communists take over South Vietnam, then I would be seen as a coward and my nation would be seen as an appeaser and we would both find it impossible to accomplish anything for anybody anywhere on the entire globe.

In the end, Johnson felt that there was no alternative but to continue the war, and if that meant more soldiers, then so be it. Escalation meant that the USA was determined to maintain its containment policy against communism. The three years which followed are described as the Americanisation of Vietnam. One puzzle for biographers is why Johnson, such a pro-active president over domestic problems, was so inactive over Vietnam. One of his biographers, Robert Dalleck, argues that:

• he knew that he was inexperienced in foreign affairs
• he found it difficult to withstand right-wing pressure
• his pride made him over-affected by anti-war demonstrations
• his 'can-do' nature made it difficult to believe that the USA could possibly be defeated.

How was the Vietnam War fought?

FOCUS ROUTE

1 Why did the Americans find it so difficult to defeat the Viet Cong (consider terrain, type of weapons, methods of attack, isolation)?
2 How did the nature of the war make American soldiers react?
3 How far were American troops successful in fighting the enemy?

ACTIVITY

Be an American general
Discuss with a partner or a group how to make the USA successful in a war against a poor, agricultural, Far East country. Look back to the map of Vietnam in Source 10.13 (page 197).
Consider:
• the country's geography
• the reasons for fighting and the pressures for victory on both sides
• what each side might fear would happen if they lost
• which weapons and tactics would be effective
• how to protect your troops and keep them supplied
• how to maintain the troops' morale and discipline.
As you read through the story of the Vietnam War think about your decisions.
• In what areas were you a good general?
• What did you forget to take into account?
• What was unexpected and difficult to plan for?
• Would you have done better than the real generals?
• What do you think of the American policy towards the Vietnam threat?

1 The military strategies
This was a war of attrition in which the North Vietnamese were attacked in two ways:

a) direct bombing
b) deployment of ground troops.

a) Direct bombing
The aim: in Operation Rolling Thunder, from March 1965 to March 1968, the USA aimed to:

• damage North Vietnam so much economically that they would negotiate a peace
• attack the Ho Chi Minh Trail of hidden paths, tunnels and waterways used by the Viet Cong to move soldiers, equipment and supplies.

TALKING POINT

What do you think are the strengths and weaknesses of the kind of journalism carried out by Larry Burrows and Michael Herr?

The method: a million tons of bombs dropped by B-52s at a cost of $30,000 a sortie, with the use of defoliation to strip leaf-cover, burn crops and expose villages. The bombing of South Vietnam was used to try to flush out Viet Cong supporters and minimise support from villagers.

The results:
- Defoliation, using toxic chemicals like Agent Orange, caused immediate and long-term sickness amongst civilians and soldiers, including Americans.
- The destruction of Vietnam's agriculture and towns.
- The North Vietnamese rebuilt roads and bridges more quickly than anticipated, moved munitions plants underground, and extended their network of tunnels and shelters.
- The attacks did not damage morale and instead seemed to intensify the will to fight.

However, the bombing continued. Between 1965 and 1973 there were three times as many bombs dropped on Vietnam as had fallen on Europe, Asia and Africa during the whole of the Second World War. Vietnam is a country in area the size of the state of Texas or almost the size of Germany today, but it has a very long coastline and the climate varies from temperate in the north to tropical in the south.

b) Ground troops deployed
The aim: to support the bombing campaign by capturing Vietnamese soldiers and damaging their support in the countryside.

The method: to continue to increase the number of troops. Numbers increased from 380,000 in 1966, to 586,000 in 1968.

The results: The Tet Offensive by the North Vietnamese over the Vietnam New Year, on 30 January 1968, proved that neither bombing nor ground forces had ended the ability or desire of the Viet Cong to continue the war. The Viet Cong attacked five of the six main cities and three-quarters of the provincial capitals. They were quickly pushed back from most, but the ancient and beautiful city of Hue was badly damaged. The Viet Cong had successfully disproved American claims that the war was almost over.

ACTIVITY

Work with a partner or a small group. You are television reporters who have to select images of the Vietnam War and present them to an audience who knows little of the conflict. Select eight images, using this book and other sources, and write the voiceover script to illustrate and link the images.

SOURCE 10.20 Wading through a swamp with a wounded soldier, 1969

204

FIGHTING THE COLD WAR – HOW SUCCESSFUL WAS THE USA, 1950–68?

SOURCE 10.21 A poster illustrating the massacre of hundreds of men, women and children at the village of My Lai, by American soldiers

SOURCE 10.22 The *New York Herald Tribune*, 25 April 1965

Two Viet Cong prisoners were interrogated on an aeroplane flying towards Saigon. The first refused to answer questions and was thrown out of the aeroplane at 3000 feet. The second immediately answered all the questions. But he, too, was thrown out.

SOURCE 10.23 From P. Caputo, *A Rumour of War*, 1977

The war was mostly a matter of enduring weeks of expectant waiting and, at random intervals, of conducting vicious manhunts through jungles and swamps where snipers harassed us constantly and booby traps cut us down one by one ... At times, the comradeship that was the war's only redeeming quality caused some of the worst crimes – acts of retribution for friends who had been killed. Some men could not withstand the stress of guerrilla-fighting; the hair-trigger alertness constantly demanded of them, the feeling that the enemy was everywhere, the inability to distinguish civilians from combatants created emotional pressures which built to such a point that trivial provocation could make these men explode like the blind destructiveness of a mortar shell ... I felt sorry for those children (soldiers arriving in Vietnam for the first time) knowing that they would all grow old in the land of endless dying. I pitied them, knowing that out of every ten, one would die, two would be maimed for life, another two would be less seriously wounded and sent out to fight again, and all the rest would be wounded in other, more hidden ways.

SOURCE 10.24 President Johnson, in early 1968, listening to a tape recording by his son-in-law, a marine serving in Vietnam. It is an image that shows Johnson's anguish at a war which had gone out of control

TALKING POINT

All wars are cruel. How would you rate the Vietnam War? What is the evidence for your opinion?

How did the USA get out of Vietnam, 1968–73?

The army response to the Tet Offensive was to ask for more troops – 206,000, or a 40 per cent increase – which would mean calling up reservists. Discussion and argument over the request lasted for 30 days. One of the strongest critics of more troops was the new Secretary of Defense, Clifford Clarke. He favoured a more restrained response. Johnson's decision was much influenced by these discussions and by the increasing hostility of the press and Congressional opposition. It was also the year of a presidential election, and this added extra domestic pressure. On 31 March Johnson rejected the request and announced there would be a partial halt to the bombing and a search for peace would start. Just as stunningly, in the same radio broadcast, he announced that he would not seek re-election as president in November. As Source 10.24 shows, the war had damaged him as it had thousands of others.

■ 10H The steps to peace

PEACE

The civil war in Vietnam continued for another two years until March 1975, when North Vietnam took control of Saigon, renamed it Ho Chi Minh City, and Vietnam was united, 30 years after its declaration of independence from France.

By the **ceasefire of 27 January 1973** – agreed by both sides it required the unilateral withdrawal of US troops from Vietnam. It was peace, but without honour.

By the **Paris Peace Talks** – stalled since 1968 because of South Vietnamese military weakness, they were restarted after more successful attacks on the North. A ceasefire was agreed in October 1972, but fighting restarted with a South Vietnamese Christmas bombing campaign against Hanoi and Haiphong.

By the **repeal of the Gulf of Tonkin Resolution** – in June, angered by Nixon's policy, Congress revoked the Tonkin Resolution and stopped any funding for attacks in Cambodia.

By **bombing raids in Cambodia** – carried out to destroy the Ho Chi Minh Trail. The raids failed, but in April 1970 Nixon sent ground troops into Cambodia. This led to many protests, especially on US university campuses.

By **reducing troop numbers** – there were 543,000 in 1969; 334,000 in 1970; and 24,200 in 1972. Their numbers were replaced by increasing the size of the South Vietnamese army.

By the **Nixon Doctrine** – which stated that the USA would help those nations willing to help themselves. So began the Vietnamisation stage of the war.

By the **election of a new president** – Richard Nixon won the 1968 presidential election on the assumption that he would end the war. It took until 1973.

206

FIGHTING THE COLD WAR – HOW SUCCESSFUL WAS THE USA, 1950–68?

WHO LOST VIET NAM?

"NOT I," SAID IKE. "I JUST SENT MONEY."

"NOT I," SAID JACK. "I JUST SENT AD-VISORS."

"NOT I," SAID LYNDON. "I JUST FOLLOWED JACK."

"NOT I," SAID DICK. "I JUST HONORED JACK AND LYNDONS COMMITMENTS."

"NOT I," SAID JERRY. "WHAT WAS THE QUESTION?"

"YOU LOST VIETNAM," SAID HENRY, "BECAUSE YOU DIDN'T TRUST YOUR LEADERS."

SOURCE 10.26   A cartoon by Jules Feiffer in 1975 entitled *Who lost Vietnam?*

Why did the US military strategy fail in the Vietnam War?

'How could so many with so much achieve so little against so few?' (the comment of General Westmoreland, the Commander in Vietnam).

■ 10I   Reasons for failure

MILITARY REASONS

1 The Viet Cong could move around in Vietnam 'like a fish in water'.
2 US soldiers served a one-year tour of duty, and inexperienced young men were suddenly faced with fighting that was more vicious and unpredictable than could be imagined.
3 Miscalculations about the most effective military operations to persuade the Viet Cong that peace talks would be preferable to more fighting.
4 The full-scale invasion of Vietnam was never possible because of the threat of nuclear escalation.
5 The determination and courage of the Vietnamese to reject foreign intervention and accept limitless casualties.
6 In such a war of attrition, time was on the side of the Vietnamese.

POLITICAL REASONS

1 The USA never committed itself to 'total victory' because of the political consideration that this might lead to Soviet or Chinese intervention and nuclear war.
2 The American public began to oppose the war and political decisions overrode military ones.
3 Continuing corruption in the South Vietnamese government made it difficult to present as an acceptable alternative to communism.
4 Missed opportunities for disengagement, particularly in 1964 when there was a choice about American action, even if it risked a communist government in Vietnam.
5 Maintaining momentum and energy in effective and flexible decision-making became harder the longer the conflict progressed. Innovative thinking became harder and failed to adjust to changing situations.
6 The government was unable to call on sufficient professional expertise because the McCarthyism of the early 1950s (see Chapter 11) had removed many Far East specialists from their jobs in government. The ones that remained were less flexible in their thinking, and supported the containment and domino theories, fearing the possible combined power of China and the Soviet Union.

ACTIVITY

Study Source 10.26 and answer the following questions:

1 Identify the presidents.
2 Do you agree with the summary of their actions?
3 What is the cartoonist critical of? Was it justified criticism?

207

FIGHTING THE COLD WAR – HOW SUCCESSFUL WAS THE USA, 1950–68?

ACTIVITY

Examine Chart 10I.

1 Which were the most important factors in the military defeat in Vietnam?

2 Select the three most important and list them in order of priority.

3 Discuss your list with a partner or a group. Do you want to change your decision?

SOURCE 10.27 Colonel Robert D. Heinl, Junior of the Marine Corps, and a veteran of Vietnam, writing in the *Armed Forces Journal*, in 1971

The morale, discipline and battleworthiness of the US armed forces are, with a few salient exceptions, lower and worse than at any time in this century and possibly in the history of the United States.

By every conceivable indicator, our army that now remains in Vietnam is in a state approaching collapse, with individual units avoiding or having refused combat, murdering their officers and non-commissioned officers, drug-ridden, and dispirited where not near-mutinous...

■ 10J What did the end of the Vietnam War mean?

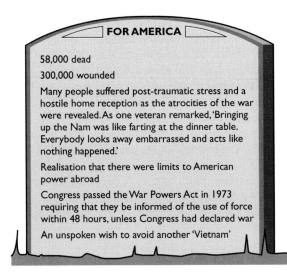

FOR AMERICA

58,000 dead

300,000 wounded

Many people suffered post-traumatic stress and a hostile home reception as the atrocities of the war were revealed. As one veteran remarked, 'Bringing up the Nam was like farting at the dinner table. Everybody looks away embarrassed and acts like nothing happened.'

Realisation that there were limits to American power abroad

Congress passed the War Powers Act in 1973 requiring that they be informed of the use of force within 48 hours, unless Congress had declared war

An unspoken wish to avoid another 'Vietnam'

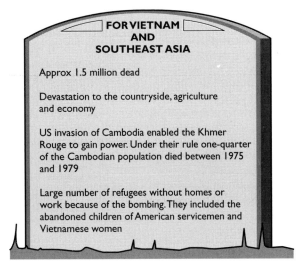

FOR VIETNAM AND SOUTHEAST ASIA

Approx 1.5 million dead

Devastation to the countryside, agriculture and economy

US invasion of Cambodia enabled the Khmer Rouge to gain power. Under their rule one-quarter of the Cambodian population died between 1975 and 1979

Large number of refugees without homes or work because of the bombing. They included the abandoned children of American servicemen and Vietnamese women

Why did the US political strategy fail?

TALKING POINTS

Of course you're biased!

Being a researcher and a historian should mean being able to collect and interpret evidence in as neutral a way as possible. However, historians have to be aware of their own bias – both in selecting the evidence they search, and in their own reactions to it. Studying wars is especially difficult. It is natural to support one side against another. No historian can be totally neutral.

Nor can *you* be in your writing. You need to think where you have prejudices and favoured interests that will affect your analysis or assessment of an event. Some topics will seem quite boring – economic policy comes first to mind! But others, involving attacks against people or your own strongly held political or religious beliefs, will involve you emotionally.

1 Can you think of areas where you react on a personal level? Can you recognise your bias?

2 Do you have a bias on the topic of Vietnam – and why?

SOURCE 10.28 These extracts were written by an American historian, William Chafe, more than ten years after the Vietnam War ended (*The Unfinished Journey*, 4th edn, 1999, pp. 296, 298, 299, 300)

In the end, American policy foundered on the flaw inherent in its premise – that a modern, industrialised, technological society could 'save', through external intervention, a society whose culture and values were totally antithetical to the American way of life. While Americans prized 'progress' and looked to the future, the Vietnamese worshipped traditionalism and the values of the past. While Americans represented the quintessence of individualism, the Vietnamese worshipped the family and the collective, not even having a word for the personal pronoun 'I'. ...

Without question, the central precondition for American involvement in Vietnam was the set of assumptions that underlay and shaped the entire history of the Cold War. Once committed to the view that the communist world was one, and systematically engaged in a worldwide conspiracy to subvert freedom, any effort in other countries that could be interpreted as hostile to the United States automatically became defined as part of that worldwide conspiracy ... containment ... became a diffuse, universal rationale for resisting any change in the international status quo. Given such a definition of the world, and the moralistic rhetoric that accompanied it, distinctions between countries and issues became blurred, and it was America's 'moral' obligation to defend 'freedom' anywhere it was threatened, regardless of how dictatorial, tyrannical, or repressive the regimes on 'our' side acted. ...

[President] Johnson could have overruled his advisors, listened to those in his inner circle who urged alternative courses of action, and found a way to extricate the US from Vietnam. Although some have argued that Johnson never knew what he was getting into, and that the final disaster of American policy in

208

FIGHTING THE COLD WAR – HOW SUCCESSFUL WAS THE USA, 1950–68?

ACTIVITY

Chafe (Source 10.28) identifies four key areas of political failure in America's war against Vietnam.

1 Write them in your own words.
2 What were the short-term effects of those failures? (The previous Activities in this section will help you.)
3 Can you guess what long-term effects there might be?

TALKING POINT

' ...We watched the United States falsification of body counts, in fact glorification of body counts. We listened while month after month we were told the back of the enemy was about to break. We fought using weapons against 'oriental human beings'. We fought using weapons against those people which I do not believe this country would dream of using were we fighting in the European theatre.' (John Kerry, the Democrat presidential candidate in 2004.)
Is this description of the Vietnam War true of all wars, or do you think the Vietnam War was a special case?

Vietnam was the accidental result of incremental decisions, each of which was reasonable, the evidence suggests that Johnson had before him accurate assessments of where his policy would lead before he made his basic decisions. ...

[President Johnson consistently] deceived the American people and Congress about his decisions. Rather than inform the public of the dimensions of the enterprise he was embarking upon, the president dissembled, insisted that no major changes had taken place, and buried his announcements of troop increases ... By indulging his obsession with retaining total control in his own hands, Johnson ... [created] a situation that guaranteed in the long run his total inability to retain credibility with the American people ...

■ Learning trouble spot

Why is the section on the Vietnam War so long?

This section on the Vietnam War can seem very long for a war in a small country that lasted only a few years, did not require a Home Front like the First World War, nor the use of nuclear weapons to end it. So why does it matter? It was the first time that the USA had been defeated in a war – and in a war against a poor Third World country that the average American could not have located on a map before 1963. It was a war in which the USA had committed vast numbers of soldiers and weaponry, and yet had lost so many troops. It was a war of brutality on both sides. It was also a war in which the Vietnamese were fighting for the same ideals as the Americans in 1776.

Americans were humiliated and angry. Television and vivid reporting had brought the war's awful reality into ordinary homes. No one could escape knowing about it. How could you have pride in your nation when you saw what it was doing? You will find out more about public opinion in Chapter 12.

E Review: How successful was the USA in fighting the Cold War, 1950–68?

America came out of the Second World War as the richest and least damaged nation amongst all the combatants. By 1968, it was still rich and internally undamaged, but it had lost the optimism and confidence of 1945. Some of the 'great expectations' that the historian James Patterson had described had been lost.

Why was the Vietnam War a turning point for the USA?

- To the rest of the world it ended the USA's unopposed power.
- Third World countries saw a way of challenging the USA.
- In America it ended the bipartisan foreign policy that had lasted since 1945.
- Ideological and economic competition continued to be seen as reasons for conflict.
- Fear and insecurity continued to affect decision-making.

The Cold War did not end until 1992, but by 1968 it had already changed the America of 1945. The Cold War world was now a different place.

ACTIVITY

Was the USA stronger or weaker as a Cold War power by 1968?
On a line, from WEAK to STRONG arrange these incidents in an assessment of American power by 1968:

a) Korean war
b) the arms race
c) the Cuban missile crisis
d) the Vietnam War
e) covert operations in Iran
f) nuclear superiority
g) summit meetings
h) alliances with Western Europe and Japan.

TALKING POINTS

What lessons do you think the USA might have learnt from its conduct of the Cold War in Europe and Asia so far? For example:

1 How far had it underestimated the strength of nationalism and social change across the world?
2 What might it choose to do differently?
3 Were military solutions too obvious and desirable for policy makers fearful of appearing to be appeasers?

Presuming that you know little of the foreign policy story that follows, you are in a similar position to policy makers of the time. It is not only what you would like to happen that should be considered, but also how to cope with the unexpected. List the lessons that you and your group decide should have been learnt by 1968. Remember to include American actions around the world, not just in Vietnam.
   As you read the rest of the foreign policy story to the end of the Cold War in 1992, you will be able to judge whether or not these lessons were learnt.

DISCUSS

Using all your notes from this chapter debate the following question:
   Was the USA successful in fighting the Cold War between 1950 and 1968?
Start with a definition of 'success' in Cold War terms. Here are some guidelines:
For the USA the Cold War was concerned with:
a) ideas
b) economic interests
c) military strategies
d) an overall desire to maintain a democratic world order.

Decide on a viewpoint and argue for it as effectively as you can.
Be prepared for possible criticisms of your opinion. How will you refute them?
Can you demonstrate empathy and avoid bias?
Make brief notes of your argument. You can check the accuracy of your assessment at the end of this book.

KEY POINTS FROM CHAPTER 10

Fighting the Cold War – how successful was the USA, 1950–68?

1 The Cold War was concerned with territorial and economic spheres of influence around the world for the USA and the USSR.

2 Its wars were fought around the world, but not in either the USA or the Soviet Union.

3 The threat of nuclear annihilation, more than negotiation and compromise, initially controlled aggression between the two nations.

4 The Korean War was the beginning of proxy wars fought by the superpowers without the risk of direct confrontation.

5 The Cuban crisis proved that there were limits to Soviet challenges to the land mass of the USA, and to the extremes of possible retaliation by the USA.

6 The Third World provided a battleground for ideological, military and economic confrontations.

7 It allowed American presidents to increase their executive powers at the expense of Congress' powers, and extended the influence of the military-industrial complex.

8 American global economic power continued to be strong.

9 The defeat in Vietnam proved that the USA was militarily vulnerable.

Did Americans live happily ever after, 1945–60?

CHAPTER OVERVIEW

The end of the Second World War brought with it a host of questions about the future for America.

■ 11A Domestic events in the presidencies of Truman (1945–52) and Eisenhower (1952–60)

Year	Domestic events
1945	Roosevelt dies in April
	Vice-President Truman sworn in as president
1946	Beginning of baby boom
	Republicans control Congress
1947	President's Committee on Civil Rights publishes *To Secure These Rights*
	Beginning of federal employee loyalty programme
	Taft–Hartley Act limits unions
	Levittown, New York built
1948	Beginning of desegregation of armed forces
1950	Rosenbergs charged with treason
	Beginning of Korean War
1951	First electronic digital computer, UNIVAC, on sale
1952	Eisenhower elected president
1953	Earl Warren appointed US chief justice
	McDonald's begins to expand
1954	*Brown v. Board of Education of Topeka* decision reverses 'separate but equal' ruling
	Senate condemns McCarthy
1955	Disneyland opens in Anaheim, California
	Montgomery bus boycott
	Salk polio vaccine developed
1956	Highway Act leads to building of inter-state highway system
	Elvis Presley releases his first single
	Eisenhower re-elected
1957	Little Rock, Arkansas school desegregation confrontations
	Martin Luther King elected leader of Southern Christian Leadership Conference (SCLC)
1958	National Aeronautics and Space Administration (NASA) founded
	Development of silicon microchip
1960	First civil rights sit-in at Greensboro, North Carolina
	Student Non-violent Co-ordinating Committee (SNCC) formed
	Kennedy elected president

What kind of America will the troops return to and what changes will they bring with them?

How will industries adjust to the end of wartime production? Will there be new products and markets to maintain prosperity?

Will the Depression come back?

Will the social welfare measures of the New Deal continue?

Can Vice-President Harry Truman be strong enough to follow Roosevelt's dynamic presidency of fifteen years?

This chapter will look at how Americans enjoyed the wealth and production that resulted from the Second World War victory. For many, being able to live 'happily ever after' was enough. They enjoyed affluent suburban living, including the delights of McDonald's and the entertainment of TV quiz shows and Westerns. This was a far cry from the chilly winds of the nuclear threat and from the lives of a significant minority who experienced: increasing urban poverty; the continuing failure to get equality for black Americans; and the beginning of new cultural challenges. To what extent were the years 1945–60 really the years of 'happy ever after'?

A The abundance of post-war USA – how did it change Americans' lives? (pp. 211–18)

B Did abundance improve life for Afro-Americans? (pp. 218–23)

C How did Americans cope with the threat of Armageddon? (pp. 223–25)

D How did the second Red Scare damage the USA? (pp. 226–29)

E Review: Did Americans live happily ever after, 1945–60? (pp. 229–31)

■ 11B 'Surely we'll be happy ever after?'

With 7 per cent of the world's population the USA had:

★ an average daily consumption of 3000 calories (50 per cent higher than in Western Europe)
★ an average per capita income of $11,450

★ 42 per cent of the world's income
★ 57 per cent of its steel production
★ 62 per cent of its oil
★ 75 per cent of its gold supply
★ 80 per cent of its cars
★ 50 per cent of its manufacturing output

★ half the population visiting the cinema every week
★ out of 38 million households 33 million owning a radio

FOCUS ROUTE

1 Note the ways in which life for Americans visibly improved – in their homes, in employment, for families.
2 What problems remained despite increased affluence?
3 Why were some aspects of American life in the fifties criticised?
4 At the end of Section A list the **three** changes that you think were the most important for their long-term impact on the American way of life. Justify each choice in a short paragraph.

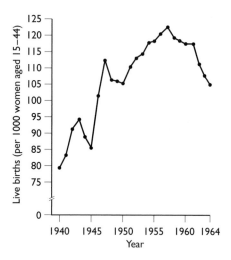

SOURCE 11.1   Birth rate, 1940–64

There was uncertainty in 1945 about what would happen next. An atmosphere of apprehension was inevitable given the cancelling of defence contracts, and unemployment for women war workers and those who had earned good wages in war-based industries. The returning 1.2 million servicemen needed work and homes. The government helped demobbed servicemen with the G.I. Bill of Rights. Its primary intent was to ease soldiers back into civilian life; but it was also concerned to protect the economy from a sudden influx of workers at the same time as defence contracts were ending. It was, in effect, indirect federal interference to keep the economy buoyant. So soldiers were able to get unemployment pay for a year and given preferential treatment for some jobs. The newly-created Veterans Administration ran hospitals for servicemen. Two of the most important aids were those of subsidies for college or training, and loans for house purchases. By 1949, veterans made up 40 per cent of college students, directly contributing to a better-educated national workforce.

At 9.00 p.m. on the evening of the 1952 presidential election a prediction was made about the likely winner. Only seven per cent of the votes had been counted and people were still voting on the west coast. The prediction was that Eisenhower would win 438 electoral college votes. CBS-TV, who were paying for the prediction, thought that it was too generous to be true and in their programme gave Eisenhower a narrower margin of victory. Eisenhower won with 442 electoral votes – only four off the original prediction. This accurate prediction was made not by a person, but by UNIVAC – the first commercial computer system. The war had accelerated technological advances, including that of computing, medicine and communications.

Why was the baby boom important?

Many changes followed in response to the 'baby boom', the term used to describe the rapid increase in the birth rate after 1945. Houses and cars were two of the essentials needed as a result. House construction was expanded because of the G.I. Bill loans, and the Federal Housing Administration, which gave home loans for 90 per cent of a mortgage and a low interest rate of four per cent. Rather than build in overcrowded urban centres, house builders bought up farm land around cities and built massive suburbs.

SOURCE 11.2   Levittown, Long Island, New York

Levittown (see Source 11.2) was one of the massive suburbs which set a model for imitation. There were homes for 80,000 families. Each building plot was a standard size (1.5m×2.5m), as was the plan and appearance of the houses. The two-bedroom Cape Cod design was much favoured, costing $7900, with all the rooms on the ground floor, plus an attic space. They had central heating, built-in bookcases and often a washing machine and fridge. Gradually amenities were added – village greens, playgrounds, bowling alleys, as well as schools and churches. Magazines offered advice to the suburban housewife about her role, 'For the sake of every member of the family, the family needs a head. That means Father, not Mother', and, 'Let's face it girls. That wonderful guy in your house – and in mine – is building your house, your happiness and the opportunities that will come to your children'.

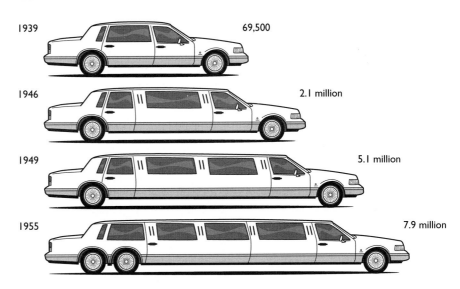

SOURCE 11.3 Car sales figures, 1939–55

Car sales were another indicator of America's increasing wealth and they were nearly all American made; by General Motors, Ford, Chrysler. They needed petrol (or 'gas' in the USA) and highways. In 1919 Eisenhower, then a young army officer, took 62 days to travel 3000 miles across the USA. In 1945 he crossed Germany and was immensely impressed with Hitler's *autobahns* – the world's first motorways, without traffic lights or crossroads. As president, ten years later, he encouraged the passing of the Interstate Highway Act, which provided $26 billion for the construction of a nationally-integrated system. The initial justification was to provide a civilian evacuation route in case of a nuclear attack, but, at the time, it became the biggest ever public works programme. Not only did it support the automobile culture, but it also had political importance. It reflected a new style of Republican government, which accepted a more extensive role for federal intervention; to protect the economy, and to maintain the social welfare changes of Roosevelt and Truman.

SOURCE 11.4 The Israeli journalist Hanoch Bartov lived in Los Angeles in the early 1960s and discovered how essential a car was (from O. and L. Handlin (eds.), *From the Outer World*, 1997, pp.293–96)

... in California, death was preferable to living without one ... The nearest supermarket was about half a kilometre south of our apartment, the regional primary school two kilometres east, and my son's kindergarten even farther away. A trip to the post office – an undertaking, to the bank – an ordeal, to work – an impossibility.

There was no public transport except hourly buses:

... gathering all the wretched of the earth, the poor and the needy, old ladies forbidden by their grandchildren to drive ... Because everyone has a car. A man invited me to his house, saying, 'We are neighbors, within ten minutes of each other'. After walking for an hour and a half I realized what he meant – 'ten minute drive within the speed limit'.

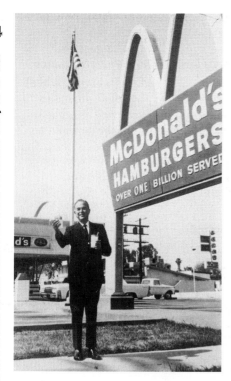

SOURCE 11.5 Ray Kroc, the man who spread the golden arches around the world

And Bartov predicted the future:

Because greater distances mean more commuting, and more commuting leads to more cars. More cars mean problems that push people even further away from the city, which chases after them.

The rising birth rate created many other markets too. People needed more food, clothes, somewhere to sleep, things to play with. The sale of cans of baby food increased from 270 million in 1940 to 1.5 billion by 1953, and the sale of toys increased from $84 million to $1.25 billion over the same period.

Entrepreneurs made and sold bicycles (sales doubled), cowboy fancy dress costumes, space science toys, and produced giant, economy and super-economy packs of nappies for families to buy in their supermarkets. Babies became both consumers, and a source of new markets.

How did consumerism change America?

In October 1956 in Edina, Minnesota you could have had a unique shopping experience. Orchids, azaleas and magnolia bloomed and canaries greeted you as you walked in an air-conditioned space basking in 72°F. Welcome to the first indoor, climate-controlled, suburban, shopping mall. Victor Gruen, its originator, had experimented with similar ideas, but this was the first which defied the extremes of Midwest weather, and encouraged Americans to combine the pleasures of the car and shopping. It did, however, threaten the profitability of city centre shopping. Ironically, ten years later, Gruen was hired to revive the unprofitable city centre of Fort Worth in Texas.

The development of television also linked Americans into a homogeneity of experience, through entertainment. By 1950, 7 million sets had been sold and by 1956 there were 442 TV stations, though most were local ones. Advertising was their only source of revenue (unlike the British BBC system), and advertisers began to strongly influence the type of programmes shown. Mass audiences were more likely for quiz shows and comedies than for plays and discussions. The sense of general well-being raised expectations and gave pride, as well as a determination not to lose what had been gained.

If you could drive to work, to shop, to take the children to school, then you could also drive to eat. America's favourite hamburger should have been known as Kroc's – but it is known as McDonald's. Californian brothers Richard and Maurice McDonald set up a drive-in service in San Bernardino with a limited menu of inexpensive hamburgers, available at the sign of the golden arches. In 1954 Ray Kroc, a milkshake-machine salesman, saw how popular the business was and set up a deal with the brothers whereby he would franchise their idea. By 1961, there were 228 outlets. When Kroc died, in 1984, there were 7500 across the world. Again, cars, a family to feed and conformity meant profits for entrepreneurs.

Population increase and America's economic strength created a consumer society. Suburbs provided an environment of prosperity and fertility. Religious attendance soared in post-war America, providing spiritual comfort, but more importantly, community strength. It was another example of a godly America versus the atheistic Soviet Union, as was Congress' decision to put 'In God We Trust' on American coinage in 1955. The Cold War was not just a test of competing military strengths. It was a test of the freedom to be able to make money and spend it without government interference. In 1950s America the concept of 'freedom' stood for everything that the Soviet Union wasn't. In the USA you could buy what you wanted, live where you wanted, travel where you wanted, work where you wanted. You were not controlled by the state as people were in the Soviet Union. Suburbia was the ideal of private space, of personal mobility and ambition, and of the value of community for personal benefits, not those dictated by the state. Affluence and abundance were America's freedom. So, if you criticised affluence and its acquisition, you were criticising the system that made the USA unique.

However, there were critics of the changes to American life. Right-wing critics saw mass culture as encouraging sexual liberation, especially among the

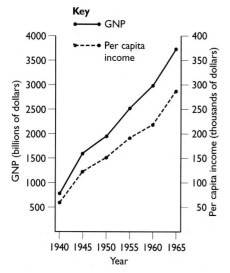

SOURCE 11.6 GNP per capita income, 1940–65

SOURCE 11.7 The picture of abundance! The ideal American family of Du Pont (a chemicals manufacturing firm) worker Steve Czekalinski with a year's supply of food, in 1951. It would have cost about $1300. Notice the amount of fresh food – a fridge would have been essential. You can easily imagine that no one with the ability to buy and enjoy this abundance would be willing to lose it

young, an increase in juvenile delinquency, and similar changes as the baby boomers reached adolescence. Left-wing critics disliked the conformity of modern mass culture so visible in television and the excesses of the consumer society. Cultural critics had three main targets – suburbia, the 'yes-man' and the housewife.

Suburbia

Critics argued that the uniform pattern of US housing helped to create a conformist neighbourhood. John Keats in *The Crack in the Picture Window*, 1956, described such suburbs as 'conceived in error, nurtured in greed, corroding everything they touch'. He saw their inhabitants living monotonous, mediocre lives, always fearing financial insecurity because of the experiences of the Depression. Routines of travel and work demanded an ability to cope with monotony for the sake of security. Other critics asserted that suburbs emphasised the nuclear family of parents with two or three children, at the expense of different types of households, such as extended families. One group deliberately excluded were black Americans. 'Chocolate cities and vanilla suburbs' was one description of this new division. Most white Americans wanted people like themselves as next door neighbours.

SOURCE 11.8 *Little Boxes*, by Malvina Reynolds, 1962. This was a popular song at the time, critical of the sameness of suburbia

*Little boxes on the hillside, little boxes
　made of ticky tacky,
Little boxes on the hillside, little boxes
　all the same.
There's a green one and a pink one
　and a blue one and a yellow one,
And they're all made out of ticky tacky
　and they all look just the same.*

The 'yes-man'

Critics argued that the corporate businesses that dominated the economy did not want individuals, but team workers willing to agree to the management's demands without asserting their opinion. David Reisman in *The Lonely Crowd*, 1950, argued that the American personality had been changed by affluence. Individualism was no longer required in an industrial capitalist system. Being liked and being able to influence others were more important. From being 'inner-directed', with a set of fixed values based on inherited traditions and Protestant ethics of work and thrift, workers had become 'other-directed'. What had happened to the idea of the solitary cowboy taking on the baddies single-handed? It may have ceased to be a reality in urban America, but it remained a popular myth and provided a staple theme for television and movie entertainment.

The suburban housewife

The popular image was of a housewife available to meet the needs of husband and children, with an immaculate home and home-made cookies prepared in anticipation of receiving visitors. It denied that education and skills had any social worth for women. It was, in fact, a time when the number of women in the workforce increased; the demands of urban living often needed two incomes. The jobs tended to be limited – clerical or service related – and rates of pay differed between men and women for the same job. Some critics were already beginning to air the ideas that would be taken up by the feminist movement in the 1960s.

SOURCE 11.9   Edith M. Stern, 'Women are Household Slaves', in M. Johnson, *Reading the American Past*, Vol. II, 2nd edn, 2002, pp.190–93

A nauseating amount of bilge is constantly being spilled all over the public press about the easy, pampered existence of the American woman. Actually, the run of the mill, not gainfully employed female who is blessed with a husband and from two to four children lead a kind of life that theoretically became passé with the Emancipation Proclamation … Its hours – at least fourteen hours a day, seven days a week – make the well-known sun-up to sundown toil of sharecroppers appear, in comparison, like a union standard … But just as slaves were in the service of individual masters, not of the community or state or nation in general, so are housewives bound to the service of individual families … It is neither freedom nor democracy when such service is based on color or sex.

As long as the institution of housewifery in its present form persists, both ideologically and practically it blocks any true liberation of women. The vote, the opportunity for economic independence, and the right to smoke cigarettes are all equally superficial veneers over a deep-rooted, ages-old concept of keeping woman in her place. Unfortunately, however, housewives not only are unorganised, but also, doubtless because of the very nature of their brain-dribbling, spirit-stifling vacation, conservative. There is therefore little prospect of the Housewives' Rebellion.

SOURCE 11.10   'The Baby Boom and the Age of Subdivision' by K. Crabgrass, in F. Binder and D. Reimers, *The Way We Live Now*, Vol. II, 4th edn, 2000, p.227

The young families who joyously moved into the new homes of the suburbs were not terribly concerned about the problems of the inner-city housing market or the snobbish views of … social critics. They were concerned about their hopes and their dreams. They were looking for good schools, private space, and personal safety, and places like Levittown could provide those amenities on a scale and at a price that crowded city neighbourhoods, both in the Old World and in the New, could not match. The single-family tract house – post World War II style – whatever its aesthetic failings, offered growing families a private haven in a heartless world.

DISCUSS

1 What can you learn about 1950s America from the kinds of culture described here and shown on p.217?
2 Which of the two cultures provides the more accurate portrayal of America in the fifties?
3 Do you think that such music, film and TV programmes really provide evidence for historians?

ACTIVITY

How to live in the nostalgic 1950s
Listen to Perry Como, Pat Boone and Rosemary Clooney.
Watch films starring Doris Day and John Wayne, Westerns like *High Noon* and romantic adventures like *South Pacific* and *The African Queen*.
Watch television shows like *I Love Lucy*.

How to live in the rebellious 1950s
Look at the work of painters such as Jackson Pollock, who rejected the conventional representation of objects and used new techniques.
Read writers such as Jack Kerouac, in *On the Road,* and poets such as Allen Ginsberg, who acted out in their lives the free-wheeling, casual style of their writing. Groups known as Beats or Beatniks became their followers.
Watch film stars such as James Dean, in *Rebel without a Cause*, and Marlon Brando in *On the Waterfront*, both moody and physical in their appeal. Marilyn Monroe, in *Seven Year Itch* and *Some Like It Hot*, presented a challenge to the respectable all-American apple-pie ideal woman of Doris Day's films.
Listen to the beginning of rock n' roll as the baby boomers became teenagers.

DISCUSS

Do you think that Section A demonstrates that Americans in the late forties and fifties were living 'happily ever after'?

SOURCE 11.12 Marilyn Monroe was blonde, brash and the pin-up of millions

SOURCE 11.13 Jackson Pollock, one of the 'abstract expressionists' at work on an 'action painting'

SOURCE 11.14 Elvis Presley performing in front of an ecstatic crowd of teenage girls in 1956. It was not only the music – a mix of blues, folk and gospel – that made an impact, but also the tight trousers, slicked-back hair and the way he moved as he sang *Jailhouse Rock* and *Blue Suede Shoes*. No white singer had so blatantly used sex appeal as part of his act, and to such a young audience. His borrowing from black music traditions had the result of making them, and black singers such as Chuck Berry and Little Richard, popular too

TALKING POINTS

Look back to your answers to the Activity on page 212. You may have considered
such changes as:

- the cost of goods and who could, and would, want to buy them
- changes in eating habits
- house building in the suburbs and new areas of the USA such as the Sun Belt of
  the south-east (delightful in winter, but unbearable in summer without air
  conditioning)
- personal mobility for work and leisure
- the beginning of computers that no longer needed large rooms in which to house
  them.

It becomes difficult to untangle the usefulness of products, as they become common-
place, from their effects on lifestyles and expectations. As new goods and ways of
organising your life become widespread, so they become embedded in normal
lifestyles. They cease to be expectations, but become instead the accepted normalities
of life.

1 Would Americans want to go back to the 'old days'?
2 Could you and your family live without television or computers or fast motorway
  routes?

B Did abundance improve life for Afro-Americans?

Did winning the war help the cause of civil rights?

FOCUS ROUTE

Make notes on the following questions.

1 In what ways did civil rights improve
  for Afro-Americans after the Second
  World War?
2 How were Afro-Americans denied
  their civil rights in the post-war
  world?
3 How were black Americans fighting
  for their rights by 1960?
4 What progress had been made
  towards equal rights by 1960?

Black American soldiers had fought (albeit in segregated units), for freedom
from fascism and dictatorships. The experience had roused their desire to
renew the fight for their freedom, which continued to be especially constrained
in the South. Yet white resistance to black equality, especially in the South,
continued. Sometimes it was brutal with instances of shootings and beatings,
sometimes it was intimidatory, sometimes it was more subtle with the refusal
of credit or the loss of jobs if black voters registered. Truman realised the
implications – how could the USA, which claimed to fight for democratic global
freedom, also blatantly deprive some of its citizens of their basic democratic
freedom to vote, as happened in many Southern states? He set up the
Committee of Civil Rights, whose report, *To Secure These Rights*, published
in 1947, exposed inequality across the nation for black citizens. Truman
related the problems to the post-war world that was rapidly becoming a
Cold War world.

SOURCE 11.15 From the report of the President's Committee on Civil Rights, *To
Secure These Rights*, 1947

*Twice before in American history the nation has found it necessary to review the
state of its civil rights ... It is our profound conviction that we have come to a
time for a third re-examination of the situation, and a sustained drive ahead.
Our reason for believing this are those of conscience, of self-interest, and of
survival in a threatening world. Or to put it in another way, we have a moral
reason, an economic reason, and an international reason for believing that the
time for action is now ... Our foreign policy is designed to make the United
States an enormous positive influence for peace and prosperity throughout the
world ... But our domestic civil rights shortcomings are a serious obstacle ...
The United States is not so strong, the final triumph of the democratic ideal is
not so inevitable that we can ignore what the world thinks of us or our record.*

A programme of reforms was devised. The president ordered the integration of
the military, which became effective during the Korean War. However, the
momentum was not maintained and, after 1952, Eisenhower preferred to rely
on gradual change rather than federal initiatives or laws.

ACTIVITY

1 Study, and solve, Puzzles One, Two, Three and Four, below.
2 What do they tell you about the practical impact of discrimination?
3 What do they tell you about the emotional impact of discrimination?

How could black Americans protest?

Puzzle One
Why did a British newspaper in 2003 devote a half-page report to the death of an elderly black woman living in Chicago?

SOURCE 11.16 Newspaper report of the death of Mamie Till Mobley, mother of Emmett Till, from the *Guardian*, 23 January 2003

And so it was that about 10,000 Chicagoans attended services, jammed the airwaves and trooped past the open coffin of Mamie Till Mobley this weekend.

Mamie sent her 14-year-old son Emmett Till to Mississippi in August 1955 with a strict warning: "If you have to get on your knees and bow when a white person goes past, do it willingly." But Emmett was a prankster and unaccustomed to the racial mores of the South. He wolf whistled at a woman in a grocery, then said "Bye, baby" in the hamlet of Money Mississippi.

Less than a week later his body was pulled out of the Tallahatchie river with a bullet in the skull, an eye gouged out and the forehead crushed on one side.

[Mamie's] decision to leave the coffin open and delay the funeral by three days exposed the rest of America and the world to what was happening in Mississippi.

Coming a year after the supreme court outlawed school segregation and less than a month before Martin Luther King rose to prominence during the Montgomery bus boycott prompted by Rosa Parks, it galvanised public outrage.

"If you were indifferent, the Till murder at 14 made you interested," the black paper the *Chicago Defender* wrote recently. "If you were a routine onlooker, the murder turned you into a revolutionary; if you were moderate, the murder turned you militant."

Puzzle Two
Why did Anne Moody hate both whites and blacks?

SOURCE 11.17 From Anne Moody, *Coming of Age in Mississippi*, 1968 in C. Carson (ed.), *Eyes on the Prize*, 1991, p.43

I was fifteen when I began to hate people. I hated the white men who murdered Emmett Till and I hated all the other whites who were responsible for the countless murders Mrs Rice [my homeroom teacher] had told me about and those I vaguely remembered from my childhood. But I also hated Negroes. I hated them for not standing up and doing something about the murders. In fact, I think I had stronger resentment toward Negroes for letting the whites kill them than toward the whites.

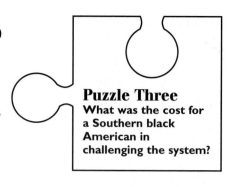

Puzzle Three
What was the cost for a Southern black American in challenging the system?

Puzzle Four
What has this poem got to do with civil rights?

J. A. DeLaine was a black church minister in South Carolina in the 1950s. He supported the NAACP, admired the courage of the activists like lawyer Thurgood Marshall, and actively tried, like him, to improve black children's education in his state. The way he was treated is described in Source 11.18.

SOURCE 11.18   R. Kluger, *Simple Justice*, 1975, p.1

They fired him from the school at which he had taught devotedly for ten years. And they fired his wife and two of his sisters and a niece. And they threatened him with bodily harm. And they sued him on trumped up charges and convicted him in a kangaroo court and left him with a judgement that denied him credit from any bank. And they burned his house to the ground while the fire department stood around watching the flames consume the night. And they stoned the church at which he pastored. And fired shotguns at him out of the dark ... all of this ... because he was black and brave. And because others had followed when he had decided the time had come to lead.

SOURCE 11.19   Langston Hughes, 'Harlem', 1951

What happens to a dream deferred?
Does it dry up
Like a raisin in the sun?
Or fester like a sore –
And then run?
Does it stink like rotten meat?
Or crust and sugar over –
like a syrupy sweet?
Maybe it just sags
like a heavy load.
Or does it explode?

■ **Learning trouble spot**

What to call non-white Americans?
The poet Langston Hughes encountered this problem. He was not black – his father had Jewish and Scottish blood, and was dark brown, whilst his mother had olive skin. He was not, therefore, by strict definition a Negro – someone with no trace of 'white' blood. He describes himself as brown or coloured. The ancestors of black Americans were descended from slaves brought from Africa. You probably know the story of eighteenth-century slave-trading. Slaves were 'black'. Although there were other Americans, like Hughes, who were neither 'white' nor 'black', they were treated as non-whites and it became accepted to use the description of 'black' as a form of shorthand. The term 'Negro' was still acceptable in the 1960s, but was later replaced by 'black' or 'Afro-American'. The term 'nigger' has always been offensive.

During the 1950s there were two major ways of challenging discrimination:

- by legal action against education restrictions, e.g. the Supreme Court decision in *Brown v. Board of Education of Topeka, Kansas* and desegregation at Little Rock, Alabama
- by community action, e.g. the Montgomery bus boycott.

a) The Supreme Court decisions
The NAACP had pursued education rights for black citizens since the 1930s. Having challenged and won equal treatment in law for university students, in the 1950s they turned to school desegregation. The case *Brown v. Board of Education of Topeka, Kansas* combined several cases of school segregation in the South, including the one that pastor DeLaine had been fighting. In 1896 the Supreme Court had ruled in the case *Plessy v. Ferguson*, which had permitted states to provide 'separate but equal' facilities, including for education. The resulting 'separate' facilities were rarely 'equal' for black people.

In May 1954, guided by the new Chief Justice Earl Warren, the Supreme Court overturned that ruling, stating, 'To separate Negro children ... solely because of their race generates a feeling of inferiority as to their status in the community that may affect their hearts and minds in ways unlikely ever to be undone ... We conclude that in the field of public education the doctrine of 'separate but equal' has no place. Separate educational facilities are inherently unequal.'

The decision was unequivocal. It also set the precedent for the desegregation of parks, beaches, public housing and transport. However, implementing the decision was often deliberately delayed, and Southern Congressmen protested at 'an abuse of judicial power'. The attempt by nine black students to enrol at the all-white Central High School in Little Rock, Arkansas, in 1957, created a crisis that brought the army onto the streets. The Governor, Orval Faubus, used state troops to bar their entry. In the face of this defiance of a court order, Eisenhower was forced, much against his wishes, to order federal troops to the town to protect the students.

SOURCE 11.20 '2-4-6-8, we ain't gonna integrate'. One of the taunts at Elizabeth Eckford as she and eight other black students tried to enrol at Little Rock's Central High School, Arkansas on 6 September 1957. Eight of the students completed their course, but troops remained there for a year; the first federal troops used, since Reconstruction, to protect the rights of blacks

Education officials in other states opposed to desegregation found more devious ways of avoiding true integration, making a mockery of court decisions and diminishing the importance of the law. The conflict did lead to the Civil Rights Act of 1957, the first such legislation since Reconstruction. It set up a Commission on Civil Rights, but had little practical impact on discrimination.

b) The Montgomery bus boycott

Tired after a long day at work, Rosa Parks took a seat on her usual bus home in Montgomery. When the bus filled, the driver demanded, as was the practice, that black passengers give up their seat to standing white passengers. Rosa Parks refused. The driver insisted. Rosa Parks refused again. So the driver called the police, she was removed from the bus and arrested. It was December

SOURCE 11.21 Rosa Parks sitting on a bus in 1956, after the boycott ended

1955. She was an NAACP activist and an ordinary citizen – the ideal person that the NAACP could use to represent the unfairness of discrimination. Over the following weekend, officials organised a massive boycott of the bus system by 50,000 black supporters in the city. They walked to work or formed car pools. The bus boycott lasted for 381 days. At the end of that long year the buses were totally desegregated as a result of court orders. The boycott had illustrated that:

- The black community were willing to forego personal comfort to assert their rights.
- Mass action could be effective, and white intolerance could be successfully challenged. As one elderly lady is reputed to have said to a reporter offering her a lift as she walked home, 'No, my feets is tired, but my soul is rested'.

ACTIVITY

1 What problems can King foresee might challenge black bus travellers (Source 11.22)?
2 What principles of behaviour are being demanded?

TALKING POINT

What is the difference between desegregation and integration?

SOURCE 11.22 An extract from Martin Luther King Jr.'s advice to black Montgomery citizens returning to travelling on buses after the boycott (from M. L. King, Jr., *Stride Toward Freedom: The Montgomery Story*, 1958). King was already establishing himself as a leader in the civil rights movement

1 Not all white people are opposed to integrated buses ...
2 The whole bus is now for the use of all people. Take a vacant seat.
3 Pray for guidance and commit yourself to complete non-violence in word and action as you enter the bus.
4 ... In all things observe ordinary rules of courtesy and good behaviour.
5 Remember that this is not a victory for Negroes alone, but for all Montgomery and the South. Do not boast! Do not brag!
6 Be quiet but friendly; proud but not arrogant; joyous, but not boisterous.

And specifically, on the bus:

If cursed, do not curse back. If pushed, do not push back. If struck do not strike back, but evidence love and goodwill at all times.

King was disappointed that his fellow white church leaders did not offer guidance to their community about appropriate ways to behave. Most of them claimed that they did not dare get involved in such a controversial issue.

■ 11C Were the protests of the 1950s effective?

It had needed the Supreme Court to overrule both lower courts and a previous Supreme Court ruling to clarify the rights of the Fourteenth Amendment.

Both legal and community action had been effective, but in particular circumstances.

It had taken the intervention of the president and federal troops to enforce desegregation in the resistant South.

The mass bus boycott had relied on there being a suitable 'victim' to be the symbol of everyday discrimination.

Neither situation had changed entrenched Southern attitudes. Black citizens still needed to prove their equality and white citizens to amend their resistance to social change. Both would be impossible without federal intervention.

Did black Americans have equality of rights by 1960? Federal intervention in education was important. Grassroots protest by ordinary black citizens was important. But in practical and legally enforced terms black Americans, especially Southern blacks, still did not have equality of rights by 1960. But the stakes had been raised, so that the new administration, after the election of 1960, would find it harder to ignore demands, and harder to stall on effective action. The movement that had started in Montgomery had a momentum that would be difficult to stop. It had raised black pride, demonstrated that peaceful mass action was possible and effective, and, so importantly, had produced an eloquent leader.

SOURCE 11.23 Martin Luther King Jr. addressing a crowd in Montgomery during the bus boycott. Martin Luther King's speech to 5000 predominantly black Montgomery citizens at Holt Street Baptist Church, on the first night of the boycott, set the tone for the civil rights fight for the next ten years

SOURCE 11.24 Martin Luther King, 5 December 1955 (quoted in C. Carson, *Eyes on the Prize*, 1991, pp.49–50)

There comes a time when people get tired of being pushed out of the glittering sunlight of life's July and left standing amidst the piercing chill of an Alpine November ... we are not here advocating violence ... we are Christian people ... The only weapon that we have in our hands this evening is the weapon of protest ... And if we are united, we can get many of the things that we not only desire but which we justly deserve ... We are not afraid of what we are doing, because we are doing it within the law ... We, the disinherited of this land, we who have been oppressed so long are tired of going through the long night of captivity. And we are reaching out for the daybreak of freedom and justice and equality ... when the history books are written in the future, somebody will have to say 'There lived a race of people, black people, ... who had the moral courage to stand up for their rights ... they injected a new meaning into the veins of history and of civilization'.

C How did Americans cope with the threat of Armageddon?

FOCUS ROUTE

1 How did Americans deal with the threat of nuclear war in a practical way?
2 What effects did this perceived threat to the American way of life have on society?

The detonation of atomic bombs above Hiroshima and Nagasaki in 1945 had brought a new weapon of awesome power to the world. Atomic bombs killed in two ways:

- the sheer magnitude of the blast and subsequent fire-storm
- nuclear fallout resulting in radiation sickness.

SOURCE 11.25 *Peace Today,* by Rube Goldberg, in the *New York Sun,* 1948

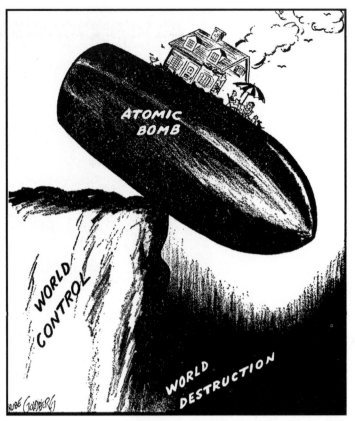

PEACE TODAY

When the Soviet Union tested its own A-bomb in 1949, it was clear that an arms race was underway (see p.189). The USA tested its first hydrogen bomb (H-bomb) on the Pacific atoll of Eniwetok, in 1952, causing the island to completely disappear, leaving a hole 1.6km long and 53m deep. Its fireball was 8km high (nearly the height of Everest) and its mushroom cloud was 40km tall and 1931km wide. When the Soviets exploded their own bomb only nine months later, it raised suspicions of spying and fears of superior Soviet scientific knowledge.

Although a Soviet attack was very unlikely, it did not stop preparations for civil defence. Protection against a fire-storm was impossible, so attention focused on fallout shelters to protect from radiation poisoning. Homes and public buildings had shelters, and children regularly practised 'duck and cover' drills in schools. The effects of the fallout were little understood.

SOURCE 11.26 'We wanted to help out what little we could'. Living in Utah, downwind of the Nevada test site (where 126 atomic bombs were tested in the atmosphere between 1951 and 1963) Isaac Nelson wanted to demonstrate his patriotism by watching the first one (quoted in C. Gallagher, *American Ground Zero,* 1993, pp.133–35)

... we were chattering like chipmunks, so excited! Pretty soon, why the whole sky just flared up in an orange-red flash, and it was so brilliant that you could easily see the trees ten miles across the valley ... Later on in the day, you'd see these fallout clouds drifting down ... it was definitely different from any rain cloud, kind of pinkish-tan color ... everyone would go out and ooh and aah just like a bunch of hicks. We was never warned that there was any danger involved in going out and being under these fallout clouds all the time I lived here ...

After a similar explosion in 1955 which Isaac's wife watched, her skin turned dark red and she became ill with headaches, nausea and diarrhoea. Within a month her hair started to fall out and she later developed a brain tumour. She never recovered from the effects of radiation poisoning and died in 1965 aged 41.

Survival Secrets for Atomic Attacks

ALWAYS PUT FIRST THINGS FIRST

Try to Get Shielded

If you have time, get down in a basement or subway. Should you unexpectedly be caught out-of-doors, seek shelter alongside a building, or jump in any handy ditch or gutter.

Drop Flat on Ground or Floor

To keep from being tossed about and to lessen the chances of being struck by falling and flying objects, flatten out at the base of a wall, or at the bottom of a bank.

Bury Your Face in Your Arms

When you drop flat, hide your eyes in the crook of your elbow. That will protect your face from flash burns, prevent temporary blindness and keep flying objects out of your eyes.

NEVER LOSE YOUR HEAD

SOURCE 11.27 *How to Respond to a Nuclear Attack*, 1950, published by the Civil Defense Agency

ACTIVITY

Study Sources 11.27 and 11.29. What do these sources suggest about how much Americans knew about the realities of nuclear weapons?

SOURCE 11.28 From the song *We Will All Go Together When We Go* (from the album *An Evening Wasted With Tom Lehrer*), issued in 1959

And we will all go together when we go.
What a comforting fact that is to know.
Universal bereavement,
An inspiring achievement,
Yes, we will all go together when we go.

We will all go together when we go.
All suffused with an incandescent glow.
No one will have the endurance
To collect on his insurance,
Lloyd's of London will be loaded when they go.

And we will all bake together when we bake.
There'll be nobody present at the wake.
With complete participation
In that grand incineration,
Nearly three billion hunks of well-done steak.

SOURCE 11.29 Louis Severance's fallout shelter, in Michigan in 1960, for a family of four. It cost him $1000 to build and had a 25cm reinforced concrete ceiling

DISCUSS

How were prosperity and daily comfort linked to the level of anxiety?

Not everyone took the threats seriously. At the end of the fifties the satirist Tom Lehrer wrote songs that were both cynical and critical. They were not popular entertainment, but spread via universities and small clubs to a wider audience. His 'survival hymn' (Source 11.28) was his response to the nuclear threat (think of the tune *She'll be coming round the mountain when she comes*).

FOCUS ROUTE

As you work through Section D make notes to answer the following questions.

1 How was the second Red Scare created and maintained?

2 Which aspects of American society were damaged?

3 Was there long-term damage to American ideals?

D How did the second Red Scare damage the USA?

What was the Red Scare?

Anti-communist and anti-radical feelings were not new in the USA. There had been the Red Scare of 1919–20 as the First World War ended and fear grew of the global spread of the Russian Revolution (see page 73). After 1945 there was still fear of a Soviet worldwide conspiracy and so, just as the military containment policy was devised against Soviet land expansion, it was believed that communist attempts to spread its influence amongst Americans had to be contained. The result was a hunt for spies and traitors, which was taken to extremes with the witch hunt tactics of Senator Joseph McCarthy, aided by the House Committee on Un-American Activities (HUAC).

As the Cold War developed it was inevitable that tensions were felt in the USA. National security became linked to loyalty, which in turn became linked to demonstrative anti-communism. These became useful tools in political arguments. Unlike Britain, the USA had not had a national, politically neutral administration in the Second World War – Democrats had dominated government since 1933. They included those with left-wing views and, during the war, the government had allied with the USSR. This made it possible for Republicans to make accusations of political bias against those who had worked with the Soviet Union, even though it was part of their war-time job.

As the tensions increased over Berlin in 1947, and Korea in 1950, Truman had to struggle to prove that he could be an eagle abroad and a liberal at home. His opponents were very willing to interpret his desire to continue the liberal social welfare policies of Roosevelt as un-American and suspiciously left-wing. Truman's Fair Deal plan of 1949 included increasing the minimum wage, broadening social security and federal aid to education. He did get some improvements in the latter two, but progress was slow because of political opposition.

■ 11D How did the Red Scare develop?

1930s

1937 House Committee on Un-American Activities (HUAC) set up to look at allegations of fascist or communist influences in trade unions and agencies of the New Deal.

1940s

1940 The Smith Act or Alien Registration Act. It was now illegal for anyone to aid, teach or advocate the overthrow of the government. All alien residents had to register their political beliefs.

1947 The Federal Employee Loyalty Program was set up by executive order. Of the 6 million government employees who were checked, 14,000 had further FBI checks and 2000 were dismissed. The government's actions made other organisations – universities, churches, political groups and local governments – start their own investigations to root out communists.

HUAC hearings on communist infiltration of Hollywood – those interviewed had to tell of their own political views and those of their friends. If they refused, as the Hollywood Ten and actresses such as Lillian Hellmann did, they could be held in contempt of Congress and jailed. An unofficial 'blacklist' was created and those named were refused work in the entertainment industry for as long as ten years.

1950s

1950 The McCarran Internal Security Act – this required members of communist organisations to register with the government and it prohibited their employment and travel.

Arrest of Julius and Ethel Rosenberg for conspiracy to commit espionage by recruiting a spy in the wartime Manhattan Project at Los Alamos.

The Korean War appeared to prove that fears of the Soviet Union's expansionist policy were real.

Senator McCarthy's list – this list comprised 205 state department officials who McCarthy claimed were communists. The names were never revealed and the number was reduced to 57 when he made a speech about it in Congress. It was enough, however, to start a four-year period of virulent anti-communist accusations.

Alger Hiss – a former state department official, was found guilty of perjury after two years of investigations by Nixon, the HUAC, and McCarthy, found that he had passed classified documents to a communist.

ACTIVITY

Why does Lillian Hellman (Source 11.30) object to the requests of the HUAC?

ACTIVITY

What is the meaning, and the reality of:
a) blacklisting
b) guilt by association?

SOURCE 11.30 Congressional record of the House Committee on Un-American Activities, *Hearings Regarding Communist Infiltration of the Hollywood Motion-Picture Industry,* 82nd Congress, 21 May 1952

But there is one principle that I do understand: I am not willing, now or in the future, to bring bad trouble to people who, in my past association with them, were completely innocent of any talk or any action that was disloyal or subversive. I do not like subversion or disloyalty in any form and if I had ever seen any I would have considered it my duty to have reported it to the proper authorities. But to hurt innocent people whom I knew many years ago in order to save myself is, to me, inhuman and indecent and dishonorable. I cannot and will not cut my conscience to fit this year's fashions, even though I long ago came to the conclusion that I was not a political person and could have no comfortable place in any political group.

I was raised in an old-fashioned American tradition and there were certain homely things that were taught to me: to try to tell the truth, not to bear false witness, not to harm my neighbour, to be loyal to my country, and so on ...

I am prepared to waive the privilege against self-incrimination and to tell you anything you wish to know about my views or actions if your Committee will agree to refrain from asking me to name other people. If the Committee is unwilling to give me this assurance, I will be forced to plead the privilege of the Fifth Amendment at the hearing.

Why were the HUAC and Senator McCarthy so powerful?

This is the **end** of the story:

- no list of communist subversives in government was published
- not one Soviet spy was uncovered by the HUAC or McCarthy (except possibly for Alger Hiss)
- there were no prosecutions for treason.

So how could one man, with the aid of a Senate committee, persecute and intimidate with exaggerated and unproven evidence, find no valid evidence and yet create the atmosphere of a witch hunt for four years?

ACTIVITY

1 Using Sources 11.32–11.38 copy and complete this chart identifying other reasons for the extent of McCarthy's power.
2 What damage do the writers think he did to America?

Reasons for the extent of McCarthy's power
The political climate meant that any accusation or implication of 'being soft' on communism was feared, especially by Democrats.
Congress claimed its right to protect the constitution and the institutions of government.
McCarthy chose easy targets, like those doing jobs involving links with communists such as the China section of the State Department, or those easily linked with left-wing/socialist/radical ideas such as trade unions and civil rights groups.

SOURCE 11.31 McCarthy with his inseparable aide, Ray Cohn on the left, and on the right a former FBI agent, Don Surine, who acted as an investigator for him. McCarthy gained the nickname the Redbaiter

SOURCE 11.32 E. Schrecker, *The Age of McCarthyism: A Brief History With Documents,* 1995

McCarthy attracted attention precisely because of his outrageousness. He knew how to manipulate the press, taking advantage of its hunger for copy and releasing sensational accusations just in time for the evening deadlines. The blatant disregard for the accuracy of his charges that distinguished him from other politicians made McCarthy notorious and frightening. Liberals loathed him and many moderates found him distasteful as well. The leaders of the Republican party, however, recognised that McCarthy could be of use. His extravagant charges amplified their own allegations that the Truman administration had lost China to the communists ... [McCarthy] had no reservations about whom he targeted, he even implied that General George Marshall, the highly respected Secretary of Defense, had been a traitor. ... McCarthyism's main impact may well have been in what did not happen rather than in what did – the social reforms that were never adopted, the diplomatic initiatives that were not pursued, the workers who were not organized into unions, the books that were not written, and the movies that were not filmed.

SOURCE 11.33 Former President Harry S. Truman in the *New York Times,* 17 November 1953

... McCarthyism ... It is the corruption of truth, the abandonment of the due process of law. It is the use of the big lie and the unfounded accusation against any citizen in the name of Americanism or security. It is the rise to power of the demagogue who lives on untruth; it is the spreading of fear and the destruction of faith in every level of society.

SOURCE 11.34 Actor Lee J. Cobb, who was blacklisted, but who then agreed a deal with the HUAC (from an interview by Victor Navasky)

When the facilities of the government of the United States are drawn on an individual it can be terrifying. The blacklist is just the opening gambit – being deprived of work. Your passport is confiscated. That's minor. But not being able to move without being tailed is something else. After a certain point it grows to implied as well as articulated threats, and people succumb. My wife did, and she was institutionalized [needed care in a mental health hospital]. In 1953 the HUAC did a deal with me. I was pretty much worn down. I had no money. I couldn't borrow any. I had the expenses of taking care of my children. Why am I subjecting my loved ones to this? If it's worth dying for, and I am just as idealistic as the next fellow. But I decided it wasn't worth dying for, and if the gesture was the way of getting out of the penitentiary I'd do it. I had to be employable again.

SOURCE 11.35 A. MacLeish, *The Conquest of America,* 1949

Never in the history of the world was one people as completely dominated, intellectually and morally, by another as the people of the United States by the people of Russia in the four years from 1946 through 1949 ... all this took place not in a time of national weakness or decay, but precisely at the moment when the United States, having engineered a tremendous triumph and fought its way to a brilliant victory in the greatest of all wars, had reached the highest point of world power ever achieved by a single state.

SOURCE 11.36 M. Norton, *et al.* (eds.), *A People and a Nation,* 6th edn, 2001, p.796

... both Truman and Eisenhower overreacted to the alleged threat of communist subversion in government. The alarmist rhetoric heightened public anxiety, and their loyalty programs ruined innocent people's lives and careers.

SOURCE 11.37 W. Chafe and H. Sitkoff (eds.), *A History of Our Time,* 4th edn, 1999, pp.3–4

... he carried to a new height the hysteria gripping the nation. McCarthy had no such list. Most of his charges were fabrications. He never uncovered a single communist spy. His investigations and exposés did not lead to the successful prosecution of a single person for treasonous or disloyal acts. Yet, the very brashness of his accusations, the abrasiveness of his insinuations, the exaggerated big lie and red smear enabled McCarthy to hold centre stage for four years ...

SOURCE 11.38 The journalist Walter Lippman in the *Washington Post,* 1 March 1954

McCarthy's influence has grown as the president [Eisenhower] has appeased him. His power will cease to grow and diminish when he is resisted, and it has been shown to our people that those to whom we look for leadership and to preserve our institutions are not afraid of him.

How did the Red Scare end?

Although Eisenhower disliked McCarthy he took no direct action to stop his activities, fearing a split within the Republican Party. Some journalists protested at McCarthy's behaviour, notably Ed Murrow, with some success, on his TV programme, *See It Now*. However, in late 1953 one of McCarthy's close associates, David Schine, was called up for army duty. Attempts to withdraw him from the draft by McCarthy failed; so McCarthy decided to investigate possible communist influence in army security. In challenging the army and with such bad manners he had gone too far. In the televised Senate hearings, which took place in April 1954 and lasted 36 days, McCarthy's bullying, hectoring and un-substantiated accusations were exposed to a now-critical national audience. The Senate responded by censuring him for unbecoming conduct and he very quickly ceased to have any political importance. He died from alcohol-related illness in 1957.

SOURCE 11.39 W. Chafe, *The Unfinished Journey*, 4th edn, 1999, pp.109–10

For American foreign policy the rhetoric of moralism led to rigidity, a loss of flexibility, and the elimination of any possibility of honest debate and criticism about the Cold War ...
Because of the anti-communist crusade, domestic dissent was stifled, civil liberties were compromised, and advocates of social reform risked being pilloried as agents of a foreign state.

E Review: Did Americans live happily ever after, 1945–60?

The Cold War was a clash of ideologies, which translated into armed conflict across the world. The Truman Doctrine, the Marshall Plan and the formation of NATO were the USA's challenges to the perceived communist threat abroad. At home, the administration challenged perceived communist forces through loyalty programmes and the search for subversives. The Cold War also made Americans want to demonstrate the value of their capitalist system. From 1945 to 1960 the economic strength of the nation meant that most Americans had an improving standard of living. No one wanted to risk losing it. Yet, the desire to keep life sweet meant there was a reluctance to realise that many Americans were suffering from urban and rural poverty, were under-educated and had their civil rights deliberately ignored. In the fifties the poor were 'invisible', partly because they were not pictured in mass entertainment. Documentary programmes about poverty did not appeal to television advertisers. Groups such as black Americans, Native Americans and Mexican migrant workers did not enjoy the benefits of a 'free' America. Yet protests were slight. It seemed as if the country was having a breathing space, a transition, after the turmoil of Depression and war, before taking action on the problems that needed to be resolved.

SOURCE 11.40   M. Norton, *et al.* (eds.), *A People and a Nation*, 6th edn, 2001, p.788

Post-war America was not only prosperous, but also proud and boastful … the American people were in the grip of 'victory culture' – that is, the belief that unending triumph was the nation's birthright and destiny. From the classroom, the pulpit and the town hall, as well as from popular culture avenues came the self-congratulatory rhetoric about American's invincibility … Americans believed that their nation was the greatest in the world, not only the most powerful but the most righteous.

SOURCE 11.41   W. Chafe, *The Unfinished Journey*, 4th edn, 1999, pp.140–41

Yet, if Eisenhower is to be given credit for the political know-how and shrewdness of his administration, he must also bear the responsibility for having ignored or suppressed profound social problems that eventually would come home to imperil the country. The economy sputtered at a growth rate of only 2.5 per cent during his administration, and despite advice to the contrary, Eisenhower refused to initiate tax cuts in the midst of two recessions. His failure on the issue of civil rights … would ensure a decade of conflict after he left office. Although in many respects he seemed the ideal president for his time, providing a symbol for serene benevolence after an era of upheaval, he failed – ultimately – to provide constructive leadership, choosing to hoard his political capital rather than spend it on behalf of critically needed moral and social departures. As with so much else during the 1950s, the appearance of comfort and complacency obscured contradictions and tensions that would inevitably surface and explode.

ACTIVITY

1   What points is each of the writers of Sources 11.39–41 making about the period?
2   Which points do you agree with? What evidence would you refer to in order to support your views?

ACTIVITY

1   You are the host of a television talk show about the fifties in the USA. Who would you want to invite onto your show? Choose two 'heroes' and two 'villains'. They could be politicians, entertainers, inventors, individuals who are clever, unpleasant or brave, or you could choose 'the man or woman in the street'. What questions would you ask them? What puzzles you about that period?
2   Select appropriate music and three photographs which symbolise the period. Now discuss your selections in a group. Does your group think that you have presented an accurate representation of the period?

Note 1: Thinking about the questions to ask helps you to identify what you do, and do not, know or understand.
Note 2: Deciding on a 'hero or villain' helps you to decide what you think is important about people's behaviour.

ACTIVITY

Write a four-paragraph answer to the following essay question:
    'Abundance united the USA in the early Cold War years.' To what extent do you agree with this statement?
Think about the three parts of the title – abundance, the Cold War, and unity.
Make brief notes on each of these to guide your answer (what were they and how were they demonstrated).
Make notes to show the inter-relationship between the three topics (a diagram might be helpful).
Structure your essay by answering these questions:

Paragraph 1 – How and why was the USA an abundant nation in this period?
Paragraph 2 – What were the developments in the Cold War that particularly affected the domestic population?
Paragraph 3 – In what ways was the nation united in this period (consider social, economic and political factors, as well as attitudes and interests)?
Paragraph 4 – Did the desire to keep abundance make people more determined to fight the Cold War and maintain national unity? Does this desire explain anti-communism, conformity and national pride?

1 The post-war era was one of increasing affluence for an increasing number of Americans.

2 Affluence changed lifestyles and created a common pattern based on suburban life, cars, television and consumer goods.

3 The baby boom generated new businesses as well as emphasising traditional family values.

4 The aggressive foreign policy towards communism was reflected in domestic policies.

5 The Red Scare of 1947–54 found little evidence of communist influence in the USA.

6 The Red Scare damaged individual careers and reputations, and threatened free speech and the right of dissent.

7 The threat of nuclear war, though exaggerated, increased demands for security.

8 Ordinary black Americans began to protest at their unequal treatment in education and leisure facilities.

9 It was clear that such protests, by black Americans, had limited success without federal government support.

10 Urban and rural poverty were growing and would have to be tackled.

12

'We shall overcome': how did the challenges of the sixties era change America?

The sixties saw the end of the post-war world. The conformity and restrictions of the late 1940s and 1950s were ended by a new young president, by baby boomers becoming protesting students and by successful civil rights legislation. It was a decade of two contrasting presidents – both Democrats, both forceful and ambitious, but both using these characteristics for different purposes and with different successes. The first, John F. Kennedy, had style, youth and glamour. The second, Lyndon B. Johnson, had immense political skill, and personal insecurities that could make him coarse and over-demanding. Their presidencies ended very differently – Kennedy was assassinated; Johnson, depressed by the Vietnam War and the public reaction against it, refused to stand for re-election. They were presidents during a time of economic success; a success which contributed to extensive social change. Yet, in 1968, the conservative beliefs of the 'silent majority' led to the election of the Republican, Richard Nixon, as president. Does this mean that Kennedy and Johnson had failed America?

This chapter will evaluate the success of the presidents in responding to the challenges to American society between 1960 and 1968. This period saw:
- the most important civil rights legislation since the end of slavery
- more social welfare change under the Great Society programme than during the first New Deal of 1933
- urban riots, in the aggressive challenges of black activists and in widespread student protests against traditional authority
- economic success, raising expectations of what the good American life should be like
- the traumatic events of the year 1968 – assassinations, riots, the reality of the Vietnam War
- the era of liberalism replaced by conservative political and economic policies.

A Was the Kennedy era more style than substance? (pp. 233–35)

B 'We shall overcome': did the civil rights activists win their fight? (pp. 235–46)

C Did President Johnson's 'Great Society' change American society? (pp. 246–51)

D 1968 – the year that went too far (or not far enough)? (pp. 252–55)

E Review: 'We shall overcome': how did the challenges of the sixties era change America? (pp. 256–57)

1 Why do political parties lose elections?
2 What possible reasons besides policy failures can you suggest to explain why the Democrats lost in 1968?

A   Was the Kennedy era more style than substance?

■ 12A The Kennedy style

To many people in 1960 Kennedy was important because he was different:

The first president to be born in the twentieth century.

The first president young enough to have fought in the Second World War (Eisenhower had been a commander, not a fighting soldier).

The youngest and, to many, the most handsome, of presidents.

His wife, Jacqueline, was attractive, well-dressed and sophisticated. Her re-decoration of the White House and the cultural entertainments she encouraged contributed a sense of fashion and modernity to the presidency.

He had two young children and was often photographed playing or sailing with them in a casual and relaxed way.

He had a sense of style – his way of speaking, his ambitions, his energy, which appealed to Americans, especially the young.

He spoke candidly to the press and was popular with them.

His closest advisors were academics, intellectuals and activists, not conservative, old-style politicians who enjoyed playing golf.

He raised expectations, for the nation and for his presidency, linked to ideas of the American dream that anything was possible.

The Kennedy 'style' was also related to the strength of the USA in 1960. It was a time of optimism.

■ 12B America in the sixties

Stable prices

Rising family incomes

More young people college-educated

Availability of cheap oil

Scientific and technological developments in electronics, chemicals, electrical goods, food processing, pharmaceuticals

Polio vaccines

First contraceptive pill for women

Rising life expectancy

Standard 40-hour week and annual paid leave

Little social class tension

High levels of church attendance

FOCUS ROUTE

As you work through Section A make notes on the following questions.

1 What did Kennedy achieve during his presidency?
2 Why did he impress Americans?
3 How did his assassination affect assessments of his presidency?

■ **Learning trouble spot**

Charisma

Kennedy is often described as having 'charisma'. This means having the ability to inspire others with enthusiasm or admiration. It is one of those characteristics that is impossible to measure and peculiar to a time and situation. Other presidents were charismatic to their time – Franklin D. Roosevelt, for example. To understand it fully you have to take other people's word for it, because a style of behaviour from the past may seem stilted or unusual in today's world. Kennedy was widely acknowledged by those who met him, or saw him on television, at home and abroad, to have charm and energy. Is there anyone in modern politics you would describe as having charisma?

■ **Learning trouble spot**

What was a liberal?

Liberal politics were those of democracy and the importance of individual rights. It is a basically optimistic set of beliefs, supporting gradual, but not radical change. The sixties in America are described as a liberal decade. They contrast with the conservative policies of the Republicans who preferred to maintain institutions as they were, and opposed intervention by 'big', i.e. federal, government.

What were Kennedy's aims for the American people and did he achieve them?

Kennedy's aims

At his inauguration Kennedy urged an extensive commitment from Americans, 'Let every nation know ... that we shall pay any price, bear any burden, meet any hardship, support any friend, oppose any foe, in order to assure the survival and the success of liberty'.

His Inaugural Address stressed dangers and the need for sacrifice, focusing on foreign policy, because he believed that the USA should contain communism aggressively. He promised heroic confrontation and raised expectations of the moral high ground of the USA, but said nothing about race or poverty at home.

Kennedy's main policy idea was the New Frontier, outlined at the Los Angeles Democratic Convention in 1960. It was a combination of policies for both domestic and foreign affairs. Domestically, he wanted a united society in order to fight communism abroad. His ideas were those of active conservatism, not radical change; of amending the system, not creating a new one. Like his Democratic predecessors, Roosevelt and Truman, he continued to improve social welfare provisions, raising the minimum wage and expanding social security benefits. However, rather like Truman, he was unable to get further measures through Congress.

Why were the aims difficult to achieve?

- Kennedy lacked Vice-President Johnson's skills in getting legislation through the Senate. He had never been particularly interested in Congressional politics, and had little control over the powerful decision-makers there.
- The narrowness of Kennedy's victory in 1960 meant that he thought there was less popular support than he needed for change. He also wanted a second term so political calculations for a victory in 1964 affected his policy making.
- Some commentators thought that his advisors, though clever and energetic, lacked knowledge about the immense variety of America. His advisors were liberal, recruited from the elite of educational institutions (Harvard, Yale, Princeton). Like Kennedy, they worked long hours, were energetic and intellectually brilliant. However, not everyone was impressed. The British journalist Henry Fairlie commented that they seemed to be, 'always taking last-minute decisions at last-minute meetings, making last-minute corrections to last-minute statements ... they were always trying to catch up with events or with each other, or even each with himself'. East coast intellectual elite-bashing was to be a successful theme in Californian Richard Nixon's second attempt at the presidency in 1968.
- Institutions like Congress and the justice system worked slowly. They could make Kennedy's promises, so energetically expressed, seem hollow because it took so long to make them happen.

How successful was Kennedy?

Given the circumstances of Kennedy's death in November 1963, his three-year presidency has been difficult to assess. It tends to be remembered for style and RHETORIC, rather than substance. This was accentuated by the comparison of the glamorous White House to the mythical court of Camelot, and by the desire of his family and friends to ensure that he was remembered with admiration. It has taken a long time for more dispassionate assessments of his life to be made.

Kennedy was slow to respond to the demands of the civil rights movement. It was only the violence shown to civil rights protests in the spring and early summer of 1963, and the encouragement of his brother Robert (who was attorney-general), that forced him to approve intervention by federal forces and to promise a Civil Rights Bill. He was uncomfortable with the planned March on Washington in 1963 (its aim was to create more pressure for a Civil Rights Act), and he tried to stop or scale it down. By November 1963, he had

235

'WE SHALL OVERCOME': HOW DID THE CHALLENGES OF THE SIXTIES ERA CHANGE AMERICA?

responded to the growing demands of the civil rights movement by promising a Civil Rights Bill.

Many liberal Democrats also felt that Kennedy was too timid and unwilling to challenge Congressional conservatives over difficult issues such as federal aid for education and health care. He reserved his aggression for foreign policy. He demonstrated his ability as a decision-maker in the Cuban missile crisis, but there is some evidence of his disquiet at the escalation of violence in Vietnam.

B 'We shall overcome': did the civil rights activists win their fight?

FOCUS ROUTE

Consider these questions as you work through Section B.

1 What did the civil rights protesters have to overcome?
2 Why was non-violent action successful between 1960 and 1965?
3 Whose support did they need to be successful?
4 What had still to be 'overcome' by the end of the sixties?

SOURCE 12.1 The first verse of *We Shall Overcome*, the most famous and widely heard civil rights song of the decade

We shall overcome,
We shall overcome,
We shall overcome some day,
Oh, deep in my heart
I do believe
We shall overcome some day.

SOURCE 12.2 The words of the former slave, Frederick Douglas, in 1857, before the Civil War

Those who profess freedom and yet deprecate agitation
Are men who want crops without plowing the ground
They want rain without thunder and lightning
They want ocean without the awful roar of its waters.
Power concedes nothing without a demand.
It never did, and it never will.

■ 12C Timeline of civil rights

1865	Thirteenth Amendment abolished slavery
1868	Fourteenth Amendment meant former slaves were citizens and the federal government had the right to intervene if a state curtailed a citizen's rights
1870	Fifteenth Amendment stated the vote not to be denied on the grounds of race
1875	Civil Rights Act to prevent discrimination in public places
1896	Supreme Court upheld *Plessy v. Ferguson*, which permitted 'separate but equal' facilities
1933	New Deal helped the poor, including black Americans
1941	President Roosevelt set up the Fair Employment Practices Commission
1946	President Truman set up President's Committee on Civil Rights
1947	The Committee's Report *To Secure These Rights* set out the federal government's responsibilities for civil rights and to establish racial equality. Truman issued Executive Orders ending racial discrimination in the federal government and the armed forces
1950	Military units in the Korean War were desegregated
1954	Supreme Court ruling on *Brown v. Board of Education of Topeka* disallowed segregation in schools
1956	Montgomery bus boycott
1957	Desegregation crisis at Little Rock, Arkansas
1958	Supreme Court ruled that school segregations were unconstitutional
1960	First sit-in to protest at segregated lunch counters at Greensboro, North Carolina
1961	Freedom Rides
1962	Supreme Court ruling in *Baker v. Carr* on the principle of one man, one vote
1963	Birmingham riots and the March on Washington, JFK promises a Civil Rights Bill
1964	Civil Rights Act
	Twenty-fourth Amendment rules as unconstitutional the imposing of a poll tax as a prerequisite for voting in a presidential election
	Freedom Summer in Mississippi
1965	Voting Rights Act
	Selma to Montgomery march
1966	Urban riots notably in Watts, Los Angeles
	Black Power movement formed
	The Supreme Court ruled that imposing a poll tax for state elections was unconstitutional
1967	Urban riots in northern cities
1968	Martin Luther King assassinated and the end of the national movement for civil rights
1972	Equal Employment Opportunities Act
1988	Civil Rights Restoration Act to counter erosion of the effectiveness of civil rights laws

236

'WE SHALL OVERCOME': HOW DID THE CHALLENGES OF THE SIXTIES ERA CHANGE AMERICA?

DO YOU KNOW THE CIVIL RIGHTS ACRONYMS?

COINTELPRO – FBI programme against domestic terrorism, but used to weaken the civil rights movement and militant black groups

CORE – Congress of Racial Equality; a non-violent organisation founded in 1942

FBI – Federal Bureau of Investigation, led by J. Edgar Hoover; official purpose is to combat domestic crime, but it was unsympathetic to the civil rights movement and militant black groups

JFK – John Fitzgerald Kennedy

LBJ – Lyndon Baines Johnson

MFDP – Mississippi Freedom Democratic Party; multi-racial political party founded in 1964

MLK – Martin Luther King

NAACP – National Association for the Advancement of Colored People, founded in 1909

NOI – Nation of Islam; organisation of black Muslims advocating separatism and economic self-help for Afro-American communities

OAAU – Organization of Afro-American Unity; black nationalist group founded by Malcolm X

SCLC – Southern Christian Leadership Conference, organisation of black ministers, formed in 1957, led by Martin Luther King and a co-ordinator of civil rights activities. Still active today

SNCC – Student Non-Violent Co-ordinating Committee, working in the 1960s for VOTER REGISTRATION

ACTIVITY

1 Using Chart 12C note which civil rights changes (and their dates) were brought about by:
   a) the law (Congress and the Supreme Court)
   b) by group action
   c) by political action.

2 What do you notice about what created change, and when?

What were they fighting for?

1 To end everyday discrimination

Civil rights activists were fighting to stop everyday acts of discrimination, which had supposedly ended a century ago, and yet were still common to most Southern blacks, and to some of those who lived in the North: the right to travel where and when they wanted; to share washing and drinking fountains; to enjoy parks and swimming pools with white citizens; to be addressed by their name and title, not 'nigger' or 'boy'; to be served at a lunch counter; to have as good an education as white children. There were many other constraints – petty and trivial on the surface, but indicating the second-class status of black Americans in most aspects of their daily lives.

2 To change attitudes

They were fighting to change the behaviour and the attitudes of white racists. After being attacked during a lunch counter sit-in in Jackson, Mississippi (see Source 12.6, page 238) a young black student wrote, 'After the sit-in, all I could think of was how sick Mississippi whites were. They believed so much in the segregated Southern way of life, they would kill to preserve it. I sat in the NAACP office and thought how many times they had killed when their way of life was threatened.' (Anne Moody, *Coming of Age in Mississippi*, 1968, p.267).

3 To vote without intimidation

They were fighting so that black citizens were not intimidated from registering to vote. It was only by voting for black politicians, or by white politicians needing black votes to win, that the needs and interests of the black community would be recognised. It had already happened in the North. It should be possible in the South, but only if Southern states were prevented from imposing restrictions or stopping the intimidation of voters.

4 For economic equality

Gradually many protesters realised that they had to fight to win better housing, health, incomes and education. Proportionally more black Americans were poorer than white Americans. This disadvantaged black Americans within society.

5 For a just society

They were fighting for justice; that black Americans should have all the legal rights, and legal protection to live their lives without fear.

ACTIVITY

Read Anne Moody's words again. Was she exaggerating? As you work through the rest of Section B, see if you can find any evidence that she was right.

Would non-violent protest be enough?

SOURCE 12.3 In 1849 the American writer Henry Thoreau had posed the question about whether CIVIL DISOBEDIENCE could be justified (from Henry Thoreau's essay, 'Civil Disobedience', 1849)

Unjust laws exist: shall we be content to obey them, or shall we endeavour to amend them, and obey them until we have succeeded, or shall we transgress them at once? Men, generally, under such a government as this, think that they ought to wait until they have persuaded the majority to alter them.

TALKING POINTS

1 Do you agree that civil disobedience is justified in certain circumstances?

2 Are there any issues where you would risk prosecution and possibly jail (as GM protesters and those opposed to motorways across nature reserves have done) to oppose a law?

Martin Luther King (1929–68)

Ralph Abernathy spoke at the commemoration service for Martin Luther King on 15 January 1969, 'He was the redeemer of the soul of America. He taught the nation that "an eye for an eye and a tooth for a tooth" if followed to their ultimate conclusion, would only end in a totally blind and toothless society. He discovered that the most potent force for revolution and reform in America is non-violence'.

Martin Luther King, born in 1929, was the son of a Baptist church pastor in Atlanta, Georgia. In 1954 he too became a pastor, in Montgomery, Alabama and was an active supporter of the NAACP. Four years later he helped to found the SCLC, was recognised as its spokesperson, and moved back to Atlanta. He gave moral and political support to the different attempts to desegregate the Southern cities, used influence in contacts with the Kennedy administration and preached the value of non-violent action. In 1964 he was awarded the Nobel Peace Prize. Like many other activists he realised the links between poverty and the second-class status of black Americans, and started a campaign in the poor areas of Northern cities. But the resistance of white officials was stronger than expected and progress was slow. At the same time, the race riots in urban areas and the growing power of new black militant groups challenged his methods and beliefs. He recognised one reason for the criticism of him, 'When hope diminishes the hate element is often turned toward those who originally built up the hope. The bitterness is often greater toward that person who built up the hope, who could say "I have a dream" but couldn't produce the dream because of the failure and the sickness of the nation to respond to the dream'. (in D. Garrow, *Bearing the Cross*, 1993, p.598).

SOURCE 12.4 The newly-formed SNCC's Statement of Purpose, 1960, outlining the rationale for non-violence by its members

Non-violence as it grows from Judaic-Christian traditions seeks a social order of justice permeated by love ... Through non-violence, courage displaces fear; love transforms hate. Acceptance dissipates prejudice; hope ends despair. Peace dominates war; faith reconciles doubt. Mutual regard cancels enmity. Justice for all overthrows injustice. The redemptive community supersedes systems of gross social immorality.

SOURCE 12.5 Martin Luther King explains the reason for non-violent action to white clergy who had criticised his actions in Birmingham in April 1963. King was writing from jail (you can find out why on page 239). He was put in solitary confinement and wrote the letter, which had to be smuggled out, on the margins of newspapers and toilet paper. As well as describing the daily humiliations that black Americans face because of their colour he explained the rationale for non-violent action (from Martin Luther King, *Why We Can't Wait*, 1984)

Non-violent direct action seeks to create such a crisis and establish such creative tension that a community that has consistently refused to negotiate is forced to confront the issue. It seeks so to dramatize the issue that it can no longer be ignored ... We know through painful experience that freedom is never voluntarily given by the oppressor; it must be demanded by the oppressed. Frankly I have never yet engaged in a direct action movement that was 'well-timed' according to the timetable of those who have not suffered unduly from the disease of segregation. For years now I have heard the words 'Wait!'. It rings in the ear of every Negro with a piercing familiarity. The 'Wait' has almost always meant 'Never' ... The nations of Asia and Africa are moving with jetlike speed toward the goal of political independence, and we still creep at horse and buggy pace toward the gaining of a cup of coffee at a lunch counter ... One day the South will know that when these disinherited children of God sat down at lunch counters they were in reality standing up for the best in the American dream and the most sacred values in our Judeo-Christian heritage, and thusly, carrying our whole nation back to those great wells of democracy which were dug deep by the Founding Fathers in the formulation of the Constitution and the Declaration of Independence.

237

'WE SHALL OVERCOME': HOW DID THE CHALLENGES OF THE SIXTIES ERA CHANGE AMERICA?

ACTIVITY

1 Are you persuaded by King's arguments (Source 12.5)?
2 What might persuade the clergy to whom he was writing?

SOURCE 12.6 Students from Tougaloo College at a Woolworth's lunch counter in Jackson, Mississippi on 28 May 1961

ACTIVITY

1 Describe what is happening in the photograph in Source 12.6. Notice the colour of the people involved, the expressions and the body language shown.
2 Read Sources 12.4 and 12.5 again. What were the beliefs that made these students appear passive?

King was always aware of how much some white segregationists hated him; to the extent of being willing to kill him. On 4 April 1968 he was shot dead aged 39. His death led to rioting in over a hundred cities, and to national mourning. King's reputation veered between him being regarded as saint-like or as being too easily subservient to white interests. He was under constant surveillance by the FBI, especially as Hoover loathed him. They had found that his personal life included relations with other women besides his wife Coretta. King knew that disclosures like this could threaten people's respect for his actions. Some other activists thought that he deliberately sought personal glory, and was prepared to be a martyr. He had an impossible task, since there always had to be compromise. Trying to draw attention to the needs of the black community needed publicity and political bargaining. However, most accounts of his life acknowledge his skills in rousing the conscience of white Americans about the injustices and malice of segregation, to the point where effective laws were passed quickly, and enforced.

How did they fight?

1 Sit-ins

The first sit-in at a lunch counter, in Greensboro, North Carolina on 1 February 1960, was unplanned. Four students from the local college refused to leave the Woolworth's counter when they were refused service because they were black. The next day they were joined by 23 more students, by 66 the next day and by 1000 at the end of the week. Over 3000 protesters were jailed, but the tactic, shown on televisions and in photographs, was popular – it spread to other Southern cities, involving up to 50,000 people; and effective – lunch counters were desegregated in 126 cities. The newly founded Student Non-Violent Co-ordinating Committee (SNCC) helped to organise support. They were a new young generation of protesters, mainly black but also with white supporters, ready to act against discrimination. If they were attacked, they went back with more supporters, even if threatened with jail, to show they would no longer be intimidated. Never before had black Americans protested with such persistence and in such numbers. They were to support their own people not because of an ideology, but because they cared about each other's daily lives.

2 Freedom Rides

In 1961 James Farmer, the director of the Congress of Racial Equality (CORE) used the idea of 'Freedom Rides' – any person, black or white, could travel anywhere in the USA by public transport – to try to force the desegregation of

SOURCE 12.7   The Freedom Riders'
burnt-out bus at Anniston, Alabama, in 1961

interstate public transport. The first
Freedom Ride was taken by seven
black and six white Americans who
used public transport to travel south
to New Orleans from Washington DC.
Attacked by white mobs, who
included members of the Ku Klux
Klan, the young riders were stoned
and beaten with clubs, bicycle chains
and baseball bats. Buses were burned
as police deliberately arrived too late
or ignored the violence (see Source
12.7). Nightly television pictures
roused the anger of many watching
and Robert Kennedy, as attorney-
general, had to send in federal
marshals to restore calm. The justice
department, under the persuasion of
Kennedy's deputy Burke Marshall,
began, by September, to enforce the
laws against such segregation.
Activists realised the value of having
media attention when there was deliberate white violence.

3 Challenging Birmingham

'The most segregated city in the United States,' was Martin Luther King's
description of Birmingham, Alabama, as he planned demonstrations, BOYCOTTS
and sit-ins in protest against its discrimination in transport and facilities, in
April 1963. He anticipated the violent reaction of the police and the Chief
Commissioner of Public Safety, Eugene 'Bull' Connor. He was not disappointed.

Using electric cattle prods, water hoses so powerful that they could strip the
bark off trees, and vicious dogs, the police attacked unarmed and peaceful
marchers. Up to 900 children were arrested for joining the marches. King was
arrested for his part in the demonstrations and it was here that he wrote his
Letter from Birmingham Jail (see page 237). The scenes were shown on nightly
news bulletins. They roused anger at home and disquiet abroad. President
Kennedy knew he would have to act. On 11 June he announced a Civil Rights
Bill. By the end of the year the Supreme Court had declared that Birmingham's
segregation laws were unconstitutional.

SOURCE 12.8   Police dogs attacking an
unarmed protester in Birmingham in April
1963

ACTIVITY

'I have a dream' – is this the greatest twentieth-century American speech?

1 What is King saying in this extract (Source 12.9)?
2 Why do you think he makes reference to a Christian God so often?
3 What is significant about the order in which he talks about places in the USA towards the end of the speech?
4 What is the mention of spirituals, at the end of the speech, designed to remind his audience of?
5 What are the clues that this is a speech and not a piece of writing?

4 March on Washington

By the summer of 1963 civil rights protests were the focus of news and discussion. In 1941 Asa Philip Randolph had threatened President Roosevelt with a march of protest on Washington. On 28 August 1963 Martin Luther King used the same idea to keep up pressure for the Civil Rights Bill. Some of the activists felt that the march was too controlled by the government (who feared a mass demonstration). But it was a remarkably peaceful day, and attracted 250,000 black and white demonstrators with representatives from all church groups and the unions. Filling the area around the Lincoln Memorial (see page 8) they listened to speeches, including King's 'I have a dream' oration. It succeeded in attracting attention to the arguments, and the power of non-violent action, of the black community.

SOURCE 12.9 King's speech from the steps of the Lincoln Memorial in J. M. Washington (ed.), *A Testament of Hope: the Essential Writings of Martin Luther King Junior*, 1963

... I still have a dream. It is a dream deeply rooted in the American dream that one day this nation will rise up and live out the true meaning of its creed – we hold these truths to be self-evident, that all men are created equal.

I have a dream that one day on the red hills of Georgia, sons of former slaves and sons of former slave-owners will be able to sit down together at the table of brotherhood.

I have a dream that one day, even the state of Mississippi, a state sweltering with the heart of injustice, sweltering with the heat of oppression, will be transformed into an oasis of freedom and justice.

I have a dream that my four little children will one day live in a nation where they will not be judged by the color of their skin but by [the] content of their character. I have a dream today!

I have a dream that one day, down in Alabama, with its vicious racists, ... little black boys and black girls will be able to join hands with little white boys and girls as sisters and brothers. I have a dream today!

I have a dream that one day every valley shall be exalted, every hill and mountain shall be made low, the rough places shall be made plain, and the crooked places shall be made straight and the glory of the Lord will be revealed and all flesh shall see it.

... With this faith we will be able to work together, to pray together, to struggle together, to go to jail together, to stand up for freedom together, knowing that we will be free one day.

So let freedom ring from the prodigious hilltops of New Hampshire.
Let freedom ring from the mighty mountains of New York.
Let freedom ring from the heightening Alleghenies of Pennsylvania.
Let freedom ring from the snow-capped Rockies of Colorado.
Let freedom ring from the curvaceous slopes of California.
But not only that.
Let freedom ring from Stone Mountain of Georgia.
Let freedom ring from Lookout Mountain of Tennessee.
Let freedom ring from every hill and molehill of Mississippi, from every mountainside, let freedom ring.

... we will be able to speed up that day when all God's children – black men and white men, Jews and Gentiles, Catholics and Protestants – will be able to join hands and to sing in the word of the old Negro spiritual, 'Free at last; thank God Almighty, we are free at last'.

This speech was meant to be heard. King spoke with all the skills and passion of the pastor that he was. The rhythm, cadence and words work together to make it a wonderful piece of oratory, and, more importantly, a powerful message about civil rights freedoms across America. However, for some young black Americans that inclusiveness and emphasis on peaceful protest was no longer sufficient.

5 Freedom Summer

In 1964 more than 1000 Northern students, many of them white, travelled to Mississippi to assist voter registration and to protest against segregation. The project had limited success because of violent white racist reaction, with churches burned, fifteen civil rights workers killed and relatively few black voters registered.

SOURCE 12.10 Deputy Sheriff Price and Sheriff Rainey, of Neshoba County, Mississippi, on trial for the murders of three civil rights activists, Michael Schwerner, James Chaney and Andrew Goodman, who had been involved with the Freedom Summer project. They disappeared on 21 June and their bodies were found two months later. The two policemen were tried in December 1967. They clearly expected the all-white jury to acquit them, as such juries always had done in cases involving crimes against black people. Instead they, and six Ku Klux Klan members they had encouraged to join the chase as the three activists drove out of Mississippi, were found guilty and sentenced to jail

DISCUSS

1 Why did the police react as they did towards the non-violent Selma march?

2 Did they, or the protesters, give the president justification for passing the Voting Rights Act?

---

6 Selma march

In Selma, Alabama, in 1965 the population was 29,000, with 15,000 black adults entitled to vote but only 335 registered to do so. Literacy tests, with different standards, were used to discriminate between the registration of white and black voters. Only individuals could challenge the registration, and it would take years for all Selma's black voters to do so. From January, groups of black Selma citizens tried to register – teachers, undertakers, beauticians. Most were attacked by the city's police and many arrested and jailed. In February, King joined the marches. In one week in that month 3000 marchers were arrested. A large protest march was organised from Selma, to the state capital at Montgomery on Sunday 7 March. As the 600 marchers crossed the Pettus Bridge out of the city they were stopped by state troopers, some of whom were on horseback. Claiming that the marchers were breaking the law, state troopers and police confronted them.

SOURCE 12.11 John Lewis described what happened after they were given a three-minute warning to disperse (in H. Hampton and S. Fayer, *Voices of Freedom*, 1990, pp.227–28)

We saw the state troopers and members of Sheriff Clarke's [Selma police chief] posse on horseback. The troopers came toward us with billy clubs, tear gas, and bullwhips, trampling us with horses. I felt like it was the last demonstration, the last protest on my part, like I was going to take my last breath from the tear gas. I saw people rolling, heard people screaming and hollering. We couldn't go forward. If we tried to go forward we would've gone into the heat of the battle. We couldn't go to the side, to the left or to the right, because we would have been going into the Alabama River, so we were beaten back down the streets of Selma, back to the church.

Lewis suffered a fractured skull in the attack and more than 50 people needed hospital treatment. It became known as 'Bloody Sunday'. The scenes outraged and sickened many television viewers, and newspapers demanded federal intervention. White supporters from the North came to Selma for a second symbolic march of 2000 marchers on 9 March.

The president called the racist Alabama Governor, George Wallace, to the White House for a three-hour condemnation, threatening to send federal troops to the state. On 15 March President Johnson spoke to Congress, 'Their cause must be our cause, too. Because it is not just Negroes, but all of us who must overcome the crippling legacy of bigotry and injustice. And, we shall overcome'.

He then introduced the Voting Rights Bill and requested Congress to pass it. In August the president signed the Act and urged, 'Let me say to every Negro in this country. You *must* register. You *must* vote. The vote is the most powerful instrument ever devised by man for breaking down injustice and destroying the terrible walls that imprison men because they are different from other men'.

■ 12D Change in voter registrations in the South

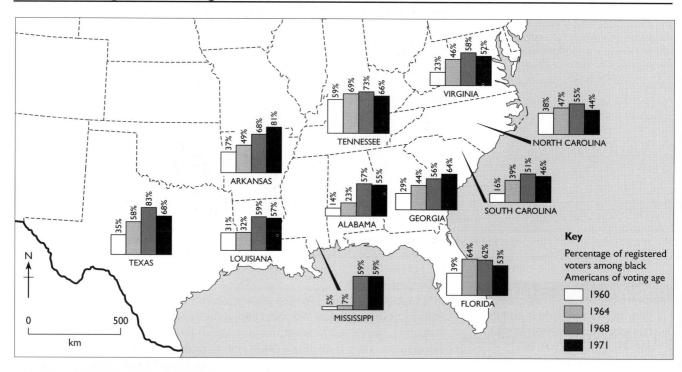

ACTIVITY

What can you deduce from the statistics in Chart 12D about how Southern black citizens responded to Johnson's demand?

7 Malcolm X

Whilst in jail Malcolm Little, who had a criminal history of petty theft, drug abuse and pimping, converted to the Muslim faith, changed his name to Malcolm X and joined the Nation of Islam, whose followers were known as Black Muslims. They believed in separation from the 'evil' white society and emphasised black pride in their heritage. They called themselves Afro-Americans and had their own moral code, though not one that valued women. Malcolm X gained a strong following in the urban ghettos, but in 1964 disagreed with the leader of the Nation of Islam, Elijah Muhammad, and supported Martin Luther King's fight for co-operation between races. However, in 1965 he was assassinated, probably by Black Muslims. He became a symbol for black defiance and black self-respect, especially for the supporters of Black Power.

8 Black Power

As white resistance to INTEGRATION continued during the 1960s optimism for peaceful change was eroded for some young black activists. They questioned whether they wanted to be part of such a society, and whether more extreme methods were needed. In 1966 Stokely Carmichael became chairman of SNCC and challenged the idea of racial integration, with arguments that black citizens needed their own power, rather than white friendship.

SOURCE 12.12 Tommie Smith and John Carlos give the Black Power salute at their victory ceremony at the Olympic Games in Mexico, 1968. They wanted to express their individuality as black Americans, but many felt that it was inappropriate at such a sporting occasion, and Smith and Carlos were suspended by the US Olympic Committee

SOURCE 12.13 Stokely Carmichael explaining Black Power in *The New York Review of Books*, 22 September 1966. He explains that no organisation so far has spoken for militant blacks: those frustrated by the violent reaction to their civil rights protests. Now the SNCC has a slogan which whites might loathe, but black people could respond to

We should begin with the basic fact that black Americans have two problems: they are poor and they are black ... black Americans are propertyless people in a country where property is valued above all ... this country does not function by morality, love or non-violence, but by power ... With power the masses could make or participate in making the decisions which govern their destinies, and thus create basic change in their day-to-day lives.

As for white America, perhaps it can stop crying out against 'black supremacy', 'black nationalism', 'racism in reverse' and start facing reality. The reality is that this nation from top to bottom, is racist; that racism is not primarily a problem of 'human relations', but of an exploitation maintained – either actively or through silence – by the society as a whole.

SOURCE 12.14 Chicago Student Non-Violent Co-ordinating Committee leaflet, 1967 (in M. P. Johnson, *Reading the American Past*, Vol. II, p.213)

We must first gain BLACK POWER here in America ... We must take over the political and economic systems where we are in the majority in the heart of every major city in the country as well as in the rural areas. We must create our own black culture to erase the lies the white man has fed our minds from the day we were born ... Malcolm X was the first black man from the ghetto in America to make a real attempt to get the white man's fist off the black man. He recognised the true dignity of man – without the white society prejudices about status, education and background that we all must purge from our minds ... The most beautiful thing that Malcolm X taught us is that once a black man discovers for himself a pride in his blackness, he can throw off the shackles of mental slavery and become a MAN in the truest sense of the word ...

DISCUSS

1 What does the author of Source 12.14 mean by 'get the white man's fist off the black man'? Why was the analogy of a fist used?
2 What does the image tell you about how this branch of the SNCC felt about white people?

ACTIVITY

1 Black Power has been described as a cry of rage. What appears to be meant by Black Power according to Sources 12.12–12.14?
2 What reasons are suggested in these sources to explain why some black activists had rejected non-violence as a tactic?
3 Source 12.14 emphasises black men. What might this emphasis signify?
4 What do you think 'freedom' means to Black Power supporters?

244

'WE SHALL OVERCOME': HOW DID THE CHALLENGES OF THE SIXTIES ERA CHANGE AMERICA?

Did they win their fight?

The Civil Rights Act, 1964

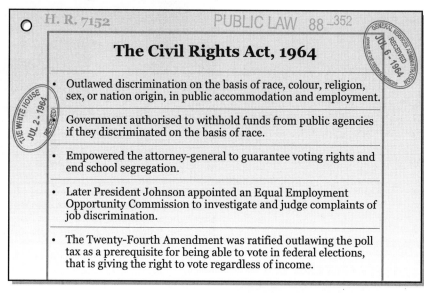

H. R. 7152   PUBLIC LAW 88–352

The Civil Rights Act, 1964

- Outlawed discrimination on the basis of race, colour, religion, sex, or nation origin, in public accommodation and employment.

- Government authorised to withhold funds from public agencies if they discriminated on the basis of race.

- Empowered the attorney-general to guarantee voting rights and end school segregation.

- Later President Johnson appointed an Equal Employment Opportunity Commission to investigate and judge complaints of job discrimination.

- The Twenty-Fourth Amendment was ratified outlawing the poll tax as a prerequisite for being able to vote in federal elections, that is giving the right to vote regardless of income.

The Voting Rights Act, 1965

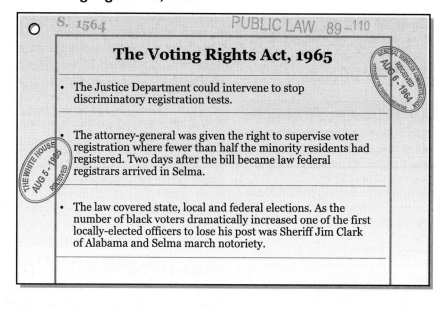

S. 1564   PUBLIC LAW 89–110

The Voting Rights Act, 1965

- The Justice Department could intervene to stop discriminatory registration tests.

- The attorney-general was given the right to supervise voter registration where fewer than half the minority residents had registered. Two days after the bill became law federal registrars arrived in Selma.

- The law covered state, local and federal elections. As the number of black voters dramatically increased one of the first locally-elected officers to lose his post was Sheriff Jim Clark of Alabama and Selma march notoriety.

The effects of the civil rights movement

Impact on other rights movements

One of the important results of the civil rights movement was that it energised other protest groups who saw that direct, group and community action could be successful. Anti-war protesters, the women's movement, Mexican migrant workers and environmental protesters were amongst those who used similar tactics. The civil rights movement had shown that grassroots action with a moral justification was very powerful in a liberal society. At the same time there were other groups who felt that non-violent protest was insufficient, particularly the BLACK PANTHERS.

Personal courage and determination

Civil rights activists had demonstrated courage and persistence, aided by liberal politicians, and especially by President Johnson's determination to enforce the end of segregation.

Raising expectations

As civil rights had to be achieved by political involvement it made other groups use similar pressure. This raised expectations that difficult problems could be solved, and that individuals were entitled to rights. When they were disappointed, there was anger and social tension, which sometimes led to violence.

Resentment

Once expectations had been raised for a better life it was hard to control them. Neither Kennedy nor Johnson had radical agendas for changing the structure of society. As long as the wealthy were protected it would be impossible for those at the bottom to dramatically improve their lives. During the long hot summers of 1965–68, in overcrowded inner-city areas, the resentment created boiled over in violence that seemed to be driven by race rather than by poverty.

Socio-economic disadvantages

Guaranteeing voting rights was essential, but it did not end the socio-economic disadvantages of decades of discrimination. Poor housing, poor health and inadequate schooling, as well as long-held racist views of white supremacy could not be quickly eroded.

Backlash

To many poor and middle-class whites, black advancement came at the expense of their economic and social security. As the challenges of the sixties began to affect their way of life it was inevitable that there would be some kind of backlash.

Could white segregationists change?

Ivan Allen was a white businessman and mayor of Atlanta from 1962–70. Initially a segregationist, when he became mayor he accepted and actively enforced desegregation policies. He took down all 'white' and 'colored' signs on the day he took office, desegregated the schools, persuaded local industries, (which included the mighty Coca-Cola corporation) to desegregate their employment, worked closely with Martin Luther King and the SCLC based in the city, and avoided the urban racial riots that affected other cities with large black populations. He showed that the Civil Rights Act and the Great Society programme (see Section C) had brought practical and federally enforced changes that could not be resisted. Unwilling co-operation could mutate into grudging acceptance and then positive action.

One of the problems for historians is judging the success of the civil rights movement. It undoubtedly led to legislation and public policies, enforced by the federal government, which radically changed the access and opportunities that black Americans had to education, employment, voting rights and housing.

Black activists have become mayors in southern cities, judges, senators and congressmen. Media stars like Oprah Winfrey demonstrate their equality. Black businesses operate across the nation. Affirmative action programmes (known

ACTIVITY

There were many heroes of the civil rights movement. Many were known only to their family and friends, or listed in jail records. Here are some of the more famous names:
John Lewis, Fannie Lou Hamer, James Meredith, Ella Baker, James Farmer, Medgar Evans, Jo Ann Robinson, Baynard Rustin, Daisy Bates, Robert Moses, E.D. Nixon

Choose two and research their achievements. Remember that what they did, and the fear they felt, was also felt by the hundreds of other 'invisible' protesters.

DISCUSS

What victories had the civil rights activists gained for Afro-Americans?

in Britain as positive discrimination) create opportunities for minority groups. But the legacy of racial hatred, and the attitude that black Americans were inferior citizens was much harder to end. Those who have benefited least are poor Afro-Americans (see Source 12.15).

SOURCE 12.15 One of the most influential books of the sixties recognised the plight of poor Afro-Americans (M. Harrington, *The Other America: Poverty in the US*, 1962, p.72)

The Negro is poor because he is black; that is obvious enough ... the Negro is black because he is poor. The laws against color can be removed, but that will leave the poverty that is the historic and institutionalized consequence of color. As long as this is the case, being born a Negro will continue to be the most profound disability that the US imposes upon a citizen.

FOCUS ROUTE

As you work through Section C make notes on the following questions:

1 What made up the Great Society programme?
2 Who was it designed to help?
3 What were its successes?
4 Why was it criticised?
5 How important was President Johnson in its creation and effectiveness?

C Did President Johnson's 'Great Society' change American society?

Sometimes a book can appear at the most opportune moment. Michael Harrington's *The Other America: Poverty in the US*, published in 1962, is one example. It examined who was poor, and why, especially when they lived in the richest nation in the world. What did he find?

- That poverty was often invisible. It was found 'off the beaten track'. It might be in remote scenic areas where visitors saw the landscape, but not the struggles of the inhabitants. It was in deprived inner-city areas abandoned by the middle classes, and only glimpsed from a car driving in from the more affluent suburbs.
- It was hidden by obesity and clothes. Obesity could suggest plenty of food, or too much cheap, unhealthy food. Mass production meant that clothes were relatively cheap, so rags and tatters no longer demonstrated poverty.
- The poor were the wrong age. They were often the elderly who had difficulty in getting far beyond their homes, or the sick, or those who lived alone and stayed close to home. They could often be all three. Children were a less invisible group, but poor housing, food and health affected their ability to benefit from school.
- They were politically invisible, usually with no party, union or organisation to speak up for them.
- They lived in a vicious circle of poverty which they could rarely break out of because they lacked the 'energy' to do so.
- They were different: 'To be impoverished is to be an internal alien, to grow up in a culture that is radically different from the one that dominated the society'.

Statistics confirmed Harrington's findings. At the beginning of the decade:

- the top 20 per cent of the population owned 77 per cent of the nation's wealth, and the bottom 20 per cent owned 0.05 per cent
- the top 10 per cent of the population earned 28 times as much as the bottom 10 per cent
- 43 per cent of black families were classed as poor, i.e. they had an annual income less than $3000
- only 1 per cent of black Americans owned businesses.

This structural imbalance in the ownership and access to wealth had lasted through the fifties, in spite of its economic growth and stability.

ACTIVITY

Make your own sketch, or create a montage of images, based on Harrington's findings.

ACTIVITY

1 What does the graph in Source 12.16 tell you about the general changes in poverty between 1959 and 1990?
2 What were the poverty levels of black Americans in 1965, 1973, 1980, 1984 and 1988?
3 How would you explain the differences?
4 Why were the levels for black Americans higher than for other groups?

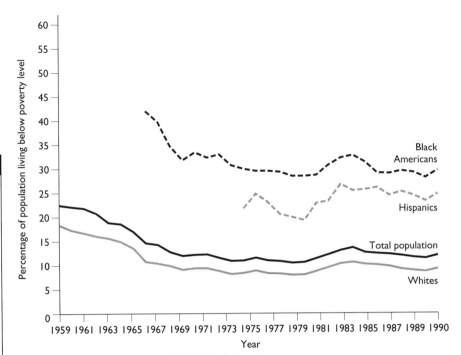

NB 1959–66 – no statistics are available for black Americans
1959–74 – no statistics are available for Hispanics

SOURCE 12.16 Poverty 1959–90

In his first State of the Union message to Congress in January 1964, Johnson announced 'unconditional war on poverty in America'. In May he addressed the students of the University of Michigan and outlined his ideas to improve society. It was an appeal to the ordinary person, and especially to the young. Johnson believed in the power of government to change lives. He was to use this power to improve the lives of the poorest in society.

SOURCE 12.17 From the *Public Papers of the President of the United States: Lyndon B. Johnson*, 1963–65

The Great Society rests on abundance and liberty for all. It demands an end to poverty and racial injustice, to which we are totally committed in our time ... The Great Society is a place where every child can find knowledge to enrich his mind and to enlarge his talents. It is a place where leisure is a welcome chance to build and reflect, not a feared cause of boredom and restlessness. It is a place where the city of man serves not only the needs of the body and the demands of commerce but the desire for beauty and the hunger for community. It is a place where man can renew contact with nature. It is a place which honors creation for its own sake and for what it adds to the understanding of the race. It is a place where men are more concerned with the quality of their goals than the quantity of their goods ... the three places where we begin to build the Great Society – in our cities, in our countryside, and in our classrooms ... Will you join in the battle to build the Great Society, to prove that our material progress is only the foundation on which we will build a richer life of mind and spirit?

Did Johnson have the ability to make his promises a reality?

LBJ became a senator for Texas in 1948 and spent the next twenty years becoming Congress' most effective politician. His ambition was to be president and he hated being Kennedy's vice-president. He was skilful because:

- he knew much about each senator, both private and public knowledge about their strengths and weaknesses

248

'WE SHALL OVERCOME': HOW DID THE CHALLENGES OF THE SIXTIES ERA CHANGE AMERICA?

SOURCE 12.18 As a man who was 1.9m tall, the LBJ 'lean' was quite effective. It was often used with the 'Johnson treatment', an almost physical attack on the person he was lobbying

TALKING POINTS

Johnson knew that he did not have the physical attractiveness of Kennedy. He did not photograph as well, he was nine years older, and had suffered a serious heart attack. Yet power has an attractiveness. Presidents know it, so do prime ministers.

1 How far do people make their judgements of politicians based on their presentation to the public?
2 Does Kennedy seem better known than Johnson because he was photogenic, or is that too shallow an assessment?

- he was brilliant at forging compromises and avoiding damaging conflict
- he worked extremely hard and paid great attention to detail
- he knew how to persuade, 'Lyndon got me by the lapels and put his face on top of mine and he talked and talked. I figured it was either getting drowned or joining'. This became known as the 'Johnson treatment', a sort of physical assault, 'encompassing, enveloping, overwhelming the recipient with the intense power of personal persuasion.' (see Source 12.18)
- he knew his skills, 'I do understand power, whatever else may be said about me. I know where to look for it and how to use it'. (to his assistant Harry McPherson)

But his sense of insecurity meant that he could be a bully. He described himself as 'a Texan ruffian among the perfumed darlings of the east'. He could make excessive demands for loyalty:

- he relied on the support of his wife, Claudia 'Lady Bird' Johnson, who tolerated his affairs, and his coarseness, and to whom he turned for reassurance
- he mistrusted the military because he knew that their loyalties were divided between their political masters and their military desires
- he wanted a total commitment from his staff, telling a staff official about the desirable requirements of a new employee, 'I want loyalty. I want him to kiss my ass in Macy's window at high noon and tell me it smells like roses' (Macy's is a large American department store, a sort of Harrods!)
- he realised that the FBI boss J. Edgar Hoover could not be trusted to support him, but decided to keep him on his side, commenting, 'Well, it's probably better to have him inside the tent pissing out, than outside pissing in'
- he found dissent difficult and preferred consensus to individualism
- he wanted what was best for the nation, to make things right, yet at the same time he underestimated the impact of social changes and tensions.

SOURCE 12.19 David Halberstam, a journalist, writing in 1969, who had worked in Vietnam and who knew Johnson and Kennedy (in D. Halberstam, *The Best and the Brightest*, 1969, pp.430–31)

He was a man of stunning force, drive and intelligence, and of equally stunning insecurity ... the country had become so large, so powerful, yet so diffuse and disharmonious that only a man of his raging, towering strengths and energies could harness the nation's potential ... He did not dream small dreams. Nor did he pursue small challenges.

SOURCE 12.20 A civil rights leader speaking at the time of Johnson's death in January 1974 (in W. Chafe, *The Unfinished Journey*, 4th edn, 1999, p.244)

When the forces demanded and the mood permitted for once an activist, human-hearted man had his hands on the levers of power ... [LBJ] was there when we and the nation needed him, and oh my God, do I wish he was here now.

SOURCE 12.21 Robert Caro, the author of a detailed three part biography of Johnson. (from R. Caro, 'The Compassion of Lyndon Johnson', in *New Yorker*, 1 April 2002)

Lyndon Johnson was the greatest champion Americans of color had in the White House during the twentieth century ... He was the lawmaker for the poor and the downtrodden and the oppressed, the restorer of at least a measure of dignity to those who so desperately needed it, the redeemer of the promises made to them by America. He ... codified compassion, the president who wrote at a least a measure of justice into the statue books by which America is governed.

SOURCE 12.22 Doris Kearns, another biographer, describes her first encounter with the president (in D. Kearns, *Lyndon Johnson and the American Dream*, 1976, p.2)

His appearance startled me. The picture in my mind had been a caricature; the sly televised politician, his features locked into virtual immobility, eyes squinting, ears that seemed to dangle like thick pendants affixed to the sides of his head. Now I saw a ruddy giant of a man with a strong mobile face, and a presence whose manifest energy dominated an entire room filled with Senators, Representatives, Cabinet officials, White House staff members, and reporters.

SOURCE 12.23 D. Kearns, *Lyndon Johnson and the American Dream*, 1976, p. 17

249

'WE SHALL OVERCOME': HOW DID THE CHALLENGES OF THE SIXTIES ERA CHANGE AMERICA?

We talked mostly in the early hours of the morning. Johnson slept poorly these days, waking up at 5.30. Terrified of lying alone in the dark, he came into my room to talk. Gradually, a curious ritual developed. I would awaken at five and get dressed. Half an hour later Johnson would knock on my door, dressed in his robe and pyjamas. As I sat in a chair by the window, he climbed into the bed, pulling the sheets up to his neck, looking like a cold and frightened child.

■ **Learning Trouble Spot**

How do biographers know?

Not many 25-year-old biographers have the sort of access to their subject that Doris Kearns had (see Source 12.23).

Not surprisingly when you read Doris Kearns' biography she records much detail given to her by Johnson of the memories and influences of his childhood and youth; the powerful, yet conflicting demands of his mother (deeply ambitious for him and rejecting if her son did not meet her high standards) and his 'man's man' of a politician/farmer father. Doris Kearns went on to work for Johnson in the White House, and was then asked by him to help set up the presidential library in Texas, and to work on his memoirs. As a biographer she had excellent access to the presidential papers and to the former president. She also admired him, and by inference, liked him. Would this affect her picture of him? Of course. The quality and reliability of her book has to be judged not only by its contents and insights, but also by the personal context in which it was written. So how can you make that judgement about biographies?

- By reading the explanations that authors give for what they do. These are usually in a preface (at the beginning) or an epilogue (at the end).
- By checking when the book was written – was the subject still alive, was it soon after their death, or many years later?
- By seeing if it has similarities with other biographers' assessments.
- By checking what sources they used. Are they varied and do they show different aspects of the person's character? Do they include family and friends as well as critics and enemies?
- By reading with an observant eye and a critical mind, you are able to stand outside the book, in a way that the biographer cannot.
- By talking to others to see if your impression and opinions are shared by them.

What did the Great Society comprise?

In 1933 President Roosevelt, Johnson's hero, had introduced the New Deal to tackle the problems of the Depression. In 1944 he had promised an 'economic bill of rights' so that all Americans should have adequate food, housing, jobs and education. Since then, little change had occurred and, as Harrington and others had shown, there was real poverty in the midst of affluence. However, the optimism and youthful energy which characterised the sixties promised change. In 1964 Johnson won a landslide victory over Barry Goldwater and had a Democratic majority in Congress. He was determined to use his success in an unconditional war on poverty.

There were three main options:

1 to redistribute society's wealth more evenly
2 to give more to the poor
3 to give the individual poor a better chance to overcome their poverty.

The Great Society programme used all three options, with especial emphasis on point 3. It best fitted the American ideal of self-help, as well as being cheaper and less disruptive to the nation's economic structure than the others.

There was also, in 1965, an Immigration Act, the first major change in immigration since 1924. It permitted more non-European immigrants, and also the admittance of the relatives of those already resident. Unwittingly it led to a more diverse population, as Asians and Latin Americans took advantage of the changes.

Social welfare legislation	Year	Effect
Economic Opportunity Act	1964	Created Office of Economic Opportunity (OEO) administering War on Poverty programmes.
Medical Care Act	1965	Created Medicaid (medical care for the poor) and Medicare (medical care for the elderly).
Minimum Wage Act	1965	Raised the minimum wage and included new groups of employees.

Education legislation	Year	Effect
Elementary and Secondary Education Act	1965	Granted federal aid to poor children.
National Endowment for the Arts and Humanities	1965	Provided federal funding for artists and scholars.
Higher Education Act	1965	Provided federal funding for post-secondary education.

Housing and urban development legislation	Year	Effect
Urban Mass Transportation Act	1964	Federal aid provided for more public transport in city centres where the poor tended to live.
Omnibus Housing Act	1964	Federal funds for public housing and rent subsidies for low-income families.
Housing and Urban Development Act	1965	Created a federal department, which gave it a higher status in government.
Metropolitan Area Redevelopment and Demonstration Cities Act	1966	Designated 150 'model cities' for combined programmes of social services, job training and housing.

Environment legislation	Year	Effect
Wilderness Preservation Act	1964	Set aside 9 million acres of federal land to be protected from commercial use.
Air and Water Quality Act	1965	Set tougher standards and required states to enforce quality controls.

ACTIVITY

Re-read Johnson's speech (Source 12.17) on page 247. How far do the Great Society programmes (Chart 12E) reflect his ideas?

ACTIVITY

1 What measures would you use to judge the effectiveness of the Great Society programmes? Check what the problems were before 1964.
2 Take two areas affected by the programmes and assess how far people's lives were changed.

TALKING POINTS

1 One of LBJ's biographers, Robert Dallek, called his volume on Johnson's time as president, *Flawed Giant*. Is this an accurate description of Johnson? You will need to look at Chapter 10 to assess his foreign policy, and this chapter to assess his domestic policy.
2 Does being 'flawed' diminish someone's achievements? Does it depend on what the flaws are?
3 Most commentators agree that as a president Johnson was incorruptible. Was this a valuable quality?

Did it change American lives?

What was the impact of the Great Society programmes?

1 The centrepiece was the Office of Economic Opportunity run by Sargent Shriver, who had run Kennedy's Peace Corps (see Chapter 10, page 193). It was innovative in its agencies. Head Start provided free nursery schools for disadvantaged children. The Job Corps provided vocational training and jobs for young people. Upward Bound helped low-income teenagers to have the skills and motivation to go to college. VISTA (Volunteers in Service to America) encouraged community service by young people in poor areas. The Community Action Programme, with the aid of lawyers, encouraged those in poor areas to take part in making decisions that affected their lives.
2 America had no National Health Service. People had to rely on savings or insurance if they needed medical care. For the poor and chronically ill, medical care was a luxury. The Medicaid and Medicare programmes, still effective today, were by 1976 providing twenty per cent of the population with medical care.

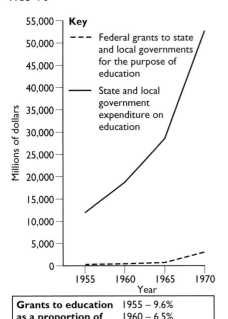

SOURCE 12.24 Spending on education 1955–70

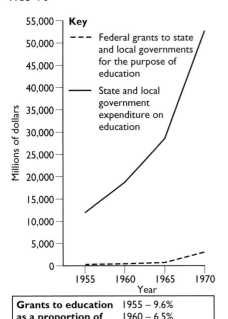

Grants to education as a proportion of all federal grants	1955 – 9.6%
	1960 – 6.5%
	1965 – 6.6%
	1970 – 12.8%

'There's Money Enough to Support Both of You—Now, Doesn't That Make You Feel Better?'

SOURCE 12.25 'There's Money Enough to Support Both of You ...', Herblock, 1967

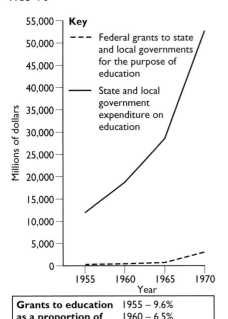

DISCUSS

Why was *national* (federal) aid to education important?

ACTIVITY

Study Source 12.25.
1 Describe the differences between the two women.
2 Who is the most powerful?
3 Who won Johnson's head and who won his heart?
4 Write a brief paragraph to describe Johnson's dilemma.

---

5 The environmental changes had been inspired by Rachel Carson's book, *Silent Spring,* which highlighted the damage done to the countryside by pesticides and pollution. Lady Bird Johnson led a beautification programme, which included planting thousands of daffodils along the major roads in Washington DC.

4 The programme put poverty, justice and access into the centre of politics. It significantly expanded the role of the federal government in initiating and protecting citizens' welfare. It proved that 'big' government was sometimes necessary for national change and benefits. Johnson was trying to fulfil his belief that it was the responsibility of the federal government to ensure that all Americans had a share of their nation's good life. More welfare legislation was passed than in Roosevelt's New Deal.

Did life get better for the poor?
- In 1959 there were an estimated 40 million poor families – in 1968 there were 25 million poor families.
- In 1959 there was no Civil Rights Act and no Voting Registration Act – in 1968 they were ratified and actively enforced.
- Society was changed irrevocably by the introduction of Medicaid and Medicare, by federal aid to education and by the guarantee of political rights and social integration for black Americans.
- The programmes did not end poverty, and failed to deal sufficiently with those least able to take up opportunities to improve their lives. It was only a brief burst of reform, but it was significant for social welfare.

Why were the programmes criticised?
Such an ambitious set of programmes inevitably had difficulties and criticisms:

- They promised too much, some were under-funded, and others were planned too hastily.
- There were fears of an over-mighty federal government and the over-centralisation of authority.
- Interest groups, such as the American Medical Association or city mayors, wanted to protect their interests against federal interference.
- The Community Action programmes could raise expectations beyond the willingness of the city councils to deliver them.
- Some middle class, conservatives and blue collar workers, felt that their hard work was undervalued, and resented 'handouts' to others.
- For radical liberals, the programmes did not go far enough, because they did not redistribute wealth.
- The Vietnam War drained money just at the time that the Great Society programmes were beginning. Tax cuts in the programme increased spending, resulting in rising prices because production could not keep up with demand. The administration was reluctant to raise taxes because that would reveal the costs of the war, still largely hidden from the public. If anything had to be cut, or under-funded, it would be the Great Society programmes. In 1966 $1.2 billion was spent on the War on Poverty programmes, and $22 billion on the War. Or as King put it, the USA spent $500,000 to kill one Vietnam enemy soldier, and $35 to assist one poor American.

DISCUSS

Should Lyndon Johnson be remembered for his Great Society programmes or for Vietnam?
Here is one historian's assessment, 'The ultimate irony was that Johnson ended up destroying himself, and that the very same qualities that brought him greatness in domestic affairs assured failure in foreign policy decisions ... in the process trying ... to transcend all human frailties and impose a solution from above that would bring the consensus he so desperately craved. His own personal sense of honor, courage, and manliness would permit no other course ... [but] every dollar that went on Vietnam was a dollar that did not go to fight the war on poverty.' (W. Chafe, *The Unfinished Journey*, 4th edn, 1999, p.301)

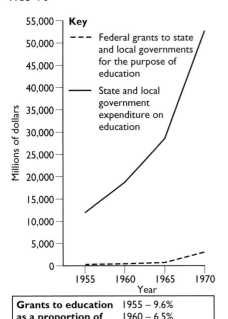

251

'WE SHALL OVERCOME': HOW DID THE CHALLENGES OF THE SIXTIES ERA CHANGE AMERICA?

252

'WE SHALL OVERCOME': HOW DID THE CHALLENGES OF THE SIXTIES ERA CHANGE AMERICA?

D 1968 – the year that went too far (or not far enough)?

FOCUS ROUTE

Make notes to answer the following.

1 What were the dramatic events that contributed to making 1968 memorable?
2 What were the underlying tensions and problems that continued or became worse?

TALKING POINTS

1 Why do you think students in the sixties protested, but students in the fifties did not, since many of the same problems (civil rights, free speech, the role of women, the Cold War) were there?
2 Are students' concerns different now from in the sixties?

DISCUSS

1 What were students protesting about?
2 How did they demonstrate their opposition?
3 Which were effective tactics and why?

ACTIVITY

What was the impact of the challenges of 1968? Copy and complete the table below.

Topic	What happened	Impact
Assassinations		
Civil rights movement		
Great Society programmes		
Baby boomers become teenagers		
Parents of baby boomers		
Vietnam War		

Why did social tensions increase?

a) Student activists

If you were eighteen in the USA in 1968 the chances were that you were a college student, along with about half of your age group. In the mid-fifties there were about 2.5 million students. By 1968 there were 7 million – more than farmers or steelworkers. Economic stability and the emphasis on home and family in the fifties had made higher education a possibility for the majority. John Kennedy with the Peace Corps, and the civil rights movement, had encouraged involvement in solving the problems of society. In 1962 at Port Huron in Michigan, the Students for a Democratic Society (SDS) was formed by Tom Hayden and 60 students. They opposed the institutions that ran America – politicians, the military, corporations – and challenged traditional authority. They wanted less centralisation and 'participatory democracy' for all. To them, freedom was the ability to be involved in decisions about your own life. They called themselves the 'New Left'.

As student numbers had grown so had the size of universities, or 'megaversities', such as the University of California at Berkeley. In December 1964 students, led by the Free Speech movement, challenged a ban on meetings there and occupied the administration building. State troopers forced them out, creating more anger because their protests were treated as criminal acts. Protests spread to other universities, with sit-ins and marches to protest at university systems, including their involvement in military research. The Vietnam War and the draft system caused particular anger.

At the beginning of the war sixteen per cent of those who had been drafted were being killed. As these numbers increased and the war continued it rose to 34 per cent in 1967 and 62 per cent in 1969. The draft drew unfairly on the population. The more wealthy could avoid the draft by student deferment (these ended in 1966) or appointments to the NATIONAL GUARD or reserve units (as did President George W. Bush). Some draftees ignored their call-up notices, or left the country or even burned their draft cards in public acts of civil disobedience. A disproportionately high number of those drafted came from poor backgrounds, making up as much as 80 per cent of enlisted men, and young black men were also called up in a disproportionate number. They were fighting for a free world whilst still suffering discrimination in the USA.

b) The 'counter-culture'

The New Left and the anti-war movement challenged accepted institutions. Some students went further and challenged accepted lifestyles. Ragged blue jeans, beads, army fatigues and long hair proclaimed a generation who wanted personal liberation through music and experimenting with sex and drugs.

'Flower power' in the Haight-Ashbury district of San Francisco was the image of the Summer of Love of 1967, with 'Make Love Not War' as its slogan. Others, dropping out of conventional culture, founded communes in rural Vermont and New Mexico, or favoured self-sufficiency by growing their own food and rejecting the commercialism they had grown up with. Organic farming and environmental concerns began to influence more people as a result. But for many the economic downturn of the next decade ended such challenges to mainstream society, as well as the unpleasantness of bad drug trips, disease and violence.

c) The anti-war movement

SOURCE 12.26   A Vietnamese prisoner seconds before he was summarily shot by the South Vietnamese Chief of Police, General Loan. This brutal violence against an unarmed man, blatantly in front of a photographer, was 'un-American' behaviour, and exposed the reality of war and the behaviour of the South Vietnamese

SOURCE 12.27   'Hey, hey LBJ, how many kids did you kill today?' This chant was often heard at student anti-Vietnam War rallies, like this one in Des Moines, in 1968

SOURCE 12.28   A protester's anger (in F. Greene, *Vietnam! Vietnam!*, 1966)

The mounting fury of the richest and most powerful country is today being directed against one of the smallest and poorest countries of the world. The average income of the people of Vietnam is about $50 a year – what the average American earns in a single week. The war today is costing the United States three million dollars an hour. What could not the Vietnamese do for their country with what we spend in one day fighting them! It is costing the United States $400,000 to kill one guerrilla – enough to pay the annual income of 8000 Vietnamese. The United States can burn and devastate; it can annihilate the Vietnamese; but it cannot conquer them.

ACTIVITY

Find the story.

One of the most disturbing stories of the Vietnam War was the brutal massacre of villagers, mainly women and children at My Lai in 1968 (see page 204). It was the journalist Seymour Hersh and the photographer Ronald L. Haeberle who exposed the atrocity, which had been covered up by the military.

1 Find out the story of what happened at My Lai.
2 What happened to the village and to the American soldiers involved?
3 Can you imagine why the story was so disturbing to Americans?
4 What did it suggest about their society?

1 The protesters about the war were originally traditional peace campaigners, including those opposed to the arms race and nuclear testing. They used methods such as vigils, small protest demonstrations and letter-writing campaigns. After 1965 the number and type of protesters grew. They included a wider range of 'ordinary' people and more students, for whom the war was part of the decade's rebellion against authority.

2 The use of the draft extended the number of families directly involved in the conflict. The number of troops required for Vietnam was more than the regular army could supply, and the number of volunteers was insufficient to make up the required numbers. So young men, many too young to vote or drink (the age limit for these was 21), were compelled to fight.

3 Television brought images of the fighting to the American public at the same time as nightly news broadcasts were getting longer. Images of fighting made good viewing, but failed to reflect the reality and tensions of this kind of war.

4 The high cost of the war, estimated at $150 billion, distorted economic plans, added to the budget deficit and fuelled inflation.

5 The war shattered the belief in a Democratic liberal consensus to make the nation better and win the war. Republicans were in power from 1968 to 1991 (apart from the presidency of the Democrat Jimmy Carter, 1976–80).

6 The conduct of the war and the withholding of information from the public by the administration deepened distrust of the government.

d) The demand for rights

Feminism – In spite of winning the right to vote and doing essential work in the Second World War, by 1950 women were still thought of mainly as homemakers and mothers, and the images of the time reflected this. Yet many were in paid work in the fifties, and this continued as the birth rate fell and the divorce rate began to rise. The pressure for change in the recognition of the reality of women's lives grew:

- In 1963 a presidential commission documented discrimination against women in education and employment.
- The Equal Pay Act of 1963 encouraged women that with this law equal pay for equal work was possible.
- Title VII in the Civil Rights Act of 1964 barred discrimination in employment on the grounds of sex, as well as race.
- Betty Friedan's book, *The Feminine Mystique*, highlighted 'the problem that has no name' – that of the mindlessness of domesticity.
- The civil rights movement demonstrated that change was possible.
- In 1966 the National Organization for Women (NOW) was formed by Friedan and others. By 1971 it had 15,000 members who wanted a more equal participation in American society.
- Women protested at the expectations of men in the New Left and civil rights movements that they should be helpmates, not equal partners. 'Women's lib' was created.
- Consciousness-raising groups shared experiences and used the slogan 'The personal is political'.
- Goals for the feminist movement generally included child care, equal pay and abortion rights.

255

'WE SHALL OVERCOME': HOW DID THE CHALLENGES OF THE SIXTIES ERA CHANGE AMERICA?

Chicanos – They were Mexican-Americans fighting to improve their lives in the South-west states. Cesar Chavez organised the United Farm Workers to represent migrant workers and won a strike against Californian grape growers for union recognition. They set an example that other minorities could follow.

e) Assassinations

The violent death of the civil rights leader Martin Luther King had always been a possibility, because he knew of the hatred some white racists felt towards all that he stood for. While assisting with a strike in Memphis, he was shot on his motel balcony on 4 April 1968, and deeply mourned by both black and white Americans. Almost more shocking was the shooting in Los Angeles of Robert Kennedy on 5 June by Sirhan Sirhan, a Palestinian opposed to Kennedy's pro-Israel beliefs. Americans struggled to understand how two Kennedy brothers could be assassinated. What kind of society did they live in? Robert Kennedy was already a popular candidate for the presidency. After his death the Democrats were desperate to find an acceptable alternative, eventually choosing Vice-President Hubert Humphrey, in preference to Eugene McCarthy and George McGovern.

Why was it the beginning of conservatism?

Resentment

The conformity of the fifties had become collective action in the sixties. It had enhanced freedom for black Americans, for women and for many of the poorest in society. But it was at a cost. At a cost of violence – against black marchers, against and by university protesters, against and by anti-war demonstrators. The deaths of Martin Luther King and Robert Kennedy seemed the end of any chance to have organised and peaceful political change to achieve a fairer society.

To those who had not been part of any of the challenges, it seemed as if their world was falling apart, made worse by nightly television broadcasts showing riots, rebellion and destruction. The sixties seemed to challenge basic American assumptions; the value of hard work and of traditional family values. 'Middle' America formed 55 per cent of the population, earning between $5000 and $15,000 p.a. They lived between the city slums and the affluent suburbs, and were usually up to their eyes in debt. They wanted the law to protect them and their property. They believed in good manners, in respect for authority and the flag. Their cultural enemies were hippies and the Black Panthers, drug-users and anti-war protesters. They were against 'them' – the urban ghetto, those on welfare or on demonstrations. The changes of the sixties left many of them confused and angry. They were not sure who to blame for social unrest, but it surely was not *their* fault. They were the 'silent majority' that Nixon appealed to in his election campaign, and they helped him to victory. Of course they were a stereotypical group, but they were the resentment and reaction by-product of social unrest.

The 1968 presidential election

Both the political parties had to cope with the growing power of pressure groups, and those best able to use the media to attract attention to their causes. The refusal of Johnson to stand for re-election, together with the shocking death of the next best candidate, Robert Kennedy, severely weakened the Democrat Party. The violence at the party's convention in Chicago, in August, further exposed them to criticism. People protesting at the decision to put forward Hubert Humphrey as a presidential candidate were treated savagely by police forces and a riot ensued.

The two candidates in November were the Republican Richard Nixon, (Eisenhower's vice-president, failed candidate against John Kennedy in 1960 and now governor of California) and Democrat Hubert Humphrey (vice-president). Humphrey lost to Nixon by only 510,000 votes out of 73 million, but it was enough to bring victory to the Republicans, and to a more conservative political agenda for the next twenty years. It was the end of the liberal sixties and the demands for a less divisive society.

SOURCE 12.29 Even President Johnson at the end of his presidency couldn't understand why there was unrest (in W. Chafe, *The Unfinished Journey*, 4th edn, 1999, pp.338–39)

I tried to make it possible for every child of every color to grow up in a nice house, eat a solid breakfast, to attend a decent school, and to get a good and lasting job. I asked so little in return. Just a little thanks. Just a little appreciation. That's all. But look at what I got instead. Riots in 175 cities. Looting. Burning. Shooting ... Young people by the thousand leaving the university, marching in the streets, chanting that horrible song about how many kids I had killed that day ... It ruined everything.

E Review: 'We shall overcome': how did the challenges of the sixties era change America?

The period 1960–68 can seem like one of continuous change. Yet there were continuities which often get overlooked in the more colourful and dramatic events shown on mass media: the routines of 'Middle' America; the Cold War; the extremes of wealth and poverty; and the economic power of the USA in the world were some of them.

ACTIVITY

What might each of the following have said about the achievements of
i)   Kennedy and
ii) Johnson as president?

a) a presidential advisor
b) a civil rights activist
c) a congressional opponent
d) an army general
e) someone unemployed

ACTIVITY

Copy and complete this table, as if you were:
a) a black student in the South
b) a white student in the North
c) a manual worker in Detroit
d) a working wife
e) an elderly man living in a city
f) a white official in Atlanta, Georgia.

Question	a)	b)	c)	d)	e)	f)
How had the sixties challenged you?						
How had your life improved?						
What had made your life more difficult?						
Was your 'freedom' strengthened or weakened during this period?						
What are you looking forward to in the next decade?						

ACTIVITY

Work in groups.

1 Individually, choose your favourite image or sound of the sixties.
2 Share your ideas with your group. Do you think that your choices together give a balanced view of the decade? If not, what else do you need to include?

1 The sixties were a time of unprecedented economic growth for most Americans.

2 The glamour and style of John F. Kennedy were not sufficient to disguise the limitations of his domestic policy by 1963.

3 The Civil Rights Act of 1964 and the Voting Rights Act of 1965 were the most important legislation to guarantee equality of citizenship for black Americans in the twentieth century.

4 In spite of a character which made him unloved by many of his supporters, Lyndon B. Johnson initiated and passed more social welfare legislation more quickly, than any other president.

5 The escalation of the Vietnam War after 1965 directly affected the availability of resources to solve domestic problems.

6 Students were at the forefront of much social and political change.

7 The civil rights movement provided an example to other groups fighting for their rights, such as women, minorities and environmentalists.

8 These movements demonstrated that a 'grassroots' campaign could be effective, and change did not have to wait for political elites to initiate it.

9 The institutions of government – the presidency, Congress and the Supreme Court – had demonstrated that they could meet social challenges.

10 There was a conservative reaction, by the end of the decade, to images of violence and of the 'counter-culture'.

13

The triumphant superpower: were the 1970s and 1980s really a success for the USA?

CHAPTER OVERVIEW

SOURCE 13.1   A remarkable photo of the five US presidents from 1968–92, at the opening of the Ronald Reagan Presidential Library. From the left:
George Bush Sr. (Republican, 1988–92),
Ronald Reagan (Republican, 1980–88),
Jimmy Carter (Democrat 1976–80),
Gerald Ford (Republican 1974–76),
Richard Nixon (Republican 1968–74)

The seventies finally ended the post-war economic boom. Economic problems in the USA were worsened by events in other countries, particularly in the Arab world. This, together with a lack of confidence in the American political system because of the Watergate scandal of Nixon's presidency, created a decade of uncertainty and stagnation. Neither Presidents Ford nor Carter were able to inspire confidence or initiate policies that made Americans feel powerful again. The decade ended with American diplomats held hostage in Iran and the mighty American government and military unable to rescue them. When Ronald Reagan arrived as president in 1980, like a cowboy hero out of Hollywood, the country was ready for his simple message – fight communism, fight big government, fight big taxes. Would it work? Did this agenda win the Cold War and overcome America's internal problems? What enemies were left for George Bush Sr. to confront?

A   Were the 1970s a disaster for America? (pp. 259–70)

B   Did conservatism improve Americans' lives, 1980–92? (pp. 270–78)

C   Did the USA win the Cold War (or did the Soviet Union lose it)? (pp. 278–82)

D   Review: The triumphant superpower: were the 1970s and 1980s really a success for the USA? (pp. 283–84)

FOCUS ROUTE

At the end of Sections A–C add events or details to your own copy of this continuum to record the successes and failures of American policies.

FAILURE   SUCCESS

TALKING POINT

Is it possible to talk about the confidence of an entire nation such as America or does this kind of generalisation cause more serious misunderstandings?

SOURCE 13.2 W. Chafe and H. Sitkoff, *A History of Our Time*, 1999, p.361

For thirty years from 1945 American politics had functioned on the premise that nothing was impossible if America wished to achieve it. We [the authors were American] would be guardians of freedom, send a man to the Moon, conquer social injustice, eliminate poverty, develop impressive technology – in short, control the universe. That sense of confidence, and of power had been the hallmark of all political factions in the country, even young radicals who thought that by their own endeavours they could change the world. In the 1970s a new sense of limits struck home … The American tendency toward what the Greeks call hubris *– the arrogant confidence that one can do anything – had come face to face with the realities of human frailty, mortality, and interdependency.*

ACTIVITY

1 What are the four main points which the authors of Source 13.2 think made post-war Americans so confident?

2 Look at Chart 13A.
   a) Which events help to explain America's loss of confidence?
   b) Which event do you think had the greatest impact on America's confidence?

FOCUS ROUTE

As you work through pages 259–70 make notes as evidence for the following statements. Then write brief paragraphs to explain why you agree or disagree with each statement.

1 Nixon's election victory in 1968 was a Democrat and a liberal defeat rather than a Republican victory.

2 Nixon successfully gave stability to the USA after the upheavals of the 1960s.

3 Nixon's behaviour in the Watergate cover-up demonstrated the strength of national institutions to force his resignation.

FOCUS ROUTE

Copy and complete the diagram below by adding details to each topic to illustrate why Americans lost confidence in their nation during the 1970s. For example, under **Middle East** you would need some information about the OPEC action and the wars between the Arab nations and Israel; under **The behaviour of the presidents** you need to include actions which disappointed or angered Americans.

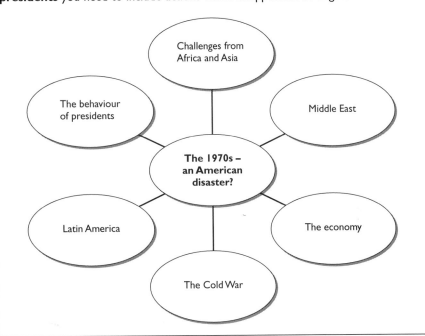

■ 13A Timeline of the 1970s

1970	US forces invade Cambodia
	Protest at Kent State University and Jackson College result in shooting of students by National Guard
1971	Twenty-sixth Amendment gives eighteen-year-olds the right to vote
	Pentagon Papers published
1972	Nixon re-elected by landslide
	Nixon visits China
	Watergate burglary
	Policy of détente
	SALT I signed
	Congress approves Equal Rights Act
1973	Paris Peace Accord begins formal end of Vietnam War
	OPEC oil prices rise
	Inflation rises
	Supreme Court decision *Roe v. Wade* allows abortion
	War Powers Act
	Gerald Ford becomes vice-president when Spiro Agnew resigns because of criminal charges
1974	Nixon resigns under threat of impeachment by the Senate
	Ford becomes president
1975	US embassy evacuated as Saigon seized by North Vietnam
	Recession
1976	Carter defeats Ford and is elected as a Democrat president
1977	Apple introduces first personal computer
	Panama Canal treaty
1979	Iranian militants take 58 American diplomats hostage in Tehran
	Soviet Union invades Afghanistan
	USA withdraws from Moscow Olympics in protest
1980	Iranian hostage crisis continues all year
	Failed military attempt to rescue them in April

Why did Richard Nixon win and then lose the presidency?

Richard Nixon won the election of 1968 promising to end the war in Vietnam and to unite Americans at home. He kept both those promises – in a way. He did pull American troops out of Vietnam and he did unite the USA, but they were united against him; national condemnation forced his resignation in 1974 because of the abuse of presidential power after the Watergate burglary.

Nixon appealed to the 'silent majority' by promising law and order, patriotism and unity after the traumas of 1968. Nixon had been in politics since being elected to Congress in 1946, where he was a vocal anti-communist. In 1952 he became Eisenhower's vice-president and was bitterly disappointed at losing the presidential election so narrowly to Kennedy in 1960. Finally, in 1968, Nixon was in the right place at the right time. The Democrats were fragmented in their purpose and leadership. Johnson's decision not to stand for re-election and the assassination of Robert Kennedy meant that the presidential Republican candidate had an excellent chance. Even so, Nixon only won by less than one per cent of the popular vote.

Nixon's main interest as president was in foreign policy, where he was encouraged and supported by Henry Kissinger, first as national security advisor, 1969–73, and then, from 1973–77, as secretary of state. Nixon's election pledge was to end the war in Vietnam. He and Kissinger realised that American power in the world had weakened. They were interested in establishing détente (see Chart 13B) with the USSR. This did not mean the end of rivalry with the Soviets, or that the USA wished to abandon the policy of containment, or that the USA wished to appear weak. Rather détente:

* attempted to stabilise international politics
* acknowledged that the Soviet Union had virtual nuclear weapons parity with the USA
* tried to reduce military expenditure as the American economy faltered
* could only have been pursued by a president as anti-communist as Nixon had been, and one who could never be seen as 'giving in' to the Soviets
* might persuade China to put pressure on North Vietnam to end the war.

Nixon's attacks on Cambodia (see Chart 13C) were made without the knowledge or permission of Congress (it was an act of war). The massive bombing raids were designed to destroy Viet Cong supply routes, but instead they seriously damaged the Cambodian agriculture and economic infrastructure, causing mass evacuation of refugees to the cities and destabilising the government. By 1975 this destabilisation had allowed the ruthless Khmer Rouge party to seize the country and enforce their 'killing fields' policy, murdering 3 million citizens by the end of the 1970s. Meanwhile, Nixon's bombing policy had little effect on North Vietnam. His policies in other parts of the world – Chile, Bangladesh and Angola, for example – similarly disregarded human rights and involved covert use of the CIA in giving support to dictators (such as Pinochet in Chile) in return for their support of the USA.

Nixon made foreign policy decisions without consulting Congress, and he relied heavily on Kissinger to support and implement them. His behaviour resulted in the accusation that he was an 'imperial' president. Nixon would have argued that secrecy was necessary for diplomatic success, that he avoided tedious opposition, and that achievements outweighed abuses. However, his critics believed that secrecy came from his paranoia about maintaining control, about preventing leaks to the press and his unwillingness to recognise who else had a right to be involved in national decision-making.

DISCUSS

1 Look back to pages 252–55 and the events of 1968. Which events worked in Nixon's favour in the election?
2 What might the narrowness of his victory suggest?

WHAT IS DÉTENTE?

Its simple meaning is that of a relaxation of tensions between rivals. In the 1970s it became a shorthand term for the attempts to establish more stable and co-operative relations between the USA and the Soviet Union.

'They worked to lessen the danger of nuclear war through the negotiation of verifiable arms control agreements, a hallmark of détente ... expanded trade links, technology transfers, and scientific sharing, while also labouring to formulate a core set of "rules" to govern their relationship.' (R. McMahon, *The Cold War, a Very Short Introduction*, 2003, p.122)

HOW WAS DÉTENTE PURSUED?

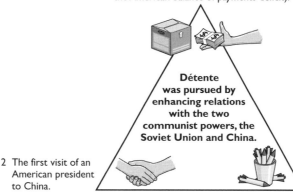

1 Increasing trade (which incidentally helped with the American balance of payments deficit).

Détente was pursued by enhancing relations with the two communist powers, the Soviet Union and China.

2 The first visit of an American president to China.

3 By slowing down the arms race through limiting the number of nuclear missiles on both sides. In May 1972, SALT I was signed by America and the USSR.

SOURCE 13.3 Richard Nixon with his wife Pat makes the first visit by an American president (and a fervent anti-communist one) to China, in 1972, where he walked on the Great Wall, the symbol of ancient Chinese technology

SALT 1

The Strategic Arms Limitation Treaty limited anti-ballistic missiles for each nation to two sites each, and imposed a five-year freeze on the number of offensive missiles each side could possess. However, it did not control the number of warheads per missile; an area in which the USA was superior. So SALT 1 limited rather than stopped the arms race.

■ 13C Was Nixon's foreign policy successful?

YES

He did get American troops out of Vietnam
He did reduce military expenditure
He did try to reduce tension with the communist states
His actions quietened protests by anti-war activists

NO

The invasion of Cambodia, intended to help end the Vietnam War, was a spectacular failure and led to mass slaughter in the country
He failed to consult Congress over key foreign policy decisions
American interventions in other parts of the world abused human rights and international law

Domestically, Nixon pursued traditional Republican policies; returning power to the states and away from the federal government, and responding to the concerns of that 'silent majority' who had elected him.

- He tried to stabilise the economy by raising interest rates, and brought in wage and price controls when inflation began to rise (which made prices rise and wages depreciate in value). However, when the controls were removed, inflation rose again to eleven per cent by 1974. The economic situation was made worse by the Middle East oil crisis (see pages 266–68) and unemployment rose to nine per cent. Welfare programmes were cut in an attempt to reduce federal expenditure.
- His Vice-President, Spiro Agnew, was used to denounce lawless behaviour, describing students as an 'effete corps of impudent snobs'.
- There were conservative appointments to the Supreme Court under the new Chief Justice Warren Burger, and restrictions on defendants' rights. The administration tried to meet the demands of the silent majority who were fearful of rising crime rates and increased drug use, particularly in the cities.

The Watergate scandal

In the 1972 election Nixon won more than 60 per cent of the popular vote against George McGovern. Yet his attempt to ensure this re-election included illegal activities – wiretaps, misuse of election funds, false rumours and forged letters against Democratic candidates. He also had a special group in the White House called the Plumbers whose task was to stop any leaks of Nixon's activities. These methods stemmed, in part, from Nixon's belief that everyone who opposed the Republicans was also opposing American values and society. He therefore refused to recognise that his actions were both illegal and immoral.

1 Nixon's character

Nixon never seemed able to lose the mocking title of 'Tricky Dicky' given to him by the press, implying that he was a man who would do anything to advance his career. Most commentators describe him as mean-spirited, a loner, ill at ease, resentful of eastern elites, intellectuals and the rich, yet tenacious and calculating.

SOURCE 13.4   M. Walker, *Makers of the American Century*, 2000, p.311

There was an inherent sadness to a man so self-controlled that he went walking on the beach in a suit and laced-up shoes, a sadness that accompanied an inner meanness of spirit that, in office, betrayed all the rest.

SOURCE 13.5   H. Brogan, *The Longman History of the United States of America*, 1999, p. 684

He was accustomed to rely entirely on his own perceptions; his decisions were mostly taken alone. Morally he was a shallow man; the only [views] he ever mentioned were those he learned from his Quaker mother and his football coach. The rich and honourable traditions of American Republicanism meant nothing to him by comparison. He had been poor, so he would never cease to be preoccupied with the rich, envying them, fearing them, craving to be one of them. He lost the presidency to John Kennedy, so the latter's good looks, wit and charm became another obsession ... [after losing the election for the governorship of California in 1962, he] blamed his defeat on a hostile press. 'Congratulations gentlemen,' he said ungraciously to reporters, 'you won't have Richard Nixon to kick around any more'.

He had fought so hard to be president yet he seemed unable to gain any satisfaction from his success. When threatened with the exposure of his complicity in the Watergate cover-up, one historian said he behaved like a cornered rat, and fought for two years denying his guilt, until forced by Congress, in August 1974, to release the 23 June 1972 tape where he was heard approving an illegal cover-up.

SOURCE 13.6 Carl Bernstein (left) and Bob Woodward, reporters on the *Washington Post* who realised, after seeing the burglars in court, that there might be a bigger story than just that of a routine break-in

The story starts with Frank Willis. He was the night guard at the Watergate buildings in downtown Washington. On his rounds on 16 June 1972 he found a lock taped open. He removed the tape. Later, on his next round, the tape had been replaced; so he called in the police. After sealing the building they searched it. In Room 723, the headquarters of the Democratic National Committee (the opposition to Nixon's Republican Party), they found five men hiding, with tools and gloves and thousands of dollars in $100 bills. They appeared to be ordinary burglars, however in court the next morning one of the burglars, James McCord, admitted that he worked for the CIA. It also transpired that all the group were employed by CREEP (the Committee to Re-elect the President), which was run by the Attorney-General John Mitchell. It was later found that the men had been in Room 723 checking illegal wiretaps that they had put on Democrats' phones earlier in the year. Who had told them to do so and who was paying them to do it?

Investigative work by Carl Bernstein and Bob Woodward of the *Washington Post* showed that the burglars were under the orders of two White House aides, Gordon Liddy and Howard Hunt, members of the Plumbers. Why did a group of burglars appear to have such close links with the administration? The journalists were helped by a mysterious source, Deep Throat (a still unidentified official), who urged them to 'Follow the money', i.e. follow where the money had come from to pay the burglars. At the trial in January 1973 (after Nixon had been re-elected), and fearful of a long sentence, McCord admitted that they had been paid to keep quiet by CREEP. It had raised massive funds from major corporations, sometimes by threats of IRS (Internal Revenue Service) and Commerce department investigations if they did not pay. Congress set up a special committee under Senator Sam Ervin to investigate the events. A White House counsel, John Dean, had already warned Nixon that there were problems; a 'cancer' at the heart of the administration. After he spoke to the committee he was sacked by the president. Nixon also forced the resignation of his two closest advisors (both of whom knew the true story of the burglary), H. R. Haldeman and John Erlichman.

The president denied any knowledge of the cover-up, declaring 'I am not a crook'. There was no clear evidence that he was – until 16 July 1973. A White House official disclosed that all the Oval Office conversations were taped. It was to be another year before those tapes were released. During that year Nixon continued to deny involvement, sacked two Watergate special prosecutors and saw his Vice-President Spiro Agnew forced to resign because of tax evasion. He insisted that the tapes were covered by executive privilege and were his

264

THE TRIUMPHANT SUPERPOWER: WERE THE 1970s AND 1980s REALLY A SUCCESS FOR THE USA?

property and not the property of Congress, but the Supreme Court ruled against him. After handing over incomplete transcripts and tapes with unexplained deletions, he was threatened with IMPEACHMENT by the Senate, on the grounds of obstruction of justice and the violation of constitutional rights (wiretapping and misuse of the FBI, the CIA and the IRS). On 5 August he finally handed over the crucial, incriminating tape. In it, on 23 June 1972, six days after the Watergate burglary, Nixon and Haldeman were heard discussing getting the CIA to tell the FBI to end their investigation of the burglary by telling them that it had been a national security operation. In fact it had been a burglary planned by those working to get Nixon re-elected; Nixon knew about it; and was a party to its cover-up.

The burglary had been an attempt to disable the Democratic National Committee, because Nixon had encouraged his aides and officials to get him re-elected at any cost. This president was prepared to see those men go to jail whilst he continued to protest his innocence, and obscured the truth for two years. On 9 August, having no other option, Nixon resigned and left the White House. His second Vice-President, Gerald Ford, was sworn in as the 38th president on the same day. Fourteen of those involved in the cover-up were jailed or fined. One month after his resignation, and much to everyone's surprise, President Ford pardoned Nixon, ensuring that he would never have to face a criminal trial.

What did Americans think of Watergate?

SOURCE 13.7 'I am not a crook', by Herblock, 1974

SOURCE 13.8 'I don't know ya ...' by Jules Feiffer, 15 July 1973

ACTIVITY

You can find out more about Watergate by reading *All the President's Men* by the two journalists, Bernstein and Woodward, who first raised suspicions about the burglary, or watch the 1976 film of the same name. It might look a little dated, but the excitement of their hunt for the truth is undiminished. What questions would you need answered before treating such a film as an accurate account?

What did Nixon think of Watergate?

SOURCE 13.9   From Nixon's diary for 1974

I am confident that the American people will see these transcripts for what they are, fragmentary records of a president and of a man suddenly confronted and having to cope with information which, if true, would have the most far-reaching consequences not only for his personal reputation, but more important, for his hopes, his plans, his goals for the people who had elected him as their leader ... through the long, painful, and difficult process revealed in these transcripts I was trying to discover what was right and to do what was right.

SOURCE 13.10   From Nixon's book *RN: The Memoirs of Richard Nixon*, 1978

My reaction to the Watergate break-in was completely pragmatic. If it was also cynical, it was a cynicism born of experience. I had been in politics too long, and had seen everything from dirty tricks to vote fraud. I could not muster outrage over a political bugging.

DISCUSS

1 How do you and your group react to the statements in Sources 13.9 and 13.10? Do you feel more sympathy for Nixon?
2 Can Nixon's behaviour be excused? Which of these statements do you agree with?
   Fawn Brodie: 'There's a little bit of Nixon in all of us.'
   John Kenneth Galbraith: 'I say, the hell there is!'

TALKING POINTS

Contrasting presidents
In 1796 the first president of the USA, George Washington, had said that 'the necessary springs of government are virtue and morality' and 'The mere politician ought to respect and cherish them'.
In 1984 Nixon said, 'Virtue is not what lifts great leaders above others.'

1 Why might a president be expected to have high moral standards? Is a president different from any other political leader or from the rest of us?
2 Who do you agree with – Washington or Nixon?

■ 13D Did Watergate change the USA?

It rid US politics of an amoral leader and his associates.

It re-established that, in a crisis, the political system of checks and balances between the executive, the judiciary and legislature, could work effectively.

It demonstrated the value of investigative journalism combined with Congressional action.

It demonstrated that US citizens had expectations of their leaders' moral standards and also did little to end the idealisation of the president.

It reinforced the suspicion of 'Washington' (i.e. big government) politics.

For some it reinforced the belief (or myth) that 'nothing had been right since JFK died' – that the sixties and seventies were a disaster for US society.

It did not stop illegal and covert actions by later presidents.

Although there were attempts to revise Nixon's record in the 1980s, and Nixon offered himself as a foreign policy expert, the events of Watergate and images of his career have been difficult to erase from the public mind.

ACTIVITY

SOURCE 13.11 Richard Nixon and his family leave the White House on 9 August 1974

1 Imagine the thoughts of the people in the picture and complete the thought bubbles. Try to include a range of reactions, justifications and personal feelings.
2 What questions would you want to ask Nixon as he left the White House?

Did presidents Ford and Carter make America feel good again?

Why was the Middle East important to the USA in the 1970s?

The USA did have its own supplies of oil, but not enough for the level of consumption by American industry and motorists. Oil was so essential for domestic needs it also affected foreign policy. There was disagreement about how to cope with oil price rises – expand production and remove price controls (Republicans) or keep price controls and conserve supplies (Democrats). At the same time there were increasing demands for environmental protection, which made exploiting oil in new areas difficult.

FOCUS ROUTE

As you work through pages 266–70 make notes on the following questions.

1 What did Ford and Carter have to do to give Americans confidence?
2 What problems did they encounter?
3 How far were they able to solve the problems?

TALKING POINT

In President Ford's administration, Donald Rumsfeld was chief of staff and Dick Cheney was deputy chief of staff. In 2001 in George W. Bush's administration, Rumsfeld was secretary of defense and Cheney was vice-president. What does this suggest to you about change and continuity in Republican politics?

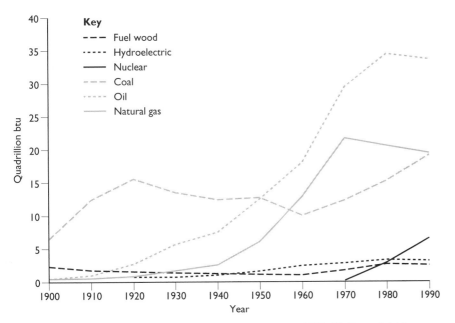

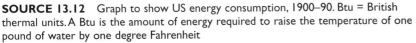

SOURCE 13.12 Graph to show US energy consumption, 1900–90. Btu = British thermal units. A Btu is the amount of energy required to raise the temperature of one pound of water by one degree Fahrenheit

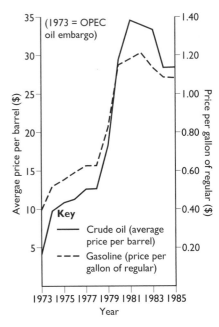

SOURCE 13.13 Graph to show oil and petroleum price increases, 1973–85

ACTIVITY

The importance of a cheap source of energy.
Study Sources 13.12 and 13.13.

1 Write a sentence about the changes in each type of energy used in the USA.
2 What was likely to be the effect of each of these changes? Think about how, and where, each of these energy sources would be used. Think about the costs – of manufacturing, driving a car, heating a home, etc.
3 How easily could the USA switch to other sources of energy? Could they meet American needs with a manufacturing economy and a high reliance on cars (both the production of them and their use by Americans)?
4 Look at the statistics on page 275 to check what happened to the American economy in this period.

In 1973 the Organization of Petroleum Exporting Countries (OPEC), producers of more than 80 per cent of the world's crude oil, put an embargo on exports of oil to the USA (20 per cent of oil imports came from OPEC states). The six-month embargo was in protest at US support for Israel in the YOM KIPPUR WAR in October. It resulted in petrol rationing, speed limits of 55 mph and the shocking realisation that the USA could be threatened in this way. The energy crisis made Americans feel vulnerable at their dependence on others for such a crucial raw material. Yet, by 1979, when oil imports had resumed, oil consumption had risen, suggesting that Americans were reluctant to change their lifestyle.

Tensions in the Middle East
At the end of the First World War the Ottoman (Turkish) Empire was defeated, and its lands to the east of the Mediterranean were shared between the Allies. Out of them were created the states of Palestine, Lebanon, Syria, Transjordan, Iraq and Kuwait. After the Second World War the British struggled to control Palestine against strong demands by Jewish activists who, after the horrors of the Holocaust, demanded that it be their own homeland. The United Nations proposed a partition of the land between Jews and Arabs. When the British withdrew from Palestine in 1947, Jewish settlers proclaimed the new state of Israel. When Israel was attacked by its Arab neighbours the USA immediately recognised the new state and offered assistance. The attack was defeated by Israel. The pattern was set for an American-backed Israel against Soviet-backed Arab states as an area of Cold War tension.

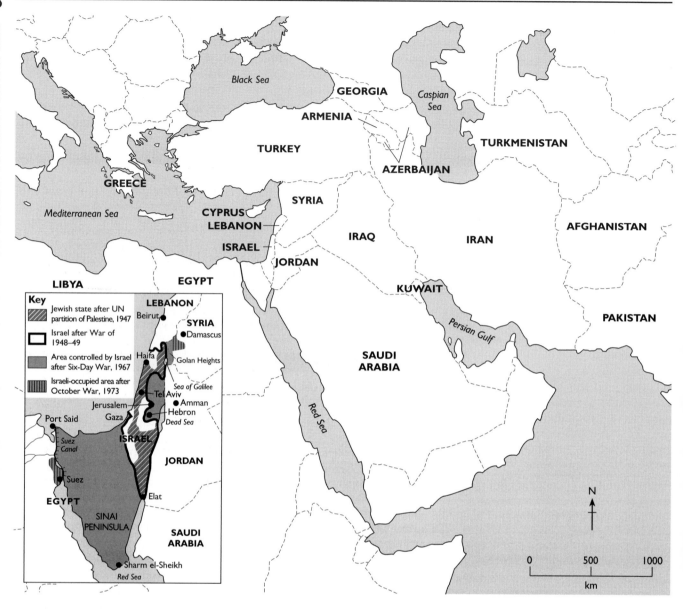

Key
- Jewish state after UN partition of Palestine, 1947
- Israel after War of 1948–49
- Area controlled by Israel after Six-Day War, 1967
- Israeli-occupied area after October War, 1973

Ford and confidence-building

Gerald Ford was a Michigan senator who supported middle-of-the-road Republican policies and opposed LIBERAL ideas. However, he was faced with the challenge of the oil price rises which resulted from the OPEC embargo on sales to the USA. Unemployment and inflation rose as productivity declined, stock market prices fell, interest rates rose and building slowed down. By 1975 there was recession, making Americans feel insecure. Ford had to go against his instincts and allow multi-billion dollar tax cuts and higher unemployment benefits. The recession eased, but the federal deficit rose (government spending exceeded its revenue). The rest of his short presidency suffered from a lack of compatible policies with Congress. Ford used his presidential veto on numerous occasions to try to block changes in the health, housing and education programmes desired by the Democratic majority in Congress. Ford did try to restore trust in government, but his rapid pardoning of Nixon, an act of generosity to try to end the disappointments of Watergate, actually undermined that.

Carter and confidence-building

Jimmy Carter tried to end the Watergate after-effects by presenting himself as an outsider to the politics of Washington. He was a wealthy peanut farmer from rural Georgia where he had been governor. Traditional Democrat groups such as Afro-Americans, Roman Catholics, and most of the South, voted for him. Once president, however, his inexperience was a handicap – he didn't know how to make the Congressional system work for him, and compounded this problem by being haphazard in his decision-making and priorities. He couldn't meet the ideals of the liberals in his party, nor could he calm the fears of those who wanted stability.

Carter's successes

Carter had strong views about protecting human rights, including in the Soviet Union, Argentina and Uruguay. Although abuses of rights were difficult to change, he did raise awareness and put it on future foreign policy agendas. He ended the dispute about control of the Panama Canal by agreeing to hand it over to Panama by 1999, as long as it remained neutral territory. He also had a major success in the Middle East where he helped to create a 'framework for peace' (the Camp David Accords), between Egypt and Israel. Egypt would recognise Israel's right to exist as a state and Israel would return the Sinai peninsula to Egypt. It was hoped this would be the beginning of further negotiations.

Carter's failures

Carter's economic policy was reactive and eroded confidence. Inflation rose, unemployment remained at seven per cent and interest rates reached a historic high of twenty per cent by 1980. He was not able to calm the energy crisis, made worse by the Iranian revolution in 1979, and the consequent threat of access to foreign oil supplies.

The event that did the most damage to his presidency was the kidnapping of US diplomats in Iran. In 1979 radical Muslim fundamentalists led by Ayatollah Rudhollah Khomeni forced the Shah of Iran to flee. There was much anti-American feeling in Iran because the USA had supplied arms to the Shah to use against his opponents. When Carter allowed the Shah to enter America on humanitarian grounds for medical treatment, Iran retaliated by seizing the US embassy in Tehran and taking 52 diplomats as hostages until the Shah was returned for trial. Carter suspended arms sales, but the crisis lasted for fourteen months. Its impact was made worse by nightly television updates. The Iranian government refused to negotiate and the crisis deepened with a failed military rescue of the hostages, which seemed to confirm Carter as ineffective. The hostages were released minutes after Carter ceased to be president and Reagan took office. The Shah of Iran died in Egypt in 1980.

By mid-1979 Carter's approval rating was lower than Nixon's during the Watergate scandal and he was doomed to defeat in the 1980 election. Since 1980 he has worked hard for the resolution of global conflicts and in 2002 he won the Nobel Peace Prize for this work.

What happened to détente?

USSR – The USA took part in the Helsinki Conference on Security and Co-operation in 1975. One of the accords accepted, as permanent, the boundaries of Germany and Eastern Europe created in 1945. The Conference welcomed détente and endorsed human rights for all. This led to the formation of Solidarity in Poland and Charter 77 in Czechoslovakia, both in turn leading to political changes in their countries which undermined communist control.

The SALT 2 treaty had been agreed for further arms limitations, but before it could be ratified by the Senate, the Soviets invaded Afghanistan in 1979. The invasion was probably driven by Soviet fears for its border security, but the USA saw it as aggressive expansionism and too close to Middle East oil producers. Therefore, the Senate refused to pass SALT 2, grain sales were reduced and the Americans refused to attend the Moscow Olympics in 1980. (The Soviet Union refused to attend the Los Angeles Olympics in 1984 in retaliation.) Tensions were high and co-operation low.

China – In 1979 the USA formally recognised the communist government in China. It led to diplomatic and trade links, and the hope that it might weaken any Soviet plans for expansion in Asia.

What was the significance of economic progress?

SOURCE 13.14   W. Chafe, *The Unfinished Journey – America Since World War Two*, 4th edn, 1999, p.432

Ultimately the 1970s became a microcosm of the unresolved conflicts within American society. No longer infused with the faith of the post-war years, Americans faced a frightening array of prospects – permanent economic stagnation, the presence of an 'underclass' that directly challenged the essence of the American dream, and bitter division over fundamental cultural values.

Progress could be measured by key indicators: the level of exports, average family income, unemployment, GNP, productivity. During the decade these indicators of progress showed a decline, threatening not only personal prosperity, but also the idea that the USA was OK. It meant that Americans had to consider whether the basic structure of their society was at fault.

269

THE TRIUMPHANT SUPERPOWER: WERE THE 1970s AND 1980s REALLY A SUCCESS FOR THE USA?

270

THE TRIUMPHANT SUPERPOWER: WERE THE 1970s AND 1980s REALLY A SUCCESS FOR THE USA?

ACTIVITY

1 Using the information on pages 259–70 note the reasons why Americans should feel a general sense of frustration and a lack of confidence by 1980.
2 Draw two American characters from the 1970s and write a dialogue between them to explain their feelings at the time.

DISCUSS

What might Americans think would make their lives better?

By the end of the 1970s:

- there were evident limits to American growth
- the economy was stagnant
- there was endemic high unemployment in some areas
- there was an energy crisis that seemed to have no solution
- no longer could Americans assume that their interests were supreme in the world
- there was a loss of optimism, direction and confidence, so important to the American sense of nationality
- the political consensus of 1945–68 had ended and no one quite knew what would replace it.

How can America accept that the rest of the world is, after 25 years, beginning to catch up with it?

Kennedy said that a 'rising tide lifts everybody', but what happens when the tide goes so far out?

Without economic growth how can the poor ever improve their lives?

How can society accept that it can no longer have guns *and* butter?

How can Western Europe and Japan produce goods more cheaply and efficiently than America?

CONSERVATISM

Conservatism is a belief in keeping the social and economic *status quo*, a general suspicion of new arrangements, and of big government that interferes with the rights of the individual.

ACTIVITY

What evidence is there in Chart 13F of:

a) political successes
b) political failures?

B Did conservatism improve Americans' lives, 1980–92?

■ 13F Timeline of the 1980s

1980	Reagan elected winning 44 states
1981	AIDS first reported in USA
	Unemployment reaches eight per cent
1982	Unemployment reaches ten per cent
	Voting Rights Act of 1965 renewed
1983	Equal Rights Amendment (that there should be no denial of rights on account of sex) fails to be ratified by sufficient number of states
1984	Reagan re-elected
1985	Mikhail Gorbachev becomes Soviet leader
1986	Tax Reform Act lowers personal income tax rates
	Iran-Contra scandal
	Republicans lose control of Senate
	Space shuttle *Challenger* explodes on take-off killing all seven astronauts
1987	Stock market crash
	INF treaty signed
1988	Bush Sr. elected president
1989	Berlin Wall pulled down
	US troops invade Panama
1990	Iraq invades Kuwait
	Re-unification of Germany
	Collapse of communist governments in Eastern Europe
	Bush raises taxes and reneges on 'No new taxes'
1991	UN-backed Gulf War against Iraq because of its invasion of Kuwait
	Iraq forces defeated by American-led Operation Desert Storm
	START I treaty reduces number of nuclear warheads
	Beginning of ethnic wars in former Yugoslavia
	USSR dissolves into independent states
1992	Los Angeles riots
	Federal deficit of $4 trillion
	Bill Clinton defeats Bush Sr. and Ross Perot to win presidential election
	Continues as president until 2000 after winning the 1996 election

271

THE TRIUMPHANT SUPERPOWER: WERE THE 1970s AND 1980s REALLY A SUCCESS FOR THE USA?

FOCUS ROUTE

As you work through Section B make notes on the following.

1 What did the New Right want?
2 How did they try to achieve their aims?

'BUSING'

'Busing' was the practice of trying to balance the racial intake of schools by busing children from one neighbourhood to another. It was feared that as white families moved to the suburbs then the inner cities would become deprived areas where only the poor (and there were still more poor black Americans than white) lived. Many parents complained that the practice prevented them from choosing the school they wanted for their children. Others did not believe in enforced racial harmony.

Who were the New Right?

Jerry Falwell was a popular 'televangelist' of the time. He popularised the evangelical form of Protestantism with its conservative beliefs in moral codes based on the Bible, attracting as much as a quarter of the population. Falwell broadcast on new TV religious networks and in 1976 founded the Moral Majority (an anti-communist pressure group and fundraising organisation supporting traditional family patterns). They were opposed to abortion, gay rights, feminism and 'busing'. Evangelical religious groups became the core of conservative political ideas known as the New Right. They were particularly effective at fundraising and the networking of supporters.

By 1980 there was a reaction against the perceived excesses of the sixties, of free love, Woodstock and the Port Huron statement (see page 252) The New Right claimed that the sixties had not improved the economy, had damaged standards and law and order and were dismissive of the traditional values of the family and church. It was time for a change.

That change was pushed along by two groups:

- economic conservatives who wanted lower taxes to give freedom to people to spend as they wanted, rather than seeing their earnings 'abused' on social welfare
- social conservatives, who wanted a return to 'family values', opposed abortion and homosexuality, and were often evangelical Christians or groups such as the Moral Majority.

Demographic change was also a factor. A larger, older population and a move from the typically liberal eastern states to the more conservative Sun Belt states of the south-west affected political strengths and demands.

Who did Reagan rescue?

To some, Reagan was 'a minor actor and a mental midget' who acted to perfection the role of president with charm and intimacy. Yet he often seemed to be detached from detail and had few confidantes among his officials; a loner, who relied on Nancy's support. His deafness could be a problem, as his speechwriter Peggy Noonan noted (see Source 13.16).

ACTIVITY

One of the most popular cartoons of Reagan is shown in Source 13.15.

1 What is the 'recovery'?
2 Why do you think Reagan is portrayed as a rooster?
3 What significance does a rising sun at dawn have?

SOURCE 13.15 *All My Own Work*, a cartoon by Ben Sargent in *Texas Monthly*, for the election of 1986

272

THE TRIUMPHANT SUPERPOWER: WERE THE 1970s AND 1980s REALLY A SUCCESS FOR THE USA?

Ronald Reagan (1911–2004)

The photo on the left shows Ronald Reagan and his wife Nancy, both former Hollywood stars, dancing at an inaugural ball. Once a cowboy fimstar it was often difficult *not* to see the president as the good guy riding to the rescue of a wagon train (i.e. the USA) surrounded by tomahawk-waving Red Indians (i.e. OPEC and Iranian fundamentalists). Europeans were somewhat bemused by his popularity, but they did not have the Wild West as part of their mythical past.

Reagan's career started with radio journalism during the Depression, and in 1937 he won a Hollywood contract and became a B-movie Hollywood star. His main roles were as good guys, with his war service consisting of making uplifting and inspirational training films in California. From 1947 he was president of the Screen Actors Guild and he gave evidence to the House Committee on Un-American Activities. It was a period when he developed his anti-communist convictions. Originally a Democrat, he changed parties in 1962, campaigned for the ultra-conservative Barry Goldwater against Johnson in 1964, and in 1966 became governor of California. In 1980 he was the obvious Republican candidate for the presidency. He brought all his acting skills to the job, being a good public speaker with simple direct messages.

It was just what many Americans wanted to hear. Audiences enjoyed his wit; 'A recession is when your neighbor loses his job. A depression is when you lose yours. A recovery is when Jimmy Carter loses his!'

FOCUS ROUTE

Make notes on the following.

1 How was Reagan different from Ford and Carter?
2 Who benefited from Reagan's policies and why?
3 Who were the losers and why?
4 In what ways was American society changed by the Reagan presidency?

SOURCE 13.16 Peggy Noonan, in W. Chafe, *The Unfinished Journey*, 4th edn, 1999, p.494

There was a quizzical look on his face as he listened to what was going on around him, and I realised: he doesn't really hear very much, and his appearance of constant good humour is connected to his deafness. He misses much of what is not said straight to him, and because of that, he keeps a pleasant look on his face as people chat around him.

Some called him the 'Teflon President' since nothing that went wrong seemed to affect him. Comments made by those who had worked for him varied (see Sources 13.17 and 13.18).

SOURCE 13.17 Frances Fitzgerald, in W. Chafe, *The Unfinished Journey*, 4th edn, 1999, p.494

The [likeness] they paint is appalling, of a president almost devoid of curiosity, reflective-ness, energy or purpose, a man full of his own preconceptions, yet easily manipulated and fooled by others.

SOURCE 13.18 G. B. Tindall and D. E. Shi, *America – A Narrative History*, Vol. II, 5th edn, 1999, p.1606

... not a deep thinker, but he was a superb analyst of the public mood, an unabashed patriot and a committed advocate of conservative principles ... also charming and cheerful, a likeable politician. Where the dour Carter denounced the evils of free enterprise capitalism and tried to scold Americans into reviving long-forgotten habits of frugality, a sunny Reagan promised a 'revolution of ideas', designed to unleash the capitalist spirit, restore national pride, and regain international respect.

He was concerned with the vision of how things should be, and could ignore the side-effects – the budget deficit, the claim that the Soviet Union was an 'evil empire' in 1982, but not by 1987, the increasing gap between rich and poor because of his tax policies. One commentator said that the Reagan years were like a drug. For a time they numbed reality and let people forget the economic decline and inequality in society.

Freedom was a key word for conservatives. They wanted freedom to be individuals, not the New Deal idea of freedom from need. Reagan's economic programmes showed this. He believed in 'the right to earn your own keep and

TALKING POINT

How fit is your leader?
It is only recently that details of the health of a president have had to be made public. Many leaders have functioned whilst ill or with chronic health problems. Reagan was 69 when he became president and 73 at his second election; the oldest president in the twentieth century. Does the age or health of a leader matter?

keep what you earn'. In foreign affairs he contrasted the freedom of the USA with repressive regimes. However, his selection of regimes for support was often for economic, political or geopolitical reasons, rather than as examplars of American democracy.

a) Reaganomics

Reaganomics were the tax cuts and budget reductions of 1981–82. They were the core policy of the Republicans in Reagan's first term. They were backed by an economic theory known as 'supply side'.

■ 13G The theory of supply side

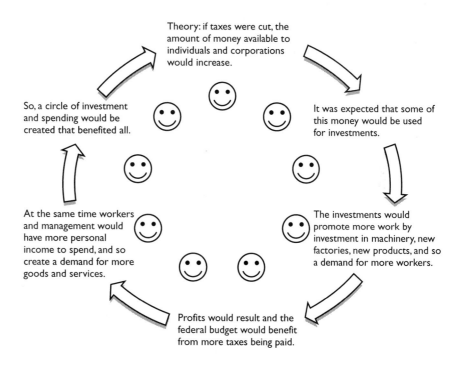

Theory: if taxes were cut, the amount of money available to individuals and corporations would increase.

It was expected that some of this money would be used for investments.

The investments would promote more work by investment in machinery, new factories, new products, and so a demand for more workers.

Profits would result and the federal budget would benefit from more taxes being paid.

At the same time workers and management would have more personal income to spend, and so create a demand for more goods and services.

So, a circle of investment and spending would be created that benefited all.

b) Reagan's second term

The second term of 1984–88 continued these policies. The administration had revived public confidence. There was satisfaction in a leader who vigorously wanted America to be better than the Soviet Union. A sense of national pride and patriotism was back in fashion. The era of self-doubt and turmoil seemed to have ended.

But the results of the economic policy were mixed:

- Reduced revenue from taxes did not balance the reduced cost of the federal aid programmes, so the federal budget went into deficit.
- The release of more money into the economy, expected because of the tax cuts, did not produce the amount of economic growth expected.
- The federal budget increased dramatically because of the increase in military spending.
- Money had to be borrowed to finance the federal budget, which resulted in more federal debt because of the interest payments on these loans.
- Inflation was halted and there was a sustained period of peacetime prosperity.
- The very rich became richer, whilst middle-class incomes remained static. The poor gained least because the cutbacks in federal aid programmes most directly affected them.

a) The Economic Tax Recovery Act of 1981 cut all personal income taxes by 25 per cent over three years. Corporation taxes were also substantially reduced. It was the largest tax cut in American history. It meant that the rich would keep more of their income than before, and that less money was going into the federal budget.

b) By 1982 there was a budget deficit of $200 billion. Reagan had three choices:

1 suspend tax cuts – unacceptable
2 cut back on rearmament – unacceptable
3 cut back on welfare and social programmes – acceptable.

c) Federal aid programmes were cut. Congress refused to cut Medicare and social security (pension and unemployment pay) to any great extent, even though they used much of the federal budget.

d) The aid programmes that were cut particularly affected poor children – school meals, education, support for single parents, aid for cheap mortgages.

e) The cuts were not sufficient to ease the budget deficit, so it continued to grow.

f) Federal income was spent on a five-year, $1.2 trillion defence programme to 'make America Number One again'. It included the 'Star Wars' plan of 1983. This was the Strategic Defense Initiative (SDI) to create a satellite and laser shield to stop incoming missiles. It has not, so far, been built.

g) Federal investment continued to support agribusiness, financial investors, energy producers and the elderly. These were the known interests of the major Republican supporters. The losers in the federal share-out of funds were the interests of Democratic voters – health, education and big cities.

h) Federal regulations in health care, the workplace and the environment were reduced, because of the belief that they were over-bureaucratic and impeded productivity, stopping enterprise and competition. Critics said that such de-regulation would mean more pollution and environmental damage.

i) The years 1980–82 were difficult with rising inflation and unemployment and a recession in 1981. By 1984 oil prices were lower, inflation was at its lowest rate – four per cent for fifteen years – unemployment was at an acceptable seven per cent.

■ Learning trouble spot

Can you balance the federal budget?

You are earning a weekly wage of £200 a week. You have weekly expenses of £300. You are soon going to be in debt. Once in debt you will find it difficult to get out of, and the longer it goes on, the bigger the debt and the bigger the problem of resolving it. You are a micro-version of the US budget deficit. The federal budget required income (from taxes) in order to pay commitments (defence, social security, education, etc.). If you cut taxes, then you cut income. This means that the federal government has less money to spend, but still the same amount of expenses. So some expenses have to be cut. But which ones? That is a political decision because it's about choices. Republicans would usually cut welfare, Democrats would increase taxes so that cuts are not necessary. Both reactions reflected the interests of their supporters, and would be done to keep them in power.

Who was left behind?

In 1980 and 1984 more than half the population eligible to vote did not do so, and therefore had no direct stake in the person governing them. Could the USA be truly democratic with such a low turn-out? Why was there such apathy to politics? Reagan had used the slogan 'It's Morning in America' for his second, and successful, election campaign. Some groups felt more that the sun was setting on their efforts to change society.

ACTIVITY

Look back to Sources 13.12 and 13.13 on page 267. What do Sources 13.12–13.13 and each of the graphs and charts in Sources 13.19–13.21 tell you about the changes in the American economy between 1980 and 1992?

SOURCE 13.19 Productivity and wages, 1982–92 (1982 = 100: this means that productivity and the real value of earnings are measured as if they were the same in 1982)

SOURCE 13.20 US trade balances, 1970–92

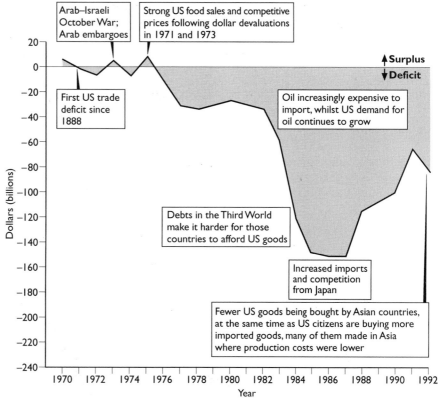

SOURCE 13.21 US federal budget deficit, 1980–92

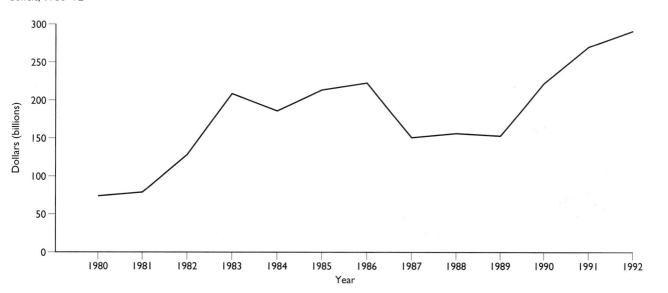

Race relations

SOURCE 13.22 Jesse Jackson in Harlem in April 1988

Civil rights were hampered by opposition to 'busing' (see page 271) and by a lack of support for affirmative action programmes. Federal courts, with conservative appointments made by Reagan, and later Bush Sr., were less prepared to enforce integration. Reagan appointed a head of the civil rights division of the Justice Department who opposed 'busing' and affirmative action, and reduced the enforcement of anti-discriminatory practices in housing and education.

In 1978 the Supreme Court had upheld affirmative action in *Baake v. The Regents of the University of California*. This permitted race or ethnicity to be a 'plus' on an applicant's form, and was an attempt to right the disadvantages of years of discrimination. However, in 1989 the Court agreed that past discriminations did not justify a racial quota. It is a debate that continues today.

Racist polarisation continued and was most vividly shown in Los Angeles in 1992 when white police were shown on video, beating an innocent black motorist, Rodney King. A white jury acquitted the police, and in fury at the disregard of justice for blacks, there were widespread riots with 51 people killed and $1 billion of damage. If the problems of racial injustice linked to poverty and social inequality had been ignored in the eighties, these riots were one of the outcomes. At the same time Black Power had shown that black violence could intimidate white Americans, and riots were a reflection of this.

Civil rights activitists were still working for integration. Jesse Jackson (see Source 13.22), an early supporter of Martin Luther King, and a pall bearer at his funeral, was the most visible civil rights activist in the eighties, and even considered standing for the presidency. He created the Rainbow Coalition, arguing that, 'Our flag is red, white and blue, but our nation is a rainbow – red, yellow, brown, black and white – and we're all precious in God's sight'. This is a little kinder than Stokely Carmichael's use of colour regarding the Vietnam War; that it was a white man's war fought by black men against yellow men by a nation that had taken over the land of red men.

Women

Women's rights groups consolidated the greater equality achieved in the seventies. There were attempts to overturn the significant Supreme Court ruling in 1973 of *Roe v. Wade*, which made unconstitutional all state laws that made abortion a crime. The Court stated that there should be no interference with a woman's 'right to privacy' and her right to choose to terminate a pregnancy. Equal pay was not achieved. Reagan was criticised for allowing welfare provision for children to be reduced.

SOURCE 13.23 When her motel room home was condemned as unfit this single mother with a one-week-old baby was evicted with no alternative accommodation. Her situation typifies the increasing problem of homelessness with too little suitable cheap housing and a growing number of single parent families usually headed by women. It became known as the 'feminisation of poverty'

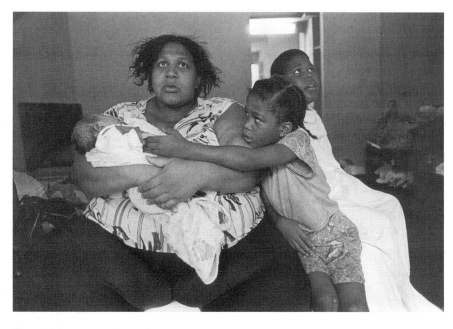

Poverty

In 1982 the Bureau of Census stated that poverty levels were at their highest since 1965. They had not reduced by 1989, suggesting that the poor had not benefited from tax cuts. In 1980 the general poverty rate was thirteen per cent, but for Hispanics (Mexican and Caribbean immigrants) it was 26 per cent and for black Americans 33 per cent. Poverty particularly affected children as poor homes and inadequate nutrition made them more likely to drop out of school and therefore be unskilled and unemployable. They could too easily be despairing or angry. Crime was inevitable. 'Rampant unemployment in a nation of boastful affluence' was the conclusion of a report by the Children's Defense Fund in 1981.

New social problems developed and were largely ignored during the eighties. AIDS was at first a mystery in 1981 and then blamed on homosexuals, before a greater understanding of its causes and risks developed in the 1990s. Drug taking and smuggling were linked to increased violence, usually involving guns. The job market changed with deindustrialisation; jobs moving to cheaper areas of production, including abroad, and an increase in low-paid, non-unionised service work, such as fast-food cafés. Such work was often seasonal and part time. As incomes for the lowest paid decreased there was an increase in homelessness. Poverty, a changing job market, and continuing racial and gender discrimination increased social inequality and tensions.

The presidency of George Bush Sr., 1988–92

George Bush Sr. had a reputation as a safe pair of hands – cautious, predictable and willing to continue with Reagan's domestic policies. He maintained limits on federal interference in citizen's lives except in one area. In 1991 Congress passed the Americans with Disabilities Act (ADA), which prohibited discrimination against people with disabilities by making all public buildings and facilities accessible and requiring businesses to hire workers without regard to their disability.

The budget deficit continued to increase and Bush was forced to retreat from his electoral promise of 'Read my lips – No new taxes'. The Gramm-Rudman or Balanced Budget and Emergency Deficit Control Act of 1985 had required the gradual elimination of the federal deficit, but by 1990 it was $200 billion. Bush had to agree to new taxes on the wealthy, a cut in military spending and increased taxes on luxury items such as yachts and expensive cars. But the budget deficit continued to rise to $300 billion as a recession developed and reduced tax income. This economic downturn was a major reason for the success of Bill Clinton in the 1992 presidential election. By 1996, Clinton had reduced the deficit to $107 billion.

■ **Learning trouble spot**

Which George Bush?
In 1988 Vice-President George H. Bush succeeded Ronald Reagan as president. He was president for one term until 1992. In 2000 his son, George W. Bush succeeded Bill Clinton (Democrat victor in the presidential elections of 1992 and 1996). In the November 2000 election Al Gore won the popular vote, but in a dispute over Florida voting, the Supreme Court ruled in Bush's favour and he was able to claim a majority in the electoral colleges and so the presidency. The first President Bush (1988–92) is now usually referred to as Bush Sr. Bush father and son are Republicans.

278

THE TRIUMPHANT SUPERPOWER: WERE THE 1970s AND 1980s REALLY A SUCCESS FOR THE USA?

ACTIVITY

Live in the eighties
- Watch contrasting films: *Wall Street, Driving Miss Daisy* and *Die Hard*.
- Play Trivial Pursuit (invented in 1982).
- Find out about the disasters of Chernobyl and *Challenger*, and their impact on society.
- Use a Post-it note (invented in 1980).

The Republican administration had changed priorities in America. The liberal agenda of social welfare and intervention for the good of all, had been replaced by a conservative one that valued individual enterprise and community action. Neither agenda helped the poor sufficiently and by 1992 the gap between the richest and the poorest in the nation had grown even wider. Did it matter? It certainly damaged individuals, but if it damaged society as well – stability, security, the ability to get on with one's life through good education and health – then it did matter to the nation, even a conservative-voting one.

C Did the USA win the Cold War (or did the Soviet Union lose it)?

Proxy wars in the Third World and Latin America

FOCUS ROUTE

Using the information on pages 278–82 make notes to answer the following questions.

1 What were the factors which affected the Soviet Union and the USA in their willingness to end the Cold War?
2 Communism had not been contained, so there were reasons to continue the Cold War. Why did it come to an end?

The Cold War continued to be fought by proxy: militarily in other lands, by economic competition across the world, and by an acceptance of changing economic realities by political leaders. Oil supplies remained a focus for the USA and the Soviet Union in asserting control in a region. Iran and Iraq (the latter, led by Saddam Hussein, with American support) were at war with each other from 1980–88, with huge casualties on both sides. US military support for Israel continued. Going into Lebanon as a peacekeeping force in 1983 the Americans became involved in the faction fighting and, after a suicide bomber killed 241 servicemen in their barracks, Reagan withdrew his army. The area continued to be violent, with little progress by any side towards a peaceful settlement of differences. In Africa heavy debts, civil wars, droughts and famines, in Ethiopia and Sudan for example, made American investment risky and reduced the sale of American goods. The USA had little political influence.

279

THE TRIUMPHANT SUPERPOWER: WERE THE 1970s AND 1980s REALLY A SUCCESS FOR THE USA?

■ 131 US involvement in Central America

America, particularly under Reagan, often interpreted nationalistic conflicts in this region as anti-American. Still determined to stop Soviet expansion, America intervened if it thought there was a possibility of Soviet support for one of the sides in the disputes. It used trade, investment and covert CIA activities to try to retain rulers sympathetic to American economic values, or if not to American economic values, to democratic ones.

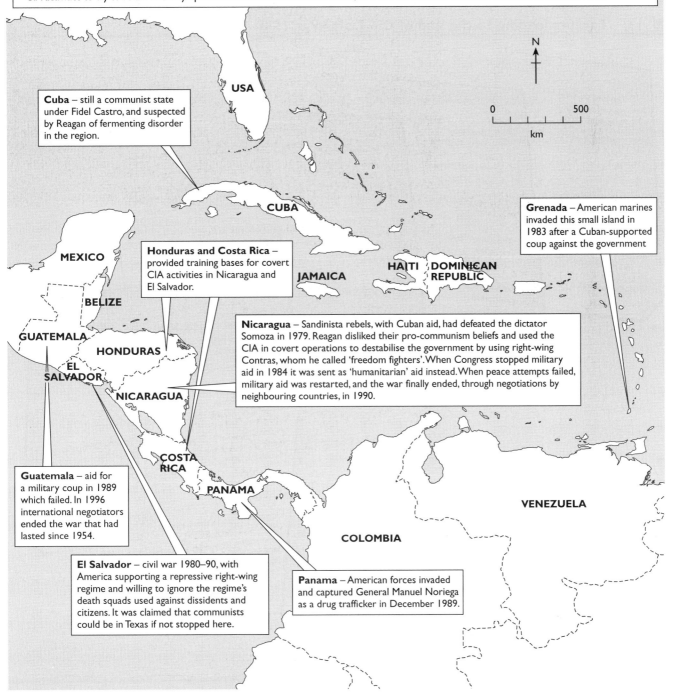

Cuba – still a communist state under Fidel Castro, and suspected by Reagan of fermenting disorder in the region.

Grenada – American marines invaded this small island in 1983 after a Cuban-supported coup against the government

Honduras and Costa Rica – provided training bases for covert CIA activities in Nicaragua and El Salvador.

Nicaragua – Sandinista rebels, with Cuban aid, had defeated the dictator Somoza in 1979. Reagan disliked their pro-communism beliefs and used the CIA in covert operations to destabilise the government by using right-wing Contras, whom he called 'freedom fighters'. When Congress stopped military aid in 1984 it was sent as 'humanitarian' aid instead. When peace attempts failed, military aid was restarted, and the war finally ended, through negotiations by neighbouring countries, in 1990.

Guatemala – aid for a military coup in 1989 which failed. In 1996 international negotiators ended the war that had lasted since 1954.

El Salvador – civil war 1980–90, with America supporting a repressive right-wing regime and willing to ignore the regime's death squads used against dissidents and citizens. It was claimed that communists could be in Texas if not stopped here.

Panama – American forces invaded and captured General Manuel Noriega as a drug trafficker in December 1989.

280

THE TRIUMPHANT SUPERPOWER: WERE THE 1970s AND 1980s REALLY A SUCCESS FOR THE USA?

FOCUS ROUTE

1 List the changes in attitude by Reagan and Gorbachev that made the end of the Cold War possible by 1990.
2 What other factors led to it ending?
3 What one crucial turning point would you identify in the period 1980–90, and why?

The Iran-Contra Scandal

Exposed in 1986, this scandal involved National Security Advisor John Poindexter, his aide Marine Lieutenant Colonel Oliver North and CIA Director William Casey. They sold weapons to Iran, in an attempt to influence the release of hostages held in Lebanon, and then, illegally, used the money from the sales to buy weapons for the Contras' attempt to rule Nicaragua. However, Congress had forbidden military aid to the Contras and Iran had been condemned as a radical and terrorist Islamic state opposed to the USA. North admitted to Congress that he had illegally destroyed incriminating documents. Reagan claimed 'I don't remember' about the deal, when he probably had been told of it. His successor, Bush Sr., who had known of the deal, pardoned most of those involved when he became president. To many it showed that there was still corruption in government, even after Watergate, but Reagan escaped the threat of impeachment.

Changes in the Soviet Union and Eastern Europe

■ 13J **Factors leading to the end of the Cold War, 1980–92**

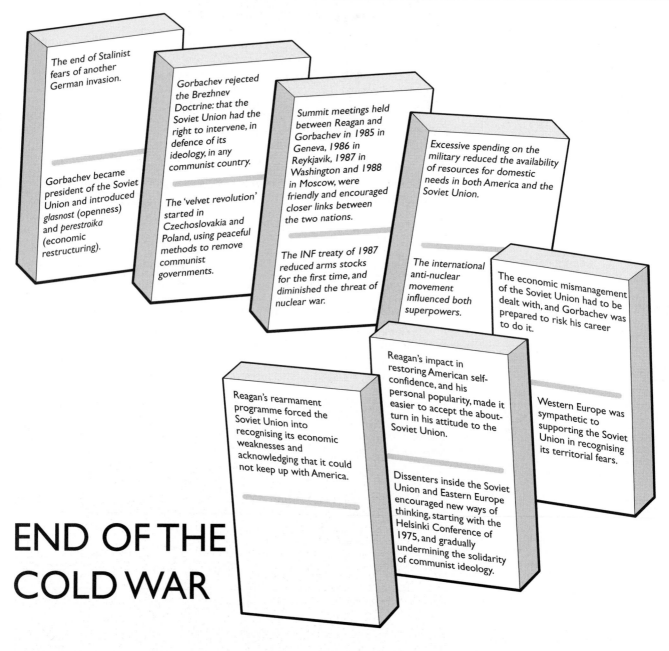

The end of Stalinist fears of another German invasion.

Gorbachev became president of the Soviet Union and introduced glasnost (openness) and perestroika (economic restructuring).

Gorbachev rejected the Brezhnev Doctrine: that the Soviet Union had the right to intervene, in defence of its ideology, in any communist country.

The 'velvet revolution' started in Czechoslovakia and Poland, using peaceful methods to remove communist governments.

Summit meetings held between Reagan and Gorbachev in 1985 in Geneva, 1986 in Reykjavik, 1987 in Washington and 1988 in Moscow, were friendly and encouraged closer links between the two nations.

The INF treaty of 1987 reduced arms stocks for the first time, and diminished the threat of nuclear war.

Excessive spending on the military reduced the availability of resources for domestic needs in both America and the Soviet Union.

The international anti-nuclear movement influenced both superpowers.

The economic mismanagement of the Soviet Union had to be dealt with, and Gorbachev was prepared to risk his career to do it.

Reagan's rearmament programme forced the Soviet Union into recognising its economic weaknesses and acknowledging that it could not keep up with America.

Reagan's impact in restoring American self-confidence, and his personal popularity, made it easier to accept the about-turn in his attitude to the Soviet Union.

Dissenters inside the Soviet Union and Eastern Europe encouraged new ways of thinking, starting with the Helsinki Conference of 1975, and gradually undermining the solidarity of communist ideology.

Western Europe was sympathetic to supporting the Soviet Union in recognising its territorial fears.

END OF THE COLD WAR

TALKING POINT

Was it easy for a right-wing president, who had also raised military spending, to end the Cold War?

How did the Cold War end?

SOURCE 13.25 President Reagan and President Gorbachev admire the architecture in Moscow's Red Square in 1988. When asked if he still thought of the Soviet Union as an 'evil empire' Reagan replied 'I was talking about another time, another era'. He offered the friendship of the American people to the peoples of the USSR

SOURCE 13.26 R. J. McMahon, *The Cold War: A Very Short Introduction*, 2003, p.162

The rapid-fire series of events that transpired between 1985 and 1990 stunned government decision-makers, foreign policy experts, and ordinary citizens alike across the world. Yet those epochal events, it is now evident, were preceded and conditioned by the new thinking about security, nuclear weapons, and domestic needs, that animated all of Gorbachev's dealings with the United States, Eastern Europe, and the world at large. Ronald Reagan, the most unequivocally anti-communist American leader of the entire Cold War era, suddenly found a Soviet leader saying yes to arms control faster than he could say no, moving to 'deideolize' Moscow's foreign policy, offering unilateral concessions on conventional armed forces, and vowing to remove Soviet troops from Afghanistan. To his great credit, Reagan proved willing first to moderate, and then to abandon, deeply held personal convictions about the malignant nature of communism, thereby permitting a genuine rapprochement to occur.

ACTIVITY

Study Source 13.26.

Why did Reagan change his thinking about the Soviet Union?

SOURCE 13.27 Delighted Berliners dance on top of the Wall in front of the Brandenburg Gate on 10 November 1989

SOURCE 13.28 A McDonald's meal enjoyed by a Soviet citizen. If global economic success was the criterion then undoubtedly the USA was the winner. To sell the food symbol of America in the capital of the former 'evil empire' was surely a sign of winning the cultural and economic battle

■ Learning trouble spot

Can you speak Russian?

'No' is the likely answer, and why should you? This is about American history, not Russian. Except, of course, that the Cold War is part of Russia's history too. In a book like this, inevitably, for reasons of space, focus and depth, the emphasis is on the US perception. Yet, particularly in trying to understand why the Cold War ended as and when it did, knowing the Russian side of the story in more detail would be very illuminating, hence the problem of reading Russian. There are a limited number of texts in English available. Without Russian it is difficult to read archive material (even if open to researchers), newspapers, memoirs, diaries, and so on. Gradually more material is likely to be translated and published. Until then you may need to keep an open mind about who won or lost the Cold War.

Did America win?

How had the Cold War affected the world?

- The Marshall Plan of 1947, anti-communist economic aid to Western Europe, brought stability and industrial prosperity. It preserved the area as a bulwark against Soviet expansion to the west, and provided a long-term region for American investment and exports.
- A similar pattern happened in the Pacific Rim centred on Japan. Both areas also provided military bases for the USA to pursue its containment policy.
- America's global presence, through the military, investment and trade brought its culture across the world as American food, drinks, clothing styles and music became universal and appealing.
- The Soviet Union was forced to modify its culture of repression.
- The secret war between the USA's CIA and the USSR's KGB (Soviet secret police) made spy novels popular, as well as permitting covert and unprincipled actions in the cause of the opposing ideologies.
- The two countries were hero and villain to each other, both believing that they had the right to establish the way the world should be governed.

◦ACTIVITY

These are only some of the global impacts of the Cold War.

1 What others would you add?
2 Choose the three most significant as they seem now. Justify your selection.

D Review: The triumphant superpower: were the 1970s and 1980s really a success for the USA?

SOURCE 13.29 M. Walker, *Makers of the Twentieth Century*, 2000, p.245

The American grand strategy, as devised by Marshall, Truman and Acheson, maintained military readiness while building Western Europe and Japan into a prosperity that would help sustain their joint burden. In this lay its endurance, its genius, and its eventual triumph. This grand strategy, based on the experience of alliance politics that Marshall had sustained in the war against Hitler, forged the West as a new and incomparable prosperous economic system. In the end, the West prevailed because it could afford guns as well as butter, aircraft carriers as well as vacations abroad, a vast expansion of wealth that secured the political support of its democracies for the strategic long haul.

The conservative 1970s and 1980s had followed the liberal challenges of the 1960s. A decade of rapid social change had been followed by over twenty years of conservative reaction. Continuing concern for civil rights, for individual needs and minority group demands struggled with an aggressive Republican emphasis on economic and individual success. At the same time, changes in world trade and production, new political groupings such as the European Economic Community (now the European Union), and more assertive independence from new nations especially in the Third World, challenged America's easy superiority of 1945. The loss of assured economic and military pre-eminence in the world left Americans confused and anxious, a feeling that was exacerbated by the quagmire of Vietnam. The cheerful confidence of Reagan and his forceful military assertiveness (although, in reality, only in small-scale confrontations) helped to ease the anxiety. The end of the Cold War was also the beginning of a different type of Soviet Union. The Cold War challenge of opposing ideologies disappeared with Gorbachev's reforms within his nation and his attitude to Eastern European satellite states.

ACTIVITY

Read Source 13.29.

1 Summarise this assessment in no more than 25 words.
2 Do you think this is a good explanation of why the USA won the Cold War?

TALKING POINTS

SOURCE 13.30 *St George Killing the Dragon*, by Vittore Carpaccio, 1516

The director of the CIA, speaking after the end of the Cold War: 'We have slain a large dragon, but we live in a jungle filled with a bewildering variety of poisonous snakes. And in many ways, the dragon was easier to keep track of.'

1 As someone currently living in the 'jungle' can you identify some of the 'snakes' faced by the USA today? (Think about: ethnic nationalism in Bosnia, war lords and fighting in west Africa, terrorism, AIDS in Africa, etc.)
2 Why might 'dragons' be easier to deal with?

284

THE TRIUMPHANT SUPERPOWER: WERE THE 1970s AND 1980s REALLY A SUCCESS FOR THE USA?

ACTIVITY

Write an essay, focused on the period 1970–92, in response to the following statement:

'By 1992 it was inevitable that the USA would be the only superpower.'

You will need to consider:

- what definition of power you will use (economic, military, cultural, nuclear strength, influence)
- what had happened in the Cold War of this period to make American power inevitable
- what challenges the USA had faced since 1970 and how it had been overcome (or not)
- was it military or economic success that made the USA a superpower by 1992?

DISCUSS

Debate the following question in groups.

The USA may have become the only superpower by 1992, but was it because of America's successful use of power, or the failure of the Soviet Union to use its power?

Consider those areas in which the USA could be deemed to have failed or be failing. Did they matter in the context of global confrontation? Do they affect American power in the world today?

TALKING POINT

'Those who desire peace should prepare for war.'
Do the 45 years of the Cold War prove that this saying is correct?

KEY POINTS FROM CHAPTER 13

The triumphant superpower: were the 1970s and 1980s really a success for the USA?

1 Liberal politics were replaced by conservative beliefs and policies after 1968.

2 Nixon demonstrated how executive power could be abused, but that constitutional institutions could stop the abuse.

3 The power of the media continued to increase and influence political behaviour and public understanding.

4 Neither President Ford nor President Carter had sufficient political power or personal strength to combat the difficulties of domestic America in the 1970s.

5 Reagan's revolution in economics was effective for the rich, but left the poor more disadvantaged.

6 The Middle East oil crisis, which began in 1973, exposed American vulnerability over energy sources. It did not, however, curb the US consumption of global oil reserves.

7 The Cold War ended with a combination of American economic and military strength and Gorbachev's determination to reform the Soviet state.

8 The conduct of the Cold War by the two superpowers had avoided nuclear war and direct confrontation with each other, but at a great cost to other nations through proxy wars and covert operations.

Section 3 Review: The most powerful nation, 1945–92

ACTIVITY

Identify at least three bullet points for each of these themes to sum up the USA's responses to these challenges. Reach your own judgement: how successfully did they respond to each challenge? These pictures will prompt you, but remember they only tell you part of the story.

How far had the USA between 1945 and 1992 successfully met the challenges of the Cold War:

- the territorial ambitions of the USSR
- the spread of communism
- extending American ideas of democracy and free market capitalism
- creating a more equal society?

SOURCE 1   Protests about the Vietnam War in 1968

SOURCE 2   The McCarthy hearings

SOURCE 3   The destruction of the Berlin Wall, November 1989   **SOURCE 4**   The March on Washington in August 1963

Over to you

SOURCE 1 President George W. Bush, re-elected in 2004

After the Cold War ended in 1992 the USA, its NATO allies and the USSR struggled to find new global roles. Should the USA follow Theodore Roosevelt's demands and be the world's policeman or follow Wilson's and be the world's peacemaker? How would the USA and the rest of the world cope with the problems of the environment that needed global solutions, with the increase in the demands of nationalism and with the continuing poverty in the under-developed areas of the world, especially in Africa which was also ravaged by AIDS? Could the USA maintain its prosperity, security and freedom in this different post-Cold War world after 1992?

In the same year George Bush Sr. failed to be re-elected and was replaced as president by the Democrat Bill Clinton. Clinton kept the USA involved in NATO and sent American troops to end the vicious ethnic war in the Balkans. He tried to extend peaceful co-operation between Israel and Palestine, but remained wary of the power of Saddam Hussein in the oil-rich state of Iraq. He reversed the Reagan/Bush federal deficit and left it in surplus by 2000. However, his attempts to improve national healthcare failed, and his relationship with a White House intern, Monica Lewinsky, damaged his reputation in the USA.

In the 2000 presidential election the Supreme Court's decision about voting returns in Florida (see page 277) gave the election to the Republican George W. Bush. He began a fiscal policy similar to that of his father. The federal surplus quickly turned into a deficit again. His foreign policy was more aggressive than Clinton's. However, his presidency will be most remembered for the events following the terrorist attack on the World Trade Center towers in New York and the Pentagon in Washington DC on 11 September 2001, when passenger planes were used as weapons and flown into buildings. More than 3000 people died in the attacks. Shown live on television, the images were seen by a stunned and disbelieving audience around the world.

Now the 'evil empire' of communism has been replaced by something less tangible and more fragmented. It caused a major shift in American foreign policy leading to proactive involvement in wars in Afghanistan and Iraq.

This story is still being written. It continues on a television screen, or in a newspaper, near you.

SOURCE 2 The unforgettable images of the attacks on the World Trade Center in New York, 11 September 2001

Appendices

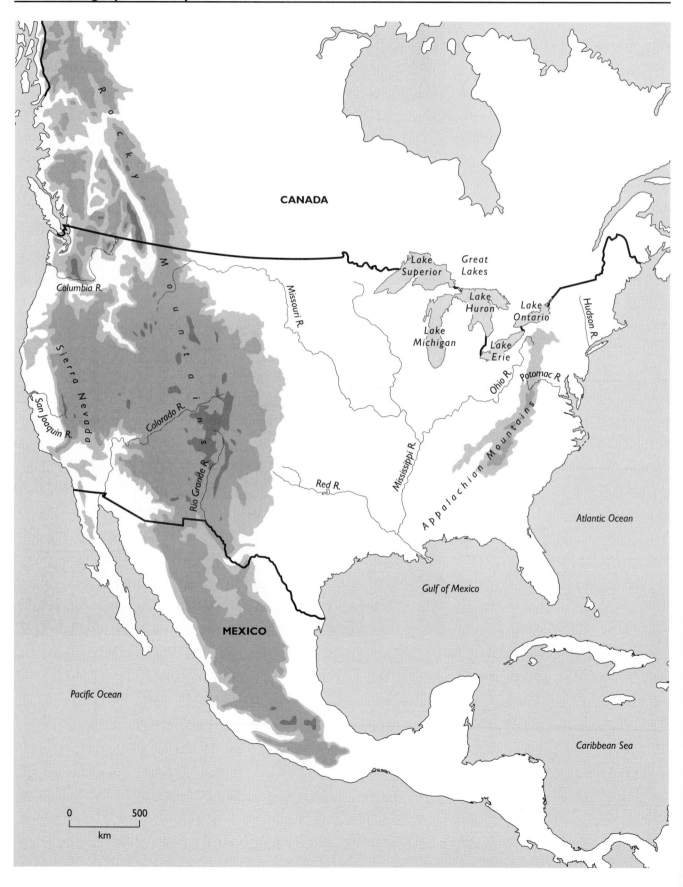

CANADA

Lake
Superior

Great
Lakes

Lake
Huron

Lake
Ontario

Lake
Michigan

Lake
Erie

Columbia R.

Missouri R.

Hudson R.

Rocky
Mountains

Sierra Nevada

Colorado R.

San Joaquin R.

Rio Grande R.

Red R.

Mississippi R.

Ohio R.

Potomac R.

Appalachian Mountains

Atlantic Ocean

MEXICO

Gulf of Mexico

Pacific Ocean

Caribbean Sea

0   500
     km

2 Political map of the USA

■ 3 The difference between federal and state government

The Constitution of the USA advocated federalism. This means that the power and functions of government were divided between the national (or federal) government based in Washington DC and the states' governments, based in the capital cities of each state. The USA began with thirteen states and now has 50. States were seen as the better protectors of individual rights against 'big' (federal) government far away in Washington DC. Distances across the nation are very great (4828km from east to west or five days' car driving or an eight-hour flight) and decisions made by Congress could seem very distant. It was the disaster of the Depression together with the powerful presidency of F. D. Roosevelt that was to end the inferiority of the national government.

■ 4 The separation of powers – the Executive, the Legislative and the Judiciary

Legislative power over Executive

Can override the presidential veto

Can impeach and remove the president

Can reject the president's appointments and refuse to ratify treaties

Can conduct investigations into the president's actions

Can refuse to pass laws or to provide funding that the president requests

Legislative

Passes federal laws

Controls federal appropriations

Approves treaties and presidential appointments

Regulates interstate commerce

Establishes lower court system

Legislative power over Judiciary

Can change size of federal court system and the number of Supreme Court justices

Can propose constitutional amendments

Can reject Supreme Court nominees

Can impeach and remove federal judges

Executive

Proposes and enforces laws

Makes foreign treaties

Commander in chief of armed forces

Appoints Supreme Court justices and federal court judges

Pardons those convicted in federal court

Executive power over Legislative

Can veto acts of Congress

Can call Congress into a special session

Carries out and interprets laws passed by Congress

Vice-president casts the tie-breaking vote in the Senate

Executive power over Judiciary

Nominates Supreme Court justices

Nominates federal judges

Can refuse to enforce Court decisions

Judicial power over Executive

Can declare executive actions unconstitutional

Has the power to issue warrants

Chief Justice presides over the impeachment of the president

Judicial power over Legislative

Can declare laws unconstitutional

Chief Justice presides over Senate during hearing to impeach the president

Judiciary

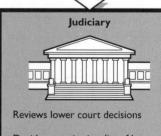

Reviews lower court decisions

Decides constitutionality of laws

Decides cases involving disputes between states

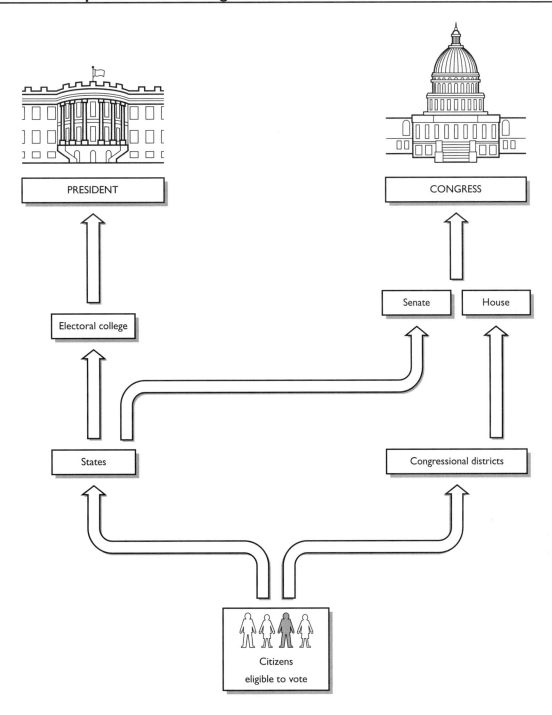

■ 6   How to amend the Constitution

The authors of the Constitution in 1789 recognised that there may be a need to alter some of it at a later date. An Amendment to the Constitution could be made if Congress agreed by a two-thirds majority in the House of Representatives and in the Senate. This then had to be ratified by at least three-quarters of the states. The Amendment would then become law. This has proved surprisingly difficult to do as only 27 amendments have been passed. Of these the Eighteenth (the prohibition of alcohol) and the Twenty-First (the repeal of prohibition), cancel each other out. The most important ones are:
Thirteenth (1865), Fourteenth (1865) and Fifteenth (1870) – concerning civil rights for former slaves
Sixteenth (1913) – collection of income tax
Nineteenth (1921) – Voting rights for women
Twentieth (1933) – Changing the start of a presidential term to January instead of March
Twenty-Second (1951) – No one can be elected president more than twice
Twenty-Sixth (1971) – Voting rights for eighteen-year-olds.

Glossary

AFL American Federation of Labor, founded in 1881

ALPHABET AGENCY popular name for the New Deal programmes and their agencies, such as the PWA (Public Works Administration) and the AAA (Agricultural Adjustment Administration)

AUTONOMY the right of self-government or individual freedom of will

BLACK CODES laws made by the Southern states in 1865–66 to keep emancipated slaves subordinate. They included laws against voting, marrying whites or testifying against white citizens. Some remained in place until the civil rights movement of the 1950s and 1960s

BLACK PANTHERS an aggressive black protest group founded in 1966 by Huey Newton and Bobby Seale, it demanded better treatment in employment, schools and housing. The behaviour of members, which included the carrying of guns, made them a threat, and police and FBI actions had destroyed them by the 1970s

BOYCOTT the refusal to purchase or use a service, to give economic power to the protester

CIO Congress of Industrial Organizations, created in 1938 from the ten major industrial unions

CIVIL DISOBEDIENCE non-violent action against a certain law as a protest against its unfairness

CONFEDERATE the eleven Southern states that left the United States in 1861, which led to the Civil War and the defeat of the Southern states, in 1865

DEFICIT BUDGET the spending of federal money whilst also lowering taxes at the same time. The plan was (and it worked for Kennedy) that lower taxes meant people had more money to spend on goods. The need for more goods meant that production was boosted, which in turn meant more workers were needed. The taxes they paid from their wages balanced the deficit.

DEMILITARISED ZONE an area in a war zone where all sides agree not to keep armed forces, as on the 38th Parallel in Korea and the 17th Parallel in Vietnam

DOMINO THEORY the Cold War theory that if one country became communist then others in the area would follow

DUST BOWL the area centred around Oklahoma, Kansas, Texas and Colorado where wind erosion and drought damage farming, as they did particularly badly in the 1930s

FBI Federal Bureau of Investigation, founded in 1908 and based in Washington DC – the chief investigator of crime within and across the USA

FEDERAL the national government, based in Washington DC, where all the main departments and offices of government are based

FOURTEEN POINTS President Wilson's plan for the peace settlement at the end of the First World War

GROVEY V. TOWNSEND CASE this case, in 1935, was the last judicial decision that narrowed the definition of the Reconstruction amendments (attempting to give equal citizenship rights to freed slaves)

HEGEMONY leadership by one state over a group of states

IMPEACHMENT trial in the Senate by Senators acting as a court

INTEGRATION the combination of facilities, previously separated on the grounds of race

LIBERALISM support for economic and social reform, with government intervention. The expansion of social services and active concern for the poor and minority groups

NATIONAL GUARD the militia of each state, controlled by the state governor. They are usually used to help the police or to assist in emergencies or disasters. They can be called into federal service under the control of the president

OLIGOPOLY a few companies controlling one industry, such as steel or oil production

PECULIAR INSTITUTION the euphemism used by Southerners before the Civil War to describe slavery

PHILANTHROPY practical benevolence through giving, usually of money, to benefit individuals, institutions and communities

RHETORIC persuasive or impressive speaking, often with the implication that it is insincere or exaggerated

SCOTTSBORO CASE this case, in Alabama, resulted in two judgements: it clarified the rights of defendants to a lawyer; and ruled that the deliberate exclusion of black Americans from Alabama juries prejudiced defendants from getting a fair trial. Both judgements had long-term significance in improving the legal process for black defendants

SEGREGATION the separation of races as dictated by laws or social custom

STATES the original thirteen colonies on the eastern seaboard, which through the Constitution became the founding states of the United States of America. There are now 50 states in all, and hence 50 stars on the American flag – the Stars and Stripes. The thirteen stripes represent the original colonies

STOCK the value or capital of a company divided into shares, which were sold to investors. The money paid by investors was then used to invest in or expand the business. Shareholders would get a share of the profits if it was successful or would lose money if it was not

SUFFRAGE the right to vote

SUN BELT southern states, such as Texas, Arizona and Florida, with hot summers and dry winters that were settled after the Second World War as new industries were established and air conditioning made life comfortable

TARIFF a tax on imported goods making them more expensive to buy, and trying to increase the sales of domestic goods

THIRD INTERNATIONAL OR 'COMINTERN' set up by the Bolsheviks in March 1919 to provide leadership and policies for the conduct of a revolutionary socialist movement with working-class support. Those who adhered to the Comintern's policies became known as communists

UNCLE SAM an affectionate term for the USA, represented by a figure dressed in stars and stripes

UNILATERALISM a foreign policy which seeks to avoid international alliances and permanent commitments, in favour of independence and freedom of action

UNION the Northern states, who won the Civil War, with President Lincoln as their leader

VOTER REGISTRATION a requirement of Americans before they can vote. In Britain you have to be on the electoral roll in order to be able to vote

WALL STREET the street where the New York Stock Exchange and many financial institutions are based. Also used as a shorthand term for American finance generally

WASHINGTON DC the capital city within its own 'mini' state of the District of Columbia, on land given by the states of Maryland and Virginia. There is also the state of Washington on the north-west coast. Adding DC indicates that you are writing about the capital city and not the state

YANKEE in the USA, someone who comes from the Northern states. In the world, a general term for Americans

YOM KIPPUR WAR a war in which Egypt and Syria invaded Israel to try to retake land taken in the Six-Day War of 1967

Bibliography and selected reading

All publishers London unless otherwise stated.

Acheson, D., *Present at the Creation, My Years at the State Department*, Hamilton, 1970

Addams, J., *Twenty Years at Hull House*, Macmillan, New York, 1911

Agee, J. and Walker, E., *Let Us Now Praise Famous Men*, Houghton Mifflin, Boston, 1941

Ambrose, S., *Eisenhower, The President*, Vol. 2, Allen & Unwin, 1984

Ambrose, S. and Brinkley, D., *Rise to Globalism: American Foreign Policy Since 1938*, Penguin, 1997

Armitage, S. and Jameson, E., *The Women's West*, University of Oklahoma Press, 1987

Badger, A. J., *The New Deal – the Depression Years, 1933–40*, Palgrave Macmillan, 1989

Bernstein, C. and Woodward, B., *All the President's Men*, Secker & Warburg, 1974

Binder, F. and Reimers, D., *The Way We Live Now*, Vol. 2, 4th edn, Houghton Mifflin, Boston, 2000

Boorstin, D. *The Americans: The Democratic Experience*, Cardinal, 1988

Boyer, P. *et al, The Enduring Vision: A History of the American People From 1865*, Vol. 2, Heath and Co., 1995

Brogan, H., *The Longman History of the United States of America*, Longman, 1999

Brown, D., *Bury My Heart at Wounded Knee: An Indian History of the American West*, Vintage, 1991

Burns, J. M., *Roosevelt: The Lion and the Fox*, Harcourt, Bruce Inc., New York, 1956

Carroll, P. and Noble, D., *The Free and the Unfree – A Progressive History of the United States*, 3rd edn, Penguin, New York, 2001

Carson, C. *et al, Eyes on the Prize – a Civil Rights Reader*, Penguin, New York, 1991

Chafe, W., *The Unfinished Journey: America Since World War Two*, 4th edn, OUP, 1999

Cook, R., *Sweet Land of Liberty? The African–American Struggle for Civil Rights in the Twentieth Century*, Pearson, 1998

Cooke, A., *Alistair Cooke's America*, BBC, 1973

Dalleck, R., *Flawed Giant: Lyndon Johnson and His Times, 1961–73*, OUP, 1988

Daniels, R., *Coming to America: A History of Immigration and Ethnicity in American Life*, 2nd edn, Perennial, 2002

Degler, C., *Out of Our Past: The Forces That Shaped Modern America*, 3rd edn, Harper, New York, 1984

Divine, R., *The Johnson Years: Foreign Policy, the Great Society, and the White House*, University of Kansas, Lawrence, 1987

Dower, J., *War Without Mercy: Race and Power in the Pacific War*, Pantheon, New York, 1986

Dumbrell, J., *The Making of American Foreign Policy: Carter to Clinton*, Manchester University Press, 1996

Evans, H., *The American Century: People, Power and Politics: An Illustrated History*, Cape, 1998

Foner, E., *Reconstruction: America's Unfinished Revolution, 1863–77*, Harper & Row, 1988

Foner, E., *The Story of American Freedom*, Papermac, 1998

Freedman, L., *Kennedy's Wars: Berlin, Cuba, Laos, and Vietnam*, OUP, 2000

Friedan, B., *The Feminine Mystique*, Penguin, 1965

Gaddis, J. L., *The United States and the Origins of the Cold War, 1941–47*, Columbia University Press, New York, 1972

Galbraith, J. K., *The Affluent Society*, Penguin, 1987

Garrow, D., *Bearing the Cross: Martin Luther King Jr. and the Southern Christian Leadership Conference*, Vintage, 1986

Griffith, R. and Baker, P., *Major Problems in American History Since 1945*, 2nd edn, Houghton Mifflin, Boston, 2001

Halberstam, D., *The Best and the Brightest*, Random House, New York, 1969

Hampton, H. and Fayer, S., *Voices of Freedom: An Oral History of the Civil Rights Movement from the 1950s Through the 1980s*, Bantam Books, New York, 1990

Handlin, O., *This Was America*, Harvard University Press, Cambridge, Mass., 1949

Harrington, M., *The Other America – Poverty in the United States*, Macmillan, New York, 1962

Hastings, M., *The Korean War*, Michael Joseph, 1987

Hellmann, L., *Scoundrel Time*, Little Brown, 1976

Herr, M., *Dispatches*, Picador, 1977

Herring, G., *America's Longest War*, McGraw-Hill, 1996

Hersh, S. M., *The Dark Side of Camelot*, Harper Collins, 1998

Hine, R. and Faragher, J., *The American West – A New Interpretative History*, Yale University Press, New Haven, 2000

Hobsbawm, E., *Age of Extremes – The Short Twentieth Century, 1914–91*, Abacus, 1995

Isserman, M. and Kazin, M., *America Divided: The Civil War of the 1960s*, OUP, 2000

Jackson, K., *Crabgrass Frontier: The Suburbanization of the United States*, OUP, 1985

Johnson, M., *Reading the American Past – Selected Historical Documents*, Vol. 2, 2nd edn, Bedford/St Martin, Boston, 2002

Jones, M. A., *The Limits of Liberty: American History, 1607–1992*, OUP, 1995

Kearns, D., *Lyndon Johnson and the American Dream*, Deutsch, 1976

Kennedy, D., *Freedom from Fear. The American People in Depression and War, 1929–45*, OUP, 1999

King, M. L. Jr., *Stride Toward Freedom – The Montgomery Story*, Harper, New York, 1958

Kluger, R., *Simple Justice – The History of Brown v. The Board of Education and Black America's Struggle for Equality*, Knopf, New York, 1975

Kolchin, P., *American Slavery, 1619–1877*, Penguin, 1995

La Feber, W., *The American Age – US Foreign Policy at Home and Abroad*, 2nd edn, Norton, New York, 1994

Lash, J., *Eleanor and Franklin*, Deutsch, 1972

Lemann, N., *The Promised Land: The Great Black Migration and How it Changed America*, Vintage, New York, 1991

Leuchtenburg, W., *Franklin D. Roosevelt and the New Deal, 1932–40*, Harper & Row, New York, 1963

Levy, P. B., *Let Freedom Ring: A Documentary History of the Modern Civil Rights Movement*, Praegar, 1992

Lorence, J., *Enduring Voices*, Vol. 2, 4th edn, Houghton Mifflin, 2000

Lowi, T. J. and Ginsberg, B., *American Government: Freedom and Power*, 6th edn, Norton and Co., 2000

Lynd, R. and Lynd, H. *Middletown: A Study in Contemporary American Culture*, Harcourt Brace, New York, 1929

McCullough, D., *Truman*, Touchstone, 1992

McMahon, R., *The Cold War: A Very Short Introduction*, OUP, 2003

McNamara, R., *In Retrospect: The Tragedy and Lessons of Vietnam*, Times Books, New York, 1995

McPherson, J. M., *Battle Cry of Freedom: The Civil War Era*, OUP, 1988

Matusow, A. J., *The Unraveling of America: A History of Liberalism in the 1960s*, Harper & Row, 1986

May, E. T., *Homeward Bound: American Families in the Cold War Era*, Basic Books, 1988

Merrill, D. and Paterson, T., *Major Problems in American Foreign Relations*, Vol. 2, 5th edn, Houghton Mifflin, Boston, 2000

Milner, C. *et al*, *The Oxford History of the American West*, OUP, New York, 1994

Moody, A., *Coming of Age in Mississippi*, Dell Publishing, New York, 1968

Morgan, I. W. and Wynn, N. A. (eds.), *America's Century: Perspectives on US History Since 1900*, Holmes & Meier, 1993

Morris, E., *The Rise of Theodore Roosevelt*, Random House, New York, 1979

Nash, G. and Jeffrey J. (eds.), *The American People: Creating a Nation and a Society*, Vol. 2, 4th edn, Longman, New York, 2003

Norton, M. *et al*, *A People and a Nation – A History of the United States*, 6th edn, Houghton Mifflin, Boston, 2001

Patterson, J. T., *America's Struggle Against Poverty, 1900–80*, Harvard University Press, Cambridge, Mass., 1986

Patterson, J. T., *Grand Expectations: The United States, 1945–74*, OUP, New York, 1996

Polenberg, R., *One Nation Divisible: Class, Race and Ethnicity in the United States Since 1938*, Penguin Books, 1981

Riches, W. T. M., *The Civil Rights Movement*, Macmillan, 1997

Riis, J., *How the Other Half Lives: Studies Among the Tenements of New York*, Charles Shribners' Sons, New York, 1890

Rowbotham, S., *A Century of Women – The History of Women in Britain and the United States*, Penguin, 1997

Schlesinger, A. M., *A Thousand Days: John F. Kennedy in the White House*, Houghton Mifflin, 1965

Schrecker, E., *The Age of McCarthyism: A Brief History With Documents*, St Martin's Press, Boston, 1995

Schulzinger, R. D., *American Diplomacy in the Twentieth Century*, 4th edn, OUP, 1998

Singh, R., *Governing America: The Politics of a Divided Democracy*, OUP, 2003

Summers, A., *The Arrogance of Power: The Secret World of Richard Nixon*, Phoenix, 2001

Terkel, S., *Hard Times: An Oral History of the Great Depression*, The New Press, New York, 1970

Terkel, S., *'The Good War': An Oral History of World War Two*, The New Press, New York, 1984

Tindall, G. and Shi, D., *America: A Narrative History*, 5th edn, Norton, New York, 1999

Walker, M., *Makers of the American Century*, Chatto & Windus, 2000

Ward, G., *The West: An Illustrated History*, Weidenfeld & Nicolson, 1996

White, R., *'It's Your Misfortune and None of My Own': A New History of the American West*, University of Oklahoma Press, 1991

Zinn, H., *A People's History of the United States: 1492–Present*, Harper Collins, 1995

Useful websites

General
The Library of Congress and the National Archives have a wealth of material to explore:
www.loc.gov
www.archives.gov
The National Park Service has a wide range of information about monuments as well as the environment:
www.nps.gov

Television channels:
www.pbs.org
www.cnn.com
www.bbc.co.uk

Universities have a wide range of electronic records, for example:
www.fordham.edu
www.stanford.edu

Presidents
www.ipl.org/ref/POTUS

Presidential libraries, for example:
www.fdrlibrary.marist.edu
www.jfklibrary.org
www.lbjlib.utexas.edu

Topics
Haymarket Bomb:
www.chicagohistory.org/dramas
New Deal: www.newdeal.feri.org
World War Two: www.ddaymuseum.org
Dropping the nuclear bomb:
www.dannen.com/decision
Marshall Plan:
www.marshallfoundation.org
Korean War: www.koreanwar.org
The 1950s: www.fiftiesweb.com
Civil Rights:
www.webcorp.com/civilrights
Watergate: www.washingtonpost.com

Text credits

p.8 source 1.6 *The Atlantic Monthly* by Frederick Douglass, 1865; **p.11** source 1.8 *The Way We Live Now*, vol II, 4th edn, Houghton Mifflin, 2000, pp.17–18; **p.21** source 2.1 *America the Beautiful* song written in 1893; **p.23** source 2.4 *The Rise of Theodore Roosevelt* by E. Morris, Random House, 1979, pp.274–5; **p.28** source 2.12 *The American Century: People, Power and Politics: An Illustrated History* by H. Evans, Cape 1998, p.7; **p.31** source 2.16 *The Virginian, Horseman of the Plain* by O. Wister; **p.32** source 2.19 *The Women's West* by S. Armitage and E. Jameson, University of Oklahoma Press, 1987, p.9; **p.33** source 2.21 *The Women's West* by S. Armitage and E. Jameson, University of Oklahoma Press, 1987, p.12; **p.45** source 3.10 *This Was America*, O. Handlin, Harvard University Press, 1949, pp.407–41; **p.45** source 3.12 *The Eight Hours Day* song quoted in *Enduring Voices* by J. Lorence, vol II, 4th edn, Houghton Mifflin, 2000, p.60; source 3.13 extract from *New Orleans Daily Democrat* in *Enduring Voices* by J. Lorence, vol II, 4th edn, Houghton Mifflin, 2000, p.59; source 3.14 extract from *The Jungle* in *Enduring Voices* by J. Lorence, vol II, 4th edn, Houghton Mifflin, 2000, p.143; **p.55** source 4.3 *A People's History of the United States: 1492–Present* by H. Zinn, HarperCollins, 1995, reprinted by Permission of The Balkin Agency, p.291; source 4.4 *A People's History of the United States: 1492–Present* by H. Zinn, HarperCollins, 1995, reprinted by Permission of The Balkin Agency, p.297; **p.58** source 4.9 *A People's History of the United States: 1492–Present* by H. Zinn, HarperCollins, 1995, reprinted by Permission of The Balkin Agency, p.302; source 4.10 *A People's History of the United States: 1492–Present* by H. Zinn, HarperCollins, 1995, reprinted by Permission of The Balkin Agency, p.308; **p.80** source 5.6 *The American Age: US Foreign Policy at Home and Abroad*, 2nd edn, Norton, 1994, p.385; **p.83** source 5.9 Norman A. Graebner in *Major Problems in American Foreign Relations* by D. Merrill and T. Paterson, vol II, 5th edn, copyright © Houghton Mifflin, 1999, pp.36–9; **p.87** source 6.5 *The American Century: People, Power and Politics: An Illustrated History* by H. Evans, Cape 1998, p.182; **p.88** source 6.9 *Middletown: A Study in American Culture* by R. S. Lynd and H. Merrell Lynd, Harcourt Brace, 1929; **p.89** source 6.10 *Reading the American Past* by M. Johnson, vol II, 2nd edn, Bedford St Martin, 2002, p.119; **p.98** source 6.19 Reinhold Niebuhr in *Reading the American Past* by M. Johnson, vol II, 2nd edn, Bedford St. Martin, Boston, 2002, © 1929 Reinhold Niebuhr, pp.123–6; **p. 108** source 7.1 Mary Agnes Hamilton from *In America Today* in *America Through British Eyes* by A. Nevins, OUP, 1968, pp.443–4; **p.111** source 7.10 William E. Leuchtenburg in *Franklin D. Roosevelt and the New Deal 1932–40*, Harper & Row, 1963, p.25; source 7.11 *Hard Times: An Oral History of World War Two* by S. Terkel, The New Press, 1970, p.227; **p.112** source 7.14 *A Study in American Culture* by R. S. Lynd and H. Merrell Lynd, Harcourt Brace, 1929; source 7.12 Mary Agnes Hamilton from *In America Today* in *America Through British Eyes* by A. Nevins, OUP, 1968, pp.443–4; **p.112** source 7.13 *Hard Times: An Oral History of World War Two* by S. Terkel, The New Press, 1970, p.107; source 7.14 *A Study in American Culture* by R. S. Lynd and H. Merrell Lynd, Harcourt Brace, 1929; **p.117** source 7.18 *Hard Times: An Oral History of World War Two* by S. Terkel, The New Press, 1970, pp.265–7; **p.121** source 7.22 Joe Marcus in *Hard Times: An Oral History of World War Two* by S. Terkel, The New Press, 1970, pp.265–7; **p. 126** source 7.27 *The New Deal: The Depression Years* by A. Badger, Palgrave Macmillan, 1989, p.311; **p.151** source 7.31 *Roosevelt: The Lion and the Fox* by J. M. Burns, vol I, Harcourt, Bruce Inc, 1956, pp.403–4; source 7.32 *Freedom from Fear. The American People in Depression and War 1929–45* by D. M. Kennedy, OUP, 1999, p.365; **p.132** source 7.33 *The Story of American Freedom* by E. Foner, Papermac, 1998, pp.203–4; source 7.34 *The New Deal: The Depression Years* by A. Badger, Palgrave Macmillan, 1989, p.8; source 7.35 Harold Ickes in *Roosevelt: The Lion and the Fox* by J. M. Burns, vol I, Harcourt, Bruce Inc, 1956, p.374; **p.148** source 8.14 'The Good War': An Oral History of World War Two* by S. Terkel, The New Press, 1984, copyright © Donaldio & Olson Inc, pp.110–11; **p.150** source 8.16 *Reading the American Past* by M. Johnson, vol II, 2nd edn, Bedford St. Martin, Boston, 2002, p.165; **p.156** source 8.31 'The Good War': An Oral History of World War Two* by S. Terkel, The New Press, 1984, copyright © Donaldio & Olson Inc, pp.117 and 122; **p.157** source 8.32 'The Good War': An Oral History of World War Two* by S. Terkel, The New Press, 1984, copyright © Donaldio & Olson Inc, p.279; source 8.34 *Freedom from Fear* by D. M. Kennedy, OUP, 1999, p.768; source 8.35 A. Brinkley in *Major Problems in American History Since 1945* by R. Griffith and P. Baker, 2nd edn, Houghton Mifflin, 2001, pp.31–2; **p.161** source 8.38 'The Good War': An Oral History of World War Two* by S. Terkel, The New Press, 1984, copyright © Donaldio & Olson Inc, pp.300–31; source 8.40 *Freedom from Fear* by D. M. Kennedy, OUP, 1999, p.857; source 8.41 *Freedom from Fear* by D. M. Kennedy, OUP, 1999, pp.852–8; source 8.42 A. Brinkley in *Major Problems in American History Since 1945* by R. Griffith and P. Baker, 2nd edn, Houghton Mifflin, 2001, p.27; **p.165** source 8.45 'The Good War': An Oral History of World War Two* by S. Terkel, The New Press, 1984, copyright © Donaldio & Olson Inc, p.197; source 8.46 'The Good War': An Oral History of World War Two* by S. Terkel, The New Press, 1984, copyright © Donaldio & Olson Inc, p.193; source 8.47 'The Good War': An Oral History of World War Two* by S. Terkel, The New Press, 1984, copyright ©

Donaldio & Olson Inc, p.166; source 8.48 'The Good War': An Oral History of World War Two* by S. Terkel, The New Press, 1984, copyright © Donaldio & Olson Inc, pp.39, 41–2, 48; source 8.49 'The Good War': An Oral History of World War Two* by S. Terkel, The New Press, 1984, copyright © Donaldio & Olson Inc, p.166; source 8.50 'The Good War': An Oral History of World War Two* by S. Terkel, The New Press, 1984, copyright © Donaldio & Olson Inc, p.287; **p.164** source 8.51 *American Diplomacy in the Twentieth Century*, 4th edn, OUP, 1998, p.200; **p.172** source 9.4 *A History of the American People* by P. Johnson, 1997, p.690; source 9.5 *Grand Expectations: The United States 1945–74* by J. Patterson, OUP, 1996, p.97; **p.177** source 9.9 extract from 'The Long Telegram' in *Major Problems in American Foreign Relations* by D. Merrill and T. Paterson, vol II, 5th edn, copyright © Houghton Mifflin, 1999, pp.210–12; **p.178** source 9.10 *Major Problems in American History Since 1945* by R. Griffith and P. Baker, 2nd edn, Houghton Mifflin, 2001, pp.87–8; **p.183** source 9.15 *Grand Expectations: The United States 1945–74* by J. Patterson, OUP, 1996, p.91; source 9.16 *Age of Extremes – The Short Twentieth Century 1945–74* by E. Hobsbawm, Abacus, 1994, p.234; source 9.17 *American Diplomacy in the Twentieth Century* by R. Schulzinger, OUP, 1998, p.12; source 9.18 *Grand Expectations: The United States 1945–74* by J. Patterson, OUP, 1996, p.135; **p.190** source 10.5 *A People and a Nation – A History of the United States* by M. B. Norton et al, 6th edn, Houghton Mifflin, 2001, p.838; source 10.6 *A People and a Nation – A History of the United States* by M. B. Norton et al, 6th edn, Houghton Mifflin, 2001, p.838; **p.200** source 10.15 *Reading the American Past* by M. Johnson, vol II, 2nd edn, Bedford St. Martin, Boston, 2002, pp.453–4; source 10.16 *In Retrospect* by R. McNamara, 1995; **p.204** source 10.21 *The New York Herald Tribune*, 25 April 1965; source 10.22 *A Rumour of War* by P. Caputo, 1977; **p.207** *The Unfinished Journey: America Since World War Two* by W. Chafe, 4th edn, OUP, 1999, pp.296, 298–300; **p.213** source 11.5 Hanoch Bartov in *From the Outer World* by O. and L. Handlin (eds.), 1997, pp.293–6; **p.216** source 11.10 Edith M. Stern in *Reading the American Past* by M. Johnson, vol II, 2nd edn, Bedford St. Martin, Boston, 2002, p.227; **p.219** source 11.18 Anne Moody in *Eyes on the Prize* by C. Carson, 1991, p.43; **p.220** source 11.19 *Simple Justice* by R. Kluger, 1975, p.1; source 11.20 *Harlem* by Langston Hughes, 1951; **p.224** source 11.27 *American Ground Zero* by C. Gallagher, 1993, pp.133–5; **p.225** source 11.29 *We Will All Go Together When We Go* (from the album *An Evening Wasted With Tom Lehrer*) © 1958 Tom Lehrer. Used by permission; **p.228** source 11.33 *The Age of McCarthyism: A Brief History with Documents* by E. Schrecker, 1995; source 11.36 *The Conquest of America* by A. MacLeish, 1949; source 11.37 *A People and a Nation – A History of the United States* by M. B. Norton et al, 6th edn, Houghton Mifflin, 2001, p.796; source 11.38 *A History of Our Time* by W. Chafe and H. Sitkoff, 4th edn, 1999, pp.3–4; source 11.39 *Washington Post*, 1 March 1954; **p.229** source 11.40 *The Unfinished Journey: America Since World War Two* by W. Chafe, 4th edn, OUP, 1999, pp.109–10; **p.230** source 11.41 *A People and a Nation – A History of the United States* by M. B. Norton et al, 6th edn, Houghton Mifflin, 2001, p.788; source 11.42 *The Unfinished Journey: America Since World War Two* by W. Chafe, 4th edn, OUP, 1999, pp.140–1; **p.237** source 12.5 *Why Can't We Wait* by Martin Luther King, Harper & Row, 1984; **p.241** source 12.11 *Voices of Freedom: An Oral History of the Civil Rights Movement from the 1950s Through the 1960s* by H. Hampton and S. Fayer, Bantam Books, 1990, pp.227–8; **p.243** source 12.13 *New York Review of Books*, 22 September 1966; source 12.14 *Reading the American Past* by M. Johnson, vol II, 2nd edn, Bedford St. Martin, Boston, 2002, p.213; **p.246** source 12.15 *The Other America: Poverty in the United States* by M. Harrington, Macmillan, 1968, p.72; **p.248** source 12.19 *The Best and the Brightest* by D. Halberstam, Random House, 1969; source 12.20 *The Unfinished Journey: America Since World War Two* by W. Chafe, 4th edn, OUP, 1999, p.244; source 12.21 *New Yorker*, 1 April 2002; source 12.22 *Lyndon Johnson and the American Dream* by D. Kearns, Deutsch, 1976; **p.249** source 12.23 *Lyndon Johnson and the American Dream* by D. Kearns, Deutsch, 1976; **p.253** *Vietnam! Vietnam!* by F. Greene, 1966; **p.255** *The Unfinished Journey: America Since World War Two* by W. Chafe, 4th edn, OUP, 1999, pp.338–9; **p.259** source 15.2 *A History of Our Time* by W. Chafe and H. Sitkoff, 1999, p.361; **p.262** source 13.4 *Makers of the American Century* by M. Walker, Chatto & Windus, 2000, p.311; source 13.5 *The Longman History of the United States of America* by H. Brogan, Longman, 1999; **p.269** source 13.15 *The Unfinished Journey: America Since World War Two* by W. Chafe, 4th edn, OUP, 1999, p.432; **p.272** source 13.17 *The Unfinished Journey: America Since World War Two* by W. Chafe, 4th edn, OUP, 1999, p.494; source 13.18 *The Unfinished Journey: America Since World War Two* by W. Chafe, 4th edn, OUP, 1999, p.494; source 13.19 *America: A Narrative History* by G. B. Tindall and D. E. Shi, vol II, 5th edn, 1999, p.1606; **p.281** source 13.28 *The Cold War: A Very Short Introduction* by R. J. McMahon, OUP, 2003, p.162; **p.283** source 13.30 *Makers of the American Century* by M. Walker, Chatto & Windus, 2000, p.245.

Index